MANY INCIDENTS AND REMINISCENCES OF
THE EARLY HISTORY OF WOOD COUNTY

TOGETHER WITH SOME OF THE HISTORIC EVENTS
OF THE MAUMEE VALLEY CONTAINED IN THIS

PIONEER SCRAP-BOOK
OF
WOOD COUNTY
OHIO
AND THE
MAUMEE VALLEY

HAVE BEEN COLLECTED FROM THE PAPERS AND MATERIAL
OF THE LATE C. W. EVERS AS GATHERED BY HIM
FOR YEARS PAST

"Lest We Forget"

Charles W. Evers

HERITAGE BOOKS
2008

HERITAGE BOOKS
AN IMPRINT OF HERITAGE BOOKS, INC.

Books, CDs, and more—Worldwide

For our listing of thousands of titles see our website
at
www.HeritageBooks.com

A Facsimile Reprint
Published 2008 by
HERITAGE BOOKS, INC.
Publishing Division
100 Railroad Ave. #104
Westminster, Maryland 21157

Copyright © 2002 Heritage Books, Inc.

Originally published
Bowling Green, O., 1910

— Publisher's Notice —
In reprints such as this, it is often not possible to remove blemishes from the original. We feel the contents of this book warrant its reissue despite these blemishes and hope you will agree and read it with pleasure.

International Standard Book Numbers
Paperbound: 978-0-7884-2151-8
Clothbound: 978-0-7884-7686-0

PREFACE

THE purpose of this book is to preserve to the people of Wood county and the Maumee Valley some of the historic facts and interesting incidents of its early days and to present them in an entertaining and readable form.

The plan of making it scrap-book-fashion originated with my father and an outline of the work had been arranged by him and left—an unfinished task.

The further preparation and compilation was then entrusted to the trained hand of Mr. F. J. Oblinger, who has, with pains-taking care, from a mass of manuscript, notes, clippings and other material, condensed the gleanings of a life time into these pages.

I am also under obligations to Mr. John E. Gunckel, of Toledo, for his kindness in permitting the use of a number of cuts from his "Early History of the Maumee Valley."

The publication I have undertaken, personally, as a memorial to my father, from whose pen most of the articles have come. Some are now in print for the first time, while others have appeared during his years of active newspaper work.

My father's labors in this direction were purely out of love for the work. All history appealed to him, but the early struggles of Wood county pioneers was a chapter so replete with tragic interest, so tinged with romance, so filled with human endeavor and its achievement that it called forth his highest admiration.

It seemed fitting, therefore, that the final effort of his life should have been a record of these events and with this thought in mind and the grateful encouragement and friendly interest extended by his old associates, both personally and as members of the Pioneer and Historical societies, I have ventured to complete the work.   MAY EVERS-ROSS.

Bowling Green, O., Nov. 17, 1909.

OUR PIONEERS

At a meeting of the Maumee Valley Pioneers some years since, Mrs. C. W. Evers wrote and read the following poem:

All honor due ye, hoary heads,
   Assembled here to-day,
A power higher than man's own
   Hath guarded your pathway;
Else not one aged pioneer
   Would answer to the call
Which brings the few remaining ones
   With each successive fall.

'Tis good to meet and here relate
   The hardships each hath borne,
You know of toils and sorrows pass'd
   O'er which none others mourn;
You know when the rude little cabins
   Loomed up in the distance afar;
Each one brought joy to your household,
   For a neighbor, a friend would be there.

'Mid joyful songs and stories
   Your evenings slowly waned,
When the choppings, and the raisings,
   And the husbands all were gained.
Think not that we would feign forget
   Your fearless courage tried,
Nor less appreciate the boon
   Your efforts have supplied.

Our eyes behold an Eden,
   Where once the forest stood,
Where generations more than one
   Have wrestled with the wood.
Where grew the bramble-bush and trees,
   Are lawns of velvet green,
Imagination scarce can paint
   The changes there have been.

Where swale and marshes yielded naught
   To energetic men,
Are orchards now of choicest fruit
   And fields of golden grain.
Not a cabin left which sheltered
   Our fathers brave and true;
They've crumbled like their owners,
   And mansions rise to view.

Products alone are not her wealth —
   Our Pioneers have cause
To justly feel a pride in those
   Who consecrate their laws.
E'en from the swamps came talent fair,
   And self-made men are here,
Schooled in a little hut of logs,
   No college then was near.

We oft bewail, declare our roads
   Are not quite smooth enough;
Well, forty years ago to-day
   Wood county roads were rough.
The farmer laid aside the wheels,
   And, mounted on his horse,
Would ride for many weary miles
   To reach the old Court House.

But now instead its dome appears,
   As centrally behest,
From seat of Justice speed the trains,
   North—South—yea, East and West.
All nature smiles upon you now,
   God bless your later years!
The time will come, we'll call in vain
   For our dear Pioneers.

WOOD COUNTY'S BIRTH

Its Development from the Misty Past—Our Love for the Memory of Our Heroic Pioneers, Whose Splendid Results We Now Enjoy

"Gimme back the dear old days—the pathway through the dells
To the schoolhouse in the blossoms; the sound of far-off bells
Tinklin' 'crost the meadows, the song of the bird an' brook,
The old-time dictionary an' the blue-back spellin' book.

"Gone, like a dream, forever—a city's hid the place
Where stood the ol' log schoolhouse, an' no familiar face
Is smilin' there in welcome beneath a mornin' sky—
There's a bridge acrost the river, an' we've crossed an' said "good-by."
—*Atlanta Constitution.*

By Charles W. Evers.

WHO is there who does not love to hear of their ancestors and their ancestral home, even if that home was ever so homely—nothing but a log cabin with a stick chimney? Even though the father and mother and grandparents, —long since passed away—were plain, every-day people, dressed in home-spun garb, yet our thoughts to our latest hour in life go back to the dear old home and to those dear old people with tenderest emotions.

Heroic, were they? Ah, yes. We of Wood county may not deny that virtue to our ancestors. Go back if you will half or three-quarters of a century and view the wilderness landscape of swamp, plain and forest as they found it, in your worst vein of imagination and say if they who buffeted with those discouragements were not untitled heroes.

The Wood county of today has much to be proud of. We need no self-glorification, but our pride may justly go back to those pioneer ancestors who amid poverty, sickness and privation of every kind laid broad and enduring, the foundation of our present prosperity.

It is the story of such as these—individuals, communities and nations, together with the land they inhabited which makes biography and history—two of the most interesting branches of human knowledge. Wood county with its accumulation, thrifty people and historic years, has an interesting contribution of this kind, now fast passing into oblivion, which if fittingly and truthfully told is well worthy a place in the annals of the nation. Much that belongs to and becomes a part of our history occurred before our land had a place marked in the Geographical Atlas.

Our homes of today lay in the track of great events. The martial tread of armies, men upon whose valor the fate of the nation hung, disturbed the silent wastes of Wood long before she had so much as a name, and the forest echoes repeated the startling roar of the cannon which proclaimed that the final contest between Civilization and Barbarism was in deadly issue at her very threshold.

The story of her early settlement and progress, while a fruitful theme for the chronicler's pen, will derive increased interest from a brief narration of some of this preceding outline history which has become a part of the written story of the nation. In this we are told that Wood county was a small fractional part of a vast extent of territory, of which the French were the first white claimants, basing their claim as other Europeans did on the right of discovery and conquest. This nominal possession had existed about one hundred years when, in 1763, the English, who were also claimants of contiguous territory, dispossessed the French, after a bloody war, of all their lands in America. That twenty years later, in 1783, England, in turn, after a war of eight years, was forced to quit-claim all her possessions south of Canada to her own rebellious Colonists, who started a new Government of their own styled The United States of America.

The open page of our history after this nominal ownership by these two most powerful and enlightened nations of Europe, for a period of one hundred and twenty years, was still a blank. No marks of civilization were left behind. Adventurous explorers and fur-traders had passed through the forests or by the river in expeditions to points beyond, but otherwise this land, since called Wood county, was nought but a vast game preserve for vagrant bands of Indian hunters.

But a change for the better is coming slowly. Civilization has set its course westward with relentless tread. War is sometimes a great educator. The various desultory expeditions in the west had been the means of promulgating wonderful stories in the east of the beauty and fertility of the western country, and shortly after the birth of the new Government a vast tide of immigration was sweeping across the Alleghanies to the fertile region of the Ohio and its tributaries.

It should be kept in mind that each of the civilized nations claiming any part of the country, held it always subject to the claims of the Indian tribes occupying it. There was this serious cloud on the title of all land in the west at that time. In the present boundaries of Ohio not less than thirteen tribes and bands laid claim to title. As will be readily foreseen the great inundation of white settlers into their fine hunting grounds soon aroused the jealousy and hostility of these tribes and stealthy murders and brutal, fiendish outrages on the whites soon followed. The Government, then under the wise administration of President Washington, had observed so far as possible a humane and pacific policy toward all the tribes and had spared no efforts to secure peace with them by treaty and purchase of their lands. But through the mischievous advice and influence of British traders, who were profiting by a lucrative traffic with the Indians, they insisted on the Ohio River as the boundary between them and the whites, and no treaty which all the tribes would respect and sanction could be made, only on this basis.

Finally an army under Gen. Harmar was sent against them, but was defeated on the Maumee near where Fort Wayne now is. Another army under Gen. St. Clair, then Governor of the Northwest Territory, was organized and sent against them. Again, the savages fell back, though by a more direct course toward the Maumee. Again the Americans met with overwhelming defeat and were routed with great slaughter and the barbarous butchery of all their unfortunate wounded and prisoners, and the loss of all their cannon and military equipage. This so emboldened the Indians that all the whites north of the Ohio were compelled for safety to shut themselves up in forts and block-houses and from all sides came loud demands for strong and vigorous measures by the Government, which was far too slow and lenient in its policy to suit the distressed settlers.

President Washington now sent for General Anthony Wayne, an old army associate of his in the Revolution. Wayne, who was a resolute man of audacious courage, came on and organized his army and though assailed and opposed by every strategem of savage warfare, he marched to the Maumee, where on the northerly bank of the Maumee about two miles below the present townsite of Waterville, August 20, 1794, he met the confederated tribes and fragments of tribes of the Northwest who had assembled their warriors to dispute his further advance by the wager of battle. Wayne assailed them with his characteristic fury and impetuosity. The issue was not long in doubt. The Indians were completely routed, many of their chiefs being killed, while the rest, when the battle was over, were flying fugitives. They had been encouraged and assisted by the British, who had a fort, in violation of their treaty with the United States, just below where Maumee is now. Some of the Indians fled there for protection but the gates were shut against them. The English commander had doubtless a pretty wholesome respect for Wayne as a soldier and did not care to take any chances in provoking him to storm the fort and therefore prudently refused to give shelter to the fugitive savages.

The Americans destroyed all cornfields and Indian villages on their return up the river, subsisting much of the time, especially while they were constructing Fort Wayne and Defiance, on the corn and vegetable patches of the Indians. After garrisoning these forts Wayne marched back to Fort Greenville, now in Darke county, and left the tribes to ponder over the situation until spring to decide whether they would make peace or have more war.

The effect of Wayne's victory over the Indians cannot be correctly measured by the number of savages slain in battle. The campaign had convinced them of their inability to successfully make war on the whites. They had seen an army come among them led by a chief whom they could neither surprise nor defeat. They had seen the hollowness of the English promises of help; when danger came they had seen the king's soldiers creep into their forts like ground hogs, and when the Indian went there for protection the gate was shut in his face and he was left to the mercy of Wayne's victorious soldiers. They had seen their cornfields laid waste, their villages burned and their women and children left destitute for the winter and had seen five garrisoned forts placed in their country to enforce peace. There was a logic in all this that the Indian could understand. He saw that he must do one of three things, make peace, leave the country, or be annihilated.

British agents still endeavored to prevent a treaty, but hollow promises and fine talk did not allay the pangs of hunger and the pinching cold of winter; and the following year the basis of a treaty was made at Greenville, Darke county, on the 3d of August, 1795, by which the Indians relinquished all claim forever to more than three-fourths of Ohio, besides sixteen cessions of land, located from each other at great distances, and distributed over an extensive area of wilderness country, the lands upon which are now established those great centers of commerce, Chicago, Detroit, Toledo and Fort Wayne, besides other distant posts, as Versailles and Mackinaw. This treaty was signed by the war chiefs of no less than twelve tribes of Indians.

Then came treaty after treaty and

grant after grant during the years that followed—Treaty of Fort Industry, 1805; at Detroit, 1807; at Brownstown, 1808; treaty where Maumee now stands, in 1817, and one of the most important to the Maumee Valley; treaty at St. Marys, 1818; treaty of Saginaw, 1819. One by one the different grants were extinguished. The Delawares ceded their reservations in 1829. The Wyandots ceded theirs by a treaty made at Upper Sandusky, March 17, 1842. This was the last Indian treaty in Ohio—a state, says Henry Howe, every foot of whose soil has been fairly purchased by treaties from its original possessors. The last Indian title extinguished was that of the Wyandots, and they left for Kansas in July, 1843.

EARLY FORMATION

Wood County Seat Once at Detroit—Struggle Over Location—Rivalry Between Orleans and Perrysburg

MR. EVERS compiled the following bit of interesting history of Wood county in its early days:

The territory now known as Wood county, belonged to the Eries, or, as some historians say, the Neuter Nation. The French explorers and missionaries first saw the shores of Lake Erie, and next to the Iroquois, invaded the country about the close of the first half of the Seventeenth Century. From the beginning of French exploration to 1713, it formed a part of the original province of Quebec; from 1713 to 1764, it was a part of Louisiana; from 1764 to 1769, under the British parliament statute, it belonged to Quebec province; from 1769 to 1778, under authority of the Virginia legislature, it was attached to Boletourt county, Va., and from 1778 to 1787, it formed a part of Illinois county, Va.

When the territory northwest of the Ohio was established in 1787, Wood county was its wildest and most inhospitable part, and later off of Wayne county (organized in 1796). The Ottawas, Miamis and other tribes, claimed it as their hunting grounds.

The First Legislature

Of Ohio, in March and April, 1803, established the counties of Green, Montgomery, Gallia, Butler, Warren, Geauga, Scioto and Franklin, and all of Wood county, south of the Fulton line was detached from the great county of Wayne. Our county seat was then at Detroit. Congress had since chopped us off, so to speak, and, like a chip from a great log, we were lying over in the state of Ohio, and our late county seat, Detroit, was in Wayne county still, but in Indiana territory. The Maumee country had been divorced. We were in that fragment of Ohio that had been Wayne county, Northwest territory, but now we were in a new state, without a seat of justice or county government, nor even a county name.

No Use For It

It is true that the hordes of Indians and few white traders and half breeds here had but little use for a county seat, but still it was the fashion to preserve the semblance of civil government, by attaching all territory to some organized county for such purposes. It had been the rule too, on the Ohio, where the settlements began, to extend the limits of the new counties to the northern boundary of the territory. So it happened, when Green and Franklin counties were organized on the northern borders of the settlements, they were extended north to the state line, possibly to include the 12 mile reserve, and took in the present territory of Wood. The present tier of eastern townships of Wood were in Franklin, with the county seat at Franklinton, now Columbus, and the remainder of Wood was attached to Green county, with seat of justice at Xenia. But the fact that this territory had two county seats caused but little inconvenience; except the U. S. Reserve it was all Indian territory; there were no taxes to pay or deeds to record. Settlements, however, were extending up the Mad river very fast, and two years later, 1805, Champaign county was formed of parts of Green and Franklin counties, and in 1817, Logan county was organized. Wood county was in Logan county from 1817 to 1820 as well as in Erie county in the territory of Michigan, for the Michigan authorities justly exercised jurisdiction over a part of it.

Dr. Horatio Conant had no sooner made his home within the old limits of Wood county, than Governor Cass commissioned him a Justice of the Peace of Erie county, with headquarters at Maumee. To oppose this action, and as soon as Waynesfield township of Logan county was established, the governor of Ohio commissioned Seneca Allen, of Fort Meigs, a Justice of the Peace for Logan county, and thus it was in two distinct jurisdictions until 1835-36, when the Toledo war woke up congress to apply a remedy.

A County of Their Own

Now that the Maumee Rapids people had a county of their own, and a seat of justice right in their midst, it might reasonably be presumed that they would, after the great inconvenience they had endured, be happy to a man. Not so. Human nature is not shaped thus. It was the same then as it is today; never satisfied. Maumee had the county seat temporarily, but not by general approval. Orleans and Perrysburg were not pleased. The settlers were pretty evenly divided on each side of the river. But in the new counties then forming, the seats of justice were fixed temporarily by the legislature until the developments of population should indicate where the proper place for the county seat would be, when three disinterested commissioners were appointed, whose duty it was to carefully investigate the situation and fix upon the location of the county seat. Had the location of the seat of justice been by a vote of the settlers, no doubt Maumee would have held it at that time.

Both Sides Were Envious

Orleans and Perrysburg, both on the south side of the river, were envious of each other and would not act in unity, and in a triangular battle, Maumee could out vote either of them. The question has often been raised in later years as to how Perrysburg got the county seat away from her stronger neighbor, Maumee, and we believe this is the first time an explanation has appeared in print.

The County Seat Located

At the session of the legislature, in the winter of 1821-22, Charles R. Sherman (father of Senator and General Sherman), Edward Paine, Jr., and Nehemiah King were appointed commissioners to fix the permanent location of the county seat of Wood county. At the May term of court in Maumee, 1822, the report of these commissioners, a copy of which had been placed on file with the clerk, was read in open court, and from which report (following the language of the journal), "it appears that the town of Perrysburg in said county of Wood, was selected as the most proper place as a seat of justice for said county of Wood, the said town of Perrysburg being as near the center of said county of Wood, as to situation, extent of population, quality of land and convenience and interest of the inhabitants of said county of Wood, as was possible, the commissioners aforesaid designate in-lot No. 387, as the most proper site for the court house of said county of Wood."

Fought Till the Last

It must not for a moment be supposed that Maumee surrendered up this coveted prize without a protest, or that Orleans looked on with an approving smile. Both opposed it with every possible influence, but Perrysburg had a powerful ally. Just at this critical juncture, the United States gave some friendly aid to her protege.

A Gift of Great Benefit

In May, 1822, Congress enacted a law vesting the title to all unsold lots and out-lots in Perrysburg, in the Commissioners of Wood county, on condition that the county seat should be permanently located there. The net proceeds of the sale of the lots were to be used in erecting public buildings, etc. There was a considerable number of these lots unsold and the gift proved of great benefit to the county in its early poverty, in getting a jail and court house without much expense to the tax-payers. Regardless of this help to the county, the decision of the commissioners who located the seat of justice, was a wise and also a just one, either in the light of the views set forth in their report, or of what subsequently occurred, the dismemberment of Wood county to form Lucas.

A Complicated Question

There was, too, at this time a complicated question of jurisdiction between Ohio and the territory of Michigan, which well nigh provoked a war 15 years later. According to the claims of Michigan, most of the territory north of the Maumee belonged to her. The final decision of the question rested with Congress, as Michigan was not yet a state. This uncertainty of jurisdiction may also have had its influence with the commission which fixed the permanent county seat at Perrysburg. It was known to the friends of the latter place, and the Hollisters, Spaffords and others, who had at that time invested in property in Perrysburg, were tacticians enough to work the point for all it was worth. Although the decision of the commission in favor of Perrysburg was made in May, 1822, there does not appear to have been any haste in the removal.

The Commissioners Meet

The first meeting of the county commissioners in Perrysburg, as shown by their journal, was on the 3rd of March following, nearly ten months after the decision had been made. Their minutes of the proceeding in Maumee, during almost three years, show a light amount of routine work. They had constructed a log jail and taken some steps looking to the establishment of roads. Their record for the entire time covers only about 20 pages, and the auditor, Ambrose Rice, received $29.75 for his services in the year ending March 4, 1822. Thomas W. Powell, then prosecuting attorney, was appointed auditor for the year 1823, and filled both offices, getting an allowance of $30 for his services as auditor, which was 25 cents more than Rice got.

SCRAP-BOOK.

THE TREATY OF MAUMEE

Most Important to Wood County—Opposed by Some of the Indian Chiefs—Thrilling Scenes—This Section at Last Placed on the Map

THE conclusion of the series of great events by which the United States acquired a clear title deed to the lands now embraced in Wood county was that of the Maumee Treaty in 1817. In September of that year Duncan McArthur and Lewis Cass, as the authorized agents of the United States, met the Wyandot, Ottawa, Chippewa, Pottawatomy, Seneca, Delaware, and Shawnee tribes to the number of about 7,000 Indians, at a treaty council at the Maumee Rapids and purchased from them all their remaining lands in Ohio except some scattering reservations. Only one of these touched the present limits of Wood county.

Of all the great treaties from that made with the Iroquois at Fort Stanwix in 1784, down to this at the Maumee Rapids, none was so important to Northwestern Ohio. Campaigns had been made and battles fought—sometimes to end in defeat, sometimes in victory. Treaty had followed treaty, but each and all had consigned this land to the sway of the savage. Almost three decades had passed from the time the Marietta Colony was planted on the Ohio in 1878, until the power of the government was invoked in bringing the unshadowed noonday light of Civilization to the Maumee country. Now, for the first time could it be said that this section stood on an equality with the rest of Ohio, free from the fetters of ownership and dominance of a race whose interests, habits, customs and mode of life were entirely opposed to the improvement of the country.

It is possible that this land was, in that early time, thought unfit for white occupation, or rather that it was better suited to the uses of Indians than whites. It was doubtless true that in some respects this portion of Ohio was not the most desirable of any in the State. That, however, coupled with the fact that it was held as Indian territory for about thirty years after settlement begun in other portions of the State, explains why some of the counties were, for a time, way behind the procession.

A line drawn from Sandusky Bay south along the west end of the Connecticut Reserve to the Greenville treaty line, near Mount Gilead, thence westerly along that line to the Indiana line, thence north to Michigan, and including all the west part of Ohio as far as Defiance, and down the Maumee to its mouth, would about embrace the Ohio land bought at that treaty, and since cut up into about eighteen counties. Wood, as she is today, lay entirely within this purchase, aside from the half of the twelve-mile square Reserve on the north side of the Maumee, bought at Wayne's treaty. The land on the north side of the Maumee, west to Defiance, was bought at the treaty of Detroit, 1807.

The treaty was regarded by the people of the state with great interest. This part of Ohio north of the Greenville line was a blank space on the map. It was simply the Indian territory and the "Black Swamp." Its name caused a shrug of terror to many. In others there was a belief that while it was not an earthly paradise, yet it was a good place to go and "grow up with the country."

The Indians too, did not agree as to the advisability of selling it. There was a division among them and some stout opposition developed at the treaty.

Signing the Treaty of 1817

Gen. Hunt, in his reminiscences, says:

There was an Indian present whose name was Mashkeman, who was a great warrior, and prided himself on being a British subject. He had been bribed to oppose the treaty. When he found the Indians giving way to Cass and McArthur, our commissioners, it made him very angry. He said in his speech that "the palefaces had cheated the red men, from their first landing on this continent. The first who came said they wanted land enough to put a foot on. They gave the Indians a beef, and were to have so much land as the hide would cover. The palefaces cut that hide into strings, and got land enough for a fort. The next time they wanted more land they bought a great pile of goods, which they offered for land. The red men took the goods, and the palefaces were to have for them so much land as a horse would travel round in a day. They cheated the red man again by having a relay of horses to travel at their utmost speed. In that way they succeeded. Now, you Cass," pointing his finger and shaking his tomahawk over Cass' head, "Now, you Cass, come here to cheat us again." Thus closing he sat down. Cass replied: "My friends, I am much pleased to find among you so great a man as Mashkeman. I am glad to see you have an orator, a man who understands how much you have been cheated by the white people, and who is fully able to cope with them—those scoundrels who have cheated you so outrageously. 'Tis true what he has said, every word true. And the first white man was your French father. The second white man was your English father you seem to think so much of.

"Now you have a father, the President, who does not want to cheat you, but wants to give you more land west of the Mississippi than you have here, and to build mills for you, and help you till the soil."

At which Mashkeman raved and frothed at the mouth. He came up to Gen. Cass, struck him on the breast with the back of his hand, raising his tomahawk with the other hand, saying, "Cass, you lie; you lie!"

Cass turned to Knaggs, who was one of the interpreters, and said: "Take that woman away and put a petticoat on her; no man would talk that way in council."

Two or three Indians and interpretors took him off out of the council. The treaty resulted in buying from the Indians the northwestern part of Ohio and the southern part of Michigan.

Another warrior, Otusso, meaning White Cloud, and his mother were also present and are thus spoken of:

Otusso, son of Kantuck-e-gau, the most eloquent warrior of his tribe, was a very intelligent Indian—quite the equal of Tecumseh in mental acumen, but lacking the force and vigor of the latter. Otusso was a descendant of the renowned Pontiac, and at the time of his death the last of his family, and the last war chief of his nation, remaining on the Maumee river.

His mother was a sort of Indian Queen and grandniece to Pontiac. She was held in great reverence by the Indians—so much so, that at the time of this treaty in 1817 (she then being very old and wrinkled and bent over with age, her hair perfectly white), no chief would sign the treaty until she had first consented and made her mark by touching her fingers to the pen. At that treaty there were 7,000 Indians gathered together. When the treaty was agreed upon, the head chiefs and warriors sat round the inner circle. She had a place among them. The remaining Indians, with the women and children, comprised a crowd outside. The chiefs sat on seats built under the roof of the council house, which was open on all sides. The whole assembly kept silence. The chiefs bowed their heads and cast their eyes to the ground and waited patiently for the old woman until she rose, went forward, and touched the pen to the treaty, after it had been read to them in her presence. Then followed the signatures of all the chiefs.

More Encouragement to Settlers

Following close after this treaty another helpful thing to the settlement took place. The Government in the previous year, 1816, had not only platted the town of Perrysburg but had resurveyed the 12-mile Reserve. It was in this survey that a change was made and the land along the river subdivided into river tracts instead of the usual form of survey.

The land office was at Wooster, Ohio, and in 1817 the sale took place, which proved of great advantage to the settlement. It gave a fixedness and permanence to the improvements started. Hitherto when all were squatters without fixed tenure there was but little incentive to go into extensive improvement. —*C. W. E.*

WOOD COUNTY BORN

In the Track of Startling Events Long Before It Had a Name

WOOD COUNTY, in name and boundary, was born into the sisterhood of Ohio counties April 1, 1820, by an act of the Ohio Assembly. She drew her first breath of official corporate life in the following month, May 12, in the second story of a little store room in Maumee. There the first Board of Commissioners (Daniel Hubbell, John Pray and W. H. Ewing) held their first meeting and made the first page of the official records of Wood county.

The beginning was small, but the expectations were proportionately great. It is safe to affirm that there was not at that time a more unpromising member in the family of Ohio counties. Possibly that gallant soldier, Captain Wood, who was Gen. Harrison's chief engineer at Fort Meigs, and who helped to defend that post in 1812, and for whom Wood county was named, did not feel very highly complimented. But were it possible that he could rise up from beside the marble shaft built to his memory on the Hudson at West Point, and view this land now touched by the magic wand of three generations, he would not be ashamed of his progressive namesake.

The biography of these hardy pioneers and the historic events of the memorable past rightly form a part of the story of Wood county. An account of the land and of the individuals and communities who occupy it makes biography and history, two of the most interesting branches of human knowledge.

Wood county, with her accumulation of historic years and thrifty, progressive people, has a contribution of this kind now fast passing into oblivion, which, if truthfully and fittingly told, is well worthy a place in our national history. Much that belongs to and becomes a part of our history occurred before our land had a place marked in the geography of the world. The homes which we enjoy to-day lay in the tracks of great events of the past.

Long before the silent wastes of Wood had even a name, the martial tread of armies responded to the call of the nation, when its destiny hung trembling in the balance. It was then the startling roar of cannon proclaimed that the final contest between Civilization and Barbarism was in deadly issue at her very threshold.—*C. W. E.*

CATHOLIC MISSIONS

First Established in Ohio—Interesting Sketch by D. W. Manchester, of Cleveland

THE following interesting sketch of the first Catholic explorers and missionaries, was furnished Mr. Evers some years ago by D. W. Manchester, Secretary and Librarian of the Western Reserve Historical Society, with headquarters at Cleveland:

There has been much published relating to early explorations in North America and the West, but a great portion from the different sources does not seem to assimilate, or there seems, rather, to be a disagreement with the whole. There has been less published, because of less general interest, perhaps, respecting the first priests and their missions; but what has been published appears to be more definite and reliable. I suppose there is no doubt that LaSalle was the first white man who "looked into the Maumee Valley," although Jolliet undoubtedly was the first Frenchman who navigated Lake Erie; and while the latter may have coasted along the southerly shore of that Lake, there is no probability that he penetrated at all the interior. There is scarcely any ground for question that LaSalle did make explorations within the present state, and he is believed to have been at Cleveland and in the vicinity of Canfield, Mahoning county. On this expedition LaSalle set out from Montreal, July, 1667, "with five Canoes and three Canoes of Sulpitians guided by some Senecas who had wintered in Canada." Col. Chas. Whittlesey, until his death president of the Western Reserve Historical Society from its organization, speaking of this expedition, the only record of which, so far as I am aware, being that of Galinee, "still in deacon's orders," who accompanied LaSalle, says, "LaSalle's plan might have been to cross Lake Ontario to Grand river, down it to the lake, thence along the north shore of Erie to the mouth of the Maumee river on the route referred to by him in 1662." The Colonel also says, "He (LaSalle) may have spent the winter (1669-70) in Ohio, where game was abundant and beaver numerous. We have no reliable evidence that he was at Montreal between July 1669 and August 1672."

There is much mystery about the movements of LaSalle, and an unfortunate lack or reliable data, arising largely from the fact that the Catholics make as little mention of him as possible after what they term his "apostasy." Gen. Garfield, in a valuable address, published as Tract 20, publications of the Historical Society, entitled "Discovery and Ownership of the Northwestern Territory and Settlement of the Western Reserve," follows much the same line of thought as Col. Whittlesey, and speaking of LaSalle's expedition says, "We find him with a small party near the western extremity of Lake Ontario boldly entering the domain of the dreaded Iroquois, traveling southward and westward through the wintry wilderness until he reached a branch of the Ohio, probably the Alleghany."

Before the death of Col. Whittlesey, Pierre Margry communicated to him an extract from an unpublished letter (without date) of LaSalle's, in which the latter mentions "the river which you see marked on my map of the southern coast of this lake (Erie), etc." The original of this letter was sent to Francis Parkman, who says, "On the map described 'Discovery of Great West' the Maumee river is clearly laid down, with a portage direct to the Ohio, which is brought close to Lake Erie." This map is clearly anterior to 1680.

I might add that an additional reason why there is so little account of LaSalle's travels and explorations, is found in the fact that a part of the papers were lost in the attack of the Iroquois on the post in 1681, and that on his assassination in 1687, his brother, the Abbe Cavalier, burned the most of the papers that were found with him.

Mr. Gillmany Shea is of the opinion that we may conclude that "unauthorized trappers, traders and Coureurs de bois, both French and English, were among the Indians in advance of the explorers."

It is a fact, I believe, that the early explorers and priests (and they were inseparable) came direct from Canada to the Northwest Territory, and Mr. Shea says that Father Joseph Le Caron was the first Catholic priest from Canada who penetrated into the present territory of the United States. He was one of four Fransiscans whom Champlain obtained from France in 1614. A year later, Le Caron was laboring among the Indians at Lake Huron; but I think there is no evidence that he was in the limits of Ohio.

Mr. Shea is unquestioned authority on Catholic missions in America, and in an article contributed by him to the Catholic Universe of Cleveland in 1881, and which paper the Rev. G. F. Houck, Chancellor of the Cleveland Diocese, which embraces thirty-three counties in Northern and Northwestern Ohio, has embodied in his book entitled "The Church in Northern Ohio," says, "The first trace of Catholic missionaries having visited the territory now within the limits of Ohio, is found as early as 1749. It was then that the Jesuit Fathers, Potier and Bonnecamp, came to evangelize the Huron Indians living along the Vermillion and Sandusky rivers, in Northern Ohio. He also states that the first permanent chapel within the confines of the present state of Ohio, was erected near Sandusky in 1751, by the Jesuit Father de la Richardie, who, with his companions, had come from Detroit and Canada to the southern shore of Lake Erie.

A part of the Huron tribe was brought by Father de la Richardie, in 1751, to Sandusky, where, under the name of Wyandots, they soon took an active part in the affairs of the West. They were also conspicuous in the last French War, and at its close were implicated in the conspiracy of Pontiac, though long checked by the influence of Father Peter Potier, S. J. During the exciting times of the war these missionaries were driven from Sandusky, Father Potier being the last Jesuit missionary among the western Hurons. He died in July, 1781. The Indian missions in and near Sandusky thence depended entirely on the priests attached to the French posts in Canada and Michigan.

When the Society of Jesus was suppressed, and Canada lost to the French, the above mentioned Indian missions were abandoned. From 1751 to 1795 no record is found of any further effort made in Northern Ohio to continue the missionary work begun by the Jesuits. In the early part of 1796 the Rev. Edmund Burke was sent by Bishop Hubert, of Quebec, from Detroit, to the northwestern part of Ohio, near Fort Miami, just built by the British government on the Maumee river, opposite the present site of Perrysburg, Wood county.

Here he resided about one year, ministering to the few Catholic soldiers in the fort, and endeavoring with little success, to christianize the Ottawa and Chippewa Indians in the neighborhood—the latter work having been for long one of his aims as a missionary priest. Father Burke left this unpromising charge about February, 1797. From that time, and until 1817, no priest was stationed in Northern Ohio, and in fact none in the entire territory of the present state of Ohio."—*D. W. Manchester.*

DISASTROUS CAMPAIGNS

Under Gens. Harmar and St. Clair—Terror of Settlers—Grief of Washington—The Man Chosen for the Emergency—Washington and Wayne Contrasted

EARLY in the year 1790, a short distance north of Marietta, twelve white settlers were inhumanly butchered and their bodies burned by the Indians. This was the beginning of what is sometimes known in history as Wayne's War. The Government still entertained hopes of avoiding a general war, but it was thought best at the same time to chastise the Indians severely for this outrage and make them feel the power of the "thirteen fires" as the Indians termed the United States. Accordingly Gen. Harmar, an old continental officer, with a battalion of regular troops and twelve hundred Kentucky and Pennsylvania volunteers, marched against the hostile warriors. These latter fell back to the Maumee at the junction of the St. Joseph and St. Mary's rivers, now Fort Wayne.

Gen. Harmar's Defeat

There, after some bad generalship by Harmar, a part of his army was ambushed by the Indians under command of a Miami chief named Little Turtle and many of the regulars with their officers killed. The volunteers saved themselves by inglorious flight.

Thus, disastrously ended the first attempt to punish the Indians. Emboldened by this victory and stimulated by the plunder it secured them the savages became more defiant and bloodthirsty than ever. The situation of the settlers at this time was one of great peril. Several desultory war expeditions by the Kentucky and Virginia volunteers were made, which resulted chiefly in destroying some Indian villages and their cornfields, but this only exasperated the revengeful savages to additional atrocities.

Gen. St. Clair's Disaster

A second expedition by the Government was commanded by Gen. Arthur St. Clair, at that time Governor of the Northwest territory. On the approach of this army the Indians, this time fell back on a more direct route to the Maumee. St. Clair, who had seen service in the war of the Revolution, was a gouty old man, lacking not only in vital energy, but in the qualities of an Indian fighter. He pursued the retreating foe until they had reached a point (since called Fort Recovery near the head of the Wabash, on the line of the present counties of Darke and Mercer), where, one morning at daylight the Americans were suddenly and unexpectedly attacked by an overwhelming force of Indians, again led by the wily chieftain Little Turtle. St. Clair's army was utterly defeated and routed with a loss in slain of over nine hundred men, nearly half of his fighting force, together with his cannon, ammunition, baggage and other equipment.

An Appalling Calamity

No such appalling, ghastly disaster had ever before befel the whites in Indian warfare; not even Braddock's defeat equaled it in loss of life.

The prisoners and wounded were put to death with the most diabolical tortures known in savage warfare, while the dead were mutilated in the most horrible manner. The eyes of these were gouged out and the sockets as well as the mouth and ears filled with earth—as if in a grim, hideous satisfaction of the white man's demand for more land. The brutality and demoniacal vengeance of the savages was never more atrociously exhibited than in this defeat and pursuit of the whites. The direful news spread rapidly from the frontier to the Atlantic and the helpless border settlers spoke of the

GENERAL ANTHONY WAYNE
Hero of The Battle of Fallen Timber. Born in Chester Co., Pa., Jan. 1, 1745.
Died at Presque Isle, Erie, Pa., Dec. 15, 1796.

calamity with bated breath and terror. The situation was now deplorable in the extreme.

Washington's Great Grief

President Washington, it is related, wrung his hands and shed tears of anguish when the news reached him and both swore and prayed in the conflict of frenzied emotions which almost distracted his mind. He was inconsolable, doubtless in part, for his share of the responsibility, in appointing a man who had proved as incompetent as St. Clair.

The whole country clamored loudly now for active and strong measures by the Government. A leader was in demand to go to the frontier, organize an army and punish and subdue the savages, an undertaking of no small magnitude as the case then stood. The President, after much serious deliberation, sent for

Gen. Anthony Wayne

A former military associate, living at Chester, Pennsylvania, a small farmer and surveyor by occupation. Wayne mounted his horse and rode to the capital city to see what his old commander wanted. He was then in the prime of life, a fighter by nature, of audacious courage and had the greatest degree of confidence in the wisdom and judgment of the President, in all things.

He promptly consented to go and fight the Indians if the President would allow him time to recruit, equip and drill his army before he was required to march against the enemy, which reasonable precaution, of course, was assented to.

Wayne and Washington

Anthony Wayne, whom President Washington had called to his aid in this grave emergency, was a rugged, picturesque character of the Revolutionary period. It seems even at this distant day, an anomaly in the character of the great President that he had always placed such implicit trust and confidence in one so much unlike himself in nearly every characteristic.

Wayne, while not dissipated, loved grog and jovial companions. Washington, was sedate, dignified and sober. Wayne was subject to startling ebullitions of profanity when angry or excited and it mattered little either who his auditors were. Washington was self-poised and devoutly religious in character.

As soldiers, too, they were unlike. Wayne in battle struck with the furry of a tempest, regardless of consequences. He was by some called reckless and had even then won the soubriquet of "Mad Anthony," which followed him to his grave. Washington was slow and deliberate, calculating carefully the effect of every movement.

Wayne had the dash and impetuosity of Murat, forming his conclusions on the impulse of the moment. Washington had the crafty strategy, foresight and inflexibility of purpose of Frederick the Great.

Wayne sought victory over his enemies by the short, sharp method of bloody annihilation. Washington compassed the destruction of his foe by adroit and far-reaching combinations and steady, hard fighting to a finish.

Each was great in his sphere. Each devoutly loved his country, and this devotion harmonized all differences or prejudices in habits and character. Such were the men of the Revolution.

Illustrative somewhat of Wayne's peculiar characteristics an incident is told of him, whether true or not, during the dark days of the Revolution.

A council of war had been held at Washington's headquarters, and Wayne, who commanded a Pennsylvania brigade some distance away, had been decided on as a suitable leader of a storming party to assault and carry the high, rocky fortress of Stony Point on the Hudson. The fortress was not only strong by nature, but was defended by six hundred trained British soldiers, and the mere thought of carrying it by a night attack was suggestive of desperate work.

Storming Stony Point

Washington sent for Wayne, with whom at that time he had but little personal acquaintance. Watching closely the effects his question would have, he said: "Gen. Wayne, I have sent for you to ask you a question; can you take your brigade and storm Stony Point?" Quick as a flash the general was on his feet and with a wicked light in his eye, staring straight into the face of the commander, he said: "General, I can storm hell, if you will lay the plan for me."

This bluff, warlike answer, in the contemplation of so hazardous an enterprise, almost startled the sedate commander, but he saw in the resolute rough and ready soldier before him the very man he had been looking for to lead the assault on Stony Point.

Wayne did not disappoint his commander's expectations. He led his men up the rocky precipice over the British parapets in the face of a deadly fire with the sweep of a rising tornado. When near the top a bullet struck Wayne on the head and knocked him down, but with a blasphemous oath on all the British he commanded his men, who thought him fatally hurt, to carry him into the fortress, where he met the English commandant, paralyzed and dumfounded at the audacity and suddenness of the attack and who surrendered without conditions. This daring and successful expedition led by Wayne, was pronounced by Gen. Charles Lee to be the most brilliant achievement of the war.

A Soldier and Leader

Wayne fought in nearly all the principal battles of the Revolution and always with distinction. If there was any desperate work to be done his was the first name mentioned. His savage attack on Cornwallis in Virginia, in which he inflicted heavy loss on the British, doubtless saved Lafayette from serious disaster in that campaign. Wayne was sent to Georgia and routed and drove from that state a large force of Indians on their way to join the British. The Georgia Legislature voted him their thanks, and also gave him a large tract of land for this service. In this campaign Wayne acquired some useful experience in Indian diplomacy and warfare, which afterwards came in good play in dealing with his Indian foes.

It should not, from these jottings of Wayne's early career, be inferred that he was a reckless or unsafe commander. There was neither lack of method nor of tactics in his mode of warfare. He was a leader and shared all the dangers and hardships of his men. He had good executive ability, unerring judgment and an acuteness of perception amounting almost to intuition. Shrewd and quick in expedient, watchful, cautious and energetic, Anthony Wayne was

A Dangerous Antagonist

Either in savage or civilized warfare. Such was the man chosen to carry the stars and stripes—the banner of Civilization to the Maumee wilderness and whose career we have deemed worthy of more than a passing notice.

In his memory, there should be here, a bronze statue the base of which should be the famous Turkey Foot Rock, which yet marks the place of his last battle.

The President was delayed in getting the necessary appropriations by Congress, but Wayne in the meantime went west to Pittsburg, preferring to recruit his army from the border men, who made better soldiers for an Indian campaign.

It will not be difficult to understand why there was at first a reluctance on the part of men to enlist to fight the savages after the disastrous termination of the two previous campaigns. It seemed, like signing one's own death warrant to enroll to fight Indians, the way things had been going. But Wayne's prestige as a soldier, with his other characteristics so well suited to western men of that time, soon won the day, and his army, which was to be called The Legion, divided into four sub-divisions, soon begun to assume fighting proportions.

Terms of Peace Rejected

In the meantime all emigration north of the Ohio had ceased. The settlers already there lived in, or close to block houses and even in this way were in peril of their lives. The Government all this time had been putting forth every effort to bring the tribes together in a grand council and, if it were possible, to yet avert a general war. Five different messengers had been sent among them on peace missions and all save one had been murdered, and this one was unable to effect any arrangement satisfactory to both sides. "The Ohio river must be the boundary or blood will flow," was the Indian ultimatum.

Wayne, while awaiting the result of the Government's peace efforts, was drilling and practicing his troops. In the early part of October, 1793, he advanced northward from the Ohio to a strong position in the enemy's country, where he established Fort Greenville, now the county seat of Darke county.

It was already too late in the season to hope to bring the campaign to a successful issue before winter, but the position of his army was such that he could afford protection to the settlements and at the same time keep his line of communications open for supplies. Gen. Wayne, therefore, decided to remain here until spring. About one thousand mounted men from Kentucky who had joined him went home for the winter, but had formed so good an opinion of his army and of Wayne's generalship, that they promised to come back in the spring, which they did with their numbers increased to 1,600 troops.

Burying St. Clair's Dead

After establishing his men securely in winter quarters Wayne sent a detachment of troops to the place of St. Clair's defeat, twenty-three miles in advance of his army, where he established another strong outpost called Fort Recovery. These troops had first to perform the melancholy duty of gathering up the bleaching skeletons of St. Clair's illfated men. No less than six hundred skulls were picked up and buried.

It was the wish of the President that Wayne should establish and garrison a chain of military posts from the Ohio to the stronghold of the Indians at the Maumee, so as to more effectually check all hostile expeditions and to make the Indians understand that the Government had power at hand and could summarily punish its enemies and also protect its friends.

The Indians had by this time become pretty well satisfied that the Government meant to deal vigorously with them and exerted themselves correspondingly.

Indian Tribes Uniting

Under the advice of Brandt, Blue Jacket, Roundhead, Little Turtle and other leading chieftains, influenced by British and Canadian emissaries, who promised them aid to drive back the hated Americans, the tribes were to all unite and make common cause against the advancing enemy.

Runners were sent to distant tribes to urge them to hurry forward their warriors for the impending struggle. The medicine men were invoked to aid by all the infernal arts of which superstition was master, to stir up the embers of hatred against the people of the thirteen (now increased to fifteen) fires, by addition of Vermont and Kentucky.

Wayne, with his knowledge of Indian

character, from the start had serious doubts of the Government's ability to effect any satisfactory treaty.

For this reason he had been restive at the restraint placed upon his movements, which practically delayed him almost a year. Still it is to the credit of the Government and humanity that nothing was left undone that could tend to avert the bloody argument of the sword.

Wayne's theory of handling savages was a good deal like the famous Methodist preacher, Peter Cartright, said about his methods of converting the rough sinners in the west at an early day. "Shake them over hell until they can smell brimstone, and then they are willing to accept salvation."—*C. W. E.*

EARLY HISTORY

Pertaining to Wood County—Wayne's Victory and Its Results—The Several Treaties That Followed, Securing This Wide Domain

IN giving the story of Wood county the reader is asked at the outset, to kindly bear in mind, that for a period of nearly one hundred and fifty years after the coming of the first whites, Wood county had neither name nor place on the Atlas of America. To make the story reasonably intelligible to the student of her history, some account of the events of that antecedent period becomes necessary. This will be given with due regard to avoiding too many tedious details.

The county as since constituted was, for more than one hundred years, a very insignificant part of a vast extent of territory under the nominal ownership of France. That ownership ceased in the year 1763 and passed to the English, who, after retaining possession twenty years, surrendered in 1783, all their lands south of Canada to the United States. That part of our history, like the unknown ages before the coming of the whites, is a blank. There are no written lines on its pages. There was nothing to write. The French and English left behind scarcely a visible trace of civilization in the Maumee country.

Adventurous explorers and fur traders had visited it, occasionally, or passed through on their journeys to distant points; that was all. The county remained in its primeval condition just as the forces of nature had left it since the dawn of creation. It was but a vast game preserve for vagrant bands of Indian hunters. Indeed this condition of things continued during the first decade of ownership by the United States, when occurrences remote from here brought about a gradual change.

The Indian tribes occupying the stretch of unbroken wilderness between the Maumee and Ohio rivers began a relentless, murderous warfare on the infant American settlements then springing up on the north side of the Ohio. This warfare, in which the tribes had the counsel and advice of mercenary British agents and traders at Detroit, was waged for the purpose of exterminating the whites or driving them to the south side of the Ohio. That was the boundary line the Indians had set, for the Americans. Treaties had been made for the purchase of the territory, but the claims of the tribes were so conflicting that one tribe would refuse to sanction or respect the agreements of another and the deadly strife continued. So numerous and warlike were the Indians that defeat or disaster had attended nearly every war expedition the Americans had sent against them. In the language of one of the Peace Commissioners sent to them by the Government, "The savages had become insolent with triumph." The settlers had fled to the forts and blockhouses for safety and it was evident that the country would have to be abandoned or the Government would have to adopt vigorous measures to break the power of the tribes, by inflicting severe chastisement upon them.

In this emergency President Washington, then at the head of the Government, sent out to the Ohio an old military associate of his in the Revolution, Gen. Anthony Wayne, a man of known fighting qualifications and by his habits, well suited to the rough and ready men on the frontier. Wayne made a success of the work he was chosen for. From the moment he organized his army and led it into the wilderness the panic-stricken settlers felt hope and confidence.

The Indians fell back slowly in the direction of the Maumee, watching for an opportunity to ambush or surprise the Americans as they had successfully done in two previous campaigns. Several savage assaults were made during the advance, but the warriors, who fought like Spartans, were so roughly handled by Wayne's soldiers that they became more cautious. All devices and stratagems of savage warfare failed them. In the language of their ablest chieftain, Little Turtle, they had met a white chief whose eyes were never closed; to whom the night and the day were alike. The more sagacious of the chiefs saw plainly that they were over-matched at last. With a sort of crude statesmanship that one cannot but admire in them, they at once cast aside all old tribal differences for the time being, sent runners to distant tribes and bands for help and put forth every effort to rally a force powerful enough to destroy the new invader. At that time the Maumee was the head of Lake Erie, in fact the whole country to Detroit was the seat of a dense Indian population.

A good descriptive writer of that time says: "The Maumee River was a delightful home and a secure retreat for our savage enemies. Its banks were studded with their villages, its rich bottom lands were covered with their corn, while their light canoes glided over a beautiful current, which was at once a convenient highway and an exhaustless reservoir of food. Forest, stream and prairie produced, spontaneously and in superabundance, game, fish, fruits, nuts —all things necessary to supply their simple wants. Here their wise men, without fear of molestation, gravely convened about their council fires, and deliberated on the means of checking and rolling back the tide of white immigration—a tide which they dimly foresaw would ultimately sweep their race from the face of the earth. From here their young warriors crept forth, and stealthily approaching the homes of their natural enemies, the palefaces, spread ruin and desolation far and wide. Here their booty and savage trophies were exhibited with the exultations and boasts of the returned 'braves.' Behind an impenetrable swamp, their women, children and property were safe during the absence of their men. Exempt from attack or pursuit, the savage here enjoyed perfect freedom, and lived in accordance with his rude instincts and the habits and customs of his tribe. Amid the scenes of his childhood, in the presence of his ancestors' graves, the red warrior, with his squaw and pappoose, surrounded by all the essentials to the enjoyment of his simple wants, here lived out the character which nature had given him. In war, this valley was his base line of attack, his source of supplies, and his secure refuge; in peace, his home."

When Wayne in the progress of his march arrived at the Maumee where Defiance is now, to his surprise he found the country had been abandoned by the enemy, but in his farther advance down the river on the northwesterly bank and when about two miles below the present town of Waterville, he found himself in the immediate presence of the confederated tribes of the northwest who had assembled their warriors in a well chosen position to dispute his further advance. The place chosen, some time previously, had been visited by a tornado that had prostrated nearly every tree in that forest and these trees lay as they fell in indescribable confusion. That battle ground has thus taken the name of "Fallen Timber," although some historians designate it as "The Battle of the Maumee," and others refer to it as "Wayne's Battle."

In the language of the missionary, Rev. James B. Finley, "It was the last united effort of Barbarism to check the swelling overflow of Civilization." This was on the 20th of August, 1794. It should be stated here also as showing the humane spirit of Washington toward these tribes, that while Gen. Wayne came with the sword of an Ajax in one hand, he carried the olive branch of peace in the other. Four days before the battle Wayne sent a peace message to the tribes, but it was treated with contempt. Wayne, after making the necessary disposition of his force, promptly assailed them. He swept everything before him. Such of the warriors as escaped the deadly bullets of the Americans sought safety in flight. Some fled to the British fort "Miami" below where Maumee now stands.

Right here occurred a thing which had much to do in subsequent negotiations between the Americans and Indians. The latter had no doubt been furnished before the battle with arms and ammunition by the English. They had also been encouraged by the English, whether from official sources or not is not so clear, that in case they met with defeat they would receive shelter at the fort. The English commandant knew that the fort was there in violation of treaty rights with the Americans. It was on American soil. He knew too, that should he give shelter to Wayne's armed enemies it would be a justifiable cause for the Americans to storm the fort. At all events he prudently kept his gates closed and left the Indians to their fate. For this act of perfidy on the part of their friends, the English, the Indians justly made loud complaint and in their treaty diplomacy with the tribes that followed the Americans made good use of it.

Gen. Wayne destroyed all the cornfields and Indian villages on both sides of the river, and everything else that could shelter or subsist an Indian that he could lay hands on far and near from the Maumee Bay to Fort Wayne and beyond, built and garrisoned Forts Wayne and Defiance and then marched back to Fort Greenville (now the site of the county seat of Darke county) and went into winter quarters, thus giving the tribes until spring to decide as to their future course; whether it should be for peace or for more war.

So horrible a visitation and such condign chastisement had never befell them before. They had met a white chieftain who defied all their arts of warfare and whipped them on their own chosen field and whose genius for destruction surpassed the Evil Spirit itself. The swampy fastnesses and the forest depths of the Maumee country proved no safe retreat for the red man. That ark of safety had been broken. Their pretended friends, the king's soldiers, had crept into their fort like cowards and left the Indians to escape the best way they could. There was a logic in all these things which the savage warriors could easily comprehend. They saw the hopelessness of further contest.

In the following spring the leading chiefs of the twelve principal tribes came in and declared for peace and during all the early part of summer these chiefs waged a diplomatic war with Gen. Wayne in defense of, and to secure all their rights which would have done credit to the statesmanship of enlightened people. They held to every vital point affecting their interests with the same desperate tenacity with which they had fought the last battle of Fallen Timber. The treaty known ever since as the Greenville treaty, when signed, gave to the United States about three-fourths of the land included within the present boundaries of Ohio in the south and eastern part.

The Greenville treaty line, which became important in subsequent surveys, and which is indicated on most Ohio maps, will be pretty correctly indicated by drawing a line from Cleveland southward to the northeast corner of Holmes county, thence west to the northwest corner of Darke county, thence south to the Ohio, at the mouth of the Kentucky river.

For this they were to receive annuities and other considerations. On the part of the United States, it relinquished all lands north and west of the Greenville treaty line, except sixteen blocks located in various places and roads thereto, known as United States Reserve lands. The Government also held a protectorate right over the relinquished territory, that is, it agreed to protect the Indians and they agreed not to sell their territory to anyone else. Among these reservations were the present sites of Fremont, Fort Wayne, Chicago, Detroit, Mackinaw, etc.

One among the largest of these blocks, or Reserves, and the one in which we are more particularly interested, in this narration, was one of twelve miles square at the foot of the rapids of the Miami of the Lake (Maumee). This Reserve includes both sides of the Maumee from the heart of the present city of Toledo to a point nearly three miles above where Waterville now is. Its southeast corner is the southeast corner of Perrysburg township, thence north, passing through the city of Toledo, twelve miles, west twelve miles, thence south twelve miles (the southwest corner is near the canal opposite the middle of Station island), thence east to place of beginning. The south line passes a little north of Hull Prairie, and crosses Station Island east of the center.

As Wood and Lucas counties have since been constructed, making the Maumee the boundary, to the east limits of the Reserve, Wood county has about two-fifths of this 92,160 acres and Lucas three-fifths. This was the first land in what is now Wood county to which the United States had a clear title and here began her settlements and civilization.

Why should we not award Mad Anthony and his hardy soldiers first honors as pioneers with the sword and cannon preceding the plow and ax? At least they may have the honor of being first here in "proceedings to quiet title." How those beleaguered people, penned up in forts, rejoiced when they heard of Wayne's decisive victory on the Maumee, and when, a year later, news of his treaty of peace reached them and they knew they could come forth in safety, how their shouts went up in gladness. An enthusiastic chronicler of that period says:

"Peace opened the garrisons, and the valleys of every river resounded with the woodman's ax. Never since the golden age of the poet did the siren song of peace reach so many ears or gladden so many hearts."

In the following year, 1796, a treaty was ratified between England and the United States under which all English troops were withdrawn to the Canada side of the boundary, thus removing another cause of dissension and distrust and giving Americans possession of Detroit. In the same year a county of colossal dimensions was organized, embracing what is since Northeastern Indiana, Northwestern Ohio and the lower Peninsula of Michigan, and named Wayne, in honor of Mad Anthony, with Detroit as the county seat. If any white man had lived where Wood county is now and been in need of a marriage license, or tax receipt or wished to attend court, his county seat would have been Detroit. The latter place had been the great focus point in the lucrative fur trade, which the French, and later on the English, had enjoyed for many years.

The Maumee Rapids, which was considered at the head of navigation, was, next to Detroit at that time, regarded as the most advantageous place on the lakes. Bright visions of the great city yet to spring up here had, even then, flitted across the brain of many an enthusiastic prophet. Wayne's men had spread marvelous stories of the beauty and fertility of the Maumee country and of the enormous catfish and muscalunge in the rivers, but always concluded their encomiums with an "if" it was not for the ague. But so long as the country remained so largely in possession of the Indians it was evident that its advancement would be retarded.

In the meantime a large per cent of the immigration was locating north of the Ohio. The west was making history. Kentucky had been admitted into the Union and in 1803 Ohio, with a population of upwards of 72,000, was admitted, with substantially her present boundary limits. This new relation at once inspired the people of Ohio with a desire to get the Indian title extinguished in their northwestern border.

In 1805 Michigan territory was organized and William Hull appointed Governor, and in the same year a treaty was held at Fort Industry (now Toledo), at which the United States purchased a strip of country along the south shore of Lake Erie about fifty miles wide, extending from the Cuyahoga river west to a point on the Lake between Sandusky Bay and the mouth of the Portage river, corresponding with the present west line of Huron and Erie counties, and south to the 41st parallel and corresponding with the present south line of Medina, Portage, Summit and Huron counties. This purchase formed the western part of what has since been known as the Western or Connecticut Reserve.

This important treaty, freeing as it did, that fine body of land covering nearly the entire Ohio front on Lake Erie, gave a new impetus to immigration from New England and New York to which the new territory was easy of access up the Lake.

In 1807 another treaty was made at Detroit by which the United States acquired that block of land lying between the Maumee river and the Canada border bounded east by the Lake and west by a line running due north from Fort Defiance.

In the year following, 1808, another treaty was made which was the beginning of what has since been one of the most important highways in the state, the Maumee and Western Reserve Road. The tribes ceded rights of way for a road 120 feet wide from the foot of the rapids to the western line of the Connecticut Reserve (east line of Sandusky county) together with a strip of land one mile wide on each side of the road grant given to aid in its construction. Thus gradually the agencies of advancing civilization are opening the way ahead.

By this time Peter Navarre and a number of other French families from Detroit, had located on the Bay and later John Anderson, a Scotch fur trader, well known among the Indians, had located a trading post at Fort Miami. Peter Manor, an adopted son of the Indian Chief Tondoganic, also located at the foot of the Rapids in 1808.

There was at this time a growing interest in this part of the Maumee country, more especially on account of the extensive fur trade with the Indians. There were then living along the Bay and river about eight thousand Ottawa Indians with some small bands of several other tribes who made their homes with the Ottawas. Considerable commerce was carried on by light sailing craft, owned mostly in Detroit, the distribution of goods in exchange for furs and other forest products forming the bulk of the trade.

This grew to such dimensions that in 1810 the Governor appointed Major Amos Spafford Collector for the Port of Miami. The Major, who also served as Postmaster, was the first civil officer in this part of Ohio. His first quarterly report shows the exports for three months to have been $5,610.85 worth of skins and furs, and $30 worth of bear's grease.

After careful research and inquiry we are of the belief that to Maj. Spafford belonged the honor of having been the first permanent occupant and owner of land in what is now Wood county—the first pioneer. Although the collector's office of the Port of Miami and the Post-office were on the north side of the river, the Major built his cabin on the south side, just above where Fort Meigs was afterward located. Like the other settlers, he became a squatter.—*C. W. E.*

WAYNE'S DARING SCOUTS

They Were the Eyes and Ears of His Army —Welles, Miller, McClellan and Others

WAYNE'S prestige as a soldier and his manly, bluff, honest nature drew about him the most adventurous, dare-devil characters on the frontier—men, who not only talked the Indian language, but in all the arts of wood craft, in war and hunting, excelled the Indians themselves.

Such men were Wm. Welles and Henry and Christopher Miller. Their comrades in these scouting expeditions were Hickman, Thorpe, May, Mahaffy and Robt. McClellan. The latter, McClellan, was doubtless the most athletic, at least the most active man on foot that ever trod the western wilderness. No white man or savage could escape if McClellan pursued, or could overtake McClellan if he chose to flee. Old Andrew Race, who was with Wayne and afterwards settled on the Maumee, told of an officer at Greenville, who had a standing offer of a fine horse to any man, red or white, who could outspeed McClellan. He would back off a few paces and spring over a covered army wagon with the ease of a deer going over a seven-rail fence. Then too, in courage and endurance McClellan was unexcelled.

To Wayne and his army these men were invaluable. They were the ears and eyes of his army. If he wanted information from the enemy's camp they brought it. If he wanted an Indian brought in alive they brought him and enjoyed the excitement and hair-breadth escapes more than the dull monotony of camp. An account of these reckless dare-devil spies who accompanied Wayne, and their many exciting adventures would make an interesting chapter in border history, but like much of that history, it has been lost. It had passed away forever when the actors themselves were gone.—*C. W. E.*

GRAND ORGANIZATION

The Maumee Valley Pioneer and Historical Association—What It Has Accomplished

THE Maumee Valley Pioneer Association was organized in 1864, and its first president was Gen. John E. Hunt. It held annual reunions from that time until Sept. 10, 1909, when it was merged into the Maumee Valley Pioneer and Historical Association, which had been incorporated in 1902, for the purpose of purchasing sites and accomplishing more practical results than could be achieved under the Pioneer Association. In regard to the work of this body, Mr. Evers says:

It is fitting that a word of commendation be spoken for the unselfish and devoted work of the Maumee Valley Pioneer and Historical Association to reclaim and preserve these historic grounds and care for the graves of those who perished in defense of their country.

Some of its members have for years lent their influence and put forth their best efforts in this work, at pecuniary loss and often under the most discouraging circumstances. And now that their indomitable efforts are being crowned with success, no one has more reason to rejoice than those faithful and indefatigable old workers, who for so many years have devoted themselves to this labor of patriotism and love.

Without these efforts Fort Meigs would never have had a monument, and the hundreds of graves thereabouts would have remained unmarked in the pasture fields as they have been in the scores of years that have passed away. All honor to the Association and their co-workers, as well as those of the Ohio Assembly, through whose patriotic action this tardy act of justice to our heroic dead was made possible. All honor, too, to the old Pioneer Association that kept alive and stimulated the interest in social and patriotic advancement.

Under the incorporation and plan of the Maumee Valley Pioneer and Historial Association, the purchase of the Kentucky burial ground was made possible. It is under this business-like method that most of the real progress has been made and so much has been accomplished. This association is still in splendid working order, not for gain or profit (for not an officer receives a dollar for his services), but to aid in every way possible to preserve and mark the historic spots in the Maumee Valley and to mark the burial places of the soldiers who laid down their lives in reclaiming the land from savagery and from the rule of kings in Europe.

As such, may not this Association claim, without overstepping the bounds of modesty, this fine monument overlooking Fort Meigs and the graves of its dead, as one of its proud achievements? But there is much yet to do. Still, with the aid Ohio has already given, the Association expects to be able to accomplish very much in the future. With these unselfish and worthy motives, the Association is most certainly entitled to public confidence and substantial support.

The officers of the Association are: President, D. K. Hollenbeck, of Perrysburg; Secretary, J. L. Pray, of Toledo. The Association holds its annual meetings in Toledo, on the 22d of February. The Fort Meigs Commission comprises the following membership: **John B. Wilson**, Chairman; **Charles W. Shoemaker**, **J. L. Pray**, and **Wm. Corlett**, Secretary.

SCRAP-BOOK.

WOOD COUNTY

Its Organization in 1820—The Counties Included in Wood—Township of Perrysburg

WOOD COUNTY was organized by an act of the Legislature of the State of Ohio, passed February 12, 1820, and took effect April 1, following. The act provided, "that all that part of the lands lately ceded by the Indians to the United States, which lies within this State, shall be erected into fourteen counties to be bounded and named as follows: No. 11, to include all of ranges nine, ten, eleven and twelve north of the second township north in said ranges, and to run north with the same to the State line, and to be known by the name of Wood." This included the county of Lucas with the exception of two small fractions taken from the counties of Henry and Ottawa. The two counties remained united until by act of the Legislature passed June 20, 1835, the county of Lucas was formed with the first county-seat at Maumee City.

In the formation of Lucas county all that part of Wood then lying north of the Maumee river was severed from the original county of Wood. The channel of the river thereby becoming the boundary between the counties. By the act providing for the original organization of Wood county, the counties of Hancock, Henry, Putnam, Paulding and Williams were attached to the county of Wood to remain until otherwise provided by law. At their meeting on the 4th day of March, 1822, the county commissioners organized the county, and the territory attached to its jurisdiction into two townships, Waynesfield and Auglaize. The township of Waynesfield was made co-extensive with the counties of Wood and Hancock, and the township of Auglaize included the counties of Williams, Putnam, Henry and Paulding.

Maumee City remained the seat of Justice of Wood county, and the courts were held at that place, and the other county business was there transacted from the organization of the county in the year 1820, until the year 1823.

By this time the settlements on the south side of the river at or near Perrysburg had become so large as to require a separate township organization, and accordingly the County Commissioners on the 28th day of May, 1823, "ordered that so much of the township of Waynesfield as is included in the county of Wood and lying on the south side of the Maumee river, be set off and organized into a township by the name of Perrysburg, and that the election of township officers be held on the 19th day of June, 1823, at the house of Samuel Spafford in said township."

This order organizing all of the county of Wood south of the Maumee river into a township, rendered the reorganization of a township for Hancock county, which up to this time had been a part of Waynesfield township, necessary, and accordingly the Commissioners organized it into a separate township by the name of Findlay. And Henry county, which by a former order had been included within Auglaize township, was erected into a separate township by the name of Damascus.

Battle at Providence, near Grand Rapids, battle on the site of Perrysburg; siege of Fort Wayne, two sieges of Ft. Meigs, Dudley's defeat near Miami, battle of River Raisin, defence of Ft. Stephenson and Perry's victory were all fought on or within 40 miles of the Maumee river.

DEDICATION

Of the Granite Monument at Fort Meigs in the Presence of Thousands—Inspiring Addresses by Representatives From Kentucky, Pennsylvania, Virginia and Ohio

THE 1st of September, 1908, will long be remembered by the citizens of Northwestern Ohio. On that day the beautiful granite monument that now adorns Fort Meigs was dedicated with inspiring ceremonies. The monument rises to the height of 82 feet, and has been erected in memory of the dead of Ohio, Kentucky, Pennsylvania and Virginia, who fell in the battle around Fort Meigs during the war of 1812-1813.

The Toledo Blade in its description of the monument and the commemorative exercises of that day, says it was on this point on the banks of the Maumee that the progress of the British was forever checked. Here the soldiers of the king, even when amalgamated with the savage hordes of the lake country, met their superiors. The onward march of British possession was first checked, then halted and then put to flight. The British held Detroit and from that outpost made strenuous effort to encroach further and further upon the lands claimed by American settlers and the American nation. The garrison in Fort Meigs, and the men under Dudley, that brave Kentuckian, and the troops under men like him, declared that the soldiers of the king could go no further. They fought, bled, and hundreds of them died, to uphold that proposition. The Fort Meigs monument says to the people of all the world: "This far the British came, further they could not go, for the volunteer soldiers, many of whom lie buried within the walls from which they fought, so declared."

The Monument

On two sides of the big shaft are bronze inscriptions, and on the others are phrases in raised granite letters. All four tell of the deeds of these men who fought and bled to save their country from the English, and who, dying, were buried on the Fort Meigs grounds, on which the monument stands.

There is nothing extravagant about the monument, no great figures surround it. It is simple; a magnificent stone column symbolic of the patriotic spirit of the people of today, and of their great love and gratitude for the hardy men of the war of 1812, who by their bravery and death, made it possible to erect a shaft in their memory on United States soil, instead of on a possession of the British.

Three hundred and twenty-two tons of Vermont granite, the whitest and purest, are in this Fort Meigs monument, and twenty-five cars were required to haul the huge blocks of stone. Forming a foundation for it is 6,000 cubic feet of concrete. The base of the shaft is 34 feet square, rising step-like for 16 feet, where rests the obelisk.

The obelisk is 66 feet in height, and from the base it tapers from six feet square to four feet square near the top. At the tip it has been cut to a perfect point. In the whole are 3,778 cubic feet of stone.

Fight for the Monument

The history of the fight for the monument is almost as interesting as the history of the battles in commemoration of which it was erected, and like the history of the war, the story of the monument fight, though bloodless, contains many records of unselfish deeds and noble efforts. Especial honor is due to the Maumee Valley Pioneer and Historical Society, to the Ohio General Assembly and to Governor Harris, for the labors of these made the magnificent shaft a possibility.

For years the graves of Ohio's dead in Fort Meigs battles were unmarked. Cattle wandered over them, slowly munching at long grass. The burial ground was a pasture. The Maumee Valley Pioneer and Historical Association protested, but its protests were little heeded. Then, lest the shame of such a condition should always rest on the heads of the people of Ohio, the association members quietly bought up land where the dead lay.

But the association wanted a monument fittingly commemorating the bravery of these heroes, to grace the vicinity of the spots where their tired bodies lay. They wanted a monument that would properly mark in the very heart of the Maumee valley region, the limit of British victory and the end of her encroachment upon American territory.

So, in the Ohio Assembly a resolution was introduced, authorizing an appropriation of $25,000 for such a shaft. It was pushed by Lucas and Wood county Senators and Representatives and adopted in 1904, but the resolution necessitated a further vote on a bill allowing the appropriation. The association worked might and main in the Assembly, night and day. In addition to the author of the measure and its chief supporter, other legislators fought for it, and Governor Harris, himself an old soldier, aided by suggestions and advice to the Commission.

Successful Issue

These efforts resulted triumphantly. The Ohio Assembly made the appropriation in March, 1906, and Governor Harris at once set to work to bring the monument plan to a completion. In accordance with a provision of the bill granting the appropriation, July 23, 1906, he appointed a commission of three, J. L. Pray, of Toledo, C. W. Shoemaker, of Waterville, and J. B. Wilson, of Bowling Green, to start the ball rolling. June 12, 1907, the ground on which the monument stands, consisting of River Tracts 65 and 66, comprising 36 acres, was purchased from the Hayes heirs for $10,800. October 22 of the same year the contract for the shaft was let by the commission to Lloyd Bros., Toledo's monument builders.

Throughout the winter, stone cutters worked on the great pieces of granite, cutting them to proper shape and size. June 15 of 1908, the stone was on the Fort Meigs grounds. Great cranes rapidly swung the blocks into place after the foundation of concrete had been completed, and August 1, the last piece was laid. It cost $14,000, or a total, with the grounds, of $24,800, $200 less than the appropriation.

While the stone for the shaft was being prepared, interested ones were still at work in the Assembly, with the result that a law was enacted providing for the care and protection of the monument and grounds. By this law an additional appropriation of $5,000 is made, to make improvements in the way of trees, fences and landscape work, and also to erect a cottage, which is now completed for the care taker of the grounds, and to be used as the headquarters of the Commission.

Unveiling the Shaft

In the morning a salute of four guns was fired by Battery B, field artillery, which came from Toledo the night before to carry out the flag raising ceremony.

A beautiful day, a lavish display of the national colors, the numerous refreshment stands and comfort tents, the encampment of the battery and the inspiring scene were enjoyed by the thousands assembled from far and near.

The features of the morning program

were the addresses of Col Bennett H. Young, of Louisville, Ky., who was a Confederate officer, and J. C. Morgan, of Maumee.

Early in the afternoon, Governor Harris, of Ohio, and his party arrived, when a salute of seventeen guns was thundered from the field pieces of battery B, under command of Captain Grant S. Taylor. When the bunting which draped the newly completed monument was drawn by the hand of David Robinson, jr., whose father was a soldier at the siege of Fort Meigs, four guns of the battery belched forth another salute and the band burst into patriotic music, which was almost drowned by the cheers from thousands.

A beautiful silk flag was presented to the State by the Toledo National Union, which was run up on the 100-foot steel flag pole that will permanently mark the site of the fort, as it stands in the exact center of the ancient strong works.

Gov. Harris Presides

The assemblage was called to order at 2 o'clock by J. B. Wilson, Chairman of the Ft. Meigs Commission, followed by an invocation by Rev. J. P. Michaelis, of Maumee.

Gov. A. L. Harris was introduced as president of the day, and in an address by Chairman Wilson the State of Ohio was presented with the completed monument, through Gov. Harris, who accepted the same in a fitting reply.

Upon the completion of the Governor's address, he introduced successively the following gentlemen, representing their states:

Hon. Robert S. Murphy, Lieutenant Governor of Pennsylvania, on behalf of the Keystone State.

Gen Bennett H. Young, of Louisville, representing Kentucky.

Major Robert W. Hunter, the representative of Virginia.

Hon. Joseph B. Foraker, of Cincinnati, representing Ohio.

All of these gentlemen gave terse, vigorous and patriotic addresses, and if frequent applause by the thousands assembled is an indication, they were thoroughly appreciated.

Rev. R. D. Hollington, of Toledo, pronounced the benediction, and the patriotic exercises were ended.

These exercises were interspersed throughout with patriotic songs, rendered by a choir of 75 voices from Waterville, which proved to be a most pleasing feature, and one that was thoroughly enjoyed.

The night previous was spent in placing markers throughout the grounds, showing different points of interest at the Fort and its surroundings, well calculated to give those visiting the spot a more intelligent view of the situation during the memorable sieges of 1813. These were arranged under the direction of the late C. W. Evers, well known as a student and expert in the pioneer history of this section of Ohio. He had worked faithfully several days in assisting the Commission to get ready for the commemoration, and paid the penalty for his unselfish and patriotic enthusiasm in promoting the Fort Meigs monument project. He was taken seriously ill and instead of witnessing the fruition of his arduous labors, he passed the weary hours in a hospital.

This work, so auspiciously inaugurated on that day, will, as the years go by, result in the further improvement of these grounds, and can not fail to elicit the interest of all the citizens of the Valley in its transformation to a scene of beauty well deserving of the memory of the heroic dead.

CENTER TONWNSHIP

Something of the Early Pioneer Days—Land Entries—First Settlers and Other Points of Interest

FIFTEEN years ago C. W. Evers gave an extended account of the early history of Center township, from which we condense the following:

Benjamin Cox was the first white settler in Center township. He built a cabin near the Portage, on the northeast quarter of section 32, now the Infirmary farm, in the latter part of 1827 or early part of 1828. Collister Haskins was under the impression that Cox did not bring his family in until 1828. Benjamin did not enter the land; still we must not grudge him the honor of being the first settler, since he located and made his improvements with that intention, but after four years sold out and moved off.

The First Land Entry

His son, Joseph Cox, however, made the first land entry in Center, January 13, 1831, the east half of southeast fourth of section 28, which, in April, 1835, he sold to Joseph Russell; the land lying on the Portage, three miles east of Main street, was for years known as the William Underwood place. A daughter of Benjamin Cox, Elizabeth, married Jacob Eberly, and was among the most respected of that galaxy of noble pioneer women, who, with their husbands, braved the deprivations of bygone days in the black swamp. Another daughter, Lydia, born at Findlay in 1817, was, according to Beardsley's history, the first white child to see the light of day in Hancock county, where the same authority credits Cox with being the first white settler. Cox, who had performed useful military service in the war of 1812, was a native of Virginia, and seems to have possessed that restless spirit of most of the old border men of that day who were never contented unless fully abreast of, or a little ahead of the westward advance of white settlements. That class usually led the van and blazed the way. Robust and fearless, these restless, adventurous fellows, were, in a sense, scouts for the more timid multitude then hastening over the Alleghenies, and, like the ocean spray, scattering itself in the valleys of the Muskingum, Scioto and the two Miamis, until in its northward and westward march, it had swept away the Greenville treaty line, advanced to and passed the Maumee.

Wrested From Savages

That hardy class of men, the coarser, stronger fibre of civilization, was not only useful, but absolutely indispensable. Their like never was before, nor can be again. The conditions which required the hard, dangerous service which they performed, have passed, never to return. The smoother grooves and easier lines on which we move today demand qualifications so varied and changed that, in our haste to keep up with the march, we almost forget that there ever was a race of pioneers, our forefathers, who lived in cabins and, with flint-lock guns, freed this land from the bondage of kings and wrested the wilderness from the dominion of barbarous savages. All honor to them. Their manhood and sterling virtues in life can never suffer by comparison with their successors. Uncrowned heroes and heroines they were. Though most of them sleep in graves unmarked with stone or bronze, we can do them the more enduring honor of passing their names and deeds down to future generations on the brightest pages of our annals. Benjamin Cox moved to Indiana, where he closed his life at an advanced age.

Built a Cabin

The next entry in Center, after Joseph Cox, was the northwest corner, 48 acres of section 31, by Joseph A. Sargent, October 31, 1832, lying on Main street next south of the Bender road. For some years this tract was owned by Nancy Flickinger. Sargent built his cabin on the west side of the street, in Plain, where he also owned land. Twelve days later, November 1, 1832, Adam Phillips entered the Infirmary tract, the improvements of which he had previously bought of Ben Cox.

The First Wagon

In the following spring, April, 1833, Phillips brought his family, wife and six children, out from Stark county, coming by way of Fremont, then Lower Sandusky. When he got as far west as Woodville with his outfit, consisting of a wagon covered with boards, and drawn by two horses and four oxen, Phillips left the road and followed the Indian trail up the Portage through the wilderness to the Cox cabin, being the first man to bring a wagon through on that route, now one of the best and most traveled roads in the county; he had taken the precaution to bring two good axmen, Jacob Phillips and George Hemminger, with him. The Phillipses were so well pleased with the location that Adam soon after bought more land. Few persons who came into Wood county at that early day were better suited to withstand the deprivations of life here than Adam and Catherine Phillips; both were rugged and determined; they were ambitious to have a prosperous home; their courage and hopes were boundless; everything in those first days looked bright; the bow of promise was great. Alas, how often that bow was to be overcast with clouds of discouragement—of sickness, of destitution—almost despair; yet this was almost the identical experience at one time or another, of all who came. Still there were few obstacles so great that Phillips would not find some way to overcome them. He was a medium sized, dark complexioned man with keen black eyes, hair long, and usually parted in the middle; he had a loud, clarion voice and though of limited education, he had a ready flow of language and when a bit excited would get off some startling figures of speech especially on religious subjects, which were always favorite themes with Adam.

The End of the World

He had a striking resemblance to some of the published pictures of Lorenzo Dow. Phillips was in many ways as eccentric as Dow, and his peculiar appearance and voice would attract attention in any crowd of men. Pages might be filled with incidents, both laughable and pathetic, told about him by his neighbors. One incident related, whether true or not, suggests how completely religious emotions took hold of him at times. It was at a period when the "Millerite" craze was being boldly promulgated, and a day had been fixed upon not far ahead, when the world was to be burned. Some of the zealous Millerites had been dinging the doctrine in Phillips' ears pretty industriously until it had to some extent become a subject of serious thought to him. One dark night about that time, as the story goes, the smoke house in the yard, where was stored the hams and bacon, took fire and the lurid glare of the rising flames soon flashed with blinding effect on Adam's bedroom window. With a piteous deep moan he sprang out of bed, shouting, "My God, Catherine, the judgment day's upon us and my soul is unprepared; call the boys," and immediately fell upon his knees, half asleep yet, and began praying so loud that no further fire alarm was needed. This story, enjoyed by none more than Adam's best friends, was told so often on him that it had doubtless like most stories, gained a little by the telling, but is given here in rather an abridged form. Phillips at once took a leading part in all improvements in the settlement; at every cabin raising or road chopping he was on hand and did his part well.

A Grand Pioneer Woman

When the great meeting was held at Ft. Meigs in 1840, he, with his neighbors cut and hauled a buckeye log as Center township's contribution for the log cabin at the fort. Of dame Phillips, his wife, it may truthfully be said, that she was a good second to Adam in all his worthy efforts. Besides the cares of a large family of children, she often had to feed from meal ground by her own hands in the mill, sold them by Cox, and also found time to do many generous deeds for her sick or otherwise needy neighbors. None went from her door unaided, if it was in her power to afford relief. With this very inadequate sketch of the Cox and Phillips, the two pioneer families of Center, it will now be in order to briefly notice some others, who came early.

These are George Stacy, Thomas Cox, William DeWitt, Thomas Slight, Jr., and Samuel Snyder, who entered lands in 1833.

Joseph Ralston, Joseph Wade, John M. Jaques, Joseph Russell, Henry Shively, Wm. Zimmerman and Adam Householder, who entered lands in 1834.

D. L. Hixon entered his land in 1835.

John Muir and William Munn made their entries in 1836.

These random notes from the land books, comprising but the small fractional part of the original entries and of the names of purchasers, are given here as showing who the first comers were. Most of these buyers named became actual residents on their land. Other early settlers, such as the Lundys, Klopfensteins, Andersons and others, not enumerated in the list, no doubt bought their lands of second hands. The chief purpose here is to show who the actual beginners were—a task not so easy after the lapse of three score years, when nearly all the actors have faded away in the corroding mists of time.

Survey and Organization

Center township, originally six miles square, was surveyed by Samuel Holmes, deputy U. S. surveyor, in 1819; that is, the exterior lines were made. In 1821 the sub-divisions were run by S. Bourne.

The county commissioners at their March session, 1835, granted the request for a township organization, under the name of Center, and ordered an election of township officers to be held, on the first Monday of April following, at the home of Adam Phillips. At the time of this action, Center was a part of Portage and had been since June, 1833, prior to which time it had been a part of Middleton, since that township was cut off from Perrysburg. When, in 1846, Webster was created, six sections were set off to that township. In 1844, on petition by the residents thereon, the south half of section 31, Middleton, was given to Center. It lies at the northwest corner on the Perrysburg road, so that as now constructed, the township comprises 30½ sections.

Converted into Roads

The trails between the settlements, at first mere foot paths, indicated by blazed trees, were gradually converted into wagon trails, barely passable, by voluntary labor among those interested. Some of these trails eventually became permanent highways, since they were usually located on the most favorable ground for the purpose. The first object of the newcomer after his cabin was built, was to get into road communication with the market, which in this case was Perrysburg. There lake boats landed regularly in the open season. The first wagon trail in Center, after Hull's trail, was from Cox's cabin up the Portage to Haskins' trading place. The next was the Phillips wagon trail, along the Portage, from Woodville.

A MEMORABLE FOURTH

In Which the Prosperity of Wood County Was the Theme

IN commemoration of the completion of the new court house, united with the celebration of the national birthday anniversary, the 4th of July, 1894, proved a day that will long be remembered by the thousands who participated. It was a day of oratory. Among other things Mr. A. B. Murphy said:

"Wood county is the garden of Ohio.
"It is unique in its history and splendid in its record. It is the parent of many of the counties of Northwestern Ohio. It is rich in soil, rich in intelligence, and rich in patriotic history. It has been the birthplace of ideas that have shaken the continent, and its soil has drank the blood of heroes, and been consecrated by the bones of patriots. It was here that a mighty party had its beginning. It was here that America's greatest leaders assembled in convention, Ewing, Harrison and Clay, and Ohio's black son, Tom Corwin, all of them long since sleeping in their graves. The children of this county ought to be taught that it is bounded on the north by Perry's Victory, and on the east by the home of Gibson, and on the south by Fort Findlay, and on the west by the battle ground of Meigs and Miami.

"The man who cannot make an honest living here cannot do so anywhere upon this round globe. This county is greater in extent than any one of those famous states of ancient Greece. It comprises more territory than Christ walked over while on earth, and has more inhabitants than that Sacred City over which He wept. It is greater in resource, and richer in fertility and more splendid in production than the Holy Land seen in the beatific dreams and visions of the prophets, and promised by Jehovah to the Hebrew Patriarchs of old. It has been redeemed by sweat and toil from the woods and the water. It has arisen as all things worth having arise, by conflict and sacrifice. Every achievement in this world represents sacrifice somewhere."

An extract from the address of Hon. B. F. James follows:

"With what loyalty and devotion such a county should be cherished.

"Young men, study more thoroughly the history of your county; ascertain the steps in its great growth; study the precepts that actuated its founders and defenders; let it inculcate in your young minds and hearts a deeper love of country, law and liberty; surely it will instill within you ideas of loyalty and the responsibilities of citizenship. May the summit of that new edifice tower no higher than your worth; may its foundations be no firmer than your convictions and truth; may the green and fertile soil of this great county, on whose bosom it reposes, and which grows great harvests, be no richer than your long and lofty labors in the service of your country and mankind. Then are you assured a fame which, mid the shadows of a century, will suffer no eclipse."

That matchless orator and loyal soldier, Gen. Wm. H. Gibson, graced the occasion with one of his masterly efforts. Among many other good things he used this language:

"This county was taken from the civil jurisdiction of Logan and at its organization in 1820, its area covered more territory than many of the European kingdoms. It contained less than five hundred people, and in 1830 eleven hundred, in 1840 less than six thousand, and in 1850 scarce ten thousand. For thirty years its progress was slow, and in 1860 the population was little over seventeen thousand. Though the savages were harmless and the frontiers were not disturbed by 'war's dread alarm,' the pioneer settlers in your county were confronted with hardships

SCRAP-BOOK.

and privations from which the stoutest hearts might recoil. No portion of Ohio presented such difficulties in its development. The adventurous men who came hither with their families to reclaim the flooded forests and water-soaked prairies, and rear their children, were and are the real heroes, entitled to our gratitude and admiration.

"In war, the imposing pageantry of field evolution, the touch of elbows with comrades and the shout of battle thrill the soldier with confident enthusiasm, and he plunges into the deadly conflict heedless of all danger. But the Wood county pioneer, remote from neighbors, toiling to open a farm in the wilderness and support and educate his children, exhibited a fortitude and heroism sublime for high purposes and manliness. A remnant of those rugged adventurers, who led the way in reclaiming 'the wilderness and solitary places' of your county, have been spared to join in this great demonstration and share the festivities of this auspicious day. We greet them as winning heroes, who have earned the gratitude of coming generations!

"With bent forms and blistered hands they planned and toiled, that this county might be gilded with inviting homes; enriched by abundant harvests, and sentineled with churches and school houses."

THE PITTSBURG BLUES

Complete List of Those Who Are Buried at Fort Meigs

THE following list of the members of the Pittsburg Blues, obtained through a Patriotic Pennsylvania Society, by the efforts of Mrs. Ellen McMahan Gaspers, was published in the Wood County Democrat of April 18, 1902. The Democrat says:

At last an authentic list of "The Pittsburg Blues," who lie buried at Fort Meigs, has been obtained through the efforts of the society known as "The Wives and Daughters of the Boys in Blue," of which Mrs. Ellen McMahan Gaspers of Detroit, formerly of Perrysburg, is president. Mrs. Gaspers wrote the mayor of Pittsburg for information as to this list. This letter was referred to Mrs. Felicia R. Johnson, president of the Pennsylvania society, U. S. D., 1812, and vice president of the national society, who secured what the Wives and Daughters of the Boys in Blue consider a priceless list.

It contains the names of volunteers famous as "The Pittsburg Blues," who fought under General Harrison. One of the three burial grounds at Ft. Meigs was assigned to the noted Blues, and there lie buried the remains of those who were killed in battle.

Here is the list of "The Pittsburg Blues," buried at Fort Meigs, as furnished by Mrs. Johnson:

James Butler, Captain.
Mathew McGee, Lieutenant.
James Irwin, Ensign.
E. Trovills, First Sergeant.
J. Williams, Second Sergeant.
J. Willock, Third Sergeant.
G. Haven, Fourth Sergeant.
N. Patterson, First Corporal.
J. Benney, Second Corporal.
S. Elliott, Third Corporal.
J. Read, Fourth Corporal.

Privates

R. Allison,
D. C. Boss,
J. Chess,
Clark,
J. Davis,
J. D. Davis,
R. McNeal,
J. McMasters,
N. Matthews,
J. Maxwell,
J. Marcy,
P. Neville,

J. Deal,
T. Dobbins,
J. Dodd,
A. Deemer,
J. Elliott,
A. English,
N. Fairfield,
S. Graham,
H. Hull,
Samuel Jones,
J. Lewis,
P. Leorlon,
F. Lonsong
N. M. McGiffin,
O. McKee,
T. McClarnin,
George McFall,
J. Newman,
E. Pratt,
J. Pollard,
C. Pentland,
M. Parker,
J. Park,
F. Ricards,
W. Richardson,
W. Richards,
G. V. Robinson,
S. Swift,
N. Thompson,
N. Vernon,
C. Widner,
J. Watt,
C. Wohrendorff,
G. Wilkins.

Mrs. Johnson, in writing Mrs. Gaspers inclosing the above list, says in part:

"My own grandfather served under General Croghan and was with him at Fort Stephenson, and I presume at Fort Meigs, so my interest is personal as well as patriotic.

"This society which I represent, is composed of the descendants of the soldiers of 1812, and we will be glad to co-operate with you in any effort to preserve the battlefields that have become resting places of those who preserved the independence of the nation.

"We have a society in Ohio—Mrs. Greves, of Cincinnati, is president. I do not know how they are working as they are rather new in organization, but will write them to help you if needed."

This letter is very gratifying to the Maumee Valley Pioneer and Historical Association, organized for the purpose of preserving the historical sites of the Maumee Valley. In this connection it should be said that the Toledo society of the "Daughters of the American Revolution" is co-operating with the Maumee Valley Pioneer and Historical Association in its efforts to preserve the historical sites of the Maumee Valley, and that matters have now begun to take definite form. It is now believed that the objects of this association will be accomplished.

PETERSBURG VOLUNTEERS

These Virginian Heroes Honored by a Granite Monument at Petersburg, Va.

DURING the preparation of this Pioneer Scrap-Book, an interesting and valuable letter was received by Wm. Corlett, Secretary of the Maumee Valley Pioneer and Historical Association, from Wm. M. Jones, Mayor of Petersburg, Virginia, in which the writer gives historical facts concerning a company of Virginia soldiers who fought under General William Henry Harrison in the war of 1812-13, and who were active in the defense of Fort Meigs and the Maumee Valley against the combined force of British and Indians. This is the first time a full roster of the officers and privates has been made known in the Maumee Valley.

Mayor Jones says that the Virginia company raised in Petersburg to assist in the defense of the Maumee Valley was composed of some of the flower of that state, and that the city of Petersburg erected a monument to their memory in the local cemetery, consisting of a granite shaft about 15 or 20 feet high, surmounted by a gilt American eagle, and on which is inscribed the following:

"Tribute to Patriotism"

"In memory of Captain Richard McRae, late commander of the Petersburg-Canada volunteers in the war with Great Britain, 1812, a corps who, under the

GRANITE MONUMENT
To Petersburg Volunteers at Petersburg, Va.

influence of holy patriotism, in the hour of their country's need, leaped from their downy beds and, foregoing domestic comforts and ease, instantly organized and took up the line of march for the Canadian frontier, when, under the supreme command of General Harrison, they met the disciplined armies of their country's enemies, on the fifth day of May, 1813, and after a bloody conflict defeated them, winning for their home the exalted and imperishable appellation of the 'Cockade City of the Union.' "

A second inscription is as follows:

"Petersburg Volunteers"

"Who embarked in the service of their country in the war of 1812 with Great Britain, on the 21st of October, 1812, and consecrated their valor at the battle of Fort Meigs, May 5, 1813—commanded by Capt. Richard McRae.

"Lieutenants—William Tisdale, Henry Cary, Shirly Tisdale.

"Sergeants—James Stevens, Robert B. Cook, Samuel Stevens, John Henderson.

"Corporals—M. B. Spatswood, John Perry, Joseph Scott, Thomas G. Scott, Joseph G. Noble, G. T. Clough.

"Musicians—Daniel Eshon, James Jackson.

"Privates"

Andrew Andrews,
Richard Adams,
John Bignall,
Richard H. Brauch,
Thomas B. Bigger,
Robert Black,
Benjamin Pegram,
Thomas W. Perry,
Daniel Booker,
George Booker,
Joseph R. Burtley,
John W. Burtley,
Edmund Brown,
Edward Mumford,
Reuben Clemments,
Moses Clemments,
James Chalmers,
Edward Chensworth,
James Cabaniss,
Edward H. Cogbill,
John H. Saunders,
William P. Rawlings,
Herbert C. Lafton,
Benjamin Lawson,
Alfred Loraine,
George P. Layburn,
William R. Leigh,
Benjamin Middleton,
Nicholas Mansenbury,
David Mann,
Anthony Mullen,
Rozer Mallory,
Joseph Mason,
Thomas Clark,
Samuel Miles,
James Page,
James Peterson,
Richard Pool,
George Burge,
William Burton,
John Potter,
John Rawlings,
George Richards,
William Lacy,
William Lanier,
John Shore,
John Shelton,
Richard Sharp,
John H. Smith,
John Spwalt,
Robert Stevens,
Ezra Stith,
James Jeffers,
Daniel Worsham,
Samuel Williams,
James Williams,
John F. Wiley,
David Williams.

On the south face of the monument are the following:

"General Orders"

"Headquarters District, 17th Oct., 1813.

"The term of service for which the Petersburg volunteers were engaged having expired, they are permitted to commence their march to Virginia as soon as they can be transferred to the south side of the lake. In granting a discharge to this patriotic and gallant corps, the general feels at a loss for words adequate to convey his sense of their exalted merits. Almost exclusively composed of individuals who had been nursed in the lap of ease, they have for twelve months borne the hardships and privations of military life, in the midst of an inhospitable wilderness, with an alacrity which has been unsurpassed. Their conduct in the field has been surpassed by no other corps, and whilst in camp they have set an example of subordination and respect for military authority to the whole army.

"The general requests Capt. McRae, his subalterns, non-commissioned officers and privates to accept his warmest thanks, and bids them an affectionate farewell.

"By command of

"William Henry Harrison.

"Robert Butler.

"Acting Assistant Adjutant General."

Edward Tiffin was the first Governor of Ohio and served from 1803 to 1807. From 1800 to 1810 the seat of government was at Chillicothe; from 1810 to 1812 in Zanesville, and from 1812 to 1816 in Chillicothe again; Columbus became the capital in 1816.

A man named Samuel Charter, living on the Foote farm, went to Girty's Island to make sugar. On his return, somewhere near Defiance he appropriated a grindstone and put it in his pirogue with the sugar. He was followed and his place searched, but no stone could be found. Many years afterward the stone was found in a dense thicket about forty rods from his cabin.

SCRAP-BOOK.

SHIBNAH SPINK

Interesting Sketch of One of the Most Active of Wood County Pioneers

FROM a lengthy sketch by C. W. Evers of the career of Shibnah Spink, who lived in Perrysburg, we condense as follows:

Shibnah Spink of Perrysburg, was one of the early settlers of the county, whose life has been so largely connected with the general history of this county that a sketch of the same must prove valuable as a contribution to the history of this section of the county.

Mr. Spink was born in Berkshire county, Massachusetts, in February, 1802, where he remained until 1811, when his father removed to Chautauqua county, New York.

In 1826, young Spink, having grown to manhood, went to Pennsylvania and took a contract on the Pennsylvania Canal, where he remained about two years, at the end of which time he went to Wooster, this State, where he remained until 1832, at which time he came to Perrysburg. At the latter place he opened a dry goods, grocery and hardware store, but the crash of 1836-'37 caught him unprepared for such an emergency and he retired from business. From 1837 to 1850 he was chiefly employed in running a steamboat during the summer and in purchasing furs during the winter.

In the summer of 1834, Mr. Addison Smith, then unmarried, came to Perrysburg to visit his sister, Mrs. Dustin. Mr. Spink's clerk in the store became frightened on account of the number of Indians encamped near the store and left, leaving Mr. Spink alone in his business suffering with the ague. Mr. Smith was in the habit of spending much of his time in the store and when Mr. Spink was too ill to wait upon customers, would go behind the counter and play the role of clerk. Finally he consented to act as clerk for Mr. Spink, and remained in the store several years. In the fall of that year Mr. Smith's sister, Mary A., came to Perrysburg to visit her brother and sister, remaining through the winter and the following summer. During this time, the friendship between Miss Smith and Mr. Spink ripened into love, and in the fall of 1835 they were married; and it is seldom that two more congenial spirits spend life together.

The Stone Road

In the winter of 1837-38 the old mud pike through the Black Swamp was so completely worn out and so impassable for loaded teams that a movement was made for the construction of a macadamized road from Lower Sandusky (now Fremont) to Perrysburg. Jessup W. Scott, Capt. David Wilkinson, John C. Spink, and Shibnah Spink, were selected to visit the Legislature at Columbus, and secure such assistance from the State as would insure the construction of the desired and much needed road.

They went in a carriage. As there had been a fall of snow and the ground was frozen they found the roads good and made the trip to the State Capital in three days. After remaining at Columbus a few days and being satisfied that the measure proposed would pass, Capt. Wilkinson and Shibnah Spink decided to return home, leaving their two companions at Columbus to see the measure through. On the day on which they started for home, the weather became warm and rain set in, rendering the roads almost impassable. On the evening of the sixth day after leaving Columbus, the two lobbyists reached home, in a sadly dilapidated condition, on foot, having left their carriage and baggage eight miles this side of Lower Sandusky. Using their blankets for saddles they mounted the horses and rode until they reached Toussaint Creek, which stream they found so swollen that it was impossible to get their horses to the bridge spanning the channel. The whole country was flooded. They put up for the night, and as the weather became cold, and there was little or no current in the vast sea of water before them, ice was formed of such thickness that in the morning it would bear a man. They were fully thirteen miles from home and the Captain was a cripple; but they decided to make the balance of their journey on foot. After breakfast the two men started, but before going far the Captain gave out and they were compelled to hire a boy and pony to bring him in. Mr. Spink walked the entire distance, reaching home with only the whip and the clothes on his back as representatives of the entire outfit of the Columbus party.

More of Pioneer Hardships

Another incident illustrative of pioneer life in this section of the country, occurred at an earlier date than the foregoing one. In the spring of 1833, Mr. Spink started out in search of cows, milk being in demand at Perrysburg. He was gone for three days through the country overcoming many obstacles and making a circuit that now could be accomplished in a few hours.

In 1839 Mr. Spink was in the employ of Judge John Hollister, who at that time owned a line of steamboats which ran between Perrysburg and Buffalo, and also transacted a large business as agent for the American Fur Company. Mr. Spink was master of the General Vance. As there were no railroads in those days, the lakes were the great commercial highways and boats ran as long as the river was open. On returning from his last trip that fall, after having been absent from his family nearly all of the season, he went into Hollister's store in the evening happy with the thought that he should have a little rest and enjoy the comforts of home, but was told that they wanted him to start the next morning for southwestern Indiana in the interest of the fur company—that somebody must go, and that he was the only person who could fill the bill. Hard as was this task and great as was his disappointment, Mr. Spink consented to go, and after remaining with his family over night, he and B. F. Hollister mounted their horses and started on the journey. The distance to be traveled was four hundred miles, and they made it in eight days, averaging fifty miles per day.

Mr. Spink remained in southern Indiana, buying furs and skins until the first of June, when, being an earnest Whig, he hastened to the monster gathering at Ft. Meigs in 1840. Although suffering from ague he made the trip in good time.

His First Public Office

In 1850, when General Taylor was President and General G. A. Jones, of Mount Vernon, was U. S. Marshal of Ohio, Mr. Spink was appointed Deputy Marshal. His duties required him to visit every house in the county for the purpose of taking the census. In 1830, when Wood county embraced what is now Lucas county, and also a portion of Fulton county, the entire population was less than 2,000, but in 1850 Mr. Spink found nearly ten thousand persons living within the present limits of this county.

Elected Sheriff

In this year Mr. Spink was elected Sheriff of Wood county. The county was strongly Democratic in politics, but his personal popularity secured success. About this time many leading Democrats became tinctured with free soil sentiments, and when the Missouri compromise measures were adopted by Congress, many of them joined with the Whigs, and the county finally passed into the hands of the Whigs, and since the organization of the Republican party has been strongly Republican. Mr. Spink contributed largely to these results. An enthusiastic partisan, liberal in his views, and genial in his manners, he was always at work and none could accomplish more. At that time the entire fees of the Sheriff's office for two years did not amount to over $500—$100 of which was received in cash and the balance mostly was never collected.

Beaten for Treasurer

At the next election after his successful canvass for Sheriff, Mr. Spink was nominated for County Treasurer by the Whigs. At that time John Bates was the strong wheel-horse of the Wood. county Democrats, and he was Mr. Spink's opponent. Bates was treasurer for a number of years and it was believed that he could neither be beaten in convention nor at the polls. Spink was equally strong with the Whigs, and the county was Democratic by about 300 majority. When the votes were counted it was found that Bates had but barely nine majority.

Elected Treasurer

When the time came for the election of Treasurer again, the Whigs nominated Mr. Spink. The Democrats were a little afraid to put forward John Bates for another trial with Spink, so they nominated Samuel Chilcote, who, it was supposed, could carry more votes than any other Democrat in the county. Chilcote was in every respect a most worthy man, but Spink beat him and was re-elected, serving four years in that office. His natural desire to accommodate the people, which often led him to advance the taxes for men throughout the county, and his well known integrity secured for him a degree of popularity with the public which is seldom enjoyed by persons so active in political work and so decided in partisan convictions.

Other Offices Filled

In 1862, under the Internal Revenue laws, Mr. Spink was appointed Deputy Assessor, a position which he filled in a creditable manner for two years, when the office was abolished. After this he turned his attention to farming, until 1871, when he was appointed Superintendent of the Western Reserve & Maumee Road, a position which he filled for nine months, after which he continued his residence in Perrysburg and for many years enjoyed the confidence and esteem of all who knew him.

A JAIL IN THE WOODS

Its Builder—How Sheriff John Webb Kept Prisoners—It Stood in a Dense Thicket

FEW of the dwellers in Wood county today will remember the old wooden jail at Perrysburg, indeed, we doubt if there are many who knew of its existence. It was built many years ago at a cost of $486, and the contractors took part of their pay in Perrysburg town lots at $12 each. It was made of square oak logs, cut mostly on the present corporation limits of Perrysburg and served its purpose as well, and was as much a terror to evil doers as are the costly structures of stone, iron and brick of the present day. Wood county's population was then less than two hundred human souls. The projectors of that jail were no doubt aware of the fact there was but little in the county at that time to steal, and that where there is no temptation there are apt to be fewer rogues. This primitive structure served as a calaboose for the confinement of some of the frisky veteran volunteers in the Michigan war, who at times indulged too freely in Maumee ague medicine and then got boisterous. It was located on Front street near the old Exchange Hotel.

Sheriff John Webb had charge of the jail, at the time George Porter was imprisoned in it, in 1830; it stood alone in a dense thicket, the brush and timber having been cleared away only far enough to admit the teams that hauled the jail timbers. The fine macadamized road now known as Front street, was only a tortuous wagon track between trees and stumps. There was no building near except the log court house. Mr. Webb lived in a little house up the river near the bayou nearly or quite half a mile from the jail, and during Porter's imprisonment Mr. Webb carried him his meals to his dismal cell in the thicket three times a day, and at night locked him in his cell and went home. Such an arrangement would not in these jail breaking times be regarded as entirely safe, but people in those days did as people do now, made the best of the means they had.

In 1823, after the county seat was removed from Maumee, "Uncle" Guy Nearing took the contract for removing the little log jail from Maumee for $45. In 1824 Nearing and Hubbell took the contract of building a court house, also for repairing the jail, which was further enlarged in 1826, or '27 by him and Elisha Martindale, though they were not the contractors, Nearing at that time being a county commissioner. The jail, as previously mentioned, was built two stories high, of logs about a foot square, secured at the ends by tenons and mortises with a wooden pin through. The floors were of the same solid square timber. The windows were but little more than long cracks where the halves of two logs had been taken out and perpendicular iron bolts passed through for security. There were two dark cells also made of strong solid square timber. The doors were rude massive wooden structures well spiked with wrought nails and swung on strong iron hinges. The roof, gables and general exterior of the building appeared similar to any hewed log cabin.—C. W. E.

OLD TIME TRAGEDY.

Atrocious Murder of Summundewat, One of the Most Noble Chiefs of the Wyandots

IN his Log Cabin sketches Mr. Evers gives the following description of the murder of Summundewat, a Wyandot chief:

During the autumn of the year 1845, Summundewat, a Wyandot chief from the Sandusky Plains, with his daughter, her husband, seven ponies, two colts, and five dogs, passed through Portage township on their way to Turkeyfoot, Henry county, on their annual fall hunt, and stopped a day or so in Portage township. While here they visited Jacob Eberly's blacksmith shop on the Portage river, one mile below the present village of Portage, for the purpose of getting a knife and hatchet made, and a gun-sight repaired.

In the employ of Eberly was a young man named John Anderson, who was quite intimate with and kept the company of one James Lyons, who lived with his widowed mother, on the middle branch of the Portage. Lyons, who was considerably older than Anderson, possessed all the elements of character for a desperado of the worst type, and dark suspicions rested on him of counterfeiting and other deviltries.

The Indians had with them two excellent coon dogs, either of which could scent a coon tree without the trouble of tracking the animal on the ground. During the visits of the Indians at Eberly's shop, Lyons had tried to buy or trade for these dogs, which he coveted very much, but without success. Lyons and Anderson both visited the camp of Summundewat, and by some means learned that the party had some money.

Shortly after the Indians left for Turkeyfoot, where they were to join another party from the Plains in a hunt. The old chief and his little party had not been gone long, when Lyons and Anderson also left. Not many days after one of these men while passing down the river was noticed to have with him Summundewat's coon dogs.

Old Benjamin Cox, who was familiar with Indian habits, and could speak their language, remarked when he saw the dogs that they must have been coaxed away, as no Indian would sell his dogs at the beginning of the hunting season.

Not many days elapsed before a startling rumor reached the settlement that Summundewat, the Indian preacher, and all his party had been murdered, and on the following Sunday, while the few scattering settlers along the river were assembled at quiet worship at a little log school house where now is the town of Portage, a party of Indians accompanied by a white trader from the Plains, and led by a chief called Snake-bones, made their appearance, causing a sensation and no little anxiety among the settlers.

Anderson Seized and Bound

After a brief halt and short parley among themselves, and a few remarks with a man whom they met, the Indians marched directly to the school house which they quietly and almost unperceived, surrounded.

Anderson, who was in the school house, was almost the first man to discover the dusky red men at the door, and divined their purpose in an instant. He grew deadly pale and shook as if awakening from a dream of horror. The chief singled out the guilty man whom he had never seen before, with that unerring certainty with which a dog tells his master. Anderson was seized and bound. At that same moment, unconscious of his danger (but with a presentiment as he afterward told, that for three days and nights somebody or some shadow was pursuing him), Lyons was one mile below on the river at Jacob Eberly's shop, trying to induce him to shoe his mare, a splendid race mare, the fleetest in the country, which Eberly did not care to do as it was Sunday. Lyons presently left and passed down the river to where Anderson lived, and waited some time for his return, but of course waited in vain.

The settlers after learning of the terrible murder that had been committed, and that the blood-stained perpetrators were from their midst, became excited almost to frenzy. Not only because of the cruel and revolting nature of the tragedy, but because it exposed them to the fury and revenge of the exasperated red men, and as may well be supposed gave every assistance in their power to give the offenders over to the law, in order that their punishment might appease the wrath of the savages.

Avenging Indians

Snake-bones had learned where Lyons lived and thither he led his party, and with that unerring certainty which had enabled him to follow the footsteps of Lyons and Anderson, from the scene of the tragedy on Turkeyfoot to Haskins settlement through unbroken forests and pathless prairies, and which seems almost an intuition, he soon revealed in that secluded cabin the evidences of terrible guilt. Mrs. Lyons lay on the bed feigning sickness. The chief made a brief survey of the cabin, and, stooping lifted a puncheon from the floor, and the two coon dogs sprung forth. He lifted the bed clothing and beheld the bloody blankets of the ill-fated Summundewat. The white spectators stood mute and aghast. In another place they found the jerked venison and furs concealed, and near by the ponies. They then retired; a short parley followed, and that night a cordon of pickets guarded that lonely cabin. Twice the two sisters of Lyons attempted to pass that line to warn their guilty brother—twice they were sent back.

Long after the shades of night had gathered over all and nothing disturbed the silence except the hum of the beetle or the song of the katydid, a horseman was heard approaching, and the rider, Jim Lyons, all unconscious of danger entered the cabin.

Lyons Captured

Scarcely had the door closed on his back ere the wary footsteps of the Wyandot chief were heard on the threshold, and all of Lyons efforts to get his favorite race mare were unavailing. She would have distanced all pursuers. She was his tried and trusted friend in case of apprehension or pursuit for crime. No telegraph or railways then to out speed her. But no—he was a prisoner, his wily captors gave him no chance of escape. He was bound hand and foot, and, with Anderson, lodged in the jail at Napoleon, the crime having been committed just within the Henry county line. The jail was a log building, and shortly after, Lyons, Anderson, and an Irishman confined on charge of murder, all escaped. Anderson was afterwards through the influence of friends, induced to give himself up, under promise that he would turn state's evidence. This was done under the belief by the settlers that there was another and third party implicated in the crime, of whose dangerous presence they desired to rid themselves.

And now, reader, would you like to hear a recital of this dark deed of blood which even at this distant day makes one shudder? If so, follow us through the

Confession of John Anderson

As has just been stated, suspicion rested on a third party. That man was John Ellsworth, who owned and lived on the farm now belonging to John Z. Smith, in Liberty township. The confession of young Anderson more than confirmed their worst suspicion. This Ellsworth, who was a little past the prime of life, was one of the most dangerous men of his time—a man who with a certain class of people could gain a strong influence, capable of strong friendship when it suited his purpose. Though professedly ignorant—so much so that he never while here, was known to write his own name or read a sentence, and yet he was one of the best educated of men. It is said that he had, before he removed to the depths of the Black Swamp, saved himself from the penitentiary on a charge of forgery by proving by bribed witnesses that he could neither read nor write, and in this state of ignorance he remained to the world about him, to the last day of his residence in Wood county.

A Polished Villain

But long after, when all old scores were outlawed, we hear of his occupying the Judge's bench in one of the Western States, to which he emigrated, and to which position he was elected. He was of fine address and plausible demeanor, yet no man more cunning in devising deep laid plots of deviltry and crime, and at the same time keeping his own skirts clear of the consequences. He was several times apprehended and imprisoned, but each time managed to break jail and get the damaging testimony disposed of, and in some way escape the law, while those of whom he had made tools would suffer the severe penalty. In fact he was supposed to be at the head of a gang of counterfeitors, horse thieves and robbers. The route of the Indians to Turkeyfoot led a little north of where Ellsworth lived.

Anderson stated that he and Lyons followed the trail until they got in the vicinity of where Ellsworth lived when they went to see him.

As soon as he learned that the Indians had money, he volunteered to go along with them, and during the journey he

Planned the Murder and Robbery

But when they reached a point near the Indians he suddenly stopped and said, "Boys, I can go no further. I am already resting under suspicion, and if this job is done, I will be the first man called upon to prove my whereabouts. I will go back and keep watch of matters until you return with the plunder, which is now to be had for the taking." Ellsworth went home and Lyons and Anderson went to the camp of the Indians, where they were well treated. The Indians, said Anderson, seemed to be suspicious of some impending evil. They were wakeful and restless at night, so much so that no opportunity offered to take their lives, until finally on the third day, under pretext of trying to find the other party of Indians, they broke up camp and moved about two miles; well had it been for them had they never stopped until they had found the other party.

Lyons and Anderson followed at a distance, blazing trees as they went, marking the route.

That night they again made their appearance at the Indian camp, pretending to be lost, tired and hungry. They were kindly received, and the poor woman busied herself in getting them something to eat, and spreading some blankets for their bed.

By previous arrangement, Lyons was to kill Summundewat and Anderson was to kill the husband of the woman and then dispatch the woman. The Indians had been broken of their rest so much that sleep soon overcame them.

A Crime of Horror

At a prearranged signal, each of the white men sunk his hatchet in the head of the sleeping men. The poor woman sprang to her feet and implored Anderson's mercy in such pitiful terms, that he hesitated. Humanity had not entirely forsaken his breast; his arm faltered. Said he, I could not strike that woman who had treated us so kindly and never had done me harm. Lyons upbraided him with a terrible oath for being chicken-hearted, and with one blow of his hatchet struck her to the earth never to rise again. They dragged the bodies a short distance and covered them beside a log. They then proceeded to gather up the effects of the murdered people, and lastly the ponies, as they were now in quite a hurry to hasten away.

So far all had gone well with them; no human eye was witness to the deed they had done. The depths of the lonely forest far, far from any settlement or habitation, was a fitting and safe place for such a crime. Safe—did we say?—no, not safe. There is an Eye that notes the fall of the sparrow, and numbers the hairs of our head. There is a Power to avenge blood beyond the ken of man. There are witnesses of all our thoughts and actions when we least suspect them. Sometimes it seems as if an overruling Hand directs mute, dumb witnesses to testify.

Just as the murderers were catching the ponies to leave, after having, as they supposed, destroyed all evidence of crime, occurred the circumstance which revealed all. Two colts that were not tethered and that followed the ponies, were very wild and fled at the approach of the white men. They could not be driven or coaxed to follow, but remained about the place whinnying and making a great fuss.

The Crime Revealed

It so happened that the other hunting party from the Plains arrived about this time and passed not far from the place, and the noise made by the colts was heard by them, and the ponies of the Indians answered the call of the colts, and the colts soon after joined and followed them. This was the first intimation to the hunters that they were in the neighborhood of the Summundewat party. Still they heard no guns and saw nothing of them. They felt certain, however, that they could not be far off, since the colts would not otherwise be there.

After a day or so one of the hunters took the trail of the colts, and following back a short distance, came to the deserted camp. He soon became satisfied that there was something wrong and reported at his camp. A number of hunters went with him and they soon found the bodies of the murdered people, and with the pursuits and results as before told. Anderson stated that not far from Ellsworth's house the crafty old villain met them and inquired, What luck? On being told what they had done, he said, How much money? They produced it; he took it, and after looking at it said, *"Boys this is no place to count money,* we will meet again;" and that was the last they saw or heard of the illgotten gold and silver.

Ellsworth Involved

The confession of Anderson implicating Ellsworth intensified public feeling to fever heat, and the officers of the law were soon after him in hot haste, but they were too late. He had gone. Rewards were offered, and he was handbilled, and finally was discovered and arrested in an out of the way town in one of the western states, but soon made his escape, and finally after Lyons and Anderson were out of reach, he boldly presented himself for trial, and of course went unconvicted and unpunished.

Anderson told how they made their escape from jail, which was built of solid square timber. With an iron poker they succeeded, by long perseverance, in burning a log of timber overhead, filling up the marks of their work with bread so as to avoid detection. On the night set for the escape, they discovered that Lyons, who was a large, full built man, could not work his body through the hole in the ceiling, but he had a will equal to the emergency. He sent Anderson through into the loft. Then stripping off all his clothes, he pushed them through, after which he thrust his body into the hole where he stood, as if he had been wedged. Then commanding Anderson to pull up and the Irishman to push up, he went through after much labor and excruciating torture, leaving a part of his skin on the rough, jagged edges of the timber.

Anderson was last heard of in Indiana, where to all who ever knew him he vanished forever, nor has search or inquiry ever been able to even get the faintest clue to him.

Ellsworth, as before stated, went west and wore the ermine of a judge, whether worthily or unworthily is a question we leave to our readers.

Lyons Lynched

Lyons finally came to the surface in California at a court organized by Judge Lynch, accused of a diabolical murder and robbery. He confessed his guilt, also to his true name, and confessed to having murdered eight men. He was hung to the limb of a tree, and his execution closed the chapter of the trio of blood-stained men, who enacted a dark tragedy which produced a state of excitement never equalled since civilization began in the "Black Swamp."

In this connection the editor of the Henry County Signal, who was well acquainted with the murdered chief, says: "Summundewat was one of the most enlightened and noble chiefs of the Wyandot nation, and was not only held in high estimation by his own people, but by all the whites that were acquainted with him as well. He had been converted to the Protestant religion, and was a leading member in the Methodist church of that nation. He was always a firm friend of the whites, and used his endeavors to maintain peace and friendly relations between his people and the 'Pale Faces' at that day. His murder caused great excitement among the Indians and the whites at his old home, and quite a number of the latter took their guns and assisted in ferreting out the murderers. These men insisted on staying and guarding the prisoners after their arrest, until court convened, fearing that they would be permitted to escape, but after some time were prevailed to leave them to the keeping of the jailor, and we know that the escape of Summundewat's murderers was connived at, and permitted by those who had them in custody."

LOGICAL REASONS

Both Historical and Sentimental, Given by C. W. Evers Why Toledo Should Be the Place for Holding the Ohio Centenary

IT will be remembered that preparations were being made to hold the commemorative centenary of Ohio's admission into the Union, at Toledo instead of Columbus, in 1903. Mr. Evers, at that time gave the following lucid points as to why Toledo should be selected without question:

If historical sentiment has anything to do with it, Toledo is the place.

Toledo is not only the proud metropolis of this section, favored by the proximity of river, bay, lake, islands and numerous railway arteries of travel and commerce, but she is rich in surrounding historic associations which inspire patriotic sentiment in the breast of every American. There is no locality in Ohio of equal historic interest.

The place where marked events in the story of a nation have transpired—where great acts of heroism, or other noble human virtues have been displayed, and have crowned momentous issues with success, always calls forth emotions of admiration.

Who that has visited Bunker Hill, the plains of Yorktown, the tomb at Mt. Vernon, or the sacred precincts of Jerusalem, has not felt this thrill of sentiment? "If such there be, go mark him well," etc.

Almost at Toledo's portals on the high bank of the Maumee is the site of Fort Miami, yet plainly distinguishable in its martial outlines of grassy embankments. It was here a party of old Count Frontenac's hardy French explorers landed in the winter of 1679-80, and unfurled the French flag—the first symbol of civilization ever planted on Ohio soil.

In the Mad Race

For empire later on, between Gaul and

Anglo-Saxon, France lost, and the tricolor gave place to the cross of St. George; twice since, this same historic spot has bristled with English cannon, contesting the mastery here with the American republic.

Farther away, across the river, but within hearing of Toledo's Sabbath bells, is another memorable landmark—Fort Meigs. Memory's filmy thread, in men yet living, almost spans the cleft of time —the short years back, when Ohio's fate hung trembling in the lurid

Smoke of Deadly Conflict

The misfortunes of war had suddenly transferred the battle ground from the Canada border to the Maumee. The sandy plains, from the River Raisin to the Maumee rapids, had drank the blood of scores and hundreds of patriotic Kentuckians who had hurried to Ohio's aid. The exultant Britons, with their hordes of Indian allies, had advanced and were at the throat of Fort Meigs, then garrisoned with a small force under General Harrison. This fort was all that stood between the defenseless settlements of southern Ohio and the infuriated savages. The heroic stand made under an almost incessant cannonade night and day, the unspoken prayers for help, the arrival of a midnight messenger bringing tidings of nearby reinforcements, and the deadly strife that ensued when that force landed at the fort are among the

Most Thrilling Episodes

Of war's dread annals. The invaders were driven back, Ohio was saved, and the story of Fort Meigs is an inspiration of patriotic sentiment, heightened greatly by a visit there.

The earth work lines, smooth and grass grown, are yet distinct in outline. Its quiet environments give scarcely a suggestion now of grim-visaged war that once frowned on its fair brow. As you glance across the beautiful sweep of water, your eye rests on the plain where Dudley's brave men were beaten down and massacred by Tecumseh's insatiate savages; where the diabolical revels of the scalp dance

Made Night Hideous

The waters, as they sweep past, seem to breathe a sad rhythm—a requiem, as it were, in memory of the heroes there, in unmarked graves.

But there are other consecrated grounds here; other mailed warriors were here. There were other tragic events, where the nation's safety hinged upon the martial valor of its patriotic sons.

Just above the fort and across the river by the road, near the margin of the water lies the huge granite boulder known far and near as

"Turkey Foot" Rock

Young man, did you ever visit that spot?

No! Then you should; there is a sulphur spring or well near—very strong. John Oviatt used to say it was here Mad Anthony let loose a big blast of sulphurous profanity because a few of the redskins got away alive. This rock is interesting in several ways. It is large; no relic hunter can carry it off; it marks the place of high tide in the battle of Fallen Timber; and let me say just here what any soldier will see at a glance, who visits this interesting field, that the Indians showed soldierly skill in selecting a defensive battle ground. Had not

Wayne's Daring Scouts

Apprised him of the situation, he might have fallen into a fatal trap, skillfully laid for him.

It is not only a battle ground monument, but is believed to be the rugged and fitting mausoleum of a sub-chief, Mas-Sas-Sa (Wyandot for turkey), of the turkey clan of the Wyandots, who was one of the unlucky fellows who tried to stop Wayne's soldiers that day. The totem, or emblem of his clan was a picture of a turkey's foot or track, which his devoted clansmen afterwards cut in this rock as a memorial to their chief.

Mas-Sas-Sa was not a leading chief, but of all the chieftains, red or white, whose deeds in war have made the Maumee historic, none other that I know of has a monument.

It is a reproach on the enterprise and patriotism of our people, that while we lavish so much on doubtful projects, we neglect to beautify these historic spots and properly commemorate the names of the heroes who came here to deliver the land from savage bondage and from conquest by kings.

It is unpleasant to think what might have happened, in case of Wayne's defeat. Did you ever think of it?

The government was weak in resources. Two American armies had been destroyed, and Wayne was leading a third one into the swampy fastnesses of the Maumee—a

Veritable River Styx

Then, the chosen rendezvous of the allied savages of the northwest, who were aided and goaded on by British agents and traders. England had advanced from the Canada border and planted her flag and garrison on the Maumee at Miami.

Behind Wayne was the buried skeletons of St. Clair's butchered army, and three feeble settlements on the Ohio from Marietta down, all cooped up in block houses. Blue Jacket and Little Turtle, insolent with victory, had made the Napoleonic decree that no American could come north of the Ohio and live. That was Ohio on that eventful August day. No wonder the victory Wayne achieved there thrilled the nation with joy and brought loud acclamations of gratitude

From All Border Settlers

Wayne was the first to plant the symbol of the new republic on the Maumee and no power has ever been able to displace it.

Anthony Wayne was a man of audacious courage, skilled in strategy, prudent in detail as Washington himself, invincible and strong of will as Kleber, impetuous in attack as Murat and profane as Swarrow. He seemed well fitted for the rough and tumble border warfare Washington chose for him.

A fitting monument should perpetuate his heroic memory on the Maumee.

Another great actor in border drama, Pontiac, the greatest red chieftain of the north, made his home with his tribe, the Ottawas, on the Maumee just below Toledo, shortly after the collapse of the startling and wide spread conspiracy which he had planned with consummate ability. His kindred lived there many years. His son Ottuso and his widow,

Kan-Tuck-E-Gun

Were at the treaty at the Maumee Rapids, 1817, and not an Indian would sign until the aged woman would first touch the pen.

Toledo is, as I just said, the focus point where more of historic interest centers than any point in Ohio. The patriotic element love and cherish these associations. It is our duty as loyal citizens to cultivate and encourage patriotism in every way. The rising generation should be taught to feel a pride in the noble deeds and virtues of their ancestors; it makes us all better citizens and makes our form of government more enduring. With Toledo's enterprise, her reputation for generous hospitality and high standard of social culture, together with her incomparable facilities for handling a crowd and making their stay comfortable, there ought to be no question of her standing at the head of the list of candidates for the Centennial.

INDIANS FOILED

In Vain Did the Strategy of the Red Hostiles Succeed with Wayne

NO sooner had Wayne's column begun its line of march through the wilderness than hostile warriors assailed the troops at every opportunity—hung on their flanks, attacked the rear guard, planned ambuscades and by every stratagem tried to draw the army into their deadly toils as they had done with Harmar and St. Clair, but in every attempt they were foiled. They always met a warm reception whenever or wherever they attacked the American line.—*C. W. E.*

PIONEER FAMILIES

That Settled on the Site of Bowling Green—The Martindales and Others

IN October, 1832, Elisha Martindale entered 40 acres of land directly west of and joining the present fair grounds, and put up a stack of wild hay at a point about due west of the floral hall, and on the west side of the present Haskins road, where the great willow tree stood, and long known as the Clinton Fay place. That was the first land entry in the present limits of Bowling Green as shown by the records.

In the spring of 1833 Martindale brought his family, and a few household effects out from Maumee, crossing the river on the ice and following, much of the way, the old army trail until he reached the cabin of a settler named Wilson on the ridge on the Haskins road, where the family stayed until a cabin could be built, except the two girls, Louisa, who later became Mrs. Van Tassel and later Thurstin and Eliza Jane, who married Warren Gunn; they were taken over to the Portage settlement and left with a family named Jaques until the cabin was ready.

Mr. Martindale, who was a man of restless energy, was nothing discouraged to find his stack of prairie hay had gone up in smoke in a big prairie fire late in the fall, started likely by Indians on their hunting excursions, but went right to work and in less than four weeks had a cabin 18x24 with "shake" roof, ready and his family moved in. They got a supply of meat from Wilson, who, with a hunter named Decker, took their pick from the bands of wild hogs that fattened on nuts and acorns in the vast forests. The girls were brought home, a shelter was made for the cow, a well dug and Bowling Green's pioneer family was settled in their new home. It was paid for and all their own.

Soon after they had got settled the oldest girl, Sally, arrived, bringing with her a gingham dress pattern and other fixings for a dress suit. In a few days William Hecox, a young man from Maumee, came with a license, and Squire Elijah Huntington, of Perrysburg, on April 15, 1833, solemnized the first marriage in Bowling Green.

The only neighbors, the Wilsons, were invited, also four friends from the mission station on the Maumee. When the young bride left the humble cabin that day on horseback sitting behind her husband on the same horse, there was no rice or second-hand shoes to throw after her; those articles were scarce then.

Other cabins followed among them that of Alfred Thurstin, in the year, 1833, who entered land and built a cabin just east of the present Reed & Merry block.
—*C. W. E. in Wood County Tribune.*

TECUMSEH
Prominent Chief of the Turtle Tribe of Indians—Killed October 5, 1813.

PETER MANOR

How He Was Remembered by His Adopted Father, the Indian Chief Tondoganie

PETER MANOR came to the river to reside in the year 1808. He had been here prior to that time but not to settle, and he had most likely acquired a knowledge of the locality through his connection with some of the French Canadian exploring parties, for at a much earlier period they had made their way up the Maumee river and carried their canoes from the head waters of the Maumee to the Wabash and passed down that river to the Ohio. Manor was adopted by the Indian chief Tondoganie and by the treaty at the foot of the Rapids of the Miami of the Lake, concluded Sept. 29, 1817, his adopted father caused a section of land to be granted to his son.

The treaty says it was granted at the special request of the Ottawas. The grant is in these words: "To Sa-wan-debans, or the Yellow Hair or Petar Manor, an adopted son of Tondoganie or the Dog, and at the special request of the Ottawas, out of the tract reserved by the treaty of Detroit, in 1807, about Roche De Boeuf, at the village of the said Dog, a section of land to contain 640 acres, to be located in a square form, on the north side of the Miami at the Wolf Rapid." This land was within the original limits of Wood county.

It was Manor who saved the settlers at the foot of the Rapids from the horhors of massacre by the Indians. He learned of the surrender of Hull from an Indian runner, and that the Indians would come in three days' time and would massacre all the Yankees in the valley. * * Manor lost no time in making this known to the settlers, and they fled, but not too soon, for they heard the yells of the savages, and saw the smoke of their log houses as they passed down the river in their frail bark. Thus tragically ended the first settlement within the limits of Wood county, and the space vacated by the destruction of their houses became the theatre of war, always dreadful, but revolting when carried on by a savage foe, and still more so, when those claiming to be Christians, use the savage scalping knife.

LITTLE TURTLE

The Wisest Indian Diplomat, Remained Faithful to the Greenville Treaty

IN making the Greenville treaty, Gen. Wayne, who was a pretty skillful, farsighted diplomatist, nearly found his match in some of the Indian chiefs who displayed wonderful tact and crude statesmanship. Especially was this true of Little Turtle, whose skill, tenacity and faithfulness in trying to guard the rights of all the tribes, won encomiums even from his enemies. It may be further said of this Indian and of his tribe, the Miamis, that after the treaty was signed they always remained faithful friends of the Americans. The same can not be said of some of the other tribes, especially the Shawanees, a portion of whom, under Tecumseh and his brother, turned against the Americans in the war with England in 1812.—*C. W. E.*

Wapakoneta was the home of Tecumseh and Logan, where their families lived. Logan, the famous Shawanese chief, was a nephew of Tecumseh, his mother being a sister of that distinguished Indian warrior.

ELOQUENCE OF TECUMSEH

His Forcible Address to Gen. Proctor in Behalf of His Warriors

WHEN Proctor began to make preparations to retreat from Malden, the quick eye of Tecumseh soon detected it. He called his warriors about him and in their behalf addressed Proctor as follows:

"Father, listen to your children! You have them now all before you. The war before this, our British father gave the hatchet to his red children, when our old chiefs were alive. They are now dead. In that war our father was thrown on his back by the Americans; and our father took them by the hand without our knowledge; and we are afraid that our father will do so again this time.

"Summer before last when I came forward with my red brethren, and was ready to take up the hatchet in favor of our British father, we were told not to be in a hurry, that he had not yet determined to fight the Americans. Listen! When war was declared, our father stood up and gave us the tomahawk, and told us that he was then ready to strike the Americans; that he wanted our assistance, and that he would certainly get our land back, which the Americans had taken from us.

"Listen! When we were last at the Rapids, it is true we gave you little assistance. It is hard to fight people who live like groundhogs. Father, listen! Our fleet has gone out; we know they have fought; we have heard the great guns; but we know nothing of what has happened to our father with one arm. (Commodore Barclay, who had lost an arm in some previous battle.) Our ships have gone one way, and we are much astonished to see our father tying up every thing and preparing to run away the other, without letting his red children know what his intentions are. You always told us to remain here and take care of our lands. It made our hearts glad to hear that was your wish. Our great father, the king, is the head, and you represent him. You always told us you would never draw your foot off British ground; but now, father, we see that you are drawing back, and we are sorry to see our father doing so without seeing the enemy. We must compare our father's conduct to a fat dog, that carries its tail on its back, but when affrighted, drops it between its legs and runs off. Father, listen! The Americans have not yet defeated us by land; neither are we sure that they have done so by water; we, therefore, wish to remain here and fight our enemy, should they make their appearance. If they defeat us, we will then retreat with our father.

"At the battle of the Rapids (Wayne's) in the last war, the Americans certainly defeated us; and when we returned to our father's fort at that place, the gates were shut against us. We were afraid that it would now be the case; but instead of that, we now see our British father preparing to march out of his garrison. Father, you have not the arms and ammunition which our great father sent for his red children. If you have an idea of going away, give them to us, and you may go and welcome, for us."

Shortly after the delivery of this speech a considerable body of Indians abandoned General Proctor, and crossed the strait to the American shore.—*C. W. E.*

The coldest day on record in this county was January 26, 1873, when the mercury stood 30 degrees below zero.

Gen. LeBaum, in 1780 attempted to capture Fort Wayne, known then as Kekionga, but was defeated and his entire command massacred.

TECUMSEH DESCRIBED

By Gen. Leslie Combs of Kentucky, as He Saw Him

GEN. LESLIE COMBS, in a letter to the Historical Record in 1871, gives the following description of the noted Indian Chief, Tecumseh:

You ask me for a description of the celebrated Indian warrior, Tecumseh, from my personal observation. I answer that I never saw the great chief but once, and then under rather exciting circumstances, but I have a vivid recollection of him from his appearance, and from intercourse with his personal friends, I am possessed of an accurate knowledge of his character.

I was, as you know, one of the prisoners taken at what is known as Dudley's defeat on the banks of the Maumee river, opposite Fort Meigs, early in May, 1813. Tecumseh had fallen upon our rear, and we were compelled to surrender. We were marched down to the old Fort Miami or Maumee, in squads, where a terrible scene awaited us.

The Indians, fully armed with guns, war clubs and tomahawks—to say nothing of scalping knives, had formed themselves into two lines in front of the gateway between which all of us were bound to pass. Many were killed or wounded in running the gauntlet. Shortly after the prisoners had entered, the Indians rushed over the walls and again surrounded us, and raised the war-whoop, at the same time making unmistakable demonstrations of violence. We all expected to be massacred, and the small British guard around us were utterly unable to afford protection. They called loudly for General Proctor and Colonel Elliot to come to our relief. At this critical moment Tecumseh came rushing in, deeply excited, and denounced the murderers of prisoners as cowards. Thus our lives were spared and we were sent down to the fleet at the mouth of Swan Creek (now Toledo) and from that place across the end of the lake to Huron and paroled.

I shall never forget the noble countenance, gallant bearing and sonorous voice of that remarkable man, while addressing his warriors in our behalf.

He was then between forty and forty-five years of age. His frame was vigorous and robust, but he was not fat, weighing about one hundred and seventy pounds. Five feet ten inches was his height. He had a high, projecting forehead, and broad, open countenance; and there was something noble and commanding in all his actions. He was brave, humane and generous, and never allowed a prisoner to be massacred if he could prevent it. At Fort Miami he saved the lives of all of us who had survived running the gauntlet. He afterwards released seven Shawanese belonging to my command, and sent them home on parole. Tecumseh was a Shawanese. His name signified in their language, Shooting Star. At the time when I saw him he held the commission of a Brigadier General in the British army. I am satisfied that he deserved all that was said of him by General Cass and Governor Harrison, previous to his death.

The names of the settlers who located within the limits of Wood county, prior to 1810, so far as can be ascertained, were Maj. Amos Spafford, Andrew Race, Thomas Leaming, Halsey W. Leaming, James Carlin, Wm. Carter, George Blalock, James Slawson, Samuel H. Ewing, Jesse Skinner, David Hull, Thomas Dick, William Peters, Ambrose Hickox, Richard Gifford; these all resided within a radius of five miles of the foot of the rapids.

DEATH OF TECUMSEH

Killed at the Battle of the River Thames and His Body Skinned

GEN. GEORGE SANDERSON, who died in 1871, at Lancaster, Ohio, was with Gen. Harrison in the battle of the river Thames, as a Captain in the regular army. Regarding Tecumseh's death Gen. Sanderson says:

My company shared in the glorious rout of Proctor and his proud army, that result being attained by the victory at the river Thames. It was on the memorable day, October 5, 1813, that Tecumseh fell. I remember Tecumseh. I saw him a number of times before the war. He was a man of huge frame, powerfully built, and was about six feet two inches in height. I saw his body on the Thames battlefield before it was cold. Whether Colonel Johnson killed him or not, I cannot say. During the battle all was smoke, noise and confusion. Indeed, I never heard any one speak of Colonel Johnson's having killed Tecumseh until years afterwards. Johnson was a brave man, and was badly wounded in the battle in a very painful part—his knuckles —and also, I think, in the body. He was carried past me on a litter. In the evening on the day of the battle I was appointed by General Harrison to guard the Indian prisoners with my company. The location was near a swamp.

As to the report of the Kentuckians having skinned Tecumseh's body, I am personally cognizant that such was the fact. I have seen many contrary reports, but they are untrue. I saw the Kentucky troops in the very act of cutting the skin from the body of the chief. They would cut strips about a half a foot in length and an inch and a half wide, which would stretch like gum elastic. I saw a piece two inches long, which, when it was dry, could be stretched nearly a foot in length. That it was Tecumseh's body which was skinned I have no doubt. I knew him. Besides the Indian prisoners under my charge continually pointed to his body, which laid close by, and uttered the most bewailing cries at his loss. By noon the day after the battle the body could hardly be recognized, it had so thoroughly been skinned. My men covered it with brush and logs, and it was probably eaten by wolves. Although many officers did not like the conduct of the Kentuckians, they dare not interfere. The troops from that state were infuriated at the massacre at the river Raisin, and their battle cry was, "Remember the River of Raisin." It was only with difficulty that the Indian prisoners could be guarded, so general was the disposition of the Kentuckians to massacre them.

ERASMUS D. PECK, M. D.

The Record of a Busy Life—One of the Leading Physicians of Our Early History

ERASMUS D. PECK, so well known to the older citizens of this county, was born at Stafford, Conn., September 16, 1808, and died December 25, 1876, at the age of 68. His medical education was obtained at Yale College and Berkshire Medical College, graduating from the latter in 1827. He came to the Maumee Valley and settled in Perrysburg in 1834, and at once engaged in the arduous duties of his profession.

Aside from his profession Dr. Peck for many years engaged in many business enterprises. Among these may be enumerated drugs, merchandise, ship building, hardware, warehousing and flour-mill. He also built the hydraulic canal at Perrysburg.

In all his money-making he turned it to some practical account. He did not keep it for show, nor wear it for ostentation. As soon as earned, it was invested in some useful occupation. There was in his composition but little of the imaginative. Dreams and visionary theories he discarded, and with wonderful tenacity clung to the practical business of the country, and through life kept every dollar employed in active business.

At the election in the spring of 1869, he was elected to Congress to fill the vacancy caused by the death of Hon. T. H. Hoag, who had beaten Mr. Ashley the fall before. He was re-elected in the fall of the next year for the full term. At both of these elections, the citizens of Perrysburg testified to the high esteem in which they held him, by largely ignoring party and casting almost the entire vote for him.

His Work During the Cholera

In a paper read before the Maumee Valley Pioneer Association on the character of Dr. Peck, among other things Hon. Asher Cook said:

"I feel the story of the doctor's life would be incomplete without some account of his noble work during the cholera, which raged with unexampled fatality at Perrysburg in the summer of 1854. Between the 20th of July and the middle of August one hundred and twenty persons died. Many of the citizens left, and of those who remained, all who did not die were engaged in taking care of the sick and burying the dead. Stores were closed and business suspended. No one came to the suffering town. Even travelers whose route lay through the town went round it. The reality of death stared every one in the face. At first the terror and excitement among the citizens were indescribable, and all who could sought safety in flight. Some of these indiscreetly advised Dr. Peck to go with them, telling him he could not stop the progress of the epidemic, and he was only exposing himself unnecessarily, where his labors would be unavailing, and in all human probability he would lose his own life without saving others. But amid all the consternation around him, he was cool, although he had greater cause of alarm than any, being constantly exposed. The door of his drug store was left open night and day, and the people helped themselves to such medicines as he would direct them to take, as he met them on his rounds to visit the sick and the dying. At the commencement of the epidemic his partner, Dr. James Robertson, was among its first victims. This left him alone to contend with this incomprehensible destroyer single-handed. But he never faltered, nor for a moment quailed before the death-dealing scourge, that was blindly putting forth its unseen power, which killed where it touched. Wearied and worn down by constant fatigue, he nevertheless rallied his powers, and hurried with unfaltering footsteps to each new demand for his aid.

"During those days and nights of terrible anxiety and suffering, he was almost constantly on the go, in no instance refusing to obey a call, until threatened with inflammation of the brain from loss of sleep. The citizens placed a guard around his house at night, to keep away callers, and allow him a few hours' rest to prepare him for the labors of the coming day.

"His answers to those who sought to induce him to abandon his duty, was: I came to Perrysburg to minister to the sick, and I shall not abandon them now when they most need my services. The physician's place is at the bedside of the sick and dying, not by the side of roses in gardens of pleasure."

MAHLON MEEKER

His Early Settlement in Plain Township—His Hard Struggle—Incidents of His Pioneer Days

MAHLON MEEKER, who came to Wood county in 1833, passed away in 1876, aged 78 years. He came from Butler county, where he left his wife and two children, until he should find and locate their future home. In company with Johnston White, a resident of Miltonville, he visited, says the Wood County Sentinel (edited by C. W. Evers), the beautiful wild meadow north of what is now Bowling Green, and discovered, accidentally, a large stool of clover in blossom, the only thing in the tame grass line he had seen since he left Butler county. He called White to him and said: "I am not afraid to trust myself on land that will grow such clover as this." That spear or stool of clover, Mr. Meeker thought, grew near where he afterward built his barn. That circumstance decided him in his location. He built his cabin there. Afterwards he went to Bucyrus and entered the land for $1.25 per acre, and owned and lived on it to the time of his death.

Startling Incident

Mrs. Meeker says after she arrived and saw what a desolate life lay before them her heart sank within her, and only for her children, she would have prayed God to relieve her from further struggle with a life of discouragement. One night shortly after her arrival and during the absence of her husband, she heard the voice of a woman screaming from a little pole shanty about a quarter of a mile distant where a family named Decker had just moved. She did not dare leave in the darkness, but next morning went over and found a dejected looking woman sitting before the fire cracking walnuts, while over against the side of her shanty on the puncheon floor, lay her husband, Jesse Decker, dead. He had died in convulsions from an overdose of turpentine taken for some bilious ailment. Mr. Meeker and a man named Howard broke their way through the ice to the Otsego mill with a yoke of oxen, got some rough boards and a few nails with which they made a rough box and hauled Decker's body to the ridge known as Union cemetery, and the burial, which was perhaps the first at that place, was conducted without ceremony.

Mr. Meeker was an excellent and exemplary citizen, a sincere friend and kind neighbor. Before his death he was the oldest pioneer of Plain township. By his enterprise in early introducing improved varieties of fruit and live stock, he contributed in no small degree to the advancement of the central part of the county and may justly be classed first among useful citizens.

"LAND SHARKS"

Mahlon Meeker's Narrow Escape from Being the Victim of One

NEARLY all the land in Plain township at one time belonged to the government and was subject to entry. Most of the settlers, at first "squatted" on a tract and began improvements, trusting to the future to get the means to enter land. But in too many cases on account of sickness or wet seasons it required their utmost efforts to gain even a tolerable subsistence, let alone getting anything ahead, and many of them lost all the fruits of their labor by those ghouls of the western frontier, called "land sharks." Mahlon Meeker narrow-

PETER NAVARRE
The Famous Scout Under General Harrison.

ly escaped becoming a victim to one of these land plunderers. He had made considerable opening before he got ready to pay for his land.

There came into the locality a fellow who pretended to be buying cattle. The stranger bought no cattle, however, but in conversation at John Wilson's, where he stopped to feed his horse, he let drop some remark by which Mrs. Wilson at once detected his business. She went at once to the Meekers, and on his return home that night she told him the business of the stranger.

Mr. Meeker went to Perrysburg that night, borrowed the money of John Hollister and immediately took an Indian trail for Bucyrus, which was the U. S. land office for this part of the state.

He rode as far as his horse could carry him the first day, then left his horse and footed it all night. He made his entry at the register office and went from there to the receiver's office. On returning shortly afterward to the register's office he was told by the officer that a man had been there only a few minutes after him to enter the same land. In his description Meeker at once recognized the bogus cattle buyer, who was just a little too late.— C. W. E.

GRAND RAPIDS

The Original Plat Made in 1831—Roads Petitioned For and Located

FIRST of the villages laid out in Weston township, was Gilead, now called Grand Rapids. The first or original plat of Gilead was made by J. N. Graham in 1831. In 1832, Guy Nearing built a saw mill at Bear Rapids on the Maumee, and with Joshua Chappel, laid out the village of Otsego, which for a time bid fair to outstrip its competitors in growth and importance, but in the progress of human affairs, the village died as did the village of Benton, which David Hedges laid out, about one and a half miles below Otsego.

All travel to and from Gilead, was along the river road to Perrysburg, at the head of navigation on the Maumee river, from which place all goods, provisions, etc., destined for the up-river settlements must be hauled, over the almost impassable roads with ox-teams, and all the peltries accumulated and produce raised must seek a market down the river in like manner.

In 1828, Alexander Brown and his father-in-law, Jos. North, were the first settlers to move back from the river into the dense forests that lay thick and dark between the river and the broad, grassy swamp known as Keeler's prairie. Mr. Brown located a heavily timbered tract of land along Beaver Creek, or as it was also then called, "Minard's Creek," and built the first cabin in a beautiful beech and maple grove. The beautiful bluff banks of Beaver Creek, covered thickly with forests of sugar maple, beech, oak and hickory timber, rapidly attracted the attention of settlers, and ere long Mr. Brown had neighbors on all sides of him.

Cutting Out First Road

The first township road petitioned for and located, was the road from Grand Rapids to a little above Potter; where it intersects the Wapakoneta road. It was located in the fall of 1830, and was the first regularly surveyed road leading from the river into the wilderness of the interior. Its length was a little over four miles and all the distance was through the most dense forest imaginable, such as the Maumee country was justly celebrated for along in the "thirties." The Wapakoneta road was not all cleared out yet at this time, so Alexander Brown took a contract to chop the timber out of a portion of the road from Gilead to the Wapakoneta road, and also for ten miles up the "Wapak" road. This furnished employment for a number of the settlers during the winter of 1830 and '31. The first choppers camped on their work. The first camp was near what is known as the John Pugh farm, in the edge of Henry county. There was at this point a deserted Indian village, and in the bark wigwams of the Indians, the choppers found shelter.

The next road laid out in the township was that very accommodating road still in use, called "the Gilead road," which ran about wherever there was dry land enough, and wherever there was a settlement, and finally brought up at Collister Haskins' place, where the Findlay road strikes the Portage river. On the surveyor's map of the road made and filed with the commissioners, the place where Ralph O. Keeler and his herders were camped on the Hollister cattle ranch, was called "Hollister's Prairie." This was the first name applied to the Keeler prairie and the settlement which afterwards became "New Westfield," Westfield, Taylortown and finally Weston. This road gave great latitude to the engineer who surveyed it, and he followed the "best" route frequently when not really the "nearest," though the old "Gilead road" is still one of the best roads as well as one of the most used roads and is the nearest route still, from "Hollister's Prairie" to Gilead. It was completed in 1834.—*C. W. E.*

AN ILLUSTRATION

Showing a Desire for Social Friendship— John Gingery's Disappointment

TO illustrate the neighborly instinct, and desire to be sociable, felt by all settlers in a new country, Uncle John Gingery tells the following story:

The choppers were at this time camped at what is known as Wilcox's bend, in Beaver Creek. One morning in midwinter found the choppers' camp bedded in a foot of snow, and a stiff blizzard blowing from the northwest. Uncle John, driven out early by the cold, set about kindling up the smouldering camp fire. While engaged at this, he heard away off to the southeast, dim through the quiet of the frosty morning air, the faint, shrill crow of a rooster. Much elated at this evidence of growing civilization, and the proximity of Christian neighbors, he at once set out in the direction indicated by the voice of the rooster, to make the acquaintance of the venturesome owners of the bird; guided by the occasional crowing, he floundered on through the deep snow, over logs and through tangled brushwood, for more than a mile, and at last pulled up at a miserable little settlement of Indians on the banks of Beaver Creek. Uncle John looked about for the rooster, and at length spied him, tied with a piece of bark by the leg to the hut of his red skinned captor. The little fellow crowed as merrily as ever he did in the civilized settlements, from which he had undoubtedly been stolen by a chicken loving Indian.

Uncle John didn't regret the tramp of over a mile, as the cheerful little bird had taught him a good lesson on making the best of circumstances, and he returned to his camp without disturbing the sleeping braves, but with a strong desire to pummel the red skin that stole the chicken. On his way back to the choppers' camp, Uncle John found that his trail had been crossed by an enormous bear's trail, but, unarmed as he was, he was glad not to have a near interview, as at that season of the year, they were apt to be hungry and ferocious.

As their job of chopping was nearly completed, Mr. Gingery and Mr. Brown arranged to visit that locality and have a grand hunt, which they did in February, camping in their old chopping camp, and securing a fine lot of bear pelts, and other game, without injury to themselves, but losing several of their dogs from the too ardent embraces of old bruin. Bear hides were worth from six to seven dollars each at Perrysburg at that time.

FISH AND AGUE

Two Distinguished Characteristics in the Early Period of Maumee Valley History

SOLDIERS who came with Mad Anthony to the Maumee country, never afterward tired of extolling its beauties, its fertility, its fine forests of oak, walnut, poplar and other valuable timber—its rivers swarming with the lovely muscalunge and sturgeon, its myriads of "red horse" (suckers), the gamey black bass and the fat, lubberly cat fish of such enormous proportions that a single fish made a meal for one of Wayne's cavalry companies at Defiance.

If the few old settlers now left on the Maumee were to explain to the present generation the numbers and size of the fish of the early times they would be suspected of having bad memories or of telling professional fisherman's "yarns."

But there were other things about these rivers not so enticing as its fish—its fever and ague. It was not usually fatal, but it was dreadfully uncomfortable. Few escaped it. Wayne's soldiers had it. He dosed them with whisky as his surgeon's reports show, but Monoghahela whisky was no match for Maumee ague in those days—in fact the fish and ague seemed to have held, for size and number, nearly relative proportions; they were hard to beat.

The soldiers and early pioneers had two theories about how they got the ague. Some thought it was carried by a malarious poison in the air, arising from decaying vegetation. Others thought it got into their systems through the fish they ate. Both sides of the question had plenty of advocates and both proved the truth or fallacy of their theory as might be, by having the ague. All had it. It was no respector of persons.

It was a singular complication or combination of attacks on the human system. The victim begun the ordeal with a feeling of extreme chilliness; lips and finger nails turned blue as if the blood were stagnant. Then greater chilliness followed by shivering and chattering of teeth. By this time the victim, feeling as if every bone in his body would break, had crawled into bed if he was fortunate enough to have one, and call for more cover, shaking meanwhile as if just out of an icy river in a bleak day.

This chilly period lasted from three-quarters of an hour to one hour or more, and was followed by a raging fever in which the patient constantly called for more water which he gulped down by the quart, and still the thirst was unquenched and unquenchable.

This fever in turn would be followed

by a relaxation of the system and the most profuse and exhausting perspiration until the sheets and clothing would be wringing wet, leaving in the clothes a disagreeable odor hard to describe, but always the same. There was no mistaking an "ague sweat" by its odor.

From this "siege" of three or four hours the patient would rise weak and dizzy and go about his or her duties and, as the ague fit only came on in most cases every other day, the patient had some respite in which to recruit a little. Usually in the "off" day the patient would be tormented with almost an uncontrollable hunger. Quinine, when it could be had was the chief antidote. The ague and chill fever as it used to be known, is seldom heard of now. With the cleaning up and drainage of the land it has passed away or taken some new form of development in the system. The last general epidemic of ague was in the wet season of 1852.—*C. W. E.*

PETER NAVARRE

The Famous Indian Interpreter and Gen. Harrison's Scout

THE stirring events of the early life of one of Maumee's most active and loyal citizens, in his day, Pierre Navarre (Peter Nevarre), should have been preserved, if it had been possible; but being an uneducated man, he was little known after the war closed except by a few of his old and intimate friends.

This energetic young Frenchman, was a favorite scout and runner of General Harrison's and other officers during the war, and was much employed, both before and after the close of the war, in carrying important dispatches for the Government, from Detroit to the settlements at the foot of the Maumee, and also to Fort Wayne, and down the Wabash and as far west as Vincennes and St. Louis. He was employed as Indian interpreter at the councils held on this and the Wabash rivers, as trusty scout sent with notice to the different tribes, when a council was to be held by the agents, or officers of the Government or army; knew all intricacies of the winding Indian trails, that led along the rivers, and across wide prairies from one point to another, and always knew where to find the different hunting parties on their remote hunting grounds.

I met, and afterwards became well acquainted with an old Pottawatomie chief, Captain Billy Colwell, on the upper Missouri, in 1840, who was well acquainted with Navarre. Capt. Colwell was in the immediate command of the Pottawatomies, at the battle of the Thames, and described Peter as one of the most active and dangerous of the scouts of Harrison on that bloody field. The chief attempted several times during the day to get a shot at the wily scout (as he was easily recognized in his highly ornamented suit of buckskin), but at each time was eluded, when the sights of his rifle were almost drawn upon him. Capt. Colwell gave Navarre credit for being the most active on foot and in general movements on a field of battle, that he ever knew. These men met frequently after the war, and became fast friends, being about the same age, both having passed through many of the same stirring scenes of that day.

These worthy men have both gone to

their long rest. Peter Navarre, lies in the little French burying ground near the mouth of the Maumee, and the old Pottawatomie chief, Capt. Colwell, is taking his last sleep, on the east bank of the Missouri, near Council Bluffs. What an interesting history could have been written of the stirring incidents of the early settlements of this country, in which these men were among the active; but they are gone, and many of the incidents of historic interest are buried with them.—D. W. H. Howard.

THE CAMPAIGN OF 1840

The Great Tide Which Carried Harrison into the Presidential Chair—The Monster Gathering at Fort Meigs—Who Placed That Log in the Well at the Fort

THE following account of the campaign of 1840, and the monster meeting at Fort Meigs in that year, was written by Mr. C. W. Evers, and published in the Sentinel some years ago:

Perhaps the most remarkable event in the political history of this country, was the campaign of 1840. General Harrison was the Whig candidate for the Presidency in 1836, but suffered defeat. The Whigs were not discouraged by their repulse in that year, nor did they lose confidence in their leader, whose war record gave him popularity with the masses of the people in all sections of the country. The campaign commenced in 1836 was not permitted to die out. The Whigs kept up their organizations, did not lay down their arms, but fortified their position and made every preparation for a renewal of the conflict in 1840, never for a moment losing confidence in their leader or abating their zeal in his support. The conflict on the part of the great leaders of the two parties was transferred from the stump to the halls of Congress, and there the battle was carried on with a zeal, eloquence and ability unequalled in any partisan struggle since the organization of the Government.

The Whigs held their National Convention at Philadelphia on the 4th of December, 1839, nearly a year before the election. This showed how earnestly they were enlisted in the fight, and the confidence which inspired their action. They felt that a long campaign would result to their advantage. They had no fear of discussion, no dread of investigation.

Log Cabins and Hard Cider

A Democratic correspondent of a Baltimore paper, before the campaign of 1840 had fairly opened, made the sneering remark that General Harrison's habits and attainments were well calculated to secure him the highest measure of happiness in a log cabin with an abundant supply of hard cider. The Whigs caught this up and from that time forward log cabins and hard cider played conspicuous parts in the campaign. Van Buren, the candidate of the Democrats, was held up as a dapper little band-box fop, using gold spoons and having not the least sympathy with the great working and producing masses of the people. This was a strong card for the Whigs and they made the most of it. At every convention log cabins were hauled in processions and hard cider was free and plentiful as water. Harrison hailing from the Buckeye State, buckeye bushes were used as the Whig emblem, and buckeyes were strung and worn as beads by the ladies attending Whig gatherings. The tide set strongly in favor of the Whigs, and even the correspondent of the Baltimore paper who spoke so sneeringly of the capacities and social character of General Harrison, was carried into the current and swept into the Whig party.

Opening of the Campaign in Ohio

The campaign was opened in Ohio by a monster ratification meeting in Columbus on Washington's birthday, February 22. On the evening of the 21st all Whig residences and business houses in the city were illuminated. The streets were thronged with people from all parts of the State, and it was necessary to open nearly every house in the then city of six thousand inhabitants to accommodate those who had arrived from a distance. The means of traveling were at that time very limited. Canals were closed, there were no railroads, stage coaches could carry but few persons, and the roads were so bad that they could make but slow progress, passengers often being compelled to get out and walk up hills or where the roads were particularly bad. But these things did not discourage the zealous Whigs. They hitched up their own teams, hired teams, and sought conveyance to the capital of the state in every conceivable manner, determined to be on hand and participate in the inauguration of that eventful campaign. Not only this, but log cabins of huge dimensions were mounted upon wheels and hauled long distances to the capital. But the most striking feature of that great gathering was the representation of Fort Meigs—being a miniature copy of the Fort in every particular, hauled by six fine horses. It was 28 feet in length, the embankments were six inches high, surmounted by pickets ten inches high. It was garrisoned by 40 men, contained seven block houses, twelve cannon, and was in every respect a complete and perfect representation of the Fort at the foot of the rapids of the Maumee river. There were three flag-staffs on the Fort 30 feet high. On one was the inscription, "Fort Meigs, besieged May, 1813"; on another was Harrison's celebrated response to the demand of the British officer for the surrender of the Fort, "Tell General Procter when he gets possession of the Fort he will gain more honor, in the estimation of his King and country, than he would acquire by a thousand capitulations," and on the other was the dying words of the brave Lawrence, "Don't give up the ship."

This miniature fort was made at Perrysburg and hauled from that place to Columbus. John C. Spink was Captain and went through with the Fort and the men. One of the guns on the Fort—a small brass piece—was cast at Toledo. The other guns were of iron and one of them was carried on the *Commodore Perry* the next season, and while being fired as the boat was coming up the lake on the fourth of July, exploded, severely wounding E. Graham, then the boat's carpenter, but subsequently treasurer of this county and Internal Revenue Assessor.

On the morning of the 22d, the large numbers of people who had collected from a distance from Columbus during the previous day and night, formed processions on the various roads leading into the capital, and, notwithstanding the rain and mud, the wildest enthusiasm prevailed, and by ten o'clock the streets of Columbus were literally filled with the drenched delegations. Numerous military companies and bands were there, and all marched through the streets in rain and mud, their enthusiasm seemingly heightened by the difficulties under which they were assembled. At that convention, after full consultation, the following resolution was adopted:

"*Resolved*, That it be recommended to the young men of the States of Ohio, Kentucky, Indiana, Illinois, Michigan,

SCRAP-BOOK.

Western New York, Pennsylvania and Virginia, to celebrate the next anniversary of the raising of the siege of Fort Meigs, in June, 1813, on the ground occupied by that Fort."

Preparing for Fort Meigs Gathering

The tide had set in so strongly in favor of the Whigs that the Democrats were thrown into confusion. They lost their temper, became demoralized, and those who did not enlist under the Whig banner conducted a guerrilla warfare, merely seeking to annoy the Whigs without securing any decided advantage. The greatest enthusiasm, amounting to almost a degree of wild excitement, pervaded the ranks of the Whigs, and from all parts of the country notes of preparation to attend the Fort Meigs demonstration were heard. Very naturally these indications of the coming gathering of the greatest partisan demonstration ever witnessed in this country excited and cheered the Whigs of Perrysburg and Maumee, encouraging them to the greatest efforts in arranging for the complete success of the important enterprise. The two villages, which were then about the only important places in the Maumee Valley, acted in concert, and no one was ever heard to complain of the manner in which they performed their part of the work.

The Log Cabin

It was decided that a huge log cabin should be erected upon the Fort, to be used as a sort of headquarters by General Harrison for reception purposes. One log for this cabin was to be furnished by each township in Wood and Lucas counties. The first log to arrive was brought from the neighborhood of the present village of Swanton. It was a fine stick of timber, about fifty feet in length. Its arrival was the signal for a jollification. The cannon was brought and taken to the Fort, followed by three barrels of hard cider. The Whigs of Maumee and Perrysburg united in this demonstration, and of course they had a jolly time, which lasted until in the evening, when many of the men and a host of boys gave evidence of familiarity with these barrels of cider.

The Fate of the First Log

After the Whigs had got over their jubilee, the next day some of them went up to the Fort to take another look at that log which had met with such a warm reception. Judge their surprise when they discovered that the guerrilla Democrats had gone to the Fort in the night and stuck said log into the Fort well. The well was about 50 or 60 feet deep. It was perhaps 15 feet from the top of the well to the water, then there was about fifteen feet of water and the balance was mud. Not only this, but the said guerrillas had bored a hole in the end of the log which projected out of the well about five feet, then they had got a hickory bush, shaved the end to fit the hole in the log and then planted said bush in the log. The bush was removed but the log could not be lifted out of the well, and it remains there to this day and is seen by all who visit the Fort. It fitly illustrates the style of warfare adopted by the Democrats in 1840.

Who Placed the Log in the Well

Until very recently only those engaged in the act knew who placed that log in the well. Time has served to cool the Whig blood which was made to boil on account of that outrage, and recently one of the actors in that drama gave us the history of how it was done and the names of those who did it. The parties who did it were Chas. F. Wilson, brother of the late Hon. Eber Wilson; Henry Ewing, Samuel Bucher, who lived in a cabin near the Fort; S. D. Westcott, a well known citizen of Perrysburg, and

John Westcott, of Vanlue, Hancock county. Just how so few men could plant so large a log in a well the reader will be curious to know. A man by the name of Radway lived on a farm about half a mile above the Fort. He had a pair of breachy oxen and was in the habit of turning them upon the commons in their yoke. These cattle were at the Fort and the guerrillas drafted them into the service. Bucher got a log chain, the oxen were hitched to the log and it was drawn into position, the butt at the well and the other end resting upon the embankment. Thus situated the men managed to raise the small end and slide the log into the well.

The Whigs were not discouraged by this little episode, but the logs kept coming in until every township had its representative for the cabin. An eye witness informs us that he never saw so fine a collection of logs. They ranged from 40 to 60 feet in length, were straight as an arrow and smooth as a ramrod. The Whigs were proud of their logs and contemplated the beautiful cabin to be made of them with great satisfaction.

Another Guerrilla Raid

It is singular that the fate of the first log did not operate to warn the Whigs against further raids from the Democratic guerrillas, but they evidently thought the success of the first venture would satisfy their enemies. In this they were deceived, for one dark night some rascals, armed with cross-cut saws, entered the Fort and cut those beautiful logs into old fashioned back logs. To this day it is not known who handled those saws. Like the man who locked his stable door after the horse was stolen, the Whigs now built a bark guard house and hired a man, armed with a shot-gun, to keep watch. Other logs were procured and a huge double cabin was erected, Geo. W. Newton, of Perrysburg, acting in the capacity of master builder, and we believe, John C. Spink, Julius Blinn, Judge Hollister, J. W. Smith and other Whigs of Perrysburg were the leading spirits in this preparatory work for the great convention.

The Demonstration

The Fort Meigs demonstration was worthy of the campaign of 1840. In fact, everything considered, it was the most remarkable political gathering ever witnessed in this country. It must be remembered that facilities for travel were very limited at that time, and that Fort Meigs was then a point on the frontier. Notwithstanding these facts, the crowd assembled was estimated at from 40,000 to 60,000 persons. It is safe to say that there were 50,000 people at the Fort on the 11th day of June, 1840. They came from all parts of the country, in all manner of conveyances. Capt. Wilkinson, with his *Commodore Perry*, escorted sixteen steamboats up the river, all loaded to their utmost capacity. Men are said to have sold their last cow to get the means to take them to that convention. Military companies from various cities were present, and a large number of bands furnished music. The processions on the roads leading to Perrysburg were simply immense, while thousands upon thousands were streaming in for two or three days before the grand demonstration, from all parts of the country. A mock siege occurred on the night of the tenth, and cannonading by the several batteries in attendance is described as having been sublimely grand. Every house and out-house in Perrysburg and Maumee was crowded with weary men who had rode in buggies and wagons hundreds of miles. Thousands slept upon the ground in the woods adjoining the Fort. The wells in the upper portion of Perrysburg were soon pumped dry in relieving the thirst of the multitude. General Harrison was present and while in

SCRAP-BOOK.

Perrysburg was the guest of Judge Hollister, who then owned and occupied the residence recently owned by H. E. Peck. In the evening, in response to the calls of a great crowd of people, he appeared upon the grounds in front of the residence and briefly addressed the multitude. The General, Tom Ewing and a large number of other distinguished Whigs were present and addressed the people at the Fort. General Harrison spent a portion of his time in Maumee, the guest of Judge Forsythe.

Thus was inaugurated and successfully concluded the greatest political demonstration, all things considered, ever witnessed on this continent.

THE WINTER OF 1842-43

Referred To by Old Settlers as a Record Breaker Wholly Unsurpassed.

THE late Mr. C. W. Evers some years since wrote up the following account of the severe winter of 1842-43, in Wood County:

J. R. Tracy of Toledo, who was an early pioneer of Bowling Green, tells some of the incidents of the memorable hard winter of 1842-3 which is referred to by all the old people as a record breaker unsurpassed since white men planted their cabins in this part of the country.

The autumn of 1842 had been a mild and delightful one. The mazy Indian summer had hung over the landscape like a protecting curtain from the chill blasts of boreas. On the 25th day of November in the after part of the day, came a change, sudden and severe. First dark, dense clouds overcast the sky; towards night rain fell. This soon changed to sleet, driven by a strong wind and so cold that men caught out with teams on the road had to leave their wagons and walk to keep from freezing. This, later turned to snow which covered the ground heavily in the morning.

That snow, increased in depth from time to time, lay until some time in April, 1843. The ice in the Maumee at Waterville, was frozen solid down to the rocks on the day of spring election in April that year.

The weather at times, in fact much of the time, was extremely cold, though there were no thermometers here then by which to gauge the temperature, as now. The mild autumn had lulled the scattering settlers into neglect and their scanty supplies of vegetables, fruit and corn fodder had been frozen solid in the unheralded storm, no more to be released till the following May. By March the scanty supply of prairie hay began to fail. The poor cattle starved, shivered and froze. Their pitiful bellowing and moans were harrowing to hear. The owners would drive them into the forest where elm and basswood trees were felled and the starving brutes ate the buds and tender twigs. Other owners later, when the ground thawed, dug prairie dock (root of the rosin weed) and fed it to their horses and cattle. Despite all the efforts hundreds of cattle perished and those that survived were mere skeletons. Hogs could get no acorns from under the icy crust and there was no corn to feed them. They crawled into bunches where they were found in the spring frozen solid as rocks. Poultry and small animals, wild and domestic, perished. Squirrels, coon and birds were found frozen in hollow trees and logs, even the muskrat in his icy home.

That was 61 years ago, but none who lived at that time will ever forget the harrowing vicissitudes of that winter and the destitution and sickness of the following spring and summer.

The present winter though unusually severe, would not, though equally as cold as that of 42-3 bear upon us of today as it did upon those scantily prepared pioneers of that time. We have warm houses, clothing and stores of supplies both for man and beast. There can be no comparison. We can never know nor even imagine the terrors of that gloomy period, to those who lived here and shared its hardships.

The unprecedented conditions that exist now in the Maumee river are only a sample of what dangerous surprises nature's working forces may bring when a certain combination of circumstances exist. Then it is that man's best efforts are set at naught. He is as puny as the fretful ant. His bridge spans are not high enough. His dykes and dams are not strong enough. His granite and steel walls are not proof against the devouring breath of flame and heat. Man's efforts only help to make the destruction greater. The Maumee is hedged and obstructed with piers, docks and earth fillings. The raging torrents armed with blocks of floating ice only mock at these artificial contrivances of man and sweep them away as if but tinsel or cobwebs. How like the ant hill or the cobweb of the spider are the works of man, in that each alike are only subject to power of destruction.

Had not man planted his cabin here nor disturbed the Maumee we would not be comparing the present winter with that of 42-43 in points of severity and destructiveness.

So long as man asserts himself along side of and against nature's modes, which will be as long as he exists, so long must he cope with hard winters, hot summers, drouth, floods and other pleasant and unpleasant manifestations of nature's caprices and whims.

SAGE CHILD TRAGEDY

Most Horrible Child Murder by a Father Whose Mind Was Wrecked by Religious Fervor

VALENTINE SAGE married a full-blooded Indian girl, adopted by and raised in the family of Rev. Isaac Van Tassel, one of the early missionaries to the Indians, on the Maumee. Sometime in 1852-3 their oldest boy named George, aged about thirteen years, took sick and died, which threw him into a despondent state of mind, and he gradually turned his thoughts to religious matters, and would shout, sing and pray alternately in the wildest manner.

Some six months afterward Sage attended a religious revival held by Rev. P. C. Baldwin, at the old Plain Church, and became so wrought up by religious excitement that he would shout and pray at the top of his voice all the way home from the church at night.

One stormy, snowy morning in March, during the progress of the meeting he arose quite early and made a fire in the stove, singing loudly all the time. Presently he went to the bed where his wife and child lay and took the child, as his wife who was awake supposed, to the stove to keep it warm while she dressed herself, but she saw him hurry out of doors. She sprang up and ran to the door just in time to see the head of her darling child dashed against a log on the wood pile. She gave an agonizing scream, when he seized the ax and compelled her to go to bed, after which he

SCRAP-BOOK.

brought the dead child to her. He sung and shouted and seemed to be entirely happy, while his wife expected every moment that either her own or some of the other children's lives would be next sacrificed. He forbid any of them leaving the house, holding the ax all the time.

Finally the oldest girl escaped from the chamber window and ran to a neighbor's, Mr. John Whitehead, about a half a mile distant. Whitehead hurried down but was threatened his life if he came even in the yard. He saw that he was powerless to relieve the prisoners in the house and that his presence only increased the rage of the madman every moment and rendered the fact of Sage's family more perilous. He hurried away for help and returned shortly after, with, we believe, Henry Huff, S. W. St. John and John Evers, all active and determined men. They came up unobserved by Sage. Two of them made an attempt to hold a parley with him, but he stood in the door brandishing his ax threatening any with death who should attempt to approach. While two of the men attracted his attention from the front, Evers climbed in at the chamber window and down the ladder, and unnoticed by Sage, stole up behind him and clasped him tightly around the waist under the arms. Even with this advantage it was hard to avoid the blows of his ax. His strength seemed superhuman. Some one finally seized him by the throat, and once out of wind they succeeded in tying him and he was sent to the jail at Perrysburg, where he afterward died a raving madman.—*C. W. E.*

HOLLISTER'S PRAIRIE

A Wild Region, Picturesque and Attractive for the Hunter of Wild Game

ABOUT eight miles southeast of Gilead lay that stretch of low grassy prairie or swamp, as it was most of the year; only in the very driest of seasons, in mid-summer did it become terra firma, its tall grass, growing from 6 to 10 feet high, and with skirting thickets and forests, furnished a paradise of security for deer and bear. The reports of this prairie, carried by hunters to the settlement at Perrysburg, attracted the attention of the Hollisters, then living there, and they located a cattle ranch with Ralph O. Keeler as partner and manager of the business. The headquarters of the ranch was on the high ridge just north of Weston, where the old Keeler homestead house formerly stood. The ridge is now a portion of the Weston cemetery. Soon the Hollisters and Keeler had large droves of cattle, roaming at will over the prairies and through the forests on what was yet all government land. The tall prairie grass furnished ample pasturage, and the sink holes in the prairie, such as the "Stone Pond" in Plain township, furnished drinking places in the driest of seasons.

Such a scene as the herds on the broad acres of pasturage, viewed from the overlooking ridges, at its best and most picturesque, might well have tempted the coolest brain to visionary dreams of Arcadian bliss, such dreams as caused the educated and wealthy German, Carl Nibelung to sink his fortune in the swampy pasture at the northeast side of the prairie, in later years.—*Sentinel, 1881.*

Wood county was organized April 1, 1820, with 13 other counties, and Maumee was the county seat until 1823.

MILTON TOWNSHIP

The Struggles of the First Settlers—Their Privations—At Work on the Hand Mill

IN the Sentinel of April 21, 1881, a pioneer says:

About the year 1834-35, began the first white settlement, in what is now known as Milton township, in Wood county, Ohio. Prior to this time it was a howling wilderness; the foot of a white man had scarcely trod on its territory. The wild Indian or red man of the forest, the bear, the wolf, the panther and wild cat, held full sway, unmolested by the approach of civilization. About this time there began to be a movement made in some of the eastern counties of Ohio, to go west. The Maumee Valley had its attractions, and the traveler in search of a home had his attention drawn to Wood county by its rich and inexhaustable soil. Landing at Perrysburg, they would wend their way up the Maumee, and striking the mouth of Beaver Creek, a mile below Grand Rapids (then Gilead), they would ascend the creek to explore the rich country before them. The earlier settlers began to locate along the creek in Henry county and soon they began to spread out over more territory.

To tell the story of pioneer life in the wilds of Milton and adjoining townships it may seem strange to some why I should connect Henry county and Liberty township and associate the names of those at such remote distances.

In those days we understood and appreciated that word neighbor. It was not used then in that narrow, contracted sense in which it is used now, but it was born of that higher and prouder philanthropy, as taught in Bible lessons, where a man fell among robbers; so we in the earlier days of our pioneer life in the wilds of Milton and adjoining townships were all neighbors, for miles and miles, and when we met, there was a happy greeting, a cordial and hearty shaking of hands, as though it really meant something.

We had no roads either, we just went zig-zag through the woods, around trees, over and around fallen timber, through the water, fighting the mosquitoes, to a neighbor's with a sack of corn on our backs to grind it on a hand mill, to get corn meal to make johnny cake for the family (it was johnny cake, coon and possum fat), and glad to get that. We had no water mills nearer than Perrysburg, and not much to get ground when we got there. And it took us from four to five days to go and come; the only conveyance was by ox teams and a cart.

Old Billy Hill (as he was familiarly known) had a hand mill, and it was kept going from morning until midnight, people coming from miles and miles around. Dozens of men and women have been there at one time waiting their turn to get their opportunity to turn the mill, and some times, when so thronged, some would leave their corn and go home to their hungry families, and come again to take their places at the mill. Of course this mill was a rude structure; four upright posts framed together and the stones set in them, and the propelling power was applied by an upright shaft, with an iron spout placed in a thimble in the upper burr, and the top held by passing through a hole in a board, and then two men taking hold of this upright shaft and turning the burr. It was a slow process, but it was the only alternative we had. This was afterward changed, so as to make it more convenient; it was arranged, so four men could take hold of cranks like a grind stone and made to grind much faster. Then we all thought that we had found a paradise.

GOING TO MILL

How Wood County Pioneers Took Their Grist to Mills on the River Raisin

A PIONEER writes to the Sentinel in 1881, the following graphic description of "going to mill":

The nearest grist mills for the settlers along the Maumee were located at the mouth of the river Raisin in Michigan, where the city of Monroe now is, and at Cold Creek in what was then Huron county—now Erie county, Ohio, near where the village of Castalia now is. The distance in either case being not far from seventy miles, and with the easy going ox teams and the horrible roads, going to mill was a vast undertaking, the journey often taking ten days or two weeks to perform even if the hungry pioneer did not have to camp out, or hunt work in the neighborhood of the mill, and wait for sufficient water to accumulate in the crazy old dams, to enable the miller to turn out their grist.

Alexander Brown, once worked, logging, at Cold Creek, and then had to turn in and help grind his own grist on Sunday, and even then did not finish before the water gave out, and he was forced to leave a portion of his grist at the mill, the miller promising to grind it and send it to Perrysburg by the first chance. Mr. Brown got his grist in a little over two months all right.

When an expedition was fitted out to go to mill either to the mouth of Raisin river or to Cold Creek, it usually became a neighborhood affair, and was considered a bigger undertaking than a trans-continental journey would now. A "team," consisting of two or three yokes of oxen, would be rigged to a wagon, and the grists of the whole neighborhood be loaded on, with feed for the cattle and a sack of potatoes, coffee pot and frying pan, and other needed camp equipage, and amidst much excitement and great shoutings of "good byes," the expedition would gaily flounder away on their trip of a week or two to mill. For the meat supply of such expeditions, the settlers depended upon the chance of game supply along the route, and usually some noted hunter accompanied the caravan as chief forager, whose unerring rifle would easily, every day, from the woods, supply the meager larder with juicy venison steaks, or a young bear roast.

Sometimes, when the country was flooded, and the rude trails through the forests back to the older settlements were impassable even to a man on horseback, the bread material of our hardy pioneers was prepared as was that of the ancient Hebrews, every family doing its own grinding, in their handmills, or as their Indian neighbors did theirs, in a sort of rude mortar attached to a spring pole, always remembering that among the Indians the ladies manipulated the hominy mill.

Uncle John Gingery has in his possession today, a coffee mill that he purchased in Wayne county, Ohio, in 1826. The old mill is still hale and hearty, and has good teeth yet for a pioneer of 57 years old. Bushels of buckwheat and corn have met the crushing influence of that old mill, and bolted through a fine meal sieve have furnished "Snap Jack" material that fried in "bar" fat, went far toward nourishing the sinewy arm of the old pioneers when by reason of the impassable condition of roads or the inclement weather, they were prevented from going to mill.

It is a matter of fact that in the Maumee Valley a greater number of battles have been fought, and with greater results than in any similar extent of territory in the Union.

ATTACKED BY WOLVES

Mahlon Meeker's Struggle at Night With a Pack of These Animals

ONE night as Mr. Meeker was going home followed by one of his dogs he suddenly heard the howl of a wolf near the trail he was following. This was instantly answered by another wolf and presently a wolf appeared in front of him. The dog slunk close to him. He had no means of defense and so knew it was just as safe to go ahead as to turn back. So he walked boldly up to the one in the trail until almost within reach of it when it sprang to one side and joined with two others in the rear, when they all broke out in a deafening, startling chorus of howls. After going a mile or so he came to where a tree had been blown down and ran into the top to get a stick. While here, four more wolves joined in the chase, and on taking the trail again they became so fierce and bold and approached so close that several times he succeeded in striking one with his club, after which they would howl and snap their teeth in disappointed rage, but continue to follow him until he arrived on the ridge at the cabin of Howard, who had a great fire in his fire place, the light of which shone through the unchinked cracks and which with two savage dogs finally scared the wolves off. Meeker thinks if he had tripped his foot and fallen they would have all attacked him at once. They were of the large brown species and seemed maddened with hunger.—C. W. E.

WILD HOGS

Some Startling Experiences With Them by Mr. Meeker

THE earliest recollections we have from the first settlers all speak of the great numbers of wild hogs that frequented the woods in the Black Swamp. They were more numerous at times than the deer and many years later they were captured in the dense woods north of what is called the "Devil's Hole."

Some of the early settlers claimed that they were not, nor could not be the progeny of the domestic hog, being entirely wild and untamable and fierce of disposition. But we incline to the belief that they were originally strays, or cast offs from the quartermaster's department of Hull's or Harrison's army. Perhaps Mad Anthony Wayne and his legion in 1794, after the victory, felt so well that they turned all their hogs loose, if any they had, to devour the Indian cornfields growing along the Maumee. At all events it is known that large droves of hogs were brought in during the war of 1812, and it is not at all unreasonable to suppose this the origin of the vast herds of wild hogs which roamed the woods many years ago. We refer to this matter in this place in connection with a couple of incidents related by Mr. Meeker.

Wild Hogs Tree a Wolf

While in search of some horses one day in company with one of the Deckers, they heard a loud commotion some distance away among the wild hogs. It grew louder and louder until their curiosity led them to cautiously approach the place or as near as they dared, when they spied a wolf on a high fallen log barely out of reach of the infuriated animals, which seemed to have gathered there by hundreds—at least the ground

SCRAP-BOOK.

was covered with them. But the wolf may have seen the men, for he sprang off his perch and was instantly torn to pieces and devoured. The hunters were only able, after the hogs left, to find a small string of his hide.

Meeker Treed by Wild Hogs

At another time Mr. Meeker was returning home when he heard the cries of a young pig, which seemed to have been deserted by the rest of the herd and was too weak to get along. Mr. Meeker took it up thinking to take it home with him, when it set up such a squeeling as soon brought the whole drove upon him. He heard them coming just in time to drop the pig and hastily climb a small tree as the excited animals gathered beneath him foaming and gnashing their teeth, while several ferocious old boars fought with each other for the privilege of gouging the bark off the tree with their tusks. After much noisy demonstrations and watching the prisoner for a time they began to drop off and finally the siege was entirely raised by the departure of the last hog —a surly old boar, a very patriarch whose large tusks and fierce mien might have well challenged comparison with any dwellers of his kind in the famous Black Swamp.—*C. W. E.*

THE MAUMEE COUNTRY

Once Regarded as One of the Most Dreary, Desolate and Uninviting Regions of Earth

THE late Dr. Geo. B. Spencer wrote to the Sentinel early in 1884, as follows:

Before the year 1820, Wood county was a part of an indefinite, undivided, unexplored wilderness, known as "Northwest Ohio," with its county seat at Bellefontaine, and but few settlements in all the "Black Swamp" of the "Miami of the Lakes." Waynesfield township of Logan county, included within its limits, all of the present counties of Wood and Hancock, and in that year, 1820, the total tax for all purposes collected in the said township was $139.45. In 1823, on the 28th day of May, the township of Waynesfield was divided by the organization of Perrysburg township, which included all of the present county of Wood.

"The Maumee Country", was by this time celebrated from one end of the United States to the other, as the most forsaken, desolate and ague-smitten wilderness of tangled forests and inhospitable swamps, only excelled in dreariness and desolation, perhaps, by the great "Dismal Swamp" of Virginia, or the unpenetrated everglades of Florida.

Hull's troops had cut and floundered a passage through this country on their way to the disgraceful surrender at Detroit, in 1812. Mad Anthony Wayne's victorious army, had 18 years before this, in 1794, followed down along the swampy "Miami of the Lakes" from Fort Defiance to Fort Miami, to punish the refractory Indians, and as the soldiers of Wayne, Hull and Harrison dispersed to their homes back in the old colonies, they carried with them their soldier stories of the horrible swamps of the "Miami of the Lakes," as the Maumee river was then called.

See how names are changed, and new words made. The river was by its earliest French settlers, called the Miami, pronounced by the French "Me-ah-me," and by the corrupted influence of the

Indians' and backwoodsmen's attempts at pronunciation, it became first "Me-aw-me" and then "Mau-mee" until now as we pronounce the "Mi-am-i" of southern Ohio and the "Maumee" of northern Ohio you wouldn't suspect any blood relation. And as "Maumee" it became a famed locality and went heralded in song and wierd story as the place where "Potatoes they grow small on Mau-mee, on Mau-mee."

But in spite of its drawbacks, and unpleasant natural features, and the unfavorable reports circulated far and wide about the country, the speculating spirit of some of Wayne's soldiers and those of the war of 1812, was attracted to the Maumee Valley by its wonderful game supply, and the hopes of a remunerative traffic in furs and peltries with the Indians, and traders; posts were established at several places in the valley immediately after the peace following the war of 1812.

Settlements started first near the shore of the lake, then gradually spreading up the rivers and tributaries. In 1821, enough settlers were located about Fort Meigs, at the foot of the rapids in the river, to demand a better means of communication with their county seat, Bellefontaine, than was presented by Hull's old trace, in its serpentine wanderings southward through this county; so what is called yet the Wapakoneta road, was petitioned for, granted, surveyed, and work begun on it in 1821. The road led from Fort Meigs along up the river on the south side, to near the mouth of Beaver Creek, then followed nearly the course of Beaver Creek, and so on south of Wapakoneta. Then the trade of the Indians at the head of the rapids, attracted settlers along up the river. At that time there were no other white settlers between that point and Fort Defiance, where the town of Defiance now is.

There was quite a good sized Indian village on the Maumee and scattering outlying settlements along up Beaver Creek, and on the sand ridges south from the river, the Indians dwelling in peace and harmony with their white neighbors.

WESTON TOWNSHIP

Gradual Accession of Settlers—Organization and the First Election

IN his reminiscences, the late Dr. G. B. Spencer wrote to the Sentinel in 1884, as follows:

Year after year during the Twenties, white settlers came, and by occasional accessions of other families, the little settlement at the mouth of Bear Creek and at the head of the rapids of the Maumee, grew, until in the spring of 1830, they demanded a township organization for themselves. The reader will please remember that up to this time all of what is now Wood county, was included in one big township called Perrysburg, which township has been divided and sub-divided since that time.

So in the spring of 1830, the settlers at the head of the rapids and mouth of Beaver Creek and at Bear Rapids or Otsego, petitioned for a new township to be called "Ottawa," and the township was duly created by the county commissioners, but before the time came to elect township officers in the spring of 1831, the name was changed from Ottawa to Weston.

The township as first organized included all of what is now Weston, Milton, Jackson and the west part of Washington townships, or a strip of land six

SCRAP-BOOK.

miles wide, and extending back from the river to what is now the southern limit of Wood county.

First Election

The first election ever held in Weston township was on the 4th day of April, 1831, when all of the voters met at the house of Edward Howard, and proceeded to elect themselves, for at that first election there were barely enough voters to intelligently fill the offices. The first officers were as follows: Trustees, Edward Howard, Wm. Pratt and Emanuel Arnold; treasurer, R. M. Howard; clerk, R. A. Howard; poor overseers, M. P. Morgan and Jas. Donaldson; constables, Wm. North and Wm. Wonderly; fence viewers, Wm. Loughry and Joseph North; Justices of the peace, Alexander Brown and Emanuel Arnold, who did not receive their commissions from the governor until in August of that year.

James Donaldson was also elected road supervisor, and the only road that came under his supervision was the road leading along down the river bank from the settlement to Fort Meigs, which was a poor excuse for a road at that time, being only partially chopped out and not worked at all. For the care of this, the only road in the township, except the Indian trails, Mr. Donaldson, received the princely salary of seventy-five cents.

The only officer who received any salary during the first year was the treasurer, R. M. Howard, who drew, all at one time, seventy-five cents. So for $1.50 Weston township was as peacefully governed as she has ever been since that date, and I find no record of any speculation or defalcation. The Fence Viewers' office in 1831 was almost a sinecure, unless they went to inspect the rude brush fences that surrounded the first clearings. But the settlements were looking up, new people coming in every year, and during the next five years, more than 50 families came into Weston township.

Start of Village

We may say then that the village of Weston was not started until in 1854 when the Taylor saw mill was put in operation. Thirty years ago the site of our town was all farm land and used as such. In 1854 Jonathan Crom built his shanty, started a saloon and kept a few groceries. Benjamin West came in 1854, and wishing to get an eligible site for his blacksmith shop, went directly across the street from Crom's saloon, and located his forge just about where Indlekofer's bar stands in his saloon today. His shop was a mere shanty. In 1855 Levi Taylor built the front half of the building now owned by Ames, and in the fall of that year, put in the first stock of dry goods and groceries that the village ever saw.

Van Tassel Killed

Many of our older citizens frequently speak of the celebrated missionary, Isaac Van Tassel, one of the pioneer preachers who frequently visited Weston and talked to the few citizens in the little old school house. He was found dead on the Gilead road, about 20 rods west of where Allen Bortell now lives. He was on his way to his home in Plain township, from Gilead. It is not known whether his horse threw him off, or whether he died suddenly of heart disease. It occurred March 2, 1849.

In 1697 French forts were built at Fort Wayne and at the foot of the Rapids.

The entire Northwestern territory for some years had but three county organizations. These were Washington, Hamilton and Wayne, the latter embracing Wood county.

ATTACKED BY SAVAGES

Settlers in Flight—Their Homes Burned—The Account of Navarre—Manor Proves a Lame Guide

THE late Hezekiah L. Hosmer said, on the authority of Peter Navarre and others, that Pierre Minard, known as Peter Manor, received the news of war from a Delaware named Sac-a-manc, who in passing through the settlement said: "I shall go to Owl Creek. I shall kill some of the Long Knives before I come back, and will show you some of their scalps. In ten days after I get back all the hostile tribes will hold a council at Malden; very soon after that, we shall come to this place and kill all the Yankees. You, Manor, are a good Frenchman, and must not tell them what I say."

Sac-a-manc returned, after an absence of six days, and showed Manor three scalps, which he said were those of a family he had murdered on Owl Creek. He repeated to Manor in confidence that it was the intention of the Indians to come to the valley in force sufficient to massacre the American settlers. This intelligence Manor communicated to Major Spafford, accompanied with advice to leave the valley immediately. The major laughed, and dismissed the subject with some remark expressive of incredulity, and Manor left him, promising that should he learn of any further cause of alarm he would let him know.

About a month after this conversation, a man by the name of Miller (some accounts say Gordon), who had lived many years with the Ottawas, and who was well known to Major Spafford, entered his house in breathless haste, and told him that at no greater distance than Monclova there was a band of fifty Pottawatomies, on the march from their country on the St. Joseph River, to join the hostile Indians at Malden, and take part in the council spoken of by Sac-a-manc. They had plundered and set fire to the buildings at Monclova, and would soon be at the foot of the Rapids.

But little time was left to escape. The major with his family and the few settlers that had remained in the valley, hastened immediately to the river, where they dislodged and launched a large barge, in which some officers had descended the river from Fort Wayne the year before. Raising a sail made of a bed blanket, they were enabled, by dint of hard rowing and a favorable breeze, to round the point and get under cover of old Fort Miami just as the Indians made their appearance on the bank, where Maumee City is built, and before the boat passed Eagle Point they saw the flames ascending from the homes they had just deserted. This little band of fugitives, favored with fair winds, made a safe passage in their crazy craft to the Quaker settlement at Milan, where they remained until after the war. Manor says they were panic-stricken, and left their horses, cattle, and most of their household goods. Their property was taken by the Indians, who completed their work by burning every dwelling, belonging to an American, in that part of the valley. This accomplished, they pursued their course to Malden, to attend the Indian council spoken of by Sac-a-manc.

Not long after Hull's surrender, the French settlers remaining at the foot of the rapids, received a call from a party of sixty Delawares, who arrived there in advance of the main body of the British army, on their march to Fort Wayne. Manor says that he, with some of his neighbors, was standing in front of Beaugrand's store, at Maumee, when the Indians came out of the woods—that they drew up in line, and each put his gun to his shoulder and aimed, as if to fire at the little group of settlers. Beaugrand came out and waved a white handkerchief. They dropped their muskets, and approached the store on a run, and remained a few minutes. An hour after their departure, about 100 British soldiers, and as many Pottawatomies and Wyandots, came up. Their first inquiry was for guides. Manor, from prudential motives was seized with sudden and severe lameness; but it would not do. The officer in command pressed him into service as a guide, and lame as he seemed, he was compelled to conduct this company to the head of the rapids. Here his lameness so increased, that his persecutors dismissed him, and he set out on his return home. At the foot of Presque Isle Hill, he met Colonel Elliott, the officer in command of the detachment, and the remainder of the troops and Indians composing it. Elliott examined him closely, and on learning that he had been employed as a guide, permitted him to go on his way.

Mr. C. W. Evers makes the following criticism in regard to the incidents above given:

The above differs from other accounts as to the time the settlers left the Rapids. In this, Mr. Hosmer quotes Manor incorrectly, no doubt. Hull had news of the declaration of war July 2nd. He surrendered his army August 16th. From Mr. Hosmer's statement, we would be led to believe that the settlers fled on hearing war had been declared. Mrs. Green and Clark both say the flight was after the surrender of Hull. Their version is doubtless the correct one. In the history of Erie county, incidental mention is made of Major Spafford being at the mouth of Huron river, with his family, in a boat, about September 1st. The reasonable inference is that he had but recently sailed from the Maumee, that is, in the latter part of August, after the surrender. The probabilities are that in the impending danger, after Hull's surrender, the settlers foresaw that they were no longer safe for even a single day; that in the confusion and anxiety of the hour each acted as his hopes or fears impelled him.

BOWLING GREEN

Something About Its Early History—The First Log Cabin—How the Town Received Its Name—Interesting Incidents of the Past

PROBABLY there has been no more accurate and succinct account of the early history of Bowling Green, than the following, penned by the late C. W. Evers, whose studious efforts in gathering every incident connected with the pioneer history of Wood county, rendered him a reliable authority in all that pertains to that early period:

Hull's March

The first time white men came to disturb the forest solitudes where Bowling Green now stands, was in June, 1812, when Hull's army passed here, marching from Dayton to Detroit.

That column of troops, preceded by guides, scouts and axmen, followed in turn by the cavalry battalion, with its gaudy pennons, escorting the commanding general with his gaily uniformed staff retinue, then the infantry, field bands, artillery and trains formed a pageant which even to-day would attract all Bowling Green to the east side of town, about where the T. & O. C. railway track lies. That is about on the line the troops held, until near Ridge street, when they turned a little to the west, coming out on the Maumee nearly opposite Waterville. That was the first wagon trail through the interior of Wood county, and the only one for the two succeeding decades. The land was then owned by the Indians. After the war, in 1817, at a treaty at the foot of the Maumee Rapids, the United States bought the land, at a price slightly less than four cents an acre, and in 1819 sent surveyors here, which was the second appearance of white men on official business. In 1821 the final surveys were completed and the plats made, when the lands were ready for market.

The Black Swamp

Unfortunately the Black Swamp country, after the war of 1812, had a worse reputation, if possible, than ever; the soldiers and others who had been here, told horrible stories about it. Few buyers of land came—none to the interior of the county. Those who stopped invariably located on or near the river; so that, aside from roving parties of Indian hunters and occasional white fur-traders, or the weekly trips of the old Bellefontaine mail carrier, the interior of the county was practically unknown and shunned by settlers for more than a decade after its survey. Prior to the year 1828, Collister Haskins, at Portage, was the only settler between Findlay and the Maumee settlement.

The First Cabin

Some few land entries were made in Plain and Center in 1831, but the pioneer entry in the present corporation of Bowling Green, was made October 29, 1832, by Elisha Martindale; the tract, 40 acres in the northwest part of town, lying on both sides of Haskins road or street, is known as the Clinton Fay place. Martindale later bought 120 acres more; he built his cabin where the present Fay house stands, near the great willow tree just west of the road, the following spring, 1833. Careful inquiry has failed to discover evidence of any cabin here prior to that date; Lee Moore, Henry Walker, Jacob Stouffer and others came and built in the summer and fall of '33. Alfred Thurstin began his cabin in November, 1833, as did Joseph Hollington sr., but so far as known the Martindale cabin was the first, and stood on the first land entry in what is now Bowling Green.

(Without going into all the particulars of the land entries given at that early day and noted by Mr. Evers, we will simply give the names of a few of those who entered land. Among them were Joseph Hollington, Benjamin Reed, J. M. and Samuel Lamb, Stephen Ward, Thomas Tracy, Henry Walker, Andrew Race, Jonathan Fay, Robert Barr, Alfred Thurstin, Lee Moore, David Hickson and others.)

A Few Came to Stay

These few notes from the land entry books, though not including all entries embraced in the present corporation of Bowling Green, neither the names of all purchasers, are yet sufficient to afford the reader some idea of the pioneer real estate men of the town and when they first came. Some, perhaps only one or two, of all those named bought merely for speculation. Most came in quest of homes. Some tried life here, got tired of it and left. Of those faithful ones who remained to buffet with adversity and fight the battle that was eventually to make a town here, of which they never even dreamed perhaps, most, alas, have passed from this stage of action; their toils and trials have ceased. They did their part bravely and well; their work of subduing the wilderness, begun more than half a century ago, and its results, are before us to-day. Their descendants and successors surely have just cause to remember them with respect and pride. If the story of their humble start in the race and their faithful stewardship to the end, shall inspire us with the ambition and will to do our part as well, then

SCRAP-BOOK.

this story will not have been told in vain.

Struck by the Panic

A glance at the old land entry books shows the rapid influx of settlers from 1833 to 1836 or 1837. That was an era of speculation. Everyone had a mania to buy land, but the money panic and business crash of 1837 brought it to a sudden end. That was a paralytic stroke from which the western country did not entirely recover until the California gold discovery, more than a decade later. Wood county was especially prostrated. There was nothing here that the people could sell, not even their homes; but there was most everything in the way of necessities even, to buy. There was in those gloomy years, little to inspire hope; much to thwart and discourage effort.

The Mail Carrier

By the middle of the year 1834 the ridges and higher spots within a radius of three miles of this place were mostly patented from the government, and in many instances the owner had built and occupied his cabin on his new purchase. This brought the population largely to the west and north, where the most ridges lay. The mail carrier between Perrysburg and Bellefontaine passed on the old army trail once each week, at first every two weeks, and this group of settlers petitioned for a postoffice in their midst; they were distrustful, however, that Collister Haskins, of Portage, might not approve of the move and went about it a little cautiously. The story of this enterprise incidentally reveals

How Bowling Green Got Its Name

The civil history of a town is but the biography of its founders and their successors, in which every incident, sometimes the most trivial, has an interest to the dwellers therein. Not only the name of a town, but what or who suggested that name, often becomes of interest.

Since Bowling Green has become the thriving seat of justice of one of the most prosperous counties in Ohio, inquiry is often made how it happened that it was so named. For the first time, in print, the story is here told, with the incidents that led to the naming, as told to the writer by two of the pioneers who had a part in it at the time, and several others personally known to all the circumstances. Bowling Green was christened after, or for the capital town of Warren county, Kentucky, by Joseph Gordon, a veteran mail carrier of the pioneer days here. Of one who performed so important a part for us in our infantile state, we naturally ask, Who was he? In his paper, the Findlay Courier, January 1847, William Mungen wrote editorially of Gordon as follows:

Who Gordon Was

"Joseph Gordon was born in Allegheny county, Pennsylvania, on the 29th day of January, 1784. In the year 1801, when but 17 years old, he commenced carrying the mail, on horseback, from Russellville, Kentucky, via Bowling Green, to Glasgow, a distance of 85 miles, once in two weeks, for which he received $12 per month. In 1802 he took a contract to carry the mail from Shelbyville, Kentucky, to Nashville, Tennessee. In consequence of the route being changed, he carried the mail only two months. From that time till October, 1804, he carried it from Shelbyville to Russellville, Ky. In October, 1804, he commenced carrying the mail on horse-back from Wheeling, Virginia, to George Beymer's in Ohio, a distance of 50 miles, with a led horse and a heavy mail on each. In 1805-6, he carried the mail from Wheeling, through St. Clairsville, Zanesville, and New Lancaster, to Chillicothe. In February, 1823, he commenced on the route between Bellefontaine and Perrysburg, a distance of 81 miles, through a wilderness, there being but one family residing in Hardin county, and but one postoffice on the route, and that (Findlay) at this place. Mr. Gordon was the only contractor on this route from February 7, 1823, to December 31, 1839. Since 1839, he has carried the mail semi-weekly from Bellefontaine to this place, 55 miles."

Few indeed have constitutions sufficiently strong to endure such labor for such a length of time. It is to such men as Gordon—to our hardy pioneers, who were ready to encounter all kinds of toil and privation, that Ohio owes her present state of prosperity and advancement. For such men we cannot but cherish sentiments of respect.

The Postoffice

Jacob Stouffer's cabin here was the central point of the new postoffice movement. Henry Walker, son-in-law of Stouffer was to be the postmaster. The Walkers and Stouffers occupied the same cabin; it stood on the high ridge just east of Main street, not far north of Merry avenue.

Gordon on one of his northward trips had stopped at Stouffer's as was his usual custom, in passing; the petition for the new office was ready, except that the movers, two or three of whom were present, had not yet agreed upon a name. The old mail carrier who stood on the cabin steps listening to the discussion, said to Stouffer, half jestingly, "if you will give me a tumbler of cider I'll give you just the name."

Drank to Bowling Green

Stouffer who had brought out a keg of cider from Columbiana county, filled a glass and handed it to Gordon; the latter briefly explaining how appropriate the name he would suggest was to the landscape about them, said with a sweep of his arm, "Here's to the new postoffice of Bowling Green," swallowed the cider and was in the act of mounting his horse when those present detained him a moment while they could write a name in the petition, which, sure enough, was the one Gordon had suggested.

The papers were soon folded and on their way to Perrysburg for some additional endorsements, after which they were sent to Washington. The office was established March 12, 1834. In 1835, when Walker sold his place, he and the Stouffers moved over to the west side of Main street, where the office was kept for a time, since which it has had many different locations and masters.

Afterwards in 1855, when the village was incorporated, there seemed no good reason why it should not take the same name as the postoffice, under which name it had been going in fact since in the early fifties. That is the way Bowling Green came to have its name.

White Hall Tavern

Aside from school and church work Bowling Green had but little history prior to the time she was incorporated, that does not properly come within the purview of the histories of Plain and Center townships. Robert Mackey's store enterprise at the Napoleon road in the south part of town, intended as the nucleus of the village of Mt. Ararat, never, under its various proprietors, met expectations. John Hannon in the north end of the street, with his tavern and blacksmith shop did not attract village neighbors about him. When, in 1847, Dr. E. D. Peck sent L. C. Locke out here to start a mercantile enterprise, most of the settlers were sure it would be a failure; the proprietors did not feel sanguine for the stock was opened on a very small scale in a little room in one corner of a tavern called then White Hall, on the west side of Main just north of the intersection of Liberty street, where a hotel called the American House has since stood. A man named Gossett kept the hotel then.

Locke's Store

Locke soon felt encouraged to call on his partner for larger quarters; then was Mt. Ararat's chance for resurrection; Locke tried to buy out Emerson, Eaton & Co., who were sort of successors to Mackey, though in a newer, better building and on the east side of Main street. The owners declined to sell and the star of Mt. Ararat sank to rise no more. Locke bought an acre of Alfred Thurstin, including that part of the east side of Main street from the First National Bank south, and taking in the opera house, and there built a store and residence under one roof; his trade was prosperous, and not long after he was appointed postmaster and a little later built and operated an ashery, the first manufacturing enterprise begun in the village, if we except Caleb Lord's cabinet shop. Locke had by his enterprise practically determined where the center of the village would be. Anyone who came in after that, and wanted to go into business, located as near Locke's as he could get.

A New Era Opened

The advent of a second railroad here opens a new chapter—a new era in the history of Bowling Green. This circumstance is of greater import to the town than the first casual thought would suggest. Not in the sense that we expect the town to be a center of vast population or a great commercial or manufacturing center. Its development in these respects rests largely with those who now rule its destiny—their enterprise, ambition and far-sightedness.

The railroad from north to south, a distance of 30 miles through a rich and largely unoccupied portion of the county, will not only develop a vastly increased trade and make better market facilities for the town, but settle forever its status as the business center—capital, of one of the largest and most prosperous agricultural counties in Ohio. As sanguine as many of our people felt on this point, it was not settled beyond cavil until this road came. This settles it and the town now stands on solid footing in this respect. It is the capital of a grand and populous county. It is the official business center and is naturally the trading center.

A number of lots were sold at public auction in Perrysburg, in 1823.

THE BELL SCHOOL HOUSE

Purpose for Which It Was Built—Much Interest Attached to It—Whereabouts of the Bell Discovered

THE Bell school house was built in 1841, says Joseph R. Tracy, on Section 26, Plain township, by John Whitehead, John E. Jenkins, carpenters, and Joseph R. Tracy and other residents assisting. The money was contributed by the leading citizens of the township, who desired to have a house for a private school, as well as for religious purposes. The bell, from which the house took its name, was formerly used on the Mission Chapel on the Maumee river. It was presented to the builders of the school house and placed in a cupola erected for the purpose. A subscription school was carried on for a number of years, after which the house passed into the possession of the common school trustees.

Some time in 1857, the house was destroyed by fire, and another building was erected for the same purposes about a mile to the west. The Methodist class that used to meet there was merged into the church at Bowling Green. The same is true of the Baptist and Congregational adherents. Each became the members of larger churches. Thus the particular necessity of this school building ceased.

The bell has been the subject of much theorizing as to what became of it. As far as can be learned, it being the property of Isaac Van Tassel, he took possession of it and removed it. Mr. J. R. Judson says it was removed in 1845 on the plea that the belfry was not safe. He says he does not know who had charge of it the next 10 or 12 years, but he is pretty certain that it was placed in the Minton school house in the late 50's. Newton Stearns says it is on the Minton school house and has not been changed. He says he bought the bell for $2 and sold it for $3 to Nate Minton. T. W. Minton, writing under date of February 1. 1909, says, "In 1870, a new school house was built on his father's farm in Plain township, five miles west of Bowling Green—that his father learned where the old mission bell was and went and bought it for something like $3.00 from a party west of Bowling Green, and if I remember correctly he presented it to the district by placing it on top of the school building and it is there today if it has not been taken down."

Mr. C. W. Evers once doubted whether the old Mission bell and that on the Minton school house was the same. But after more thorough investigation and the statements of those upon whom he could rely he was less skeptical and admitted the probability that they were the same. Mr. Evers attended school in the old Bell school house in 1846-7, and had many tender associations in all that pertained to it. In writing of the bell he says: "Its silvery peals swelled up from that little forest-hidden chapel over forest and glade, and bore the glad tidings to the scattered settlers, far and near, that some one would preach, some one would sing, and some one would pray that day at the 'Bell'. That bell was the pioneer evangelist of this kind in Wood county, or for that matter in Northwestern Ohio. It came with the vanguard of Civilization."

LAST OF BIG GAME

The Last Bear That Was Killed Within the Limits of Wood County

IN the Sentinel of November 27, 1884, Mr. Evers gives substantially the story, as told by Wm. Mears and J. G. Ralston, of the killing of the last bear ever slain in Wood county:

It was late in the fall of 1858; there was a nice tracking snow on the ground. Wash. G. Avery, who then lived on his farm north of town, was out hunting; had wounded a deer and was following in its track when, about three o'clock in the afternoon he came across a big brown bear poking along in the woods. Mr. Avery thought no more about his deer, but immediately turned his attention to the "bigger game." His gun was a small one, and not just the thing to tackle a bear with, but Wash did not stop to think of that, but pulled up and blazed away. The ball struck the bear in the thigh, inflicting a flesh wound of no consequence, and bruin set off in an easterly direction. Wash went over to Joe Ralston's on Sugar Ridge, and got Joe and

Geo. Walker, who were there visiting, and the three set out in pursuit. They followed the trail as far as the McCutchenville road over in Webster, and then, it being late in the night and all hands being tired, they went to the Ten Mile house and stayed until morning. At daylight they were again on the trail, the crowd re-enforced by the addition of Jesse Williams, a harness maker from Perrysburg, and a friend of his. They followed the trail to the Ottawa county line, where they found that the bear had taken the back track, crossing the McCutchenville road within a mile or so of where they had started in the morning. As they crossed the road, they found that some one else, with a dog had taken the trail.

Jesse Williams said it was old Jake Hedinger, an old hunter who lived in the vicinity; said he knew his track. Away they all started on the dead run, whooping and halloing to Hedinger to stop and wait for them, but he did not stop. They finally heard the dogs and taking a short cut came up with Hedinger. They found where the bear had attempted to climb two different cottonwood trees, but had been pulled down by Hedinger's big dog, and had been obliged to continue his flight by the near approach of the men. He finally came out and crossed the plank road at the intersection of Center and Middleton township lines. When the men came out on the plank road Williams and his friend followed the trail after the dogs, and Ralston went down the plank road to watch what was then called the Rudolph road.

Wm. Avery, Wm. Mears, and Benj. Johnson had been hunting that day in east of the John Hood place, north of the bend. Mr. Mears had killed a turkey gobbler that weighed 55 lbs., and they were returning homeward. Mr. Johnson had left them and gone home, and the others met Joe just as he turned off from the plank road, and an explanation ensued, when Mears and Wm. Avery agreed to join the bear hunt. They agreed that the bear which had gone away in west of the road would attempt to get back to the Devil's Hole, and that they had better station themselves along what was known as the Rudolph ditch. Ralston, Mears and Wm. Avery accordingly went over on the ditch. Joe Ralston took up his station on the ditch-bank, while Wm. Avery stood about 15 rods east of Joe, and Mears about the same distance east of Avery. As it began to get dusk they heard the dogs coming, yelping at every jump. Pretty soon bruin came in sight of Joe, lumbering along to within a few yards of him, with back bowed up, mouth open and tongue hanging out, looking tired and savage. Joe pulled up his gun—and it snapped. Tried it again, but it was no good. By this time the bear had passed on to Mr. Avery, who, owing to the gathering darkness could not see to shoot very good. He fired, however, striking the bear in the back, but not inflicting a serious wound. Now came Mr. Mears' turn. He waited until the bear was within a few feet of him, and had just cleared a 14-foot ditch at a bound, when he put a half-ounce ball through his heart. Bruin fell, apparently dead, and the dogs coming up at that instant, sailed in, and then immediately sailed out again, for, with his last strength, the bear struck one of them a terrible blow with his paw, knocking him about 20 feet away, whereupon the two dogs set off through the woods, howling as if "the old Nick" was after them.

When they found that the bear was dead, Mears, Avery and Ralston set up a shout of triumph which soon brought Wash., Williams and Hedinger to the scene. After a consultation it was decided to take the bear up to Thomas' tavern and there divide up. They accordingly dragged the carcass through the snow to the place of destination.

Arriving at the tavern, those who felt

disposed to do so celebrated the occasion by indulging in a little tangle-foot, after which they divided the bear, which weighed about 250 pounds. Wash. took the hide, and the meat was divided among the others, after which all went home, tired and worn out, but well pleased with the day's adventure.

This is the story of the last "big game" ever brought down, or which probably ever will be brought down in Wood county.

TURKEY FOOT ROCK

A Boulder Monument Commemorative of Wayne's Great Victory

THE large boulder called "Turkey Foot Rock" which lays on the north bank of the Maumee denotes the point on the river where Gen. Wayne gained a decisive victory over the combined Indian tribes of the Northwest, on August 20, 1794. The Indians were principally directed and commanded by Blue Jacket and Little Turtle, and the tribes engaged included the Shawanese, Miamis, Wyandotts, Pottawattomies, Delawares, Chippewas, Ottawas and a few Senecas and other remnants of tribes. The Wyandotts, a once powerful tribe lost all their chiefs, nine in number, at that battle, and tradition says that one of the bravest of their clan, called "Turkey Foot," was slain by Wayne's infuriated followers near this rock and that after Wayne, whom the Indians called the "Whirlwind" was gone, the few scattering members of the Wyandott nation repaired to the spot where their beloved chief had fallen and carved the representation of a huge turkey's foot on the rough boulder with their hatchets. This roughly chiseled turkey's foot is still to be seen, although the rock has been sadly defaced by sacrilegious and disrespectful hands.

The armies of Harmer and St. Clair had been butchered and destroyed, and the savages, encouraged by the British agents, were exultant and blood thirsty. But an avenging Nemesis was after them at last. The highest tribute paid to Wayne's generalship, was by Little Turtle in a council speech the night previous to the battle, which he was not in favor of. Said he, "the Americans are now led by a chief who never sleeps. The night and the day are alike to him. During all the time he has been marching on our villages we have been unable to surprise him. Think well of it." But the counsel of Blue Jacket who was more bloody and precipitate prevailed. The Indians were overpowered, out generaled, driven into the river and almost annihilated, and the glad tidings were heralded across the Alleghanies in shouts of triumph. That boulder is a mute reminder of the battle of Fallen Timber.

A Piece of Fiction

In a communication to the Sentinel, the late C. W. Evers thus disposed of the prevalent theory that Turkey Foot was an Indian chief:

I notice in your daily of June 15 that Dr. Dwight Canfield in his review of the battle of Fallen Timber has fallen into the usual mistake of people who write about Turkey Foot rock. There is such a rock as we all know, but that there was a "noted Indian chief" named Turkey Foot, as he stated and as many others have done, I deny. I know I am going in the face of a long standing legend—breaking an idol as it were; but it is best, that we get our history of the long ago correct before it is too late.

If any one interested, will take the trouble to consult a book written per-

TURKEY FOOT ROCK
At the Presque Isle Hill, Where It Marks the Site of the Battle of Fallen Timber

SCRAP-BOOK.

haps some time in 1830 or possibly earlier when the Indians were still here, by T. M. Coffinberry, called the Forest Rangers, foot note, page— (I have not the book before me, though several of them are owned in Toledo) they will get the facts, regarding Turkey Foot rock. Mr. Coffinberry was a lawyer, lived at Perrysburg, was well educated and mingled, out of curiosity perhaps, much with the Indians, and knew their habits, customs and history quite well.

According to his statement, I give the substance rather than his words, the Indian killed, at or near the big boulder, August 20, 1794, was a sub-chief of the turkey clan of the Wyandott tribe, whose totem or coat of arms or monogram was the imprint of a turkey's foot. Each tribe is divided into more or less clans; the beaver, the muskrat, the eagle, the dog, the bear, or any favorite object may be adopted as the emblem of a clan. A turkey in Wyandott is Massas.

This warrior, killed that day was evidently popular and beloved of his clan for they not only carved the emblem of the clan, a turkey's footprint on the big granite boulder, but always, when passing that way, some of his kin or clan would stop and leave some little tribute of their affection, oftener plug tobacco than anything else.

Thus it was the stone took the name Turkey Foot rock. There was no noted chief of that name. No treaty record with the Indians bears such a name. No such name is mentioned in the many fights before Wayne's battle. If he had been a noted warrior, some where his name would appear. It is just a fiction of some of the white men of the later years and with some has grown into an honest belief as is the case with many other fictions we cling to as truths.

There is a turkey foot rock. It is a land mark denoting the high tide spot of Wayne's battle. Near it a brave of the turkey clan was killed. He was popular and his clansmen cut the clan emblem, the print of a turkey's foot, on the stone and very naturally it has gone by the name Turkey Foot rock. Its chief importance, however, is that it marks the place of one of the great battles of the border war period.

Until recently it was the only battle ground in this part of the Maumee valley that had a marker of any sort.

The old rock should be cared for and preserved and above all when we take our school history pupils to these historic places we should give them the history straight—unmixed with any fiction or carelessly drawn conclusions formed without due investigation.

UNBROKEN FORESTS

Black Snakes, Rattlers, Wolves and Other Pests That Annoyed Early Settlers

AN old pioneer of Perry township, in writing to the Sentinel, says that prior to the year 1830, the southern part of Wood county as far as known was without a living white settler. Its forests of oak, walnut, beech and poplar were primeval in beauty, and teemed with bears, wolves, deer and other animals, while countless multitudes of wild geese and ducks quacked in the tangled undergrowth along the various branches of the Portage.

About the year 1830 solitary hunters would come in occasionally and chase a bear or herd of deer, but for the most part it remained an unbroken wilderness, and although speculators and those contemplating actual settlement had entered lands, they were laughed at for their credulity if they asserted it would ever be a habitable region. The "Munchausen" stories of the Black Swamp represented it as being occupied by a species of genii closely allied to mother Eve's persuader. Black snakes were said to attain *constrictor* proportions, while the dread rattler was supposed to hiss forked lightning from every stump and crevice. Gradually, however, these stories became "old," and some adventurous spirits began to talk seriously of making a "clearing."

The cholera which made its first appearance in the United States in 1831, spread north with great rapidity and dire effects. At the old town of Gallipolis on the Ohio, its advent was felt and sent many northward, who preferred any hardship to a tussle with the dread malady.

Named Millgrove

In the election of '34 the number of voters had increased to twenty-eight, and during the fall and winter the settlement at the McCormick entry was sufficiently large to warrant James McCormick in surveying a piece of his land and laying it out in lots. He secured the services of Davis, and lots were laid on the McCutchenville road, and the road to Fremont and the streets named Main and Sandusky. Since that time several additions have been made and new streets laid out. McCormick named the town Mill Grove, to which has been suffixed West to distinguish it from Mill Grove in Morgan county. The sale of lots was slow and building slower.

The Wolves

One of the greatest pests to the raising of any kind of stock were wolves, the forests seemed literally alive with them, and in the winter they were ravenous, attacking every living animal from a chicken to even the settler himself. Gradually, however, they disappeared, drew deeper into the forest, and it has been many years since the wolf lost his identity in the county. Settlers used different modes to protect their stock from them, the steel trap and chain being very effective. Many daring exploits are related of the old hunters then young men, chuck full of grit. One is worth relating.

George McCormick at that time a mere boy, went out one morning to see his trap, and found a very large wolf fast but unhurt. Now as there were some new settlers just come in, George determined they should have a close view of a live wolf. After considerable planning he succeeded in tying the wolf's mouth and feet. He then very coolly strapped him on his back and walked home, a distance of over a mile.

THE HOLLINGTONS

Like Other Early Settlers They Shared in the Sufferings of Pioneer Life

AMONG the list of early settlers of Plain township, may be mentioned Richard Hollington, who came out to the Maumee country in the year 1834, by the lake, and almost directly from England. He entered 400 acres of land, embracing what is now a fine farm south of Bowling Green. Mr. Hollington selected a spot about one-fourth of a mile west of the Findlay road as his future abiding place, and in course of time had a fine orchard of apple trees planted from the old Station orchard on the Maumee.

After contracting with a man named McKnight, for the building of a log house, and buying two yoke of oxen (the first ever owned in the township) he re-

SCRAP-BOOK.

turned to Buffalo for his family, whom he had preceded in search of a home.

He had a wife and five children, four sons and one daughter. Richard, the eldest son, then 13 years of age, became a resident of Williams county, this State. Mary became the wife of Hon. Octavius Waters, of Fulton county. Joseph was a resident of Bowling Green. William, the youngest of the family, became a resident of Missouri.

Ambrose, next to the youngest, will be remembered by many of the present day throughout this section of Ohio, as Rev. Ambrose Hollington, who was classed among the most eloquent of pulpit orators. His son, Dr. R. D. Hollington, of St. Paul's M. E. church, Toledo, is destined to become as famed as his father.

Privation and Inexperience

In due time the Hollingtons arrived at the dock in Perrysburg, where the rough side of life's reality in the Black Swamp, set in.

Mr. Hollington had in the old country been a tradesman, while his wife, who was a well educated woman, had been accustomed to all the comforts and conveniences of life. But her piano had been left across the ocean, and the only music she would be likely to hear for many long months would be a medley of uncouth sounds of frogs, mosquitoes, wild beasts and birds. Hollington knew nothing of woodcraft, did not know how to use an ax, in fact with his wife, he was entering upon an undertaking rendered doubly trying because of their inexperience.

After a toilsome journey through swamps and forests, they finally arrived at the cabin of Joseph Mitchell, who had settled a short time previous near the south boundary of the township, and about two miles north of Cass' Corners, in Liberty township. The Mitchells had barely got their cabin covered. A place for a door and small window had been cut out, but lumber for a door or glass for windows were practically out of the question then, nor had the cabin even a puncheon floor, but such as they had the early settlers shared freely with each other, or with the stranger who came among them.

It was here in mid-winter, after the last weary day of their long journey was done, that the Hollingtons began fully to take in the situation. They had reached the goal of their ambition, free America, where every man is a law unto himself, no kingly power, no necks galled with the yoke of oppression, no excisemen, a land of plenty and unmixed happiness. But alas, how different the picture of fancy and the homely reality.

A Triumph Through Tears

Mrs. Hollington, of all the souls gathered there, was the most disheartened and most keenly realized their disconsolate situation. Overcome at last by her feelings, she sank down on one of the floor sleepers and burst out crying. But her grief was not the grief of despair. It was a transition in her life pilgrimage. This evanescent storm of tears seems to have washed away all the weaker elements of her womanly nature, and instead of the dependent, timid woman, she became the strong arm, the pillar of strength in that household; when her husband grew despondent, she spoke words of encouragement to him. With each new and trying vicissitude, her courage arose. No trial seemed too great for her fortitude. She seemed suddenly to have been imbued with that strength of character and tenacity of purpose which can surmount every difficulty, and which in all ages of the world has made men heroes.

The family remained at Mitchell's about six weeks, and their own house still being incompleted, they moved with what few articles they had, to the cabin of Lee Moore, just in the south edge of the present town of Bowling Green.—*C. W. E.*

INDIAN ASSOCIATES

In Milton Township—Hardships of Settlers—Expert Hunter—Coon Pot Pie—Rev. Joseph Badger

IN the Sentinel of November 29, 1883, Mr. Evers says that James Hutchinson, sr., and family, and sons Andrew and James and families, who came from Summit county, Ohio, in April, 1834, were the first settlers within the borders of what is now known as Milton township. The family of Mr. Hutchinson, besides his wife and two married sons, consisted of three daughters. Andrew and wife had twelve children. In James Hutchinson, jr's, family were only himself and wife.

These families found Milton to be an unbroken forest, the home of the red man and the abiding place of the deer, wolf and bear. Not a tree had been cut in the township, unless by hunters, and everything was in a state of nature. They came with five yoke of oxen and one span of horses, making their journey from Summit county in ten days; they took what is now the Maumee and Western Reserve road to Perrysburg, then almost bottomless with mud, thirty miles in length and supplied with a tavern to every mile, and one to spare. At times on their journey the wagons would get stuck, compelling them to put all five yoke of oxen to one wagon to pull it out. From Perrysburg they traveled most of the way over what was known as "Hull's Trace" to Lee Moore's place, in the south part of Bowling Green. From there Mr. Moore piloted them by the way of the sand ridge to their future home, and for many a mile they were obliged to cut their way through the woods, step by step.

The three men with the help of the women, on their arrival, immediately set to work to build a cabin, which they completed in forty-eight hours ready for occupancy, and in which they slept on the second night spent on the premises. This cabin, the first in the township, stood on the farm entered by Mr. Hutchinson, sr.

Indian Associates

After getting a good start on this farm each of the sons entered a piece of land and built a cabin for himself. The only associates of these families until the next settlers moved in, were the Indians, who of course, were very numerous. The Indians had a camp for years on the place owned later by Morris Brown and by H. C. Strow, and after being disturbed there, camped for a long time on the east side of the Van Tassel farm.

The settlers' children and Indian pappooses would play together day after day just as neighbors' children do now. The Indians learned the sports of the whites and vice versa. The Indians lived mostly on hominy and wild game, such as venison, coon, wood-chuck, 'possum, musk-rat, etc. Andrew Hutchinson states that he had often when visiting their camps, seen large copper kettles (which they obtained from the government) containing perhaps eight or ten fat coon each, mixed with hominy and water, swung over a fire and boiling like a young volcano. The coon would be skinned and quartered, then thrown in the kettle head, feet, claws and all. Mr. Hutchinson relates that his brother James went back to Summit county and married a rather fashionable young lady who came out to the Wood county wilderness to share the trials of the pioneer life with her husband. About the first Sunday she was there they went to visit their neighbors—red neighbors, and of course were invited to stay to dinner. The young Summit county bride took a look into one of the kettles and got a full sniff of the steaming coon pot-pie which so sickened her that she had to be taken off home which amused the Indians very much.

Expert Hunter

Mr. Andrew Hutchinson, who, with his father and brother were, as before stated, the first settlers of the township, is yet living (1883) at Milton Center, and though 74 years old, told us a few days since that he had cleared 12 acres of land the past year. Mr. Hutchinson when young was one of the best hunters in northwestern Ohio. He supplied most of his pioneer neighbors with their meat, such as venison, turkeys and other wild game, and they in turn would work on his farm to pay him for hunting; "Change works" it was called. He was schooled in the art of hunting by the Indians, and hunted with them day after day. In giving him instructions about hunting they would say: "White man hunt deer slow, go still. When see deer watch him close. When deer look up, white man stop, stand straight; when get close take good aim, fire, and down come deer." He evidently followed their instructions well, as he said he had killed probably not less than 2,000 deer in his time.

Rev. Joseph Badger

Some time later Rev. Joseph Badger and family, moved in from near the old "Missionary Station" and lived on the farm now owned by M. B. Todd. Father Badger was a soldier in the Revolutionary war, chaplain in a regiment of Harrison's army in the war of 1812 and he was also present at the siege of Fort Meigs, near which place his ashes now repose (the Perrysburg cemetery). He was a man of deep piety, greatly respected by all, kind and generous, was never known to refuse a favor, and would render assistance to an Indian or even a dog. The esteem in which he was held can be aptly illustrated by the following fact. He was on principle opposed to hunting on the Sabbath, as was the custom of many of the hardy, careless pioneers. But they knew Mr. Badger's opposition to the practice and if they chanced to pass near his house on a Sabbath hunt they would always as a matter of respect to his feelings, leave the road and go around his house in the woods and thus escape his observation.

TINGE OF ROMANCE

The Story of Horace Cady—Why the Young Frenchman, James Bloom, Came to Wood

HORACE CADY was an eastern man and at one time quite wealthy. He lost heavily in a large speculation and as is always the case his position and the prestige of his family among the wealthy social circles of the east diminished with his fortune. He chanced to come west with a friend and while in this county became favorably impressed with it as a refuge for his family from the outside world and settled here in 1832 or '33. Leaving his family he started for South America with the hope of regaining his lost fortune.

While on his way to Valparaiso, he came across a dashing and spirited young Frenchman of high parentage and wealth who was also on a tour of speculation in Lima, Peru. He became much attached to the young man and after they had been in South America some time, Cady not making any advancement in his project and the young Frenchman losing heavily in his operations, they concluded to return to the United States and Cady invited his friend to accompany him to his home in this county, which he did.

The young Frenchman, with his high ideas and aristocratic notions was not favorably impressed with the country but what was lacking in this was made up by the presence at Cady's home of a fine looking and accomplished daughter to whom he soon become greatly attached and in a short time married and settled for life in Liberty. The young Frenchman was James Bloom and the daughter, Harriet Cady, became Mrs. Harriet Bloom.

Though this story may not be correct in every particular, it in main explains how Mr. Bloom came to reside in Liberty. He was evidently never cut out for a farmer and the style of life he was compelled to live, in the early days here, failed to bring prosperity. He died about 1870 at an old age, and his remains now lie in the Liberty township cemetery.

To tell how these first settlers toiled to make comfortable homes of their "farms in the wilderness" of the privations and hardships they endured, of their great distance from family supplies, etc., would be simply a repetition of what has been said of other localities. Two things, however, worthy of mention that used to be the greatest enemies of the early settlers were the

Ague and Mosquitoes

Ask any old settler of Liberty to-day about the mosquitoes and he will tell you the swamps along the Portage river in those days bred the best specimens of mosquitoes the world ever saw. They were of the Jumbo type, blessed with long lives, powerful endurance and a perseverance equaled only by the settlers themselves. And as the latter sat around their cabin homes on warm, pleasant evenings, their only mode of protection from the ravages of these little persecutors would be to build a "smudge" and envelop themselves in the smoke arising from the same, like a ham in a smoke house. As a breeder of malarial complaints the Portage had an established reputation. As soon as the summer and fall months rolled past they would bring with them malarial fevers of the most dreaded type and ague in all the stages and forms known. Whole families would be stricken down at one time and many of them died from the dread complaint. Dr. Eli Manville, father of the late Dr. A. J. Manville, was the first doctor to practice in this community and the way he fed quinine to his patients was a caution, but he was a blessing to the community, saved many lives and is gratefully remembered by his few surviving patients of 70 years ago.—*C. W. E.*

MIAMI OF THE LAKE

A Paper Published at Perrysburg 72 Years Ago—Gleanings from Wood County's Oldest Newspaper

WRITING to the Wood County Democrat, a correspondent gives the following sketch of interest:

Rumaging through a trunk of old time records recently, several copies of a Perrysburg newspaper came into view, called "Miami of the Lake." These copies were dated in March and April of 1837—about 72 years ago. J. H. McBride was the editor and publisher.

The first page of these numbers is largely made up of literary matter, both prose and poetry. One article by Judge Story is entitled, "What is to Become of This Country?" He refers to the na-

SCRAP-BOOK.

tions of the old world—to Greece, Rome, Italy, Venice, Genoa—one time republics, that have passed away. He closes in an impassioned appeal in the following language:

"I call upon you, fathers, by the shades of your ancestors, by the dear ashes which repose in this precious soil, by all you hope to be, resist every project of disunion, resist every attempt to fetter your conscience, or smother our public schools, or extinguish your system of public instruction."

After proceeding at some length in his appeal to the fathers, the mothers and the young men of America, he thus concludes:

"Life can never be too short, which brings nothing but disgrace and oppression. Death never comes too soon, if necessary, in defense of the liberties of our country."

In the number of April 5, 1837, an important discovery is announced—"the greatest since the days of Franklin." James P. Espy, Esq., has ascertained that the weather is regulated by fixed, unalterable laws—easily understood, so that the captain of a vessel may tell whether there is a storm raging anywhere within 500 miles of him, and how he may direct his course so as to avoid it.

The proceedings of the Ohio legislators in both the senate and house of representatives are given at considerable length, occupying nearly a page. The paper is a four page folio, with six columns to a page.

At the head of the editorial columns delinquent subscribers are stirred up—money is needed, "badly needed." The panic of 1837 was then spreading over the country, and "the money market at New York was hourly becoming more alarming."

Hon. John Hollister was the representative of this district, and the district embraced nine northern counties, in which was included some of the most important works of internal improvement in the state. In speaking of Hollister, the editor says: "There has been a straight forward and honorable course adopted and pursued by the representative from this district, in all matters of legislation, which has received the approbation of political enemies as well as political friends."

In another editorial the condition of the Western Reserve Road is scored in the severest language. Says the editor, "It is only those who have become stalled in the mud, in endeavoring to work their way through this Ohio Golgotha, that can draw a true picture of this stigma upon the character of the state." Again he says: "Teams are not unfrequently five days in passing through this section of the road of thirty-one miles in extent!"

From an editorial on the money panic may be found the following:

"One firm in New York alone has paid the enormous sum of $30,000, usury money the past year."

"The most wealthy and prudent firms are disheartened and ready to yield to the pressure of the times."

"The rich men are now made poor, and the poor made beggars."

"Every man in the country is now made to suffer except the broker and extortioner."

"Every day matters grow worse, and as the exchanges are still becoming more deranged, thick gloom and darkness rests upon the future."

Petitions from many points were presented to the Ohio Legislature for the construction of the Wabash and Erie canal on the southeast side of the Maumee river from Defiance to the lake, which location was never realized.

In markets fresh beef and pork quoted at 8 to 12c; butter 20 to 25c; eggs, 12 to 15c; flour, per bbl., $11.50.

In the Perrysburg marine list arrivals of vessels from March 30 to April 4, were steamboats General Jackson and Oliver Newberry from Detroit, with passengers; steamboat Cincinnati from Cleveland, with passengers; also schooner Delphos from Cleveland with pork, flour and merchandise.

During the same time the departures were steamboats General Jackson and Cincinnati for Detroit, with passengers; steamboat Oliver Newberry, for Cleveland and Erie, with passengers, and the schooner Caroline, for Cleveland.

A. Hills, postmaster advertises nearly 200 letters remaining in office April 1, 1837.

The fourth page is mostly devoted to advertisements.

J. Chappel, sheriff, advertises a number of sales.

Some ten or twelve legal notices are scattered through the paper.

Independent voters are notified that John C. Smith is a candidate for Mayor.

Among the merchants advertising their goods, Woodruff & Spafford, Russell & Brigham, Beach & Bennett, J. Hollister & Co., Doan & Earl, Oren Clark and Spink & Smith.

Jones & Tucker and Earl Brothers advertise their stores at Waterville.

Forwarding and Commission merchants of Maumee and Perrysburg, comprise the following firms: John Hollister & Co., and Doan & Earl, of Perrysburg; J. J. Bingham, Forsyth & Hazard, Cook and Kirtland and J. A. Scott, of Maumee. These firms publish their prices at length for storage, wharfage and commissions.

D. Wilkison, Master, advertises that the steamer Commodore Perry will leave Buffalo every Monday evening for Detroit and Perrysburg. Will leave Detroit every Thursday morning and Perrysburg every Thursday afternoon for Buffalo.

Charles Stoner offers six cents reward for a runaway apprentice.

Leander Ransom, acting commissioner of the Board of Public Works advertises that "sealed proposals will be received at the town of Maumee in Lucas county, Ohio, on the 15th day of May, 1837, for the construction of so much of the line of the Wabash and Erie Canal, as lies between the head of the Rapids of the Maumee River and the eastern termination of said Canal near the town of Manhattan, at the head of the Maumee Bay."

Several advertisements appear from Detroit, Erie, Pa., and other places.

The following are the legal firms whose cards appear under the head of "Law Advertisements."

Henry Reed, jr., Horace Sessions, Henry Bennett, H. C. Stowel & J. D. Brown, J. C. Spink & A. C. Coffinbury, Isaac Stetson and Mason Brayman, the latter located in Buffalo.

There are many points of interest embraced in this relic of two generations ago, and not desiring to prove tedious with further detail, the foregoing is probably sufficient to indicate the activities of the first settlers and business men at Perrysburg and along the Maumee river.—*F. J. O.*

Some geologists are of the opinion that Lake Erie, at one time, extended westward as far as the source of the Maumee, citing as evidence the existence of various "moraines" yet plainly visible in that vicinity.

The first school house in the east part of Middleton township was a small log building built by joint contributions of the settlers on Section 24, in 1844, and Mrs. Amelius Robertson, who was then Margery Frazier, just from Glasgow, Scotland, was the first teacher. It was also for some years used as the first church for that community, until a society was organized at Haskins.

THE TOWN OF BENTON

Why It Was so Named—Samuel Ewing Killed

THE town of Benton, one of the "has-beens," was located a short distance west of Tontogany, and David Hedges was its proprietor. It was laid out during the best days of Thomas Benton, "Old Bullion" as he was called. Hedges was a Jackson Democrat, and a great admirer of old "Tom," and named the town in his memory.

The building used as Hedges' store was moved away and was afterward used for a barn by Henry Nearing, on the Hedges farm, owned by Morehouse heirs. Mrs. Gen. Commager, of Toledo, was a daughter of Hedges. The stone house on the place was built by him in 1834 or '35. Mr. John Whitehead, now of Tontogany, who had just come on from New Jersey, helped to do the carpenter work. The saw mill at this point did not stand very long.

The ruins of the cellar under the store building is all the vestige left of the town of Benton. It did not even live to get a saloon. The store house was moved and is now used as a barn at the stone house.

The Hedges place has a strong claim for priority of settlement in Washington township, though our chronicler has in the recent sketch of the township, given the preference to the Chris Gundy farm located on by Michael Sypher in the spring of 1830.

In 1819 Samuel Ewing, father of Anthony Ewing, and of the late W. H. Ewing (Uncle Hank, near Hull's Prairie) settled on this place, then called Wolf Rapids.

Killed at Rush-Te-Boo

Ewing lived here until 1823, when one day while at Richardson's tavern at Rush-te-boo, the same place where Porter shot Richardson, Ewing and a man named French got into an altercation and French struck Ewing in such a manner as to dislocate his neck, killing him instantly. French was imprisoned on charge of murder in the little log jail at Maumee and escaped one night and never was heard of after.—*Sentinel, 1883.*

BATTLE OF GRAND RAPIDS

A Fierce and Savage Battle That Has Not Figured Largely in the War of 1812

GEN. LIDA of the United States troops gave the following account of a fierce battle with the Indians in the war of 1812, on the site of the present village of Grand Rapids. It was not until 45 years afterwards that he related this account of that battle. He said:

"One of the toughest and most hotly contested little battles ever fought in our Indian wars occurred just where your little village of Gilead now stands. A company of U. S. troops, of which I was one, was ordered from Defiance to Fort Meigs. We passed down the north bank of the river. About noon on a certain day, we came opposite the island that is in the river there. Our commander chose this as a safe place to rest and eat dinner. About two hours were consumed in this way, and then we made preparations to continue our journey. Equipped as we were with the trappings of soldiers and the necessaries for an extended march our freedom of locomotion was not a little encumbered. We proceeded to cross the Rapids to the south bank, but only a little over half the distance had been accomplished, when, without a moment's warning, from the top of the bank and beautiful grove over the bottom from the river to the bluff behind, belched forth a volley of musketry wounding several of our men, but killing none outright. The foes, of course, were Indians, who appeared to be a host in number. They had been lying in close concealment, but after the first discharge could be seen, and I remember, to me at least, every tree in the bottom seemed to conceal an Indian. We promptly took refuge under cover of the bank before they could load and fire again. The river bank here was bluffy and perhaps 15 feet in height. We found immediate protection here from the enemy's fire, and began making our way gradually down the river to a ravine about 80 rods distant, carrying our wounded with us.

"This ravine was a dense thicket of brushwood and larger trees, while, from the high ground to the river was free from brush; the trees were principally maple and made a beautiful looking grove, which for six hours we were compelled to turn into a bloody battle field. Before night the dead and dying had been strewn from one end of the bottom to the other. As soon as we had succeeded in establishing ourselves in the shelter of the ravine, we began to be aggressive in our operations, forcing our way up the bottom, keeping ourselves in the protection of every friendly covert afforded by thicket, tree and hollow, and compelled the savage foe to retire from place to place; driving them steadily up the bottom until we reached a point about a hundred or more rods from our place of starting, where two or three mound like knobs with ravines and thickets furnished capital rallying points for the Indians. Taking advantage of this they, with redoubled exertion, forced us back over all the ground we had gained. In like manner we must have passed back and forth over the battle ground five or six times during the afternoon. Each time we fell back we were careful to carry our dead and wounded with us—as far as possible—to our rallying point below.

"On that hotly contested ground many met in hand to hand encounter, at short intervals throughout the entire afternoon. Amid the sharp crack of rifles came the battle shout of the whites, the warhoop of the savage, and the death yell! No one can realize the horrible and blood-curdling sensation produced by the death yell of an Indian, except, one who has seen and heard for himself. The groans of wounded and dying, and that green bottom land grove, all this, comes up before me to-day, as vividly as they were produced in that battle on the lonely banks of the Maumee over forty-five years ago, and I say again it was a battle well worthy of the name. I had been in a dozen battles and skirmishes before that, and several after, but none were as active and fierce, in contest; so tenacious and stubborn in holding every advantage, considering the number of combatants engaged and length of time fought incessantly. The soldiers numbered about one hundred and twenty-five and of the Indians, no doubt, they were double that many. The closing act in this forest tragedy occurred, as dusk was coming on, by our force driving the Indians to the bluffs before mentioned. We then retired to our ravine to watch the night through. The Indians did not follow us, and during night for some reason, withdrew from the vicinity entirely, leaving us to bury our dead and go on our way unmolested."

In the course of narrating this bloody encounter, Gen. Lida became quite absorbed with the memories of the past. Evidently this incident of all others in his life impressed him the most. He had been a soldier under Wayne and seen much of Indian warfare.

SCRAP-BOOK.

MERCER SETTLEMENT

Advent of Caleb Mercer—A Plucky Youngster—Lost in the Woods—Turkey Fight

CALEB MERCER was the second of the Mercer family to come to Wood county, and arrived here at the age of 19, in March 1834. He started out as a mere boy from his home in Columbiana county, to seek his fortune in the wilderness of western Ohio. All he brought with him was his "knapsack" and gun, and money enough to enter a small piece of land. He was nine days on his journey of 200 miles, and spent his first night in Wood county at the house of Ashael Powers, the first settler at the "forks" in Freedom township, and from there went to his brother, George Mercer, in Liberty, who had at this time been here about a year. It is needless to say it required pluck for a mere boy to start out alone, on foot, to make a long journey into an unknown and almost uninhabited wilderness, through mud and water, and leave behind friends and relatives, to seek a home in the forest familiar only to the red man and the objects of his prey.

Young Mercer immediately on his arrival located land in Section 14, of Liberty, and set out in a day or two, again on foot, for Bucyrus, a distance of 60 miles, to enter the land at the land office. He left the house of Collister Haskins about 10 o'clock one cloudy March day, intending to reach Fostoria, then called Rome, that night. After he had proceeded on his journey about five miles, by the way of an Indian trail leading in a southeasterly direction, he heard a queer noise in the woods off to one side of the trail, and being curious as to its cause, he proceeded to investigate and found it was caused by a flock of nearly

Three Hundred Wild Turkeys

That were fighting a terrible battle. He said he had never seen such a sight in his life, and it is probable that two strange flocks had come together, and the matter of chief gobbler was being decided.

After dispersing the battle of turkeys he turned to find the trail he had left, but much to his dismay he was unable to find it. He wandered about for some time and soon became confused and lost. After a time he struck a creek, the meandering of which he aimlessly followed until about dark, when the welcome sound of a cow bell struck his ear. Following the sound he soon came upon a cow, and near by perceived the blue smoke curling up from a cabin, which he thinks must have stood near the Hancock county line. Upon going to the little hut he found a man and woman just preparing to abandon their home in the wilderness the next morning. Mercer asked for something to eat and lodgment for the night, and was informed they hadn't "a bite in the house to eat," but that he might remain over night, which he did.

The next morning he got his bearings, and struck for Rome which he reached that afternoon, when he got something to eat, the first nourishment he had had since his departure from Haskins' about thirty hours before. From Rome he proceeded to Bucyrus, entered his land and returned to his brother's again on foot. It might be stated here, that Mr. Mercer traveled the road between Columbiana county and Wood county, a distance of 200 miles, on foot five times, and between Bucyrus and here, 60 miles, on foot six times.

The same spring, '34, he cleared five acres of land on his new farm and built a cabin. The five acres he planted to corn and a small patch of potatoes. The corn crop was devoured by the squirrels and coon, but he managed to save a few potatoes.

The following fall he went back to Columbiana county for his father (Wm. Mercer) and mother, who returned with him, accompanied by his sister Lucretia, and brothers Abram and Charles. They all took up their abode in the cabin he had built the previous spring. They drove through with them a herd of 40 cattle, probably the largest number ever brought to the county up to that time. They, however, had much difficulty in keeping the cattle through that winter, a number of which strayed away and never were found. Thus began the Mercer settlement in Liberty.—*C. W. E.*

OIL IN WOOD COUNTY

Brief Summary of Its History—Wood in the Very Center of Oil Production

MANY of the residents of this portion of Ohio well remember the intense excitement twenty-five years ago in the eighties upon the discovery of oil in Wood county. Pen cannot describe the wild, feverish unrest and anxiety that prevailed among all citizens. Investors and speculators were attracted to the county by hundreds. It was the day of the gusher. While oil was struck in different counties in Northwestern Ohio, Wood county, in the heart of the Black Swamp proved to be the "King Bee"— the greatest oil producing county in the history of crude oil probably on the continent at that time. No county equaled it then even in Pennsylvania. Oil was found in no less than sixteen townships, indicating that hundreds of feet beneath us was a vast lake of oil.

In those days Bloom, Henry, Liberty, Portage and Jackson townships were regarded as gusher territory, while remarkable producers were also found in Plain, Middleton, Montgomery, Freedom and Perry townships. Prices for land went skyward. Farms that previously could have been purchased for $10 to $25 and $50 an acre, could not be touched for less than hundreds of dollars per acre. One incident may suffice to show this. One farmer who had a tract of 50 acres, who would have gladly disposed of his farm at $50 an acre, declared he would not sell under $30,000 and he didn't care for that. This is not an isolated instance, but there were many of the same kind. Such was the excitement at that time that it was difficult to secure land at any price. Values went to a high level throughout the county, although in the passage of years, there has been a decline from the high standard of that period, yet they are maintained today at a high level, when compared with prices before the oil period, and that high level is normal and will so continue.

More than half of the oil producers in the Wood county field came from Pennsylvania, experts in the business. They not only came themselves, but brought their household goods, their families, and all the property they had; they have settled in the towns; they have become permanent residents and tax payers; they are helping build up the towns and are increasing the duplicates with refineries, their pipe lines and all of their property, which would not be there a moment if it were not for the oil development. They have added to the wealth of the state— it is difficult to say how much, but an ex-auditor of Wood claims that in this county alone these producers increase the value on the tax duplicate of more than five million dollars, more than that of any other property or interest in the county.

There were in those early days many gushers. One developed at Hammansburg in December of 1886 will suffice as a sample of those spouters. William Carothers, an experienced driller, had the contract for sinking the well and the work was in charge of C. Ash. They drilled 400 feet through lime stone and 770 feet through slate. At this point they struck the Trenton rock, and said Mr. Ash, "we drilled in this awhile and had about given up getting anything. We were losing hope every minute and Monday afternoon, the 6th, at 5 o'clock, we were just 30 feet in the Trenton when we heard a noise in the well which began to fill. We stopped the drill and were hardly out of the way when the oil spouted up over the derrick and 85 feet in the air. We quickly put the fire out under the boiler and withdrew from the field. The flow was so continuous that we were not able to get our tools out until Thursday.

A representative of the Sentinel visited the gusher when it had been flowing for four days at intervals averaging about 18 minutes, and he says it seemed surely that if there was one there were 4,000 barrels of oil running on the ground. A wagon path in the woods was nearly a foot deep in oil, which run each way for many rods from the well. A half acre of land was covered with it, and a man walking a log made a misstep onto the ground and went over his boot top. The derrick and surrounding trees were dripping with the crude material and the men at work were covered with it.

This was the first well of any importance drilled in the county, and in 1887 four gushers were completed, yielding 1,200, 4,800, 1,500 and 800 barrels respectively. Two gushers in 1888 gave 3,000 and 1,250 barrels. Eight gushers in 1889 yielded 27,100 barrels. In 1890 one gusher gave 600 barrels. Nearly a score of wells drilled in 1891 yielded 7,300 barrels. In 1892 twenty gushers yielded 36,600 barrels. In 1893 there were recorded 22 gushers yielding 16,000 barrels. In 1894 four gushers yielded 3,300 barrels. Several gushers were recorded in 1895 yielding 4,000 barrels. Other gushers were recorded in the years 1896, 1897 and 1898, yielding an average of 500 barrels each. In 1901 a 1,200 barrel producer was drilled in Liberty township. These figures are taken from the oil reports as given in the newspapers at that time. Hundreds of other gushers too numerous to mention were completed throughout Wood county, making it one of the wealthiest counties in the state.

Since then the oil industry has continued to be a paying one. Here is what an old oil expert says with regard to the future of Wood county: "With the richest land, with inexhaustible soil, with a county agriculturally standing at the head, and add to it the natural gas advantages which is bound to bring manufacturing, and oil with the attendant business outgrowing therefrom—I say, with all these things taken into consideration, I know of no spot in America with a brighter future. Real estate in any event is bound to boom and good results follow from what has already taken place."

The earliest tradition has it that at one time there was a continuous water route from the Lakes to the Mississippi, navigable for canoes with the exception of a "portage" about nine miles across at the head of the Maumee, and that this "portage" was owned or controlled by an Indian woman who exacted tribute for all goods that were transferred across it.

EARLY SCHOOL DAYS

The "Little Red School House" of the Past —The Enjoyment of Spelling Matches

MANY there are who may yet remember something of the educational facilities sixty or seventy years ago. Then they knew nothing of the grades in schools. The settlers were few in number, their wants were few and these were bountifully supplied. The benches were crude, seats had no backs, and yet there was little or no complaint, as they knew of nothing better in the way of conveniences. Pupils were compelled to trudge through brush and mud and cold from one to three miles or more.

The average wage paid to the teacher then was $10 a month of 26 days, and three months was about the limit of the contract. Included probably in the contract was that of "boarding 'round," as was the custom in those days.

One of the customs of that time was to bar the school master out of the house, and keep him out until he yielded to the demands of the scholars to treat them to apples, candies, raisins, or such luxuries as could then be had.

Gov. Foster in speaking of those early days, himself a teacher in that early day, says that James Pillars, who afterwards graced the bench for ten years, as the Common Pleas Judge of this judicial district, when a young man contracted to teach a school for ten dollars per month, of twenty-six days; one-half to be paid in cash, and the other half in provisions.

In those days the great feature of our schools was the attention given to spelling. It is seriously doubted whether the schools of the present day can produce so much excellence in spelling as did those of that day. One-fourth of the time, probably, was devoted to spelling exercises, and in addition, at least one night of each week was devoted to what was known as spelling matches. These were attended by the best spellers from the neighboring schools. The highest ambition of the pupil was to be the best speller in school.

In an address on those early days, the late Gov. Foster says that he is perfectly safe in saying that he attended spelling school three nights out of a week, during the three months of school for several years—visiting alternately three different school houses. He believed that his sister, Emily, was the best speller of all, and she was under twelve years of age. The larger scholars used to carry her on their backs as they went to the different schools on foot, the only way of going to these meetings. The Governor relates this incident in his boyhood school days. "I remember of going one night, to the Kiser school house, through the woods the most of the way, and alone, to attend a spelling match. I broke through the ice, and was wet up to my knees when I reached the place; yet I do not think I ever felt better repaid for a day's work than I did over my success on that occasion, for I spelled down the entire school."

Those good old days are only reminiscences now in the dim and distant past. "Good old days" may be said deliberately and seriously without exaggeration, for it is very doubtful if any of the pupils of the present day experience more delight and genuine pleasure in any equal number of days at the present time.

At the meeting of the Commissioners, May 5, 1820, Attorney McCurdy presented an order of Court for $20, his compensation as prosecuting attorney of Wood county, for the May term of 1820.

SCRAP-BOOK.

HENRY DUBBS

One of the Early Settlers of Liberty—With His Son Lewis Built a Tannery.

HENRY DUBBS was the first settler in the west part of Liberty township. He came from Ashland county and entered the land upon which he built his home. He had one son Lewis, now deceased, and two daughters, Ann, who married Ebenezer Donaldson of Grand Rapids, and Sarah, who married Daniel Barton of Milton township.

Mr. Dubbs and his son Lewis, were tanners by trade and soon after their arrival, built a tannery on their lands, probably the first in the county, and did a large and successful business.

Lewis Dubbs was Justice of the Peace in Liberty for 27 years. He was prominent in advancing the best interests of the early settlement and a leader in public improvements; educated, kind and generous, and his name is remembered with respect by those who know him.—*C. W. E.*

MAIL ROUTE

Established in 1829 Between Perrysburg and Bellefontaine

AS this northwestern part of Ohio began to be opened up a mail route was established on March 12, 1829, between Perrysburg and Bellefontaine, and the first post office in the interior of Wood county was located where Portage now is, with Collister Haskins for postmaster. Soon after this Haskins built a log store on the south bank of the Portage river and stocked it with goods best adapted to his customers, a majority of whom were Indians and with whom he built up a large fur trade.

Thus it will be seen that Haskins was not only the first resident of Liberty township, but also established the first store in Portage and might be called the founder of the only village in Liberty township. This store was probably the third regular trading point started in Wood county, others being at Perrysburg and Grand Rapids.

The first mail carrier on the route above mentioned was James Gordon who carried the mail on horseback, made one trip a week each way and usually arrived at Haskins at noon where he took his dinner.—*C. W. E.*

INDIAN SKELETON

Exhumed Over Thirty Years Ago—Somewhat of a Mystery That May Never Be Solved

IN the spring of 1879, a skeleton was exhumed five miles west of Bowling Green, by brick yard men, who were engaged in excavating sand for their yard on the top of a somewhat noted sand dune, on the north side of Keeler prairie, known to the early settlers by the Indian name of Shut-nok.

In the Sentinel Mr. Evers says this skeleton is supposed to be the remains of an Indian, or some other human of giant stature. He had been buried with his head to the west. Between his legs sat a two gallon brass kettle in a good state of preservation excepting the bottom, which is partially gone. Inside this kettle set a small iron kettle which is nearly consumed by rust, except the bail.

Near the side of the skeleton lay a rust-eaten tomahawk, scalping knife and a flint steel for lighting fire, also a stone smoke pipe. The bones, of which but few if any are missing, even to the toe and finger bones, are in an excellent state of preservation and indicate by their size that they were once the mechanism of a powerful man. The skull on which still clings some frizzy substance like hair, is one which phrenologists would say indicated the Indian to have been no common fellow in his tribe. It is a well-shaped, large skull for an Indian, though the prominent cheek bones and low forehead are distinctly recognizable. The fellow had, in his day, an excellent set of teeth—small, sound and evenly set, though well worn and only two missing out of the two and thirty. One arm had, in his lifetime, been broken and the bone had knit together very clumsily, deforming the arm by a great bulge and crook. In the back of his skull is a small hole, but whether this hole had anything to do with his taking off, is an uncertainty.

Mr. Avery says from the best information he can get from the old settlers, the grave has been there not less than 45 years, that is, no burial has taken place there since the neighborhood was settled. He also thinks that the grave was not less than four feet deep originally, something not usual in Indian burials.

Avoided by Indians

Shut-nok, on which this grave was found, is, or was before its surface was disturbed by the plow, the highest sand mound in Wood county. How it came to bear this name, none of the old settlers seem to know, though the belief has been current and has been handed down from generation to generation that it bore the name of a chief of one of the fragmentary tribes inhabiting the Maumee country after Anthony Wayne broke their power in 1794. There are others who have been led to believe this spot was the burial place of a chief whose name it bore. But why a chief or any other influential man in his tribe should be buried in this then lonely place when the burial ground was only a few miles away on the Maumee, we cannot understand.

There is another story that comes to us more directly from an early chronicler, who was once connected with the Indian mission at the Station Island. He states that the Indians avoided the place under the superstitious belief that the Great Spirit had set its seal of displeasure—a curse upon the place for some sin committed by his children, the secret of which was hidden beneath the grassy surface of the mound.

An Indian Legend

In this connection a story is circulated that the chief Tondoganie had a daughter either his own or an adopted daughter—a beautiful girl who was loved by a young Indian of the Shawanee tribe, and of noble birth, but whose tribe had dwindled down to only a fragment, so that he had lost his greatness in the eyes of the chief Tondoganie, who looked upon him with disfavor. The young Indian's love was reciprocated by the girl, and was a secret between them. Her lover's home was at Sandusky plains along with the great chief Black Hoof or Tarhe, but he often made visits to the Maumee ostensibly to fish, but for no other purpose than to see the dark eyed maiden. This secret love was detected by the quick perceptions of the chief, and with flashing eye and angry voice, he pointed the young man to the plains and told him to GO and never return. Both the lovers knew the penalty of disobeying.

The girl secretly stole away and followed her lover in the direction of his home until they reached a high mound, the highest perhaps in the county, on the north side of what is now known as the Keeler Prairie, when she bade him farewell, and watched his receding form until he passed from her sight forever. The heart broken girl returned to her father's wigwam, but fell into a despondent state of mind and could not be roused. She would be missed at times for days and nights together, and some of Tondoganie's runners reported to him that she was wont to stand on the high mound looking to the south chanting a mournful song. Finally she was missed and came back no more and a superstition prevailed that in the darkness of night the figure of an Indian girl with her blanket about her shoulders, could be seen on the mound and that strange sounds as of some one singing a funeral dirge could be heard echoing in the grove below. The mound has ever since gone by the name of Shut-nok, said to be the name of the girl.

The same authority for the above account, stated that Tondoganie's anger was such because of the love of the girl against his wish, that he called upon some of the young men of his band to rid him of the cause. These young men stealthily dogged the movements of the girl until they discovered the place where she met her lover, whom they waylaid, murdered and buried in the mound, and on the final disappearance of the girl the chief forbid his tribe from visiting the place which only brought him memories of remorse and sorrow.

Such is one of the stories handed down from mouth to ear and which may have lost many details of what was a tragic romance, or it may, as is often the case, have gained much by repetition.

A FIERCE BATTLE

Fought in the Fall of 1812 on the Ground Which Perrysburg Now Occupies

IT may not be generally known that the site of the present town of Perrysburg was once the scene of a fierce battle between the Indians and Americans, but such is the fact. The news of the cowardly surrender of Gen. Hull at Detroit in August, 1812, spread like the wind throughout Ohio, and struck the frontier settlers with dismay. It aroused the people from their lethargy, and showed the government the necessity of greater activity and skill in the conduct of the war. In the fall of 1812, General Tupper, of Gallia county, raised 1,000 men, mainly from the counties of Gallia, Lawrence, Jackson, and marched to the foot of the rapids of the Maumee river. From Urbana they followed Hull's trail. As they approached the river the Indians appeared on the opposite bank. Tupper endeavored to cross the river in the night, but owing to the rapid current and the inexperience of his men, he failed and went into camp on the ground where Perrysburg now stands. The enemy soon after collected a superior force, and attacked him in his camp but after a short, sharp engagement, they were defeated with considerable loss and returned to Detroit. The Americans fell back on Fort McArthur.

In 1701 Cadillac, with a Jesuit missionary and 100 men, laid the foundation of Detroit, naming it Ponchartrain.

THE DREAD CHOLERA

Dr. Kinnaman, First Practicing Physician in Perry—Rude Tools for Surgical Operation

IN October, 1835, says a correspondent of the Sentinel in 1877, O. Diver entered 80 acres one-half mile south of Mill Grove, this being undoubtedly the last entry near Mill Grove.

About this time the cholera made its appearance at Rome (now Fostoria) and Risdon in Seneca county, but few died. However, its advent sent terror to the hearts of the settlers in Perry, who with or without—for they were often without —quinine, could battle the "shakes" from July to late in September, and without a physician would successfully cope with the malarial fevers that followed.

Cholera, however, the very word itself made the boldest quake. Dr. John Kinnaman a graduate of Philadelphia College was the first practicing physician. He was a young man highly educated and a lover of his profession. His coming was hailed with delight by the settlers. He located about two miles south of Mill Grove. A very large walnut stump served him for a laboratory, drug repository and general reception room. He laid out a town at this point and named it Royalton, but it died in its infancy shortly after the demise of its founder.

Dr. Kinnaman's patients were scattered over the entire southern part of the county, and his indefatigability in riding was wonderful and denoted a man of iron nerve. Many times in riding he would cut down a tree, hitch his horse to one of its branches and let him browse until his patient was out of danger, often from eight to ten hours.

The following is an instance of this man's nerve and ability in his profession. Swane a settler of Perry was hurt by the falling of a tree. In a few days it was found necessary to amputate the leg. Dr. Kinnaman was sent for and arrived. Without any assistance and with no surgical implements but a razor and old saw, the Doctor amputated the limb neatly and speedily, and the man got well.

Dr. Kinnaman died in '38 a victim of excessive attention to medical study and overwork.

PASSED AWAY

A Once Powerful Tribe That Enjoyed a Happy Life Close to Nature

THE first settlers of Washington township, found here the remnants of a once powerful tribe of Indians. Their old men and warriors had listened to the counsels and obeyed the commands of their great Chief Tondoganie. Their wigwams were in the belt of timber which skirted the river; and the broad prairie which has become so fertile under skillful cultivation, afforded them hunting grounds and space for the young warrior to practice himself in imaginary battles to improve his skill in an art which fortunately, he has never since had an opportunity to practice.

The river and creek furnished them with fish, and on the flowery banks they passed a happy, indolent life. They were the remnants of a race which according to the laws of nature, had had its time on earth, and in obedience to that inexorable law, they were fast yielding to those who were to succeed them and here they lived to meet and see the mighty race of men who were to take their places. For ages they have lived on the bounties of nature without making her any return.

They were a race governed by instinct; they made no advance in agriculture, commerce or the arts. The son made his canoe and armed himself with the bow and arrow as his father had done, as mechanically and with as little improvement as the young robin builds its nest in imitation of the parent bird. Their time had come; their race was doomed; and here on the banks of this beautiful stream, where the dark eyed Indian maiden had taught the young chief to love her, a fairer maiden was to take her place and by the graces of a purer virtue, teach a noble heart to love her.

A SUMMER OF GLOOM

When Northern Ohio and Indiana Suffered— The Cholera Scourge in Perrysburg In 1854

OLDER citizens will undoubtedly remember the fatal summer of 1854. It was indeed a summer of sorrow and gloom. This was not only true of Northern Ohio, but of Northern Indiana as well. Not a village between Buffalo and Chicago that did not furnish its quota of suffering and death from the malarial poison that impregnated the very atmosphere, spreading intermittent and typhoid fevers, as well as that dreaded scourge, cholera. These afflictions became epidemic, and in some localities there were not enough persons well to take care of the sick.

Take Goshen, Indiana, population 1,500 then. For two months there was a funeral daily, sometimes two or three. Not a family escaped affliction. Two cabinet shops were busy night and day making coffins, and physicians had mighty little rest from their strenuous labors.

Probably no town suffered like Perrysburg. The scourge started, it seems from a ball that was held on the night of the 4th of July, when the first case of cholera made its appearance, and from that time until the 19th of August following there were 117 deaths—at least that is the number buried in Fort Meigs cemetery, and there may have been many more. Among that number are included Albert D. Wright, editor of the Northwestern Democrat, Dr. James Robertson, Dr. Frederick, Jarvis Spafford, John J. Spink, and many others. The deaths were startling in their suddenness and sadness. The epidemic was one of great virulence. So great were the ravages of this terrible visitation at that place, that it put a check upon business of every kind, no paper was issued and no other business transacted for seven weeks or longer, excepting that of caring for the sick and the burial of the dead. Included among those who passed away were some of the most active business men of the place. Dr. E. D. Peck and Dr. James Robertson were on duty night and day, the latter falling a victim to the scourge in the very midst of his strenuous labors. Two-thirds of the residents fled from the town, leaving a comparative few to fight the dread epidemic. Among those noble men and women, aside from the physicians may be mentioned Joshua Chappel, Seth Bruce, N. H. Callard, Mrs. A. E. Frederick and Mrs. Amelia Perrin, who were volunteer nurses during the terrible calamity. There may have been a few others, but we have not their names. All these have passed away, but they nobly performed their duty during their life's span. Perrysburg was indeed "a deserted village." Grand Rapids fared but little better, with a score or more of cases and a number of deaths, the disease beginning like Perrysburg at a 4th of July ball. Never perhaps in the history of the cholera were its ravages so fatal as in Perrysburg, and never did the few who remained meet death with more resolution or endure suffering with greater fortitude.

Seth Bruce made coffins in the hall of the log court house and no victim was buried without a coffin being furnished. Only one person of all that number died alone, a young man who had a room in a tenement house. He breathed his last before the return of his attendant, who had gone for medicine. The women were patient and heroic in their care for the sick, and there were brave, noble men who remained and stood beside them in the terrible conflict.

The physical condition of the inhabitants, reduced by fever and ague, and their systems poisoned by well water rather than by miasmatic exhalations, left them an easy prey to the ravages of this sweeping epidemic.

WOOD COUNTY FAIRS

A Grand Feature of the County's Prosperity —Origin and History of These Exhibitions

THERE is no question of the fact that much of the superiority of the agricultural products of Wood county has been due to the stimulating influences exerted by the Agricultural Society. It has lifted the science of agriculture to a higher plane. It has brought forth observation, comparison, thought and efforts on the part of the farmer as well as those interested in mechanics and arts. Each one learns something of value from a competitor, while it is apparent that there has been much of benefit from the results of combined effort.

The following account of its early origin and history is taken from the premium list published in 1877:

Middleton township, at an early period in the history of the county, contained a number of intelligent and enterprising citizens. In these respects, it surpassed any other township in the county, and it was natural that the movement for the organization of a County Agricultural Society should originate there. On the 26th day of April, 1851, a meeting of the farmers and mechanics of the township was held, at which David Creps presided and H. H. Pain acted as Secretary. The object of the movement was stated to be the promotion of the interests of farmers and mechanics, and it was decided to call a mass meeting of the people of the county at Bowling Green, on the second Monday of June, 1851.

In addition to the President and Secretary, the following citizens of Middleton township signed the call for the mass meeting, viz; David Whitney, Henry Sarvis, Henry Hood, James McGinness, Francis E. Meagley, Patrick McIsaac, Robert Clark, Wm. Ewing, John Hood and Martin Byers. The call was subsequently signed by the following persons: E. Huntington, John Bates, John Brownsberger, David Ladd, J. Spafford, James Hood, Asher Cook, James Hall, John Groves, Joseph A. Creps, Gabriel Yount, Henry Crook, L. F. Robertson, Amelius Robertson, James W. Frazer, and John Taylor.

On the 9th of June, the people convened at the Methodist Meeting House,

SCRAP-BOOK.

in Bowling Green, when Emelius Wood was chosen chairman and Asher Cook Secretary. J. R. Tracy, Henry Hood, Patrick McIsaac, James Bloom and Geo. Powers, were appointed a committee to draft a constitution for the Wood County Agricultural Society. David Whitney, John Bates, N. D. Blinn and S. W. St. John were appointed a committee, to nominate officers for the following year. Thomas Jolly, L. C. Lock, and Henry Groves, were appointed a committee to "procure suitable persons to address the meeting and explain the objects of the contemplated organization." In the afternoon, in response to the request of the last named committee, the meeting was addressed by Messrs. Elliott, Cook and Bloom. The committee for that purpose reported a constitution, made up of 12 articles, which was adopted and signed by 56 persons, who became members of the society.

Then a series of by-laws were adopted. The following persons were appointed a committee in each township to collect statistical information to be reported to the Secretary of the Society:

Perrysburg—N. D. Blinn, Asher Cook and James Hood.

Middleton—D. Whitney, Henry Sarvis and Patrick McIsaac.

Washington—Martin Warner, Jr., John Bamber and Geo. Warner.

Weston—B. Bassett, S. Jefferson and Benj. Olney.

Liberty—James Bloom, Henry Groves and John C. Wooster.

Plain—S. W. St. John, Nathan Minton and J. R. Tracy.

Center—L. C. Lock, Lee Moore and Henry Shively.

Portage—Collister Haskins.

Bloom—E. Gorton.

This was an important work, but there is no evidence that any of the committees were ever heard from in an official capacity. The following officers were chosen for the ensuing year: President, John McMahan; Vice-President, W. R. Peck; Recording Secretary, E. Elliott; Corresponding Secretary, George Powers; Treasurer, John Bates; Managers, Benj. Olney, David Ladd, Edwin Gorton, Henry Hood and John Groves.

Aside from the fact that a meeting was held on the 26th of July, 1851, to arrange for holding the first Fair, and also the fact that the Fair for 1852 is designated as the "second Fair," there is no recorded evidence that a Fair was held in 1851, nor is there any record of the place where it was held, though probably the first County Fair was held at Bowling Green.

The foregoing facts respecting the organization of the Society are quite complete, except the almost total omission of reference to the first Fair, in which the people of to-day would feel a lively interest. Subsequent Fairs were ignored by the Society's secretaries with equal care, and the points of real interest are thus largely omitted. The second Fair was held at Perrysburg, the third was held at Bowling Green, the fourth and fifth at Portageville, and the sixth and seventh at Bowling Green. At the seventh annual meeting of the Society, the board elected for the ensuing year was authorized to "procure suitable grounds for the Annual Fair and permanently locate the same."

At a meeting held in July, 1858, a vote was taken upon the permanent location of the Fair, when Bowling Green received five votes and Portageville two votes. The next Fair was held at Bowling Green, but the permanent location of the Fair was not satisfactory to rival villages. Portageville inaugurated an independent Fair, and in 1860 the County Society held their Fair at Perrysburg.

Subsequently, perhaps in 1865 or 1866, the Society purchased grounds at Tontogany and permanently located the Fair at that point. This result grew out of the county seat contest and is understood to have been brought about by Perrysburg in the hope that it might result to the disadvantage of Bowling Green. The latter village naturally felt resentful and organized an Independent Society, but it proved a losing operation and was soon abandoned.

Space will not permit further record of the Society's history here, but it may not be improper to mention the fact that the fairs of Wood county have compared favorably with any exhibitions of a similar character in the state. With the richest of soil in the hands of intelligent and enterprising farmers, the products of Wood county have excited the pride of citizens of the county and commanded the admiration of strangers. At state fairs, Wood county has carried off her full share of premiums, and seldom fails in a competition with other localities where she has a fair chance.

Further Growth

In addition to this piece of ancient history it may be said that this Society has grown and expanded with the years and its exhibitions hold their own in popularity and are visited by hundreds throughout the State. It stands in the van of all similar exhibitions in Northwestern Ohio.

Within a few years past the needle work, art and educational exhibits have proven to be a strong feature and have attracted the interests of thousands of visitors. The erection of buildings and other equipment are added from year to year, and this expansion can not fail to give added interest to all classes of our people, and thus keep pace with the progress and prosperity of all. Under the stimulus of the great and instructive exhibitions, such as have been given, new ideas are brought out, new sciences developed and better and more profitable methods learned, and we will go on in the march of progress until we of to-day will be as far behind in comparison as that first Fair here years ago is behind to-day.—C. W. E.

AN HISTORICAL CRISIS

The importance of the victory at Ft. Meigs to the nation is thus summarized by a pioneer chronicler of the times:

As a pivotal point in the war of 1812, no battle was of greater importance than the battle of Ft. Meigs. Had Gen. Harrison been compelled to surrender, the battle of the Thames would never have been won. Perry's conflict on Lake Erie would never have been fought, the whole Northwest would have been in the hands of the British and Indians, and the frontiers along the whole continent would not have been safe for an hour against the attacks of the wily savages. Gen. Jackson might have been defeated at New Orleans, the British under Prevost and Ross might have won at Ogdensburg, or captured Baltimore. Gen. Brown and Gen. Scott might have lost Lundy's Lane, and still the defeats would have left the nation safe. But the capture of Ft. Meigs by Gen. Proctor would have lighted the torch all over the Northwest. It would have made the British masters of Michigan, Ohio, Indiana, Illinois and Kentucky. It would have enabled the allies to push on to the foot of the Alleghanies and even the Eastern states would not have been proof against the attacks of Proctor and his savages. Fort Meigs is indeed historic ground.

Hull's trace through Wood county was designated many years ago by the discovery of a large pile of gun barrels, locks, flints and bayonets near Portage. The discovery was made by a little girl in search of cows. At another time the entire iron work of an army wagon was found near the same place.

THE MAUMEE PIONEERS

Written by Mrs. Kate B. Sherwood for the Reunion of the Maumee Valley Pioneers, Held in Toledo, February 22, 1880, and Recited by Mrs. Elizabeth Mansfield Irving

Come, friends, around this festal board,
    Where peace and plenty smile
And memories in each bosom stored
    Are quickening the while;
Come, let your hearts go back again,
    With more of joy than tears,
Unto that sturdy race of men,
    The Maumee Pioneers.

Let others tell the tales of Dee,
    The Danube and the Don,
The Rhine that ripples to the sea,
    The Iser rolling on;—
New England's glades and palisades,
    Virginia's vaunted years,—
We'll tell of sturdier men and maids,
    The Maumee Pioneers.

We'll tell how came the brave La Salle,
    Two hundred years ago,
To list St. Mary's madrigal,
    Responsive to St. Joe;
To speak the vows that woke the trance
    Of long unfruitful years,
And give to Frontenac and France
    The Maumee Pioneers.

Of Couthemanche whose lonely fort
    A century before,
Stood guard where Fort Miami's port
    Heard British cannon roar;
How stripped Perrot the faggot sees
    Flash through Miami's jeers,
'Till save the swift Outagamis,
    The Maumee Pioneers.

I mind me in those bloody days
    Of Foxes, Sacs and Sioux,
Of Miamis and Ottawas,
    And Iroquois and Pous,
An Indian woman 'tis we see
    Before her Priest in tears;
Her prayers have saved from massacre
    The Maumee Pioneers.

Our feet are on historic ground.
    The very streets we tread
Re-echo to a solemn sound
    Above the shroudless dead.
Now French, now British we define,
    Now red ally appears,—
They form a vast and shadowy line,
    The Maumee Pioneers.

Here sleeps the braves of Pontiac,
    There Harmar's hosts go down,
And bold "Mad Anthony" brings back
    The knights of old renown;
There Harrison's battalions glance
    Along the burnt frontiers,
And in the trail of arms advance
    The Maumee Pioneers.

Fort Meigs and Fort Miami show
    A sweet and solemn truce,
And old Fort Industry I trow
    Has met a nobler use;
So we above our levelled graves,
    Across the flood of years,
May name with once dishonored braves
    The Maumee Pioneers.

For valor's not of any race,
    And right of grace has none,
If Wayne is given a hero's place,
    Tecumseh's fame is won;
If Wells be praised for warlike deeds
    That wring the heart with tears,
Then Simon Girty's fealty leads
    The Maumee Pioneers.

The days of bow and spear are fled,
    Of tent and bark tepee,
The ax is ringing in their stead,
    The woodman zones his tree;
And where the Indian village stood
    The cabin chinked appears,
And white-haired children scour the wood,—
    The Maumee Pioneers.

They fight no barbed and painted foe,
  They run no gauntlet where
The Indian tomahawk is slow
  A captured foe to spare;
They fly no cruel massacre
  Of plundering buccaneers;
But deadlier foes they stricken see,
  The Maumee Pioneers.

They fought the famine and the cold,
  They conquered field and flood,
They drove the murrain from the fold,
  The fever from the blood;
Their triumphs blossom in the vales,
  And blush along the piers,
And fleck the lake with snowy sails,
  The Maumee Pioneers.

The wind is up, the sails are spread,
  The gales of traffic blow;
The Yankee comes with level head,
  The Teuton sure and slow;
The thrifty Scot, the Irish true,—
  And Quaker grace appears
A wholesome leaven running through
  The Maumee Pioneers.

O free born sires! from whom there runs
  A tide of valor through
The hearts of sons' remotest sons!
  O wives, and daughters true!—
Who toil and spin, and spin and pray,
  And hiding homesick tears
Keep heart and hope that crown to-day
  The Maumee Pioneers!

Blow soft above their lowly grave,
  O North wind swift and keen!
And South wind that the lily waves
  Keep aye their grasses green!
O Spirit of the Centuries!
  Blow on his heart who hears,
And wake to fragrant memories
  The Maumee Pioneers!

BUT THE SHOT MISSED

On a clear, bright morning in the early spring of 1813, writes a pioneer chronicler, Gen. Harrison was standing on the earth works of Ft. Meigs. As he stood there his eye rested on scenes which have since become famous in the history of the state and nation. In the clear sunlight every foot of ground for miles around was visible. At his feet flowed the rapids and to the southward the river was lost behind the hills. Forests stretched away in every direction. Through an opening among the trees an Indian chief and a companion were seen. A sentry fired and the parties disappeared. Had the aim been more true and the arm of the sentry been more steady a vast amount of bloodshed and cruelty might have been averted, for that Indian chief was the notorious Tecumseh, his companion—the hated Proctor.

At one time during the siege of Fort Meigs the ammunition was nearly all gone, and Gen. Harrison offered a gill of whisky to any man who would bring in a cannon ball from outside the fort. The soldiers kept a score to see who would bring in the most, and in this manner cannon balls were obtained only to throw them over at the British batteries.

MAUMEE RIVER AND VALLEY
View Taken from British Point, Maumee City—Foot of the Rapids

COL. SELDEN A. DAY

This Young Officer of the U. S. Artillery Had Charge of Jefferson Davis at Fort Monroe

COLONEL SELDEN ALLEN DAY and his talented wife, Helen H. Gardener, will be remembered by many of the citizens of Bowling Green, as they visited Wood county several years since, when the accomplished lady gave a lecture. As writer, author and speaker, she is widely known on account of the many books she has published of a semi-medical nature along the line of heredity. They are written in such form and language as to make them understood and appreciated by the general reader. Her success is demonstrated by the fact that the products of her pen, put out partly as fiction, occupy the reference shelves of Cornell university and other scientific libraries of national reputation. All this has required much earnest study on the part of this earnest writer, to whose work is attached more than a literary value.

No less interest attaches to Colonel Day than to his talented wife and he is known from the Atlantic to the Pacific seaboard, where he commanded Fort Mason, San Francisco, for four years. His military career began in 1861, when he raised a volunteer company at the first call for troops, serving continuously in the field until the close of the war and was finally made captain for "gallant and meritorious service during the war." Colonel Day's record in the war with Spain was also notably brilliant. He commanded the first troops that entered Porto Rico and on July 28, 1898, ran up the American flag on the custom house, the first American flag raised over the island possessions. In addition to his career as a soldier, Colonel Day is the successful inventor of a series of military and scientific appliances.

Mr. Day chanced to be the first officer of the prison guard at Fort Monroe, when Jefferson Davis was brought there a prisoner after the close of the war. Notwithstanding the account of Ben Perley Poore of the distinguished prisoner being put in irons, the experience of Col. Day, while he was in charge of Mr. Davis, shows that the prisoner was of a most tractable and gentlemanly disposition. Here are extracts from a letter written by Colonel Day in February, 1890, from Fort Schuyler, New York:

Day's Letter

An article in a New York paper headed "Grateful to his Guard," alludes to kindness on my part to the distinguished prisoner, the late Jefferson Davis, while he was confined at Fort Monroe. While I did my duty as best I could I disclaim now, as I did then, the idea of kindness in doing what any man ought to have done for another whom the fortunes of war had placed in his keeping. The kindness in the case was rather the other way. Although I had seen four years of solid war, I was still a youngster in the service, while his experience included the entire range of promotion from West Point cadet to Secretary of War, and extended from the fall of Richmond back to and through the war with Mexico.

It so happened that I was the first officer of the prison guard, detailed from the regulars when we came to Fort Monroe after the close of the war, and of course I took charge of the State prisoners, Messrs. Davis and Clay. This was after their removal from the casemates to Carroll Hall. Mr. Davis' room, or cell, was on the second floor, and adjoining it was a room occupied by the officer of the guard.

Though many a time during the early part of the late war I had, as a young volunteer, trudging along on the march under the weight of knapsack and gun, joined in the chorus: "We'll hang Jeff Davis on a sour apple tree," yet, when brought face to face and introduced to him by the officer, whom I relieved as his custodian, I need hardly say I recognized a gentleman and treated him accordingly. This was the sum total of my kindness to him. No one could have been more particular or careful that the orders governing the prison should be carried out than was the prisoner himself.

One little incident may serve to show how delicately the prisoner had to be dealt with. His cell was scantily furnished with only an iron single bedstead, a hospital mattress, a small table or stand, bucket, bowl and pitcher, and two straight-backed, hard wooden kitchen chairs—one for the prisoner and the other for any visitor he might have; and the visitors were few and far between. We, officers of the guard, used to have our easy rocking chairs brought from our quarters (nine were in the same building) to sit in during our hours of duty, sending them back when relieved. One day I offered to exchange my easy chair for one of his for the time being. "No!" said he, "these are the ones furnished by the authorities for my use, and it might not be right to exchange them." "Oh," said I, "if need be I will speak to the General about it, and I have no doubt it will be all right." "No," he said, "don't do it on any account," and I knew he meant it. Still, I did not feel quite easy in my rocking chair, seeing him sitting bolt upright reading day after day on his hard seat. One evening as I was about leaving, my colored servant had not come up, as was usual, to take away my things, so gathering up my books and papers, and with both hands full, I said, "Mr. Davis, John has not come for my things, won't you be kind enough to take charge of my chair until I send for it." "Certainly," said he, and emptying one of my hands into the other, I dragged it into his room, came out, closed the door and bade him "good evening," just as my relief entered the outer room. The next night when I came on guard again, the prisoner was standing at the grating looking out, pipe in hand, and said after greeting, "I have your chair here." "Oh, yes!" said I, looking over my shoulder into my room, "but I see John has brought up another, just keep it, won't you, until I want it."

Mr. Davis made no reply, but he gave me a look that will remain in my memory, as a ray of sunshine. He had seen through my little ruse.

After Mr. Davis was given the parole of the fort, all was changed for him, as well as for us of the garrison. We officers then got more than "one night in bed," as the soldiers say, and the duty was not so hard.

Mrs. Davis joined her husband and they were assigned a set of officers' quarters, which by the way, included his old "prison cell," and they lived like "white folk." With Mrs. Davis came their little daughter ("Pi" we called her then), now "Miss Winnie," or the "Daughter of the Confederacy," as she is sometimes spoken of. With them also for a time was Mrs. Davis' sister, Miss Maggie Howell, all of whom made a sunny addition to the social life of the garrison in a quiet and becoming way, and they changed the atmosphere for Mr. Davis in many respects.

I could fill a volume of reminiscences and incidents connected with our involuntary intimacy during Mr. Davis' imprisonment, at Fort Monroe, but I will mention only one more in closing this letter. Mr. Davis had a grim sense of the humorous under all circumstances. On one occasion Doctor Craven, who had been the post surgeon and attended Mr.

SCRAP-BOOK.

Davis during his severe illness in the casemates, came back to Fort Monroe on a visit, and called upon the prisoner in his cell. In the course of conversation the doctor said, "Do you know, Mr. Davis, that at one time, over there in the casemate, I really thought you were going to die?"

"Ah, doctor," said Mr. Davis, "that is the last thing I am going to do."

"UNCLE" GUY NEARING

A Remarkable Man—His Athletic Build and Strength—Interesting Incidents in His Life

IN the Sentinel of December 20, 1883, Mr. Evers gave an extended account of "Uncle" Guy Nearing, as he was called by the early settlers, and "Nawash" by the Indians, from which we clip the following:

Guy Nearing in his early manhood came to the Maumee country from Cayuga county, N. Y. The date was about the year 1817, and he first located on what is now the Forest Pratt place, Perrysburg. Nearing was a remarkable man in many respects, and is better remembered and oftener and more kindly spoken of by the early settlers than any one who lived on the Maumee.

In physical make up he was a man of almost gigantic stature and strength; broad shouldered and bony; he scarcely knew his own strength, and his power of endurance was something wonderful. He was a sort of local Hercules of that day, and a terror to the Indians, great and small. His qualities of head and heart were no less marked than his physical powers. He inherently loved and trusted his fellow men. He had great big bumps of generosity, and benevolence. He always had a cheering word for the despondent and friendless, and would divide his last piece of corn bread with the needy.

It is not denied by his many friends that he possessed a "rough side," and was given sometimes to fearful ebullitions of temper, and startling profanity, nor that he was averse occasionally to having a good time, when, more than at any other time he prided himself on his athletic powers, and feats of great strength.

At a Circus

One day he was in Perrysburg after it had become quite a village, attending a circus, an event he never missed if he heard of it in time. He was leaning against the cage in which was a large zebra and the keeper cautioned the spectators lest the animal which was vicious, should kick some of them. In an instant Uncle Guy thrust his hand into the cage and seized the zebra's hind leg which he pulled out between the bars and held with one hand in spite of the animal's wild struggles. Guy would have done the same with a young lion only that the keeper prevented him.

Cut His Toe Off

Though rather slow to anger he was like most of that kind of persons very wrathy when he did get warmed up. It is told of him that the little toe on one of his feet had a habit of getting on top of the next toe and the friction of the boot kept it constantly sore. In a fit of anger one day he jerked off his boot, seized a chisel and mallet and off went the offending toe, to trouble him no more.

Always Kind to All

Still with all his eccentricities and faults, he was, as before mentioned, a kind-hearted sympathetic man. If a stranger moving in, needed help to get his wagon out of the mud, Guy would take his team and assist him without pay or thanks. If a newcomer wanted to find land for a home, Guy would leave his own affairs and go with him, board him besides, accepting no compensation, especially from the poor. If the pioneer needed help to raise his log cabin, Guy would take his men and go and help him. Anything he had or could do was always at the command of a needy neighbor or stranger. Such a man was "Uncle" Guy Nearing. He was fitted by all his physical and mental qualities for a leading and useful man amid the rugged vicissitudes incident to pioneer life, and well he filled the bill.

Two years after Nearing came, his family followed, wife and three children. There were two sons and a daughter. Minerva afterward married Wm. Ewing. Neptune Nearing, one of the sons, father of G. C. Nearing, now of Bowling Green, settled at an early day on the ridge and prairie three miles west of Bowling Green, or where the town now is.

Another son, Henry, who is well known and respected in the north part of the county, and who in stature and appearance, much resembles his father, lives now near White House, Lucas county.

Thrashed an Indian

Here is an incident by Henry Nearing, explaining why his father, "Uncle" Guy, was called "Big Nawash."

Nearing's cabin was on the route followed by the Indians in passing up and down the river. The red men, while unusually quite peaceful, got fire water down at Hollister's trading post sometimes and some of the bucks were a trifle ugly. A big buck of some prowess and athletic pretensions who frequently, when tipsy, would boast of blood-thirsty deeds he had perpetrated on white men at the massacre at River Raisin, one day entered Nearing's cabin where he saw no one in the room but a couple of women, and drew his hunting knife and began to talk Indian and make murderous flourishes. The women were terrified, as the old buck had a satanic gleam in his eye which was threatening to behold. They concealed their terror as well as they could until one of them on some pretext slipped out and told "Uncle" Guy, who was making an ax handle in a shed near by. Guy was angry in a minute, and seizing a big black whip, he went round to the door and pulled the buck out, and between the sounds of the terrific blows of the whip on old Nawash's breech clout and his hideous screams, there was a small bedlam there for a little while. An account of the incident soon went up and down the river and reached the other Indians. This buck was a sort of revengeful fellow and some of Guy's neighbors did not know but he might try to retaliate, but he was too much humiliated, and in a day or so came back and shook hands with Uncle Guy and said, "Me bad Injun! me good now." Pointing to Nearing he said "You big Nawash." After that Nearing was nicknamed "Big Nawash," and quarrelsome Indian bucks never troubled his family again.

Contractor and Builder

In the latter part of 1825 Nearing took a contract to build five miles of the Maumee and Western Reserve pike, which he did not complete till 1827, and at about the same time he took five miles of the Maumee and Monroe pike.

In 1823 when the county seat was moved from Maumee to Perrysburg, there was not much to move except the little log calaboose. This, Nearing hauled over for which, and the rebuilding, he received $45.

In 1824 he helped to build for Wood county its first court house, a little log structure located on Front street, Perrysburg, but torn down some years ago. In

1826 and '27, he and Elisha Martindale built a new log jail near the court house and took their pay in part, in town lots at $12 apiece.

On Christmas day 1829, Uncle Guy with his men and teams, went to Bear Rapids, since called Otsego, and built a cabin on the hill, to board and lodge his help in. He had previously bought 60 acres of land there, of the Mason estate. Stickney had also built a cabin near there, to prospect for free stone, and expected to open a grind stone quarry.

Built a Mill

By New Near's day, 1830, all was in readiness, and next day all hands began work on timber for a dam. The winter was mild and dry, and the river low. By May Nearing had a dam in, and a saw mill in operation, and by the middle of June a grist mill with one run of stone, and by September a second run of stone with bolting facilities. This was a great help and convenience to the pioneers, and people patronized the mill from a distance of 20 to 30 miles. Nearing owned the mill until the spring of 1833, when he sold it to a New Yorker named Asa Gilbert, and the mill went by the name of Gilbert's mill. Later Gilbert sold to a man named Flanders, who lost the mill by a great freshet. Flanders rebuilt it and a little later the mill passed into the hands of Samuel Clymer, who owned it until the freshets finally destroyed both mill and dam and it was never rebuilt. The old mill, the builders, and owners have all passed away and the town of Otsego, a name once familiar to all the early settlers, is a thing of the past and exists like many of the noble race of hardy men and women of that early day only in memory.

"WORST OF ALL ROADS"

Graphic Description of the Maumee and Western Reserve Road

AGREEABLE to the treaty of Brownstown in 1808, the Indian tribes ceded a tract of land for a road 120 feet wide from the foot of the Maumee Rapids to the western line of the Connecticut Reserve, and all the land within one mile of said road on each side thereof for the purpose of establishing settlements along the same. By an act of Congress December 11, 1811, the President was authorized to appoint three commissioners to survey and mark the road. It seems this work was not satisfactory. Hence Congress passed an act on April 16, 1816, authorizing the President to make such alteration in the survey as he may deem proper.

Nothing, however, seemed to have been done, for February 28, 1823, Congress passed an act granting to the State of Ohio all the land for this purpose obtained by the treaty of Brownstown. By an act of the Legislature, the State of Ohio accepted the grant made to her by the last recited act of Congress, and at once set about building the road.

In locating this road it was so laid out as to pass through Perrysburg and Lower Sandusky. The contracts were let and work commenced in the year 1824, but the road was not completed until the year 1826, if, indeed, such a road could be called completed, but such as it was, it was accepted and, for years served as the thoroughfare over which the thousands in search of a paradise in the West, were obliged to travel the almost impassable Black Swamp.

It would be difficult to describe this worst of all roads, and the agony bordering on despair to which the emigrant was reduced in his effort to pass over to the land flowing with milk and honey beyond. It is said nature is equal to all emergencies, and it proved so here. On the desert the caravan may stop at any point and pitch their tents, but travelers wading all day in mud and water, require a place of rest for the night, where they can dry as well as rest their weary limbs. On the route of this road, their wants in this respect were well supplied, for there was a tavern to each mile of the distance between Perrysburg and Lower Sandusky, and travelers were sometimes compelled to stay two nights at the same tavern, notwithstanding the most vigorous efforts to proceed. Things remained in this situation until the year 1838 when the state commenced to macadamize the road, which was completed in the year 1841, and from that time to the present has been one of the best roads in Ohio. From this period the real prosperity of Wood county began, and was materially aided by the completion of the Wabash and Erie Canal a few years later.

LAKE COMMERCE

An Extensive Commercial Traffic Carried on at Perrysburg at an Early Date

BETWEEN the years 1828 and 1840 there was transacted at Perrysburg as large a commercial business as any port on Lake Erie, excepting Buffalo and Cleveland. This business was transacted chiefly through the forwarding and commission houses of Hollister & Smith, and Bingham & Co. Through these houses nearly all the goods consigned to Northern Indiana, and a large portion of Northwestern Ohio, and Southern Michigan were forwarded by teams from Perrysburg, to the head of the rapids of the Maumee river, where they were taken on keel boats, pirogues and flat boats, and transported to Fort Wayne, and thence distributed to their several destinations. These boats returning brought back furs, skins and dried meats, which were brought to Perrysburg by the teams which had carried goods to the head of the rapids. From 1835 to 1840, this business, together with the emigration which came to this port by water, afforded a very lucrative business for nearly all the schooners and steamboats in the service.

There were between the above dates steam boats enough running from Perrysburg to Buffalo, to form a daily line had they been so arranged, besides many schooners, as the steamers could not carry all the freight offering for this port. In addition to the above, there was a daily line of steam boats running between Perrysburg and Detroit. It may be asked, what has become of this commerce? The answer is, it still exists, but the headquarters have been removed, and other modes of transit have driven the steam boats and vessels from the river.

The last siege of Ft. Meigs lasted about eight days and was most obstinately resisted by Gen. Clay. The siege was finally abandoned by Gen. Proctor after 200 men and officers had been killed and wounded. No less than six wagon loads of balls and unexploded shells were picked up and utilized by the Americans.

AN AMUSING INCIDENT

John C. Spink's First Introduction to This Region—His "Maiden" Speech

THE late N. H. Callard furnishes the following incident of an early date: Among the earliest lawyers residing in Wood county may be named John C. Spink and Willard V. Way. The latter mentions in his notes a ludicrous incident that occurred to Spink when on his way from Wooster to Perrysburg to commence the practice of law. As showing the condition of travel through the Black Swamp, and its inconveniences of transit it is worthy of note. It was on this occasion that he made his first or maiden speech as a lawyer.

Spink was on his way in company with a young preacher, who like himself, had left his home for the first time. He stated that the roads were simply terrible, being like a sea of mud and water. At that time many immigrants were moving from the eastern parts of Ohio to places further west. It was frequently the case that they could not advance with their wagons more than two or three miles a day, and they would return at night to the same tavern they had left in the morning. Spink and the preacher had left what is now Fremont in the morning and reached a small log tavern at Sugar Creek a few miles west late in the evening. They found the house crowded with moving families, with apparently no room for them to find a bed. At that time there were only two beds in the house. They could not well return neither could they advance with the chance of getting better accommodation, as they would have to flounder in the mud. The landlord, however, was equal to the emergency. He did not want to lose two guests so prominent as the lawyer and the preacher and assured them that he would give them a good bed. They took their supper and on getting into the sitting room found that the movers had all disappeared. How this had been done they could not tell. That, however, was soon revealed. They were shown to the only spare bed in the house which was located on the off side from the door, and they discovered there were ten females and four males extended on the floor covered by their own bed clothes, he and the preacher making the number sixteen in what was but a small room. They picked their way through the sleepers as best they could, when getting to the bed side they found just light enough from the burning wood in the fire place opposite them as to show everything in the room. It appeared to them as if all eyes were upon them, and they were at a loss to know how they could get into bed. The preacher suggested to Spink that he would take off his coat and that he Spink should hold it as a screen between them and the floor occupants. That was speedily done, the preacher jumped into bed on the off side and covered himself up, and left Spink in the lurch. This took him by surprise—he was at a loss what to do. He could not go to bed with his clothes on him as they were wet and covered with mud. He concluded that as a lawyer he should have to make his living by his wits, and he might as well begin then and there as at any time, and make a speech, yes, a maiden speech, supposing that they were as wide awake as himself. His speech was brief and to the point, he said:

"Ladies, this is my bed, and there is nothing to screen me from your observation while I get into it. This is my first introduction to a new country life, and probably it is yours, as you appear to be moving, I will therefore take it as a great favor if you will kindly duck your heads under the clothes while I get into bed." All heads were instantly covered, he got into bed and concluded that he had made a great fool of himself, for they were all of them asleep, and he had waked them up by his speech. This he ever after declared to be his maiden speech as a lawyer.

Mr. Spink was highly successful as a criminal lawyer, his reputation extending throughout the northwest. The late James Murray of Sidney, Ex-Attorney General of Ohio, was a student at law with him. Spink died in 1853, in the zenith of his fame.

RECOVERING A STOLEN HORSE

THE following incident is related by Gen. John E. Hunt:

In July, 1812, my brother bought a very fine horse, which had been driven with the army from Dayton. It was a large, elegant dapple grey, and he rode it acting as the aid of Gen. Hull at the surrender. Soon after the British took the town the Indians stole the horse, saddle and bridle from my brother's stable. He went to the store next morning looking very much down at the loss of his fine horse. There he met Jack Brandy. Jake says, "Harry Hunt, what's the matter with you? You have a very long face this morning." Says my brother: "Jack, the Indians have stolen my big horse!" Jack says: "Dam rascal! Maybe me find him. Give me some money, some meat and some bread." My brother gave him $5 in silver and what else he wanted. Jack mounted his pony and started up the River Rouge.

The next day he crossed an Indian trail, and discovered that one of their horses had large iron shoes. He followed the track and that evening camped with the party. After eating, they wanted to know where he was going. He said he was directed to go to Chicago to call the Indians in to fight the Long Knives. They told him they had a very fine American horse. Jack says, "My horse is tired. If he is a good horse maybe in the morning me swap with you," and added, shaking his silver in his pouch, "and give some boot." In the morning, after an early breakfast, Jack told them to put the saddle and bridle on the horse. "Well me try him, see if he is a good horse." He mounted, and it was the last they saw of Jack or the horse. We were standing in front of my brother's store about sundown the next day, when we saw an Indian coming up the road on horseback. It proved to be Jack on my brother's grey horse. When he jumped off and delivered him to my brother, he said, "Harry Hunt, you see now, Jack Brandy can't lie."

LIBERTY TOWNSHIP

Settlement Begun in 1824—Collister Haskins First Settler—Organization of Township

THE first white settler in what is now Liberty township was Collister Haskins, in the spring of 1824. In the following September, with the help of kind Indians and friends from Waterville, he built a log cabin on the west side of the established route of the Findlay pike and on the south bank of the Portage river, and moved in with his family, who had resided in Waterville.

Let the mind of the reader imagine Wood county one vast unbroken forest of virgin timber, without a white inhabitant (except as their cabins now and then dotted the bank of the Maumee river), the stillness of which was only marred by the presence of the red man who built his camp fire unmolested, and where the wolf, deer, bear and other animals roamed in their natural state; a wilderness unpenetrated by a single well defined road; a wilderness containing 390,000 acres, in the center of which is one solitary cabin, with none other nearer on the north than Waterville, thirteen miles distant, and none on the south nearer than Fort Findlay, "twenty miles away," and they have the home of Collister Haskins in 1824. And oft' was the time of an evening, when this solitary white man of the interior, with his little family, would be gathered about his cabin fire that the Indians would congregate about him and curiously survey his surroundings and as they became more familiar, converse as best they could upon topics of mutual interest. In Mr. Haskins' family besides himself and wife, were three daughters, Sarah, Wealthy and Cynthia, and one son, Henry. Sarah was the first white child born in Liberty township.

The next settler, or rather squatter, in Liberty was J. M. Jacques, who came from New York and built a cabin.

Jacques only remained about three years, for in the spring of 1833 John Sargent moved in from Ross county and entered the land upon which Jacques had located, paid him for his improvements and moved into the cabin he (Jacques) had built. In Mr. Sargent's family were three sons and two daughters.

The Mercers

The next settler in Liberty was Geo. Mercer, the first of the large Mercer settlement in that township, to locate there, who came from New Lisbon, also in the spring of 1833, and entered the land upon which he made his home. He came with two yoke of oxen and a wagon by the way of Woodville, making the trip of 200 miles from New Lisbon in 11 days. From Woodville he came up the Portage river on a road cut through a few days previous by Adam Phillips, who settled in Portage township, and the next day cut a road from there to Mr. Haskins', making the trip from Woodville in two days. His family stayed at Mr. Haskins' and he immediately set to work with the assistance of Peter Johnson and Adam Phillips of Portage township, and Mr. Haskins, and soon had a pole cabin built on his own land and moved in with his family. The same spring he "broke up" 15 acres of prairie land belonging to Mr. Haskins and planted it to corn; using five stout yoke of oxen and a big old-fashioned wooden plow to break up the prairie and says he raised about half a crop. He raised a family of nine children.

The advent of new settlers into this community was now not so infrequent and on the first day of April, 1834, there were eight families in Liberty, as follows: Collister Haskins, John Sargent, Thos. Cox, Geo. Mercer, Caleb Mercer, Horace Cady, Henry Groves, John Groves and James Birdsell, and late in the same year came Henry Dubbs, John McMahan, Joseph Mitchell, Wm. Mercer and John Mercer. Wm. Mercer was the head and father of the Mercer family, which settlement in Liberty numbers nearly 200.

Liberty Township Organized

A sufficient number of settlers having moved in, a petition was presented to the commissioners on March 20, 1835, for the organization of a township, to be called Liberty. The petition was granted and the first township election held on the first Monday in April, 1835, which resulted in the election of the following officers: Trustees, James Birdsell, Henry Groves and Geo. Ellsworth; clerk, Reuben Strait; treasurer, Hugh Arbuckle; justices of the peace, James Birdsell and John Groves. The poll books of this election contains the names of 22 electors.

Their choice for treasurer proved to be an injudicious one. He was a native of Scotland, a fine scholar and apparently a gentleman. He was in the stock business in company with a Messrs Reed & Bishop of Urbana. During the year he was serving the township as treasurer, he sold a quantity of the partnership stock, pocketed the money and "migrated." At the time he left he also took $28.00 of the township funds, fortunately all there was in the treasury at that time. Mr. John McMahan and Henry Dubbs were his bondsmen and jointly made up the same to the township, but not without some pointed remarks about the defaulter. John Sargent was elected his successor the spring following and held the office for twenty years.—*C. W. E.*

ORGANIZATION OF OHIO

PURSUANT to a proclamation of the Territorial Governor, members of a constitutional convention assembled at Chillicothe, November 1, 1802, and during this session of 29 days formed the first constitution of the state of Ohio as the state was named.

The state government was organized under the constitution so formed on March 3, 1803.

The Bill of Rights, which is a part of the constitution, includes, among other things, substantially the provisions of the ordinance of 1787; but to two provisions of this Bill of Rights particular attention is called, viz, to sections 25 and 26.

The first, section 25 provides, "That no law shall be passed to prevent the poor, in the several counties and townships within the state, from an equal participation in the schools, academies, colleges and universities within this state, which are endowed, in whole or in part from the revenue arising from donations made by the United States, for the support of schools and colleges; and the doors of the said schools, academies and universities shall be open for the reception of scholars, students and teachers of every grade, without any distinction or preference whatever, contrary to the intent for which said donations were made."

The second, section 26, provides, "That laws shall be passed by the legislature which shall secure to each and every denomination of religious societies, in each surveyed township, which is now or may hereafter be formed in the state, an equal participation, according to their number of adherents, of the profits arising from the land granted by congress for the support of religion, agreeable to the ordinance or act of congress making the appropriation."

It will thus be seen these are the fundamental principles on which the northwest territory, and the state of Ohio have been established.

AS TO HULL'S TRACE

IN a recent number of the Sentinel, a pioneer makes the following correction regarding Hull's trace:

Hull's trace in Portage after crossing the stream, turned its course west of north, passing through the village of Portage near the old ashery, M. E. church and Quaintances' lime kiln, passing north on the limestone ridge, crossing the east part of the farm owned by Noah Foltz, also the premises of Jas. Taborn (deceased), which was the original Parshall lot. Parshall had a large family, all girls. These young women and their parents had been living in their log cabin near the northwest corner of Portage township. One day, while Sarah was taking a stroll east of their cabin, she walked out on a fallen tree in the top of which she found a load of muskets. The news soon spread that "Sall" Parshall had found 40 muskets. (Quite a prize, over $200 worth if they had not been damaged.) Hull's trail here crossed through the point of timber between the Little Prairie and another that lay in the southwest corner of Center township, passing close to the west of the original John Taborn cabin across the original Thomas Rigly lot, and so on towards the Pernot farm. The loss of the army trail near the Haskins saw mill, and the mistake made by S. B. Abbott and others, was the mistaking our pioneer trail down stream past the "Aborginal Grave Yard" for Hull's trace. The same is true of the pioneer trail or road made by John Gallatin and others across the east end of the Sizer farm, a branch pioneer road into that of Hull's army road.

THE LOST CHILD

An Agonizing Search by Hundreds for a Little Tot Alone in the Woods for Eleven Days

AN old pioneer gives, in the Weston Avalanche, the following somewhat sensational account of the search for a lost child in the wilds of Wood county, seventy-five years ago:

The child was that of Frederick Frankfauder, who lived in Bloom township, in this county. In the year 1835, some time in the month of November of that year, on Sunday (as was their custom), Mr. Frankfauder and wife went to their place of worship, and did not return home until late in the evening. During their absence the children were gathering hickory nuts, under a tree standing in the fence corner close by the woods. There were a number of children on both sides of the fence, and the little girl, five years and six months old, was with them gathering nuts, and probably on the side of the fence next to the woods. The children did not miss her until the parents came home at night. You can imagine the feelings of that family when they found that little Margaret was truly lost, night on hand and very dark. They sent to the nearest neighbors for help in the hunt. They started with torches in hand and calling her by name, and ringing bells, but all without success.

Then they sent word to Ft. Ball, Tiffin, Findlay and Perrysburg, to the search. They came with their teams, feed and provisions, to assist. The company so engaged, numbered about two hundred and fifty persons. About the third day they found tracks north of Woodbury, crossing Hull's trail, that they knew to be her tracks certainly, as a little dog was with her, and they saw his tracks also.

Then the excitement grew intense; they continued the search west and north of the windfall, and bordering on the prairie, but found no sign of her, till the seventh day, when they found tracks in the windfall south of John McMahan's. There she lost her little dog, she afterwards said, "as I lay by a fire I saw a big dog come and they took Penny and killed him." They were wolves. Then all began to despair but the parents. Some left for home while others continued the search.

Reader, pause and think! How must the parents have felt, when all began to despair; when a fruitless search was kept up for eight or ten days, when all gave up in despair, but a praying father, who said that his trust was in the Lord; that He would restore the child to his arms in answer to his unceasing prayers. What hope was there? The child gone ten days, in a wilderness like the Black Swamp forty years ago, plenty of Indians, bears, and wolves; and the worst of all, the wild hog.

On the eleventh day they sent a man around by Portage, up the Ellsworth ridge, then to Hutchinson's in Milton, and to Major McMillen's. Just before he arrived, Orlando McMillen and Samuel Clark got home from hunting cattle, and McMillen asked his mother if Indian children had blue eyes; she said, "No, why do you ask?" He said that he and Mr. Clark had seen one that had blue eyes, and they gave it a biscuit, and it ate it greedily. They thought it an Indian child, as they could not understand her language. I will just say she was German, and did not understand English.

This report of the lost child explained the whole matter to them. Mr. G. Alberty and Mr. McMillen started at once in pursuit of the child, over to John Dubbs'. There they saw a man by the name of Henderson Carrothers, who was chopping in a clearing for Dubbs; he said that he saw a child playing on a log, on the north side of the clearing, an hour or so ago, but thought that it was an Indian child. So they all went to look after the child and in a few minutes they found her in the woods on the north side of the clearing, and they soon saw that she was the long lost child, as she had deep blue eyes.

You can imagine the joy and rejoicing when they found her; they took her to Mr. Dubbs' and sent word at once to her bereaved parents, who got word in the fore part of the night. You can't imagine how the parents and friends passed that night, as there was joy mixed with doubt. Before daylight Mr. Mahlon Whitaker and Mr. Frankfauder were plunging through the woods to Mr. Dubbs'. They made the distance in double quick time, and found the child all right, but quite wild and strange.

The little one had wandered 14 miles for 11 days amid the terrors of the Black Swamp. That child lived to be a woman, was married and passed away some years ago.

JIM SLATER'S CURSE

Is There an Avenging Nemesis Hanging Over Bairdstown on Account of the Curse of a Ruined Man?

THE following weird, uncanny incident came in the experience of Mr. C. W. Evers, during his term of sheriff in the later sixties, when the county seat was at Perrysburg. The raving agony of Slater, crazed with his losses, his bitterness in being ruined by a crime of which he was undoubtedly innocent, together with the curse he pronounced upon the place and all connected with his downfall—these are the facts. The retribution that followed those connected with Slater's persecution and the calamitous incidents that have attached to the vicinity of Bairdstown, so strikingly described by the facile pen of Mr. Evers, strongly reminds one of Hamlet, when he says:

"There are more things in heaven and earth, Horatio,
Than are dreampt of in your philosophy."

"Say, my boy," said an ex-sheriff to a reporter some years ago, "do you believe in retribution through Providential agency here on this earth, for sins done by the sons of Adam? If you do, possibly I can give you a partial solution to the serious misfortunes of our neighbors at Bairdstown."

"Explain and we'll see," said the scribe.

"Well, these late calamities to the town and the mystery of their origin has set me to thinking of the place when there was no town there; and if one was inclined to be superstitious it would not be very difficult to believe that evil spirits come back from the dominions of the dead and curse the haunts of living men with deeds of vengeance."

But I'll give you the story as I recall it, and you may draw your own conclusions.

Away back about the close of the war with Mexico, the quarter section of land where Bairdstown is, was owned by an old man named

Jim Slater

Old Jim was not considered very bright, or rather, some of his neighbors doubted at times if his mind—reason—was rightly balanced. He was rough and uncouth in manner, inclined to be irritable and violent, when he imagined he was being imposed upon; but with his family, worked hard, and lived poorly. In this uphill struggle, his wife, who was an estimable woman, far above Slater, sickened and died. Soon after this Slater's misfortunes began. William McMurray, a neighbor, put in a piece of wheat on Slater's land on shares. At harvesting, Slater objected to the grain being hauled off the farm for threshing. A sharp war of words and much feeling grew out of this trivial affair. Slater in his ungovernable anger, swore that the wheat would never do his neighbor any good. Possibly he took the case into justice court. I believe he did, and got non-suited or beaten.

So the matter rested until some weeks later, when one night the wheat stacks were burned, and a new harness and some other articles were stolen from McMurray's or D. Wineland's barn, near by.

Slater, who was not a favorite among his neighbors, was of course set upon at once among the gossips, as the instigator, if not the direct agent in burning the stacks; all because of the constructive threat made. No other evidences could be found against him except that assertion, made in anger; and on this slender thread and a good deal of prejudice, he was arrested, and tried before a justice, and I believe bound over to court. David Hays of Fostoria, who made some pretensions to a slight acquaintance with Blackstone, pettifogged Slater's case.

At the next term of common pleas court, Slater was indicted; the late George Strain being the prosecuting attorney. After heavy expense in lawyer fees and other ways, Slater was acquitted. David Hays and Dodge & Tyler defended his case.

Public sentiment was divided as to Slater's guilt, and strangely too, McMurray, who with Slater was the loser by the fire, did not believe Slater guilty, though at a loss to explain the origin of the fire, which was clearly the work of an incendiary. This prosecution, or persecution as Slater termed it, was the cause of his ruin. The lawyers got notes, secured by mortgages on his farm, and an old creditor in Tiffin, with a mortgage of four or five hundred dollars, got uneasy and began proceedings of foreclosure. This scared small creditors and they began a crusade in justice court against the unfortunate man, probably on the old rule, "kick a man when he's down." Slater tried to fight them off. He was combative and Hays, his lawyer, was a ready servant to help him, but alas! in deeper, in nearly every instance. At last and not long either, the evil day came and the sheriff with an order of sale in which were marshaled all the liens, came with appraisers to value the property. I can see Slater yet as he sat on a log near his cabin, sullen and dispirited while the appraisers near by were trying to fix upon a value. He scarcely spoke during the time we were there. He asked if he could take off the growing crops. He said he had not slept nights because of this trouble and the only hope he had was that none of the neighbors would bid on the farm when it was offered.

The day of sale came. There was only one buyer. John Baird, a prosperous farmer, living some two miles from Slater's, bid in the land.

A day or so after the sale, as I sat at the office table writing (this was while the court house was in Perrysburg) I heard a shuffling step at the door, at my back. I turned my head and said "Good morning, Mr. Slater!" for it was he. He said nothing, but silently took a chair near the table. After a little he said, "Sheriff, did my place sell?" "Yes." "Who bought it?" I told him. He said, "I heard so, and came clear here to see if it was true." He dropped his head on his arm on the table and trembled as though suffering agonizing bodily pain. He did not speak for many minutes. I felt so much moved by his distress that I could scarcely go on with my work. I had from the first believed him innocent of the crime which brought this trouble on him. I had had little experience in detecting criminals, but from the first I felt that Slater was the unfortunate victim of circumstances which almost completely screened the real perpetrator of the crime, whoever it might be.

After his agitation had subsided a little, I told him there was yet time to save his place—that he should not give it up so—that he could probably borrow money to cancel the judgment liens and secure the lender by a mortgage on the land as soon as the liens were off. That if these liens were paid before the first day of court, the judge would not confirm the sale.

"No! No!" he said, "I cannot do it; I have no friends. All are down on me. No one has a good word for me; even my lawyer is against me; I am robbed of my place and driven from my home. There is no law, divine or human, that will justify this robbery. If there is a just God, he will curse the place to the last end of eternity as a warning. That farm will never do John Baird any good. He has been against me. He wanted my place; he has got it, and the curse of a wronged man goes with the place and all who have had a hand in robbing me."

I do not pretend to give Slater's exact words, nor could I possibly give even a faint expression of his intense agitation, bitterness and despair. Words of encouragement or kindness were alike useless. The fires of hope and ambition were quenched—drowned forever in his breast.

* * * * * * * *

James Slater died a pauper. He lies buried at the infirmary.

On his old farm is Bairdstown. When the B. & O. railroad located its line through there, John Baird with the enterprise characteristic of himself, laid out a town and beside giving it his name, promoted the growth with all his energy. He built a fine flouring mill, hotel, etc., and the town grew rapidly.

About this time misfortunes, one after another began to stop at Baird's door. His downward career, as did Slater's and as do most men's, commenced in litigation. Law suit after law suit harrassed him. Creditors pressed him from every side. Judgments and executions disturbed his sleep until he did not know which way to turn. One or two of his sons became unsteady in habits, being a hindrance instead of a help to the father in his troubles. Next in the line of bad luck his fine mill burned, attributed at the time to incendiarism, the first I believe in that line of calamities which later on have so frequently been visited upon the ill-fated town. Finally as if in sheer desperation at the bootless fight he was making against fate, Baird gathered up what little he could from the wreck, and taking his estimable wife and daughter, went to Arkansas and engaged in hotel keeping. But fate still had misfortunes in store for him. His daughter sickened and died and later on the final blow, the loss of his beloved but heartbroken wife. Stripped of family and property, broken in spirit and bowed with age, Baird returned to Ohio, where with relatives, in the southern part of the state, if living, he makes his home.

David Hays, Slater's lawyer, fell, too, into hard lines. He was at one time the owner of much property, but fortune, ever fickle in her ways, turned against him and, like Baird, for a time he felt like "calling upon the rocks to cover him" from the clutch of remorseless creditors.

But at the last, by a lucky turn in the tide—a sudden advance in some city property he owned—he reached shore with something saved from the wreck, though, in the meantime, he had the sad misfortune to lose his wife—a most worthy woman—who died bereft of her reason, her death having been preceded only a short time by that of their only daughter.

George Strain, the prosecuting attorney who drew the indictment and prosecuted Slater, went insane, later on, and died, afterwards in an insane asylum. What has been the fate of the jurors who indicted the unfortunate man, I have not inquired. In fact, I have not cared to pursue the unpleasant subject further, lest the truth might reveal a like sad state of affairs clear through.

It is a little singular, too, that, with rare exceptions, nearly every enterprise, nearly every business man, no matter how worthy, starting in Bairdstown, has met with disaster or ill-success, sooner or later.

The recent fires, from whatever mysterious cause, are, to all appearances, but the greater culmination of misfortunes, of which previous ones have been as but muttering warning of the slumbering volcano beneath.

It is but proper to state here upon the authority of Frank W. Dunn, who related the fact to me only a day or so since, that a woman now living in Kansas, but who lived near Slater at the time of the stack burning, wrote a full account of the burning and theft, to William McMurray before his death. Her statement corroborated as it was by circumstances, was doubtless true and was the first positive testimony as to Slater's innocence of the crime. But it came too late. The woman as is well shown in her letter, had good reasons for not daring to reveal her story at the time.

A TEN YEARS' STRUGGLE

The Intense Strife in Removal of the County Seat Half a Century Ago

IT has ever been the experience that in every instance involving the removal of a county seat from one locality to another, strife and opposition have been engendered, and the removal of the county seat from Perrysburg to Bowling Green was no exception to this fact. Probably no removal was ever productive of more intense feeling or more bitter denunciation on both sides in that memorable contest. Ananias held full sway, and to such an extent that enmities were provoked and friendships estranged. For the time the prosperity of the county was measurably checked, and the turmoil tended to weaken the population morally, politically and financially as well.

Fifty years have passed away since that time and many of our older citizens still remember that prolonged struggle. It began in 1865, and was not definitely and permanently settled until in the fall of 1875. The first election was held in 1866, and resulted in favor of the removal from Perrysburg to Bowling Green. The citizens of Bowling Green entered into a bond to build as good a court house and jail at Bowling Green as those at Perrysburg were at the time they were built, on condition that the material of the old buildings at Perrysburg and the lots on which they stood be given to the removal interest. If the conditions were fulfilled the county was not to be taxed for court house and jail.

But the people were taxed, and under the following circumstances: The commissioners stepped in and demanded to be heard as the guardians of the county's interests. They changed the location from the one chosen where the foundation could be laid on the solid rock; the size of the court house, under their direction, was also enlarged. They demanded that the county required better and more commodious buildings than those at Perrysburg. The removal interest adopted the suggestions and demands of the county commissioners and built accordingly. The commissioners also demanded many other improvements and proposed to pay for the same out of the county treasury. They took into account the increasing business of a large, rich and rapidly developing county, and their action was taken after a conference with a number of the best and most judicious men of the county. None of these improvements were contemplated by the signers of the bond. For these improvements the people were taxed $3,006.

The removal interest proceeded in good faith to carry out their pledge in the bond. When they were ready they made complete arrangements to carry the old material from Perrysburg to Bowling Green, but were then prevented by the court, invoked by the anti-removal interest, and they never received one cent from the sale of the property of the county at Perrysburg. Thus this condition on which the bond hinged was not available.

The auditor was then directed to advertise for bids under the authority of the commissioners, and an entire new jail was built for the contract price of $14,506, which was $494 less than the Bowling Green bond, and much less than the estimate made of the county buildings at Perrysburg. Thus there was no bad faith whatever on the part of the removal interest as was charged in the heat of that contest.

Judge Phelps, probate judge, removed his office from Perrysburg as soon as the court house at Bowling Green was ready, transacting business there a year or more before the other offices were removed in 1870.

The year following the court house was destroyed by fire, but after considerable litigation an enabling act was secured to give the people another opportunity to vote on the removal question, this time to take the county offices back to Perrysburg. The Perrysburg interest had rebuilt their court house more substantial and in better condition than ever, and the vote on removal was again taken on the 12th of October, 1875.

It resulted in a large vote throughout the county—it may be said an extraordinarily large vote—but the vote in Perrysburg capped the climax. Out of a vote that would be a large one at 1,000, the ballot box, when opened, revealed the number of ballots cast in favor of removal—3,016!

The vote on governor at that election was very close, and when Ezra S. Dodd, of Toledo, heard of Perrysburg's vote, he at once sent a telegram to John G.

SCRAP-BOOK.

Thompson, chairman of the Democratic state executive committee asking, "Would 1,000 from Wood be of any good?" That has now passed into quite a familiar phrase. Mr. Dodd left Toledo as soon as he sent the telegram, and it was surmised by the chairman of the Republican executive committee in Toledo, Rev. Robert McCune, that Dodd had struck out for Bowling Green. Accordingly the writer with George S. Canfield, was dispatched to Bowling Green, leaving Toledo at 11 o'clock that night in a disagreeable rain. We remained until the votes were all received, but Dodd had not put in an appearance.

The vote of Perrysburg was thrown out without much ceremony, and the vote against removal proved to be a large, unmistakable majority. Thus ended that memorable struggle, and the present prosperity of Wood county strongly affirms the wisdom of that decision by the people.

CAPT. DAVID WILKINSON

One of the Veteran Steamboat Pioneers of the Maumee Valley

ON Monday, September 8, 1873, at his residence in Perrysburg, Captain David Wilkinson, in the 74th year of his age, passed away.

The relatives and a very large circle of friends were called upon to mourn the loss of another pioneer of the Maumee valley. A few days before Mr. Wilkinson was visited with a stroke of paralysis which affected his left side and rendered him helpless and almost insensible, in which condition he remained until death had relieved him from his suffering. His wife and five children were all present during his last moments.

The funeral services took place from his late residence on Front street, and were conducted by the members of Phoenix Lodge No. 123, Free and Accepted Masons, of which lodge he was a charter member. The Rev. G. A. Adams officiated as chaplain. The remains were followed to the cemetery by a very large concourse of relatives and friends, and were deposited in the grave with the accustomed Masonic honors.

The editors of the Toledo Blade and Commercial were familiar with the early history of the deceased, and the following extracts are taken from the eulogy of each.

From the Blade.—One by one the pioneers of the Maumee valley are passing away, and today there are few left to relate the incidents and struggles through which the early settlers of this now fertile and prosperous section of the state, were called to pass. Yesterday (Monday) closed the life of another one of those who lived to see their hopes respecting the Maumee valley more than realized. Captain David Wilkinson of Perrysburg, is no more. The captain was born in February, 1800, at or near Buffalo, and the writer of this has often heard him speak of the early days as in the village of Buffalo during the war of 1812. At an early age he went upon the lake as a sailor, and in 1815 he sailed up the Maumee river on the schooner Black Snake, commanded by his uncle, Jacob Wilkinson. This was a small craft to venture upon the lake, being of but twenty-five tons burden. At that time, where Perrysburg now stands, nothing but a wild forest was to be seen. This little schooner as we learn from a memorandum furnished by Capt. Wilkinson to H. S. Knapp, Esq., for his history of the Maumee valley, brought up as passengers the family of Mulhollen, who kept the noted tavern at Vienna some years later, also a Mr. Hunter and family, Scott Robb, and a Mr. Hopkins, who settled on land above the present village of Perrysburg. At that time, Fort Meigs contained about forty soldiers, who were taken to Detroit by the schooner on her return trip.

From the Commercial.—The deceased was in his 74th year, having been born in the year 1800. His first advent to the Maumee valley was in 1815, as a hand on board the schooner Black Snake, a craft of about 25 tons, commanded by Jacob Wilkinson, an uncle, which brought several passengers, who landed at Perrysburg, and most of them became settlers of the town and vicinity. This was during the year in which the war with England closed, and Fort Meigs, above Perrysburg, was still garrisoned by United States troops. The chief industrial interest at that time was fishing. In 1817 the young navigator, though but 17 years old, was promoted to the command of the Black Snake. In 1818 he took command of the schooner Pilot, which plied between the river and Buffalo, and continued to sail different vessels until 1835. Among these crafts was the Eagle, a schooner built in 1828 at Port Lawrence (now Toledo). In 1835 he became the commander of the steamer Commodore Perry, which he sailed for ten years, when he took charge of the Superior, in which he remained until 1852, when he left the lakes. Since that time he has devoted himself to the cultivation of his farm and to the charge of the Light-house in the Maumee Bay, near Manhattan.

Deceased was a man of great kindness of heart and geniality in disposition, whereby he won his way to the esteem of all acquaintances; while by his integrity and honorable dealing he commanded the confidence of his fellow men in an eminent degree. His independence of character ever prompted him to self-reliance and unremitting effort. After a residence in the Valley of 58 years, he passed away amid a state of things in extraordinary contrast with the scene which presented itself to his youthful eyes. He leaves five children —two sons and three daughters—to mourn the departure of one who never failed in his duty to them, and whose advantages in life have been mainly due to his unceasing care. Few, indeed, of his earliest contemporaries now remain, and the last of them will soon follow him. Be it the care of those who have or shall come after them not to forget the debt due to their early enterprise and sacrifices.

Capt. Wilkinson is said to have made the first chart of the Maumee river and bay, which was adopted by the government, and was in general use until a more accurate one was made many years later.

MAIL CARRYING

The Struggles and Hardships Endured by Mail Carriers in the Early Thirties

THAT old pioneer, Noah Reed, thus speaks of the trials of the mail carriers in the early history of Wood county:

In the year 1832—the year of the "Black Hawk war"—in the first week of that year, Hiram Wade made his first trip as a mail carrier under Guy Nearing who had the mail contract. The route was from Perrysburg to Lima. His first trip was a pleasant one. On his second trip he got through to Lima all right, but on his return to Perrysburg he encamped on a sand ridge near the center of Wood county, and during the night the wolves in large numbers

SCRAP-BOOK.

flocked so closely about him that he was compelled to build a fire between a large stump and the butt of a whitewood log that was hollow as a shell. He was somewhat frightened, and for greater security he crawled into the log to keep clear of the wolves. Finally the log itself caught fire and he was obliged to desert his quarters. However, Wade did not get out of that log unscathed. His face and hands were badly burned, the mail bag scorched, and two large holes were burned through his blanket. That was his last trip.

Next my brother, L. W. Reed carried the mail two trips, which resulted in a lameness of his horse. He met with a mishap in which he nearly drowned both himself and horse, and lost the mail bag, which was recovered a few days later full of water. On his second trip there was no mail to collect on his way to Lima and on his return he had but two letters —one for Gilead and one for Perrysburg. That was his last trip.

Next A. B. Crosby made one trip.

Next was Hiram Fane, who made a trip, but he had no bad luck. Following him was a man, whose name I have forgotten. He came very near being drowned and his horse crippled in the Blanchard river. He left the horse and hung the saddle on a tree. This man simply undertook the job of carrying the mail out of curiosity, to see whether it was as difficult as had been reported by Wade and Reed. He found out, and his curiosity was fully satisfied.

Now, I undertook the work of carrying the mail. I made my first trip during the last week in February of 1832, and carried the mail until the last of November of that year without any injury to my horse. However, quite frequently I was compelled to break the ice for myself and horse, and had great difficulty in crossing the Blanchard. On one occasion I was utterly unable to cross that stream on account of the extraordinary high water, and could not make the trip. For this the government kept back $50 of my hard earnings in that perilous trip.

REV. JOSEPH BADGER

Thrilling Incident in His Life When Attacked by Wolves

THIS gentleman, so well known and identified with the early history of Wood county, had his home in Gustavus, Trumbull county, where he began his unselfish labors as early as 1804. A highly educated man, a graduate of one of the great Eastern colleges, he yet chose to tread the thorny path of a pioneer missionary, enduring the hardships and facing the dangers of the western forest that he might do good unto his fellowmen. In 1835 he removed to Wood county, where he died fourteen years later, in 1849, at the advanced age of 89.

One Sunday morning from his pulpit in Gustavus, he related the following thrilling adventure:

"I had started to come through from Ashtabula, but there being no path I got ahead but slowly, and I can not say how far I had come when darkness came upon me. As I could make no headway through a pathless wood I tied my horse so that it could feed about some, and then lay down on the grass to rest. Ere long I was aroused by the cry of a wolf. This cry was answered, and soon it seemed that a hundred ravenous wolves were howling for their prey. I quickly arose, tied my horse more firmly, and, feeling about in the darkness, found a stout limb, which I cut for a cudgel and prepared for an encounter with the enemy.

"The wolves formed a circle about me. I drew near to my horse and walked around him constantly. The wolves came so near that I could hear the snapping of their jaws. All night long I kept up this walk, beating the trees with my stick and shouting to keep the hungry animals at bay. My horse trembled, but trusting to my protection did not try to get away.

"In the first gray light of morning the wolves began to creep slowly away. Their cries grew fainter and fainter in the distance and I found that they had left me. Blessing God for the countless manifestations of his goodness in preserving me through this and similar perils I was again proceeding on my way when once more the barking of wolves resounded through the forest. There was little opportunity for me to hasten, as fallen trees, brush and bushes were in the way. The pursuers were coming quite near and their howling rent the air, when suddenly there was a crashing near me and like a flash of light a fine, full grown deer leaped out, bubbles of white foam falling from his mouth, and panting for breath. He thrust his head alongside my faithful horse and so came beside me until we reached a clearing probably four miles from the place where I had spent the night. The hungry wolves were again baffled and retired to await the coming of another night in which to continue their search for food."

STRANGE INCIDENT

A Memorable Little Cabin—Three Lives Snuffed Out, and Under a Veil of Mystery

ON the right hand, or east side of the Haskins road, about two and a fourth miles from Bowling Green, the passerby may have noticed on the crown of the sand ridge, just inside the field, a little old dilapidated, deserted log cabin.

It has stood there for years and years, like a faithful sentry noting the progress of surrounding events, and the days of its existence exceed that of any other cabin in Plain township. It was for many years previous to the drainage of the country adjacent, a sort of Mt. Ararat to the unfortunate travelers on the "old" Miltonville road. Many a weary man has sought rest in that little homely cabin. It was long known as the Wilson place, and was built by a man named Wilson, and was for a time made to do extensive hotel duty. All classes per force patronized it—emigrants from afar as well as local dignitaries, sought friendly shelter in its narrow limits.

The Spinks, Hollisters, Robys, Spaffords, Drs. Dustin, Peck Burritt and Conant, Collister Haskins, W. V. Way, Count Coffinberry, Ralph Keeler, all the leading men of that day, had sought shelter under the roof of that diminutive cabin on the sand ridge. True it was but one story high and nearly all of one end was taken up by a great fire place, but for all that it was the only dry place the benighted traveler, with his weary horse, could find. Stay he must, and some nights there were almost as many sleepers snoring away as there were split puncheons in the rude floor, on which the guests had to lay, for bedsteads were scarce in those days.

Involved in a Law Suit

But enough about the old cabin. It was in the year 1840, the year in which

Gen. Harrison was elected President, that the two Harris brothers, Seth and James, moved into the cabin, which had been abandoned by its former occupants. James Harris was a bachelor and lived in his brother's family, and the brothers worked together. They had a short time previous lived in Liberty township, either on the premises or not far from where the late James Bloom lived. Bloom and the Harris' had become involved in a law suit, which suit had been taken up and was pending trial in the county court at Perrysburg. Court was in session, and both parties, plaintiff and defendants were there ready for trial.

Before the case was called up, however, the parties to the suit had effected a settlement, though considerable bad feeling had been worked up in the mean time. It was the current talk at the time, that all the parties met at the tavern and took a drink, after which the Harris' started home. On the road home, Seth Harris was

Taken Very Sick

And as soon as they reached the cabin James Harris went for a doctor Rice, who lived where Portageville now is. Before he arrived at the cabin with the doctor, James Harris also was taken very sick with similar symptoms to those of his brother Seth. All the efforts and skill of the doctor could, nor did not relieve them, and Seth died in great agony, and twelve hours after, his brother James was laid on the bed beside him a corpse.

Mr. Ralston, who was about the nearest neighbor, except Eli Martindale, on the present Clinton Fay farm, was alone in the cabin, washing the body of James Harris and was in the act of putting a clean shirt on him, when Dr. Rice arrived, bringing with him another physician named Thomas and a half gallon jug of whisky. Rice told Ralston not to dress the body as he desired to cut the man open and find if possible what caused his death.

Suspicion

Rice, it seems, had suspicions that the two men's lives had been cut short by something they had drank or eaten. He got a butcher knife and sharpened it, but before he was ready to operate, Dr. Thomas was taken with a shake of the ague and had to lay down. Rice ripped open the stomach of the dead man and could discover nothing wrong as he said, though his frequent drafts on the half gallon jug, did not improve his sense of vision any.

He then turned and cut open the breast and throat clear to the chin, Ralston holding the chest open while the heart, liver and lungs were examined. During the savage operation with the butcher knife, Rice scratched one of his fingers on the jagged breast bone of the dead man, but paid no further attention to it than to clap his finger to his mouth and suck the oozing blood from the skin abrasion.

The lungs of the man were discolored and showed an unnatural condition, but Rice pronounced that he could find no trace of poison, and soon after he and Thomas left. Mr. Ralston took the carved body of Harris and washed, arranged and wrapped it as well as he could, and the bodies of the two men were taken from the cabin and buried.

The Doctor Succumbs

Three days after their burial, Mr. Ralston was in Portage, and learned that Dr. Rice was lying in a critical condition. He called in to see him and the doctors were just in the act of amputating the frantic man's arm, which, from the small finger wound received while operating on Harris's body, had become intensely inflamed, mortification followed, and the flesh came from the arm in chunks and flakes while the doctors were performing the amputation, which was effected near the shoulder, to arrest if possible the further progress of the poison; but it was too late. The poison had taken possession of his whole system, blood, brain and muscle. Rice was a doomed man and survived the cutting off of his arm only a short time, when he too, died in great agony, helped and hurried off, no doubt, by the hard usage of himself including the too free use of whisky.

Thus three strong, healthy men were suddenly snatched from the sparsely settled neighborhood—from life to death, and the living, neither then nor since were able to satisfactorily answer the question, what caused their sudden death?—*C. W. E.*

CYGNET'S CALAMITY

Flames Destroy Human Lives and Wipe Out Much Property Nearly a Score of Years Ago

ON the morning of the 30th of January, 1891, Cygnet was visited by a most disastrous conflagration. The Wood County Democrat chronicled the fact that three lives had been snuffed out and $50,000 worth of property destroyed. Here follows The Democrat's account:

Cygnet, as is well known, is an oil town and is one of the incidents of the discovery of oil in Ohio.

All the buildings in the town were hastily and poorly constructed affairs, and many of them were more or less saturated with the oil that not only permeates the earth, but also the very atmosphere, and deadens and discolors the genial current waters.

Buildings of that variety are easy prey to the fire-fiend, and most woefully did he perform his deplorable mission today. The business portion of the town comprises only one street which is intersected about middle by the T., C. & C. railroad. West of the railroad on the north side of the street, a disastrous fire occurred this morning, destroying $50,000 worth of property and ushering three human beings into eternity.

The fire originated in the millinery store of Mrs. Maloney and was not discovered until it had gained an impetus that was irresistible. It was 5:30 when the flames asserted their presence in the bed room of Mrs. Maloney, who was occupying a bed on the first floor with her domestic, Mattie Stackhouse. The fire caused an explosion of gas which awakened her to the danger of her situation. She immediately awakened Miss Stackhouse and her five-year-old son and the two hastily donned their dresses and fled to the rear of the building, taking the boy with them. When they got out of doors the two women looked back into the burning building, and saw Francis Slattery, a brother of Mrs. Maloney, crawling about on the second floor covered with flames. They called to him to come out of a certain door, but he was probably unconscious. Slattery was sleeping on the second floor with Mr. Maloney and Mr. Maloney's 15-months-old child, and the three were burned to a crisp.

Mr. Maloney was 30 years old and was a boiler maker by trade. Mrs. Maloney kept a millinery store on the first floor of the ill-fated building.

The flames spread before the influence of a western wind towards the east, and in an hour had destroyed several of the principal buildings of the town. In less than an hour, the whole block was a smoldering ruin.

The baby was burned up completely, nothing but its skull being found in the debris. The town is full of people come to see the great conflagration.

SCRAP-BOOK.

A FALSE ALARM

An Indian Rumor Frightened Settlers—And This Was the "Blackhawk War"

THE "Blackhawk War" in 1832, was no war at all. All it amounted to was a senseless rumor that thoroughly alarmed the settlers for a short time. In his pioneer recollections, Noah Reed gives the following version of the incident:

"In the summer of 1832, as some of the Pottawatomies were out hunting they ran across some of our young Ottawa Indians. They conveyed to them the alarming intelligence that the bloodthirsty Blackhawk of Illinois, was on his way to this point, and his purpose was to kill every Indian woman and child. This intelligence so frightened the Ottawa Indians that they scattered in every direction in their canoes or by other methods of escape. Many of them slept in their canoes. The Ottawas spread the rumor far and near, and were so positive of the truth of the report that the white settlers were thrown into a state of anxiety and dread. Some of them were so alarmed that they buried and hid their property, and then went to Nearing's Mill as a place of safety. Some fled to Beaver Creek for greater safety, and placed guards on duty so that they might be duly warned of the approach of the savage chief and his warriors.

"Uncle Guy Nearing learning of the consternation that prevailed among the settlers, and regarding the rumor as nothing more than an idle report, without even the semblance of truth, determined to have some sport with those who had barricaded themselves within the mill at Damascus. One night at 10 o'clock he came riding like Jehu of old, splashing the water and singing in the Indian style until he came up to the guard. 'Who comes there?' was the prompt query of the guard. 'Nowash,' answered Uncle Guy, giving his Indian name. This act on the part of Uncle Guy convinced the guard that the rumor of Blackhawk coming was a silly hoax, and those who were huddled in the mill began to regard the matter in a different light, and in some embarrassment they concluded to return to their homes, confident that all their fright was needless. And this was the sum and substance of the so-called 'Blackhawk War' on Beaver Creek."

JONATHAN SALSBURY

An Athlete for Work—Never Idle—In an Evil Hour He Was Stripped of His Possessions

JONATHAN SALSBURY and the Salsbury farm in Liberty township, will long be remembered by the old settlers. Old man Salsbury, as he was familiarly called many years ago, was rather a remarkable man and had endured hard work and man-killing hardships enough to have killed four or five ordinary men.

In the spring of 1834 he bought 880 acres of timber land in Liberty township, then a wilderness, the patents for which were signed by Andrew Jackson. He immediately set to work to clear and improve the tract and after staying on it about 30 years had improved over 300 acres. Aside from the work on his farm, wherever there were extensive contracts for work such as teams could be used on with advantage, Jonathan Salsbury was a competitor. When the people began to open artificial water courses in Wood county, and the prairie or swamp lands were to be brought under cultivation, Salsbury found a field in which he was peculiarly a success. He fitted up an enormous plow that was gauged and guided by wheels and capable of cutting and turning a furrow 32 inches wide, and so constructed as to require nobody to "hold the plow," in fact the plow had no handles. To this breaking machine six pairs of oxen and one span of horses were hitched, and when under full headway no ordinary root, sapling or grub would disturb its progress. The cutter and shear were kept filed sharp and it was not necessary to grub land for this sort of a plow.

Always at It

When Salsbury started on a job it mattered not to him about the weather. Rain, snow, mud or water never deterred him from pushing the work from break of day in the morning until after dark at night.

We remember on one occasion when he broke 100 acres of land for Dr. Cass on the Keeler prairie, to have passed across the prairie after night and seen the old man camped under his wagon with scarcely bedding to keep him off the wet ground. A cheerless fire flickered up a little light occasionally, and but for the barking of his dog, his only companion, no one would have supposed a human being to have been within two miles of the place. His team grazed on the prairie near by, and before other people had taken their breakfast in the morning, Salsbury had made one "bout" with his big plow and a full half acre of prairie had been turned upside down.

When George Williams began on the prairie east of here years ago, he contracted with Salsbury to plow a half section of land (320 acres). The old man came with his big plow and team the 17th day of March, and never left even to go home, until the work was completed on the 4th day of July. His feet were wet a great portion of the time, and yet he never was sick.

Salsbury was not one of your men that worked hard for a season and then idled away months of time. He was always on the move. Scarcely an hour of the night in the working season on the farm that he was not up and out looking after stock, crops or fences—fact, those who knew him best wondered when he slept or how he existed, leading such a hard, grudging, toiling dog's life. Yet when he was nearing his ninetieth year he seemed as smart and active as ever.

The Plague Spot of His Life

With his large landed estate at the start, and his working habits, dogged perseverance, he had a good start, it will be inferred, to make a fortune, and to which his industry and slavish services undoubtedly entitled him, if, indeed, worldly pelf can be called a compensation for such a life. Yes, he made a fortune, but it went from him in an unfortunate hour, else he had been the richest man in the county, and yet, after a long life of drudgery, he has but little of this world's goods to show for it, hardly a sure reliance for his old age. While conversing with him he was reticent on this subject, but we will tell it briefly, and let the story not be lost on those who hear it.

Jonathan Salsbury was induced to invest in a lottery. He was uneducated and credulous and avaricious. Like two-thirds of the sons of Adam, he was ready to invest in any speculation or game which promised a good deal for nothing or, next to it, a small investment. Dr. Roback of Cincinnati, is the man to whom Salsbury attributes his misfortune. First $100, then $500, $1,000, $1,500, until over $3,000 was gone. The trick was baited and the old man drew a lucky ticket or so. Then he lost. Then the man who was leading him on pretended by some power of necromancy or legerdemain to be able to forecast the lucky numbers. These Salsbury reached for to recover what he had already lost, and of

SCRAP-BOOK. 143

course drew blanks. All was gone now, and he as a last resort caused Roback's arrest on a criminal charge, and the sheriff brought the prisoner to Perrysburg, accompanied by his lawyer, the late Hon. George E. Pugh. The prisoner was so hedged about, that the law or testimony could not reach him and he went free.—*C. W. E.*

IMPREGNABLE

Against the Vicious Assaults of Great Britain and Her Allied Savages Stood Ft. Meigs

NO greater victory, none of more transcending import is recorded in our nation's history than that of the sieges of Fort Meigs. It was the purpose of Gen. Harrison, the commander-in-chief, to retake Detroit which had been so ingloriously surrendered by Gen. Hull. Harrison had been appointed Governor of the Northwestern territory, including Indiana, Illinois, Michigan and Wisconsin—having done much civil and military service, well known to history.

Victory of Tippecanoe

On the 5th of November, 1811, Governor Harrison marched with some regulars and militia, 800 strong, upon the Prophet's town (the brother of Tecumseh), on the Tippecanoe river, in Indiana, where he was entrenched. The Indians were defeated and dispersed, their leader, the Prophet, being killed. This overawed the Indians, who were in almost entire possession of the whole territory, but war with England being imminent, they refused a peace.

Hull's Surrender

War with England was declared June 12, 1812. Gen. Hull was sent with his army to Detroit to conquer western Canada. In August following he surrendered his entire army, Detroit and the Northwestern territory to Gen. Brock, of the British army. This surrender filled the whole country with surprise, alarm and indignation, and he was everywhere denounced as a traitor, in spite of his patriotic services during the Revolution. He was courtmartialed on two charges, treason and cowardice. He was condemned to be shot but was afterwards reprieved.

Winchester's Defeat

In an address of Cassius M. Clay, in 1891, he said that on the first day of January, 1813, the Northwest army under Brig.-Gen. Harrison rested, with the left wing, commanded by Gen. Winchester at Fort Defiance, on the Maumee river, and the right wing under the commander-in-chief at Upper Sandusky. Detroit being the objective point of attack, Winchester was ordered to march with his brigade of Kentuckians and regulars, commanded on the left by Col. Lewis, to reach the rapids and await Harrison's arrival. But Winchester on the 14th, hearing of the weak garrison of Frenchtown, on the river Raisin, in Michigan, detached Col. Lewis to capture it, which was done on the 18th of January, 1813.

Winchester, hearing of the capture, marched to the support of Lewis, refused to enter his pickets, and camped his regiment on the plains outside, because he would not take post on the left of Lewis —military etiquette ordering—and he slept at a farmhouse a mile distant from Col. Wells' regiment.

Massacre at River Raisin

A British force under General Proctor, marched with regulars and Indians in the night of the 21st, assaulted Lewis' fort, and were repulsed with great slaughter. They then turned on Wells' regiment and cut it to pieces, taking many prisoners, among them Col. Wells himself. The whole British force, with six field pieces, was turned upon Lewis, who surrendered under promise of the protection of civilized warfare. The generals, colonels and men were saved as stipulated, but all the wounded were massacred in Frenchtown. There was no guard left, and two houses full of the wounded were burned.

Siege of Fort Meigs

Defeat after defeat seemed to be the lot of the American forces, and after the battle and massacre at Frenchtown, Gen. Harrison was compelled to abandon the recapture of Detroit and to stand on the defensive. During the spring of 1813, he pushed forward to completion the work on Fort Meigs, so-called in honor of Gov. R. J. Meigs, of Ohio. This was a work of no small magnitude and moment. For no sooner had the ice commenced to move in the river and lake than the British general, Proctor, formed his plans for the invasion of the Maumee Valley. By threats, by entreaties, by cunning schemes and false promises, Proctor secured the assistance and fired the zeal of Tecumseh, promising to turn over to the Indians Fort Meigs, its garrison and immense stores, and the savages, fresh from the bloody scenes of Raisin Valley and Frenchtown, were only too ready to join in the crusade for plunder.

Gen. Proctor embarked from Detroit with 2,000 regulars and Indians, in the last week of April, 1813, and occupied Fort Miami, when the savages indulged in their favorite pastime of skirmishing, pillaging and scalping in the vicinity.

Meanwhile, on the 1st, 2d and 3d of May, the British and their allies were pouring hot shot into the fort. Batteries had been erected just across the river, and the firing was something terrible. Only the strong earthworks saved the Americans from death and destruction. Round and round, the Indians skirmished, picking off the American soldiers whenever they had a chance, while the British kept up an untiring cannonade.

Gen. Harrison had dispatched a messenger, Major Oliver, to Gen. Clay, who was at Fort Defiance, and on the night of May 4, came the cheering news that Clay was above Fort Meigs with 1,200 men. The historian Collins in his Kentucky History says:

"Gen. Harrison, with the rapid resolution of military genius, dispatched by Capt. Hamilton an order to Clay, to land 800 men upon the northern shore, opposite the fort, to carry the British batteries there placed; to spike the cannons and destroy the carriages, after which they were immediately to regain their boats and cross over to the fort. Hamilton, ascending the river in a canoe, delivered the orders to Clay. But he, with that sagacity which distinguished his life, sent Hamilton to deliver Harrison's order to Col. William Dudley himself. Dudley captured the batteries and filled his orders literally—all but the important one. Led off by the artifices of Indian warfare, he was killed with all his force, save about 150 men. Clay landed his 1,200 men."

In a letter written by Gen. Clay to a friend in Kentucky, dated July 8, 1813, while he was in command at Ft. Meigs, he says:

"On the day of the action, Maj. David Trimble accompanied me to cover the retreat of the remnant of Col. Dudley's regiment, and behaved with great coolness and gallantry. * * * Here the Kentuckians drove Tecumseh, where the hottest battle was fought, and then he crossed the river, and with their whole force overthrew Col. Dudley."

The Bed-Rock of History

Acting under General Harrison's or-

FORT MEIGS
As It Appeared From the River

SCRAP-BOOK.

ders, on May 5, 1813, with 1,200 men, Green Clay, defeated the immortal Tecumseh and the British forces, 3,000 men, in open daylight, drove them over the river, and saved 150 Kentucky soldiers, the remnant of his brigade, from death. This was the first real victory, within the lines of this address, since the declaration of war, January 12, 1812.

Col. Dudley's Fatal Error

After the British batteries opposite Fort Meigs were dismantled, the guns spiked and the flags pulled down, in obedience to orders, a writer in the Toledo Blade gives this account of Dudley's disaster:

"Capt. Coombs and 30 riflemen were in advance of the main body when the Indians in ambush turned on Coombs. Dudley saw the danger and ordered his men to their assistance. The Indians were driven back and Coombs was saved.

"But it was only for a moment. The Indians re-enforced turned. Dudley and his men were scattered through the woods. They were surrounded. Fighting desperately some of the command were pushed back towards the boats. All along the river they were driven backward and forward, fighting, struggling bravely and contesting every inch of the ground. But Dudley fell a victim to the savages while 630 out of 800 who landed with him, were either killed, wounded or taken prisoners.

"Gen. Harrison, with indescribable anguish, saw this advance movement from Fort Meigs and saw what must be the inevitable result. He tried to signal Dudley's command back, but in vain, and all the orders sent were not received. Col. Dudley had sacrificed almost all his army to save Coombs and his riflemen from destruction. When too late he tried to call his men back, but the Kentuckians, confident of success, only pushed on deeper into the forest, and to their own ruin.

"Col. Dudley, when last seen, was fighting the Indians single-handed in the swamp. He died surrounded by the savages whom he had killed. But they had their revenge. His body was slashed and in many places large pieces were cut out—pieces which it is thought the savages in their drunken madness cooked and ate."

But the sorties from Ft. Meigs were successful. The British were driven from their batteries, and forced to beat a hasty retreat by the remainder of the Kentuckians commanded by Col. Boswell, Maj. Johnson and Maj. Alexander. The siege was raised. The fort was saved.

The Second Siege

Gen. Green Clay was in command of Fort Meigs during the second siege, Gen. Harrison was at Lower Sandusky. On the 20th of July the British again ascended the Maumee river. The united forces of Proctor and Tecumseh amounted to more than 5,000, while the Americans at the fort amounted to but a few hundred, Gen. Harrison having withdrawn the American forces to other forts in Ohio.

When Gen. Harrison heard of the movements of the British, he sent Capt. McCune to the assistance of the garrison. His knowledge of the plans of the enemy prevented a wholesale slaughter of the soldiers at the fort.

A Cunning Device Failed

Tecumseh had planned a cunning strategem which almost proved successful. The British infantry were secreted in a ravine near the fort, the cavalry in the woods, and the Indians in the forest back from the fort. The British and their allies commenced a sham battle among themselves. So cunningly was the scheme planned, and so skilfully was the fraud managed that it deceived the garrison, but not their commander. The men demanded permission to go out and assist in the battle, and were indignant when this permission was denied. Had not a shower put a stop to the sham battle, the men would probably have been led into an ambush and the fort taken.

A Desperate Resolve

But the soldiers in Ft. Meigs would never have fallen into the hands of the enemy alive. Preparations were made to fire the magazine in case the allies succeeded in storming the fort and thus all would have perished together. It is more than probable that Proctor learned of their resolve, for he must have guessed that after the terrible scenes at the River Raisin and Maumee the garrison would never fall into his hands alive. On July 28, Proctor discontinued the siege, and discouraged and disheartened, retreated down the river in his boats.

WOLF HUNTING

The Method and Cunning of John Carter in His Expeditions

JOHN CARTER became famous in the forties in southern Wood county as a leader among all those engaged in the dangerous sport of hunting wolves. One of his many exploits will serve to show his style and craft in this, his chosen avocation.

It was in the early summer of 1839, John Carter called at the cabin of John Johnston, who had just settled on the bank of the middle branch of the Portage river, about three miles east of the village of that name, and desired to make his headquarters there while he scoured the swamps further up the river in search of wolves.

He would remain at the house all day until at dark, and often not until the family had retired would he strike for the woods; and the wilder the location the better. He threaded his way through that swamp where the old corduroy road was afterward constructed—on further, in a southwesterly direction until he reached a point in that region of fat mosquitoes, indicated on our old maps of Wood county as a lake and called "Inundated." Here in this inaccessible region, in the weird stillness of darkness and desolation, Carter began howling in imitation of a wolf which he could imitate with such accuracy as to defy detection of almost any man, and easily deceived the unsuspecting wolves. He had not howled long before he was answered. Now mark his cunning. He blazed several trees as nearly as was possible in the darkness, in the direction of the sound and laid by for the next night. Soon as the woods were still and night had shrouded the trees with their thick green foliage, in darkness almost tangible, Carter again took his station at a point at right angles with the line of blazes made the first night, and again began to howl. Again he was answered and blazed his trees in the direction of his answers and awaited the return of daylight.

The next day he followed the lines indicated by the trees he had marked until they intersected each other, and not a rod from that point in a great hollow log, he found the old she wolf and four cubs. From the glare of the fire of the eyes of the old wolf he was able to plant a ball in her skull, and then crawling in on his hands and knees he finished the cubs with his tomahawk.

Mr. Carter continued hunting until 1847, when he closed his hunting in Wood county, as the following last affidavit of his, taken from the records of the clerk's office, will show:

The State of Ohio, Wood County, ss.:

You, John Carter, do solemnly swear,

that the six scalps of wolves taken within the county of Wood by you within twenty days last past, and you verily believe under the age of six months, and that you have not spared the life of any she wolf within your power to kill, with the design to increase the breed; and have received an order for $15.00.

Sworn and subscribed before me, this 2d day of June, 1847.
THOS. UTLEY, Clerk.

The last wolf scalp redeemed in Wood county was Dec. 20, 1871, and presented by Leonard Rush, and the stub in the clerk's office is signed by Geo. Weddel, clerk.—*C. W. E.*

TRAFFIC IN 1833

Experience of Mahlon Meeker—First Log House Built in Plain Township

MAHLON MEEKER who came from Butler county in 1833, left his family and brought with him only a few head of cattle, remaining on the river most of the summer, working for Guy Nearing, Elias Hedges and others. Toward fall he went out to the prairies to cut hay for his cattle and make preparations to build a cabin, after which he and a man named Howard, took a wagon load of white bass which they bought of John Hollister at Perrysburg, to Bellefontaine and West Liberty by way of Fremont and Fort Ball. With this they bought twelve barrels of flour and ten gallons of whisky and started back. When near Bellefontaine, Howard proposed that he could drive the three yoke of oxen home and Meeker could go down to Butler and see his family and arrange for their coming out to the Maumee, which was accordingly done and Meeker started southward.

After making a short visit Mr. Meeker soon found himself again on the prairies in Wood county. Howard had got back and disposed of all the flour excepting sixty pounds; this, with a keg of whisky, being all Mr. Meeker got out of the load. He was now ready to raise his cabin, a work which among the early settlers was attended with no little difficulty on account of living so far apart. Meeker had to get all his help from the river, some of the men coming from Perrysburg, and even then they would not consent to come, so busy were they, unless he would raise on Sunday, which of course he had to do. So on Saturday afternoon he made a shelter of poles and prairie grass, and with a supply of bread and meat and some blankets for the raisers and a dozen or so bunches of pea-vine grass, which he had mowed and placed about against small saplings for the horses, preparation for his help was made; early in the evening they began to arrive by the Indian trail in ones, twos and fours until sixteen had arrived. By the first light next morning they were at work, and now as this was the first systematic house raising in Plain township, we subjoin the names of the party as near as Mr. Meeker can recollect.

Elijah Herrick, Guy Nearing, Michael Sypher, John Whitehead, John Howard, Epaphroditus Foote, Jesse Decker, Levi Decker, Moses Decker, Nathaniel Decker, James Spafford, Eber Wilson, Charles Wilson, Johnston White.

By two o'clock the cabin was up, the roof (of shakes) on, and all cobbed off, with weight poles in good shape. Some of the men had got pretty hilarious by this time, not just because of the good work they had done, but because of frequent visits to the ten gallon keg, which in those days was an indispensable aid on occasions of this kind.

After the work was done, Mr. Meeker announced that he had found a bee-tree near by, and if they would like some honey, he would lead them to it. A vote was taken, and carried in favor of the sweet undertaking. The honey proved to be of the finest kind. One man made a paddle, and as fast as the honey was put in a pail, stirred it up well, after which the pail was filled with whisky. Then a commissary was chosen, with instructions to administer to each man present, a tin cup full, no more, no less, after which they mounted their horses, and started home, on the Indian trail with such whoops and shouts as would have startled a native denizen of the forest. Shortly afterward Mrs. Meeker arrived with their five children, and a few household articles, and made the new cabin their home.—*From Evers' Log Cabin Sketches.*

MISSION STATION

Some Doubt About Its Benefit to the Indians

NOAH REED hauled the brick for the Station chimneys from Daniel Hubbell's brick yard at Port Miami, there being seven loads, for which he received pay mostly in second-hand clothing and stockings for the Nearing family. This clothing had been sent by the Home Mission for the heathen—probably white heathen. Mr. Reed thinks this Mission was of no great benefit to the Indians. The Mission Board through their agent, got into litigation with David Hedges and others. The island, about which they went to law with Hedges, was returned to the Government Survey as a sand bar. Hedges bought his claim from the Indians.

EDSON GOIT

One of the Honest, Sterling Characters That Are Beloved

EDSON GOIT was a man of strong physical constitution, tireless energy, vast will power and of great industry and endurance. Combined with these he had honor and integrity of the highest order, and his impulses toward his fellow men were generous and noble.

Mr. Goit was born in Oswego county, New York, in 1808. While he was yet an infant his father died and during his boyhood he had but little time or opportunity to improve his mind by the aid of books; but such chance as he had, he improved to the best possible advantage and by the time he was 20 years old he taught a district school, and before he was of age started for the western country, finally reaching Tiffin.

He worked at odd jobs, taught school in both Tiffin and Fremont, then unpretentious villages, and in the meantime read law with Abel T. Rawson. In due course of time he was admitted to the bar to practice law and opened an office at Findlay. He made his home in the family of the late L. Q. Rawson. After six months of studious days and anxious nights—six months of patient waiting for a client, none came. Six months were gone—nearly all his scanty means were gone—his clothes were well worn and only a single dollar had he earned. After he had sat down with the family at the breakfast table one morning, he told them that it was to be his last meal with them as he had decided to leave the place.

While they were yet at the table there came a rap at the door. A stranger was there and wanted to know if a lawyer boarded at the house. The stranger was from the east and he had come on to collect a claim against a man who was teaching school not far away, and who owned 40 acres of land near the town. The case was somewhat complicated and papers had to be taken out. Goit prepared the papers through the day and a constable was quietly sent for so as to give no alarm or warning to the man of the birch-tree government. Everything being all ready they pounced down on him at night, and the result was that the stranger got the 40 acres of land, the teacher skipped out for some reason and Goit got as fee ten dollars and an ax. Then the district had no teacher and who could be a more proper man to fill out the term than Goit, which he did to the satisfaction of all concerned.

In 1833 he married Miss Jane Patterson and from this time on he was prosperous. By the year 1840 he had accumulated quite a competence, owning at that time nearly 2,000 acres of the best land in and about Findlay, and having in ready cash over $10,000.

His future, however, was wrecked in mercantile business and indorsing for others. The rascality of a partner brought him to Bowling Green, where he secured a portion of that due him.

Through all his misfortunes Mr. Goit left in his later days a comfortable competence for himself and remaining family and as he himself said a short time before his death, "after so many ups and downs in my life I am glad to know that if I do not get well I shall at least die square with the world."—C. W. E.

NOT ALL A DREAM

More Things in Heaven and Earth, Horatio, Than Dreamed of in Thy Philosophy

ON the morning of the 3d of December, 1877, the citizens of Bowling Green were startled by the sudden death of the wife of Albert E. Royce, a prominent business man. She was sick but a few days, and her ailment was not considered serious as she was in possession of all her faculties of mind up to the very last, and was up on her feet only a short time previous to her death.

She was known, respected and liked by every one. Her kindly presence and cheerful aid, said the Sentinel, was always ready where she could be of use or do good in the community, and few could be taken from our midst who would be more sadly missed. As she lay in the burial casket, apparently in the fullness of health, it seemed impossible to realize otherwise than that her eyes were gently closed in sleep, so natural and painless was the expression of her lifeless face.

A strange coincidence in connection with her death was related by her husband and friends, and given from the pulpit during the funeral services. Somewhere near three years before she had a dream in which it was foretold her that she would be taken sick on the 27th of November, 1877, and that she would die on the 3d of December following. This dream she related to her husband who made light of it as did her parents and immediate friends when she told them the story; but with her it was not so. The matter appeared to weigh upon her mind, and several times during that time she spoke to her husband about it, reminding him that the time was drawing near. Very naturally he laughed the matter off, and even when on the 27th ult. she was taken suddenly ill and again referred to the dream, her friends could not be persuaded that there was anything in it. But when the morning of December 3d had arrived, and at about 10 o'clock she quietly passed away, and her gentle spirit took its flight, then only, were the sorrow-stricken relatives forced to acknowledge the dreadful accuracy of her dream.

This statement is literally true as given, and is one of the mysteries that must remain forever unexplained.

AN ODD GENIUS

"Judge" Lord of Perrysburg, the Butt of Local Ridicule

AMONG the early oddities, says Hezekiah L. Hosmer, which a thirst for adventure or a spirit of enterprise brought to Perrysburg, was one Frederick Lord, better known to old residents as Judge Lord. He came from Maine, from one of whose universities he was a graduate, walking all the way with a pack on his back. He arrived in Perrysburg destitute, money gone and clothing tattered. Failing to obtain a situation as a student in a law office, he took a small piece of land and cultivated it to onions. These, eked out by an occasional loaf, constituted his principal diet.

The neighbors regarded him as the very genius of famine, for he never forsook an undrained coffee-pot or left the cat her portion. After a while he applied to the trustees for the district school. Judge Hollister's ingenious argument that "every man is good for something," prevailed, and he obtained the position, which he filled acceptably, until his admission to the bar. Meantime, however, he became unconsciously, the butt of local waggery and ridicule, and the inglorious hero of many laughable occurrences.

On one occasion he was appointed leading affirmative disputant in the debating club, to open that much mooted question, "Was the English Government justifiable in banishing Napoleon to St. Helena?" The audience had assembled and President Wheeler called upon Lord, who, fully prepared, commenced his argument. When fairly under way, one of the members suddenly sprang a question of order, and others in the secret joined in discussing it, until the evening was spent and its further consideration adjourned till the next meeting. Other preliminary questions were introduced in succession, each one so timed as to break in upon and arrest the argument which Lord was almost bursting to deliver. He bore with these delays and annoyances through three or four meetings of the club; but finally Lord's patience was exhausted. Waiving the interruption, and with his arm extended towards his tormentors, in a voice hoarse with passion, he shouted:

"Mr. President: There is a point beyond which human nature will not pass, and I give these gentlemen due and timely notice that we are now upon the very v-e-rge of that point."

The violent gesture and bodily contortion with which this menace was emphasized, rendered the scene intensely ludicrous, and elicited from the audience a perfect yell of applause. The speaker, however, delivered his argument without further hindrance.

Soon after his admission, Judge Lord opened a law office at Napoleon. Here he fell naturally into drinking habits, in which he indulged at the expense of his associate. When William Sheffield put out his legal shingle, Lord called on him, and after a brief interview, told him he had an important confidential communication to make to him. They walked some distance into the forest skirting the town in perfect silence, Sheffield meantime pondering over the supposed gravity of Lord's relation. Seating themselves on a log, Lord opened the subject somewhat after the following manner:

"Sheffield, you know you are a young man, just setting out in life, and have not had as much experience in the world as I have. I know these fellows pretty well, and don't want to see you taken in, and I thought I might do you great favor by telling you on the start what you ought to do. Just as fast as you make acquaintances here you will be asked to drink with them. It is their social custom, and they will expect you to treat them in return, and it's pretty expensive. Now, my advice is, that you buy your liquor by the gallon, take the jug to your office, and whenever you feel obliged to treat your friends, just take them to the office and treat them there. It won't cost a quarter as much as to pay for drinks at a grocery. As a matter of economy you'll find it a very judicious arrangement."

Lord soon left Napoleon and settled in one of the new counties in Michigan. He was elected county treasurer, and at last accounts had become a man of more wealth and influence than many of those who laughed at his oddities many years before.

REV. ROLLA H. CHUBB

One of the Venerable M. E. Ministers of the Maumee Valley

FEW men in the Maumee Valley were better known in Northwestern Ohio than Rev. Rolla H. Chubb. Born in Poultney, Vt., Sept. 18, 1812, he came west with his father at an early age, who had charge of an Indian station on Lake Superior, where he remained about five years, after which he accompanied his brother to Michigan. When quite young he had followed the footsteps of his father, joining the M. E. church, was admitted to conference, and from that time on until about 1867, he was actively engaged in the ministry, when he retired from active work and was enrolled among the superannuated ministers of the conference. From 1838 to 1855 Mr. Chubb was prominent among the itinerant ministers of the M. E. church in the Maumee Valley, and traveled Wood county on a four or six weeks' circuit, when he encountered all the perplexing embarrassments incident to those early pioneer days, and his life and adventures as a minister of these swamps, would make a volume quite as interesting, and in many instances as pathetic or thrilling as a romance. There may now be living some who remember Rev. Rolla H. Chubb when he was young and in his full strength of manhood, and all can attest the wonderful pulpit oratory with which he was endowed. With clear conceptions, strong convictions, a retentive memory, and a mind to grasp the contents of libraries, and that power of language always at his command, he became eminent as a public speaker.

His sermon preached at Greenwich, Huron county, O., during the war, was characteristic of the man, and was widely copied in the public journals. He was in attendance at the Ft. Meigs celebration in 1840, and about that time became acquainted with Olive Ewing (sister of Judge Ewing), whom he married March 16, 1841. She died July 14, 1863, at Ashland, O., leaving four children, three daughters, Mrs. Emily Peacock, residing at Gallatin, Tennessee; Mrs. Maria Bristol, of Fremont, Ohio; Mrs. W. S. Eberly, and one son, Henry, of Perrysburg, Ohio. On October 4, 1865, he married Miss

Mary C. Hamer, of Ottawa, O., and moved back to Perrysburg. His last regular appointment was Freeport, in 1868. He moved to Delaware, O., in 1883, to give his children an opportunity of attending the college there. He died Friday night, Nov. 7, 1884, after a short illness, and his remains were brought to Perrysburg and interred in Ft. Meigs cemetery.—*Wood County Republican.*

WOOD COUNTY MASONRY

History of the Masonic Order in Northwestern Ohio for Almost Seven Decades

IN October, 1907, Grand Rapids celebrated the fiftieth anniversary of its Masonic Lodge organization. Grand Rapids Lodge had its origin in Wood County Lodge No. 112. Among the exercises was an address by George A. Bell, in which he gave the following interesting history concerning Freemasonry in northwestern Ohio:

"It is quite probable that the history of Freemasonry in northwestern Ohio began when Army Lodge, No. 23, spread its charter at Fort Meigs, in 1813, and worked there until the fort was abandoned. Next, in 1818, the grand lodge of Ohio chartered Northern Light, No. 40, at Maumee. This lodge was active until 1828. A new charter, however, was granted in 1845, and the lodge was allowed to retain its old number.

"From 1828 to 1842, there was not a single Masonic body in 22 counties of northwestern Ohio, and strange to relate, the first lodge sprang up in the midst of the Black Swamp of Wood county.

"In October, 1843, the grand lodge chartered Wood County Lodge, No. 112, naming Martin Warner, Emelius Wood, Morris Brown, Morrison McMillen, James Curtis, Leonard Perrin, David Maginnis and Sylvester Hatch as charter members.

"The first home of Wood County Lodge was in the second story of the home of Emelius Wood, a primitive log house which stood—and still stands—upon the bank of Tontogany creek a short distance north of the present village of Tontogany. It was an ideal location; first because it was comparatively central, and, second, you could, as a rule, get there from three different directions without swimming your horse. Being at the confluence of the two Green Encampment trails, the Perrysburg people could take the one which left the river at Miltonville, and the Gilead (Grand Rapids) people could take that which left the river a short distance east from South Otsego; then, when the five trails joined at Wood's, the combined trail went on into Plain township.

"For six years Wood County Lodge worked in the loft of Wood's dwelling, and then removed to Eaton's Corners— later known as Selkirk's Corners, now a part of the city of Bowling Green.

"Of the Gilead people who took the degrees in Wood County Lodge, the first was Alvin Gillett, father of Jay L. Gillett, of Toledo, Emanuel Arnold, John Edgar and Omar C. Carr and S. H. Steedman.

"In July, 1856, the five brethren last above mentioned, together with Emelius Wood, Everett R. Wood and Daniel Barton, also of Wood County Lodge, A. J. Gardner, of Youngstown, Selah A. Bacon, a past master of New England, No. 4, of Worthington, Ohio, and Samuel Blythe, from Steubenville Lodge, No. 45, petitioned and received a dispensation for a lodge, to be known as Grand Rapids Lodge, and to be located at Gilead (Grand Rapids), Wood County. The dispensation arrived July 31, naming S. A. Bacon as the first senior warden and Alvin Gillett as first junior warden.

"The charter was received November 4, 1856, bearing date of October 3, and naming S. A. Bacon, A. J. Gardner, Alvin Gillett, Emelius Wood, E. R. Wood, John P. Nye and Samuel Blythe charter members. The three stationed officers were named as in the dispensation, and the minor officers also held over. The officers were installed by R. W. Bro. Hez. L. Hosmer, of Toledo. He was a prime mover in the organization of Phoenix Lodge No. 123, of Perrysburg, of Fort Meigs chapter, and of all the Toledo bodies up to 1862, when he was appointed chief justice for Montana territory, and it is of record that he gathered together the Masons of that vast territory and instituted lodge, chapter and council at Virginia City.

"Speaking of individual Masons, the two pastmasters, who were prime movers in the organization of Grand Rapids Lodge, S. A. Bacon and Emelius Wood, had a remarkable Masonic career. Mr. Bacon was born at Granby, Conn., in 1797, and received the Master's degree there in 1818; removing to Franklin county, Ohio, he affiliated with New England Lodge No. 4, and was for several years its master; removing to Henry county, half a mile west of this village, he assisted, as shown, in the organization of this lodge and was for four years its master. Mr. Bacon's death occurred in March, 1883, he being 86 years of age, and for 65 years a Master Mason. Emelius Wood was born in 1797, and is said to have been the third white child born in the old fort at Marietta. He was educated at Athens and received the degrees in Paramuthia No. 25, in 1818; later he went to Somerset, the then county seat of the new county of Perry, where he served as county surveyor for some twelve years. His wife dying in 1833, he removed in 1834, with his two sons, A. J. and E. R., to Wood county, and settled on the bank of Tontogany creek, as we have mentioned. Here he married a Miss North, and a number of children were born, the eldest being the well known surveyor, William H. Wood, of Bowling Green. Brother Wood was a principal mover in the organization of Wood County Lodge, was its master in 1847, 1848 and 1855. He was the first justice and the first school examiner of Washington township. He died in 1875, aged 78, having been a Master Mason for 57 years.

"Fifty years to those who are past the meridian of life seems but a brief period, and yet, looking backward, many things may happen in fifty years. In 1856 the territory of Grand Rapids Lodge extended from Fulton Lodge, Delta, on the north, to Kalida, Putnam county, on the south, and east and west from Bowling Green to Napoleon. Up to date it has given of its territory to Deshler, Holgate, Liberty Center, Waterville, Tontogany and Weston. That shows some change, but let us contemplate Wood County Lodge again for a moment; it is just 13 years older than Grand Rapids lodge. When Wood county was constituted, its territory comprised more than ten thousand square miles, figuring from door to door of nearest lodges, but to-day that territory contains 110 lodges and more than 12,000 members."

It is not an exaggerated belief that had Hull's army, which passed through the site of Bowling Green, almost a century ago, been led by a man of the nerve of Anthony Wayne, that a portion of Canada would to-day be a part of the United States. Hull's disastrous failure compelled the few settlers at the Maumee Rapids to leave and the whole northwest was opened to the merciless raids of savages. It was indeed a national calamity.

HON. THOS. W. POWELL

A Veteran Pioneer Lawyer, at One Time Identified with Wood County History

DECEMBER 12, 1882, says the Cleveland Herald, Hon. Thomas W. Powell died at his residence in Delaware, at the advanced age of eighty-five years. For several years he had been almost blind. His name stands foremost as one of the greatest thinkers of the State. The following history was given by Hon. James R. Hubble:

Hon. Thomas W. Powell was born in South Wales in 1797. In 1801 he came with his parents to America and settled in Utica, N. Y., in the Mohawk Valley. During the war with Great Britain, although a mere youth, he drove his father's team with the baggage of a regiment, to Sacketts Harbor, and in the spring of 1813 entered the place at the close of the battle. In 1814 he was appointed by the military authorities to carry dispatches to Plattsburg, and at the close of that battle entered the town with dispatches to Gen. McCombs.

In the year 1819 he came to Ohio and studied law in the office of Hon. James W. Lathrop, at Canton, and in 1820 was admitted to the bar. He removed to Perrysburg, on the Maumee, where he filled successively the offices of Prosecuting Attorney and County Auditor of Wood county.

In the discharge of his official duties, he was noted for his probity and industry as well as his abilities. In 1830 he removed to Delaware, where he resided until his death.

INDIAN JUSTICE

How a Chief Carried Out the Law of His Tribe

ONEQUIT, a chief of a tribe of Indians that occupied Station Island above Waterville, proved to be judge and executioner, as the following incident will show, as related by an early settler:

An Indian, who had been guilty of some crime, was brought before Onequit for trial. The cause was duly heard with Indian solemnity, after which Onequit retired, smokng over his deliberations. The result of this deliberation was that the chief took down his rifle and shot and killed the convicted red man.

Onequit himself was then brought before a magistrate near Miltonville to answer for the crime of murder. The chief admitted the killing of the Indian, but claimed that he had acted only within the laws of his tribe. On this showing he was acquitted and released.

NOTABLE ADDRESSES

From Two Commanders That Thrilled the Soldiers With Enthusiasm

GEN. CLAY and his Kentuckians were at Ft. Defiance in April, 1813, having followed in Gen. Winchester's footsteps, and when he closed a ringing denunciation of the British treachery at the River Raisin, his men were ready for action. Said their general: "Kentuckians stand high in the estimation of our common country. Our brothers in arms who have gone before us to the scene of action have acquired a fame which should never be forgotten by you, a fame worthy of your emulation. Should we encounter the enemy, *remember the fate*

GEN. WM. H. HARRISON

of your butchered brothers at the River Raisin—that British treachery produced their slaughter." And the Kentuckians remembered it.

Gen. Harrison's Address

Standing in sight of the battle field of Fallen Timber and under the severe cannonade from the British batteries across the river, Gen. Harrison thus addressed his men, some of whom had fallen wounded, and others who were fainting and tired of the conflict:

"Can the citizens of a free country, who have taken up arms to defend its rights, think of submitting to an army composed of mercenary soldiers, reluctant Canadians, goaded to the field by the bayonet, and of wretched, naked savages? Can the breast of an American soldier when he casts his eyes to the opposite shore, the scene of his country's triumphs over the same foe, be influenced by any other feeling than the hope of glory? Is not this army composed of the same materials with that which fought and conquered under the immortal Wayne? Yes, fellow soldiers, your general sees your faces beam with the same fire that he witnessed on that occasion; and although it would be the height of presumption to compare himself with that hero, he boasts of being that hero's pupil. To your posts then fellow citizens and remember the eyes of your country are upon you."

In after years in conversing with a friend about the siege of Fort Meigs, he said: "It was the greatest speech of my life."

TWO LOST GIRLS

Thrilling Episode Related by J. F. Dubbs in the Early History of the County

THE following interesting reminiscence comes from J. F. Dubbs an esteemed pioneer of Milton Center and was written by C. W. Evers:

In 1836, the old Revolutionary soldier and Missionary, Rev. Joseph Badger built a cabin and settled on a ridge at the west end of the Wadsworth prairie, overlooking the great marsh, stretching out miles to the eastward. When, a few years after his health failed and he moved his family away, the vacant cabin became a sort of rendezvous for counterfeiters, and other law-breakers. They were finally broken up and driven away.

In 1851, Nathaniel Badger, nephew of the old missionary, came and fixed up the cabin, got married and lived there a year or so. Nathaniel had a sister Stella, a teacher, who lived in Plain township. One bright morning in June, Stella and a lady cousin from "York State," nicely mounted on horseback, rode up to our cabin, on the north side of the prairie to inquire if it would be possible for them to follow the old Indian trail straight across to the Badger cabin. I was a young man at that time and far too much interested in the two nicely dressed young ladies to see them try to pass over that dangerous miry trail, and at once advised them to go around by the usual wagon trail, which was of itself bad enough; they took my advice.

That evening my brothers, Lewis and John, W. R. Carothers and myself were chatting around a mosquito smoke at my father's, when, about 9 o'clock we heard some one hallooing in the distance. I told the boys of the incident of the morning—that two girls had rode over to Badger's, which was about two miles from our place. Carothers at once said, "that is surely a woman's voice"; we started at once for the prairie, taking with us our two well trained dogs.

When we got through the woods to the prairie we could hear the cries, but very indistinctly, away to the east of us; we shouted so lustily that we made ourselves heard plainly by the lost wanderer, who at once turned back toward us.

Soon the dogs were barking, away out in the gloomy waste in a somewhat different direction. When Lewis and Carothers got to them, they found the intelligent brutes had done their part well and faithfully. As if guided by some instinct, almost providential, in this case, the dogs in some unexplained, or I should say unexplainable way, had understood what we wanted them to do and had done it, thereby saving a human life.

There, in a grassless spot, in the oozy mire and water, her head barely above the slimy surface, speechless and exhausted, was one of the girls—the one from New York. She probably could not have survived an hour longer. I need not relate our difficulties in getting the poor girl out for she was perfectly helpless to walk for sometime, even if she had been on good ground.

Soon after, Stella, whose shouts had first warned us of their danger, was found, and not long after, brother John and I and the dogs found the horses, grazing in a place where the water was shallow, and got them out to the woods. Stella then told us how it all happened: They had prolonged their stay at Badger's until quite late and then to gain time had attempted to make a short cut by the Indian trail to our house. The trail crossed a neck of prairie about half a mile wide; it was here they lost their course and went too far east. The prairie, at that time of the year, was wet in those days; no one who has not seen the Wadsworth, or Liberty prairie as we sometimes called it, in its natural state, before our drainage system went into effect, can form any true conception of its condition, nor picture to himself the magnitude of the change since. The water was from one to three feet deep, the grass from three to eight feet high;

a great part of the prairie was swampy. It was infested with all sorts of beasts, birds and reptiles common to this country at that time. Wolves, snakes, turtles, frogs, cranes, pumpers, deer flies and last, but worst in early summer, were the endless swarms of ravenous mosquitoes. Then the heavy fogs which curtained this gloomy wilderness made the aspect so dismal and forbidding that the strongest man might well recoil from its treacherous borders.

Not long after the horses left the trail, they began to swamp down and the riders were unseated from their saddles with no possibility of mounting, even if it had been desirable to do so. In attempting to lead the horses the girls had their skirts trod on and torn off at the waist and were in danger themselves of being tramped into the mire by the floundering animals.

By this time they had worked so far east as to be in about the worst part of the swamp, probably not far west of the notorious "Stoga Hole." Here the New York girl gave up to die. Stella left her friend and the horses and started as she supposed in the direction of her brother's cabin; but how could a woman, wading in water to her knees, in coarse rank grass higher than her head, blinded by mosquitoes and fog, take a course without a single landmark to guide her? She could not even see the woods that bordered the swamp. Fortunately she steered to the woods on the north side, but in a direction almost opposite from what she had intended, and came out about three-fourths of a mile from our house, where she was wandering about when her screams attracted our attention as previously mentioned. After we all got together on dry ground, the girls, whose deplorable plight was mercifully shielded by the darkness, pleaded with us to be taken to the Badger cabin, but we persuaded them to go to our house nearer by, where they were taken in hand by the women, made as comfortable as possible, and next morning were able to continue their journey home.

One of those girls of nearly half a century ago, Stella, married Dr. Stephen Olney, brother of Professor Edward Olney, of Michigan university, and at this time, 1894, is living in widowhood in one of the thriving cities of New Jersey. Her rosy cheeks of yore are faded; her dark hair long since has turned gray; the voice that was strong enough to carry its pitiful appeal through the Cimmerian darkness for help nearly a mile away, is feeble now; memory too fails, but not the remembrance of that dreadful night experience in the "Black Swamp" of Wood county.

In thus imperfectly giving the details of this and other incidents, I have sought to also convey to the younger generation a dim, outline picture of the country as the pioneers first found it; also some of the inconveniences and hardships met with. Each passing day and year in our lives has its sore trials, mingled with its sunshine and joy. Each country has its drawbacks, but I think now, in looking back over my three score years' experience, and that of my old neighbors here, that Wood county's early settlers had more than their full share of trials. The county was too, from causes only slightly alluded to in this narration, in very bad repute. This bad name followed it hurtfully for years after, and kept improvements back until many fell, weary and discouraged in the conflict. But all honor to the old pioneers, and the new ones too; it is different now. Wood county is, at last, the first; and the miry swamp, where we found the lost girls, groans each recurring autumn under its load of golden grain; and the successors of those first pioneers would hesitate to swap situations with the most favored husbandmen in the land.

THE OLD EXCHANGE BELL

Something of Its History and What Became of It

A CORRESPONDENT of the Elmore Independent says that in the year 1832 or 1833, Mr. Jarvis Spafford built a hotel in Perrysburg, and it was a very fine hotel—even a model one in those days. In order to make it complete he had to have a bell on top of the house. There happened to be a man by the name of S. Davis who had a bell foundry in Detroit, Mich., then Michigan Territory. Mr. Spafford went to Detroit, saw Mr. Davis and made a contract to cast him a tavern bell. For want of material to make a bell of the desired size, Mr. Spafford put in 36 Spanish dollars, which were melted and run into the bell. In the year 1834 the bell was cast; the name of S. Davis, Detroit, Michigan Territory, and the year, in large, bold letters, appear on the bell. After due time Mr. Spafford got the bell home, and it was a great curiosity there in the wilderness, the whole country abounding with Indians and wild animals. However, Mr. Spafford had the bell hung up in a tree in front of his house, to ring when it was time for meals.

The Indians used to gather around the tree to see and hear the bell ring; they would even climb up on the tree to get hold of it to ring it themselves, to the great annoyance of Mr. Spafford and his customers, as they supposed meals were ready when the bell rang. This annoyed Mr. Spafford so much that he was compelled to drive the Indians away by force, but they, not being easily scared, came one night and stole the bell and carried it off to Upper Sandusky, which was the headquarters for all the Indians in this section of the country in those days. When Mr. Spafford missed the bell he was much worried, and offered a big reward for the thief and return of his property.

As the bell cost him $75, he felt the loss of his investment, as well as the enjoyment and convenience of it, but he was not long in finding the trail of the bell from friendly Indians. He secured the services of a half-breed, by the name of Sam Brady, an old scout, who had killed as many Indians and some white men, as any other man in those days. Mr. Frank Hollister, the first white man who settled at Perrysburg, and bought furs from the Indians, knew about all of them, and had slept in almost every Indian wigwam on the Maumee river. The three started in search of the bell, and were three days making the trip from Perrysburg to the plains of Upper Sandusky, camping out every night, with Sam Brady to pilot them through. On the morning of the fourth day, to their great surprise, they heard the sound of the bell, and leaving their camp with their scanty breakfast half cooked, they struck out fully determined to get the bell. After half an hour's traveling through the deep grass and thick underbrush, with rifle in hand to shoot the first Indian they met, they came to the missing bell. To their great amazement they found it tied around an Indian pony's neck, which was considered the leading pony of the plains. Mr. Spafford says that it did not take Mr. Brady long to bring down the pony with his rifle, cut the sinew that the bell was fastened to, and soon shouldered it and started back to camp, to finish their breakfast of jerked venison and whisky.

After finishing the meal, they started back for home, a happy trio. In the meantime they kept a sharp lookout on their retreat, but met with no interruption, and arrived home safe and whole, but worn out by fatigue and hunger, still full of glee and "good whisky."

Mr. Spafford, in order to keep the Indians from stealing the bell again, went to Detroit to a blacksmith, and got a heavy iron bar, one inch square, made in a half circle, with a cross-bar, and hung the bell in the circle, spiked it on top of his tavern, and the bell hung there until the death of Jarvis Spafford, and for several years after. The property then fell into the hands of Willis Norton, sheriff of Wood county, and for a number of years he kept the house and bell. Finally the hotel business died out and Mr. Norton had a good deal of sickness and reverses and left Perrysburg, went west of Ft. Wayne, on a small farm, taking the bell with him, with the full intention of keeping it as long as he lived, but his health failed him, necessaries of life were hard to get, and getting an offer for the old bell from the oldest landlord in northern Ohio, who knew the bell ever since it was hung upon the old Exchange, he concluded to sell it to his old friend, D. M. Day, of Elmore, Ottawa county, O., where it can be seen and heard three times a day, on top of the Elmore House.

GEORGE HOPPER

His Experience with Hardships and Wolves in Early Years

GEORGE HOPPER, an early settler, died at his home in Troy township, February 7, 1879. He came to this country from England, and reached Perrysburg in the year 1836, engaging in the service of the firm of Smith & Hollister in their large warehouse. He remained with them three years, at the end of which time he took 160 acres of land in Troy township for his pay, on which he made his home until his death.

Mr. Hopper and his wife, like most of

SCRAP-BOOK.

the people of that date in Wood county, had to put up with hardships and inconveniences, which to this generation of people would seem unbearable. Mr. and Mrs. Hopper related as a fact that during their first settlement in the woods and for years after, they seldom passed a night without being disturbed by the unwelcome and dismal howl of wolves. Sometimes these ravenous brutes would come into their door yard and make the night a hideous pandemonium. On one occasion Mr. Hopper had been to Perrysburg to get some provisions and was belated and came home unconscious that he was pursued until he entered his cabin door, when he heard the brutes jumping the fence, and no sooner had he closed the door behind him than they opened in an unearthly chorus, startling enough to make a dead man's hair stand on end. This sort of solitary life was continued until 1847, when Samuel Shreiner moved in, he being their first neighbor nearer than the Gorrills. In all his obligations of citizenship Mr. Hopper was a model man, upright and honest, and commanded the respect and esteem of his neighbors and all who knew him.—*Wood County Sentinel.*

A SHAKING SCOURGE

Chills, Fever and Ague the Result of Malaria of the Black Swamp

NOT the least of the ills encountered by the early settlers in the Black Swamp, was the scourge of sickness, chiefly fever and ague, which widely prevailed. These ills were caused by the malaria of that day.

It took from three to five years to get acclimated; every year from about the first of July until frost and cold made its appearance, the people had the ague, and they looked for it just as much, and it came with the same regularity, as summer and fall came. An old pioneer says: It took hold of a person and literally shook him up. I have seen fellows go to bed with the ague, and when the shake came on the very bed and floor would rattle. So violent was the disease that at times their teeth would rattle.

Many times whole families would be down at one time, so that one could not give another a drink of water. The ague usually came on every other day, and when there were not people enough they had to have it every day, for sometimes there appeared to be about two agues for one man; and oftentimes they had to have it twice in one day. The well day as we used to call the day we missed it, men would be able to do some light work, and it may seem strange, but the day the chill was to come on you could look out from 10 a. m. until 2 p. m., and you could see the boys come in to take their shake, as much so as to take their dinners. We were not troubled much in those days from any disease of a malignant form. Aside from the ague, we had some bilious, intermittent and remittent fevers. We had no need of a doctor to bleed the patient, for the pesky mosquitoes did all the bleeding that was necessary.

Dr. H. Burritt was the physician; he then lived at Gilead (now Grand Rapids), and he also kept the postoffice. Oh, how he used to swear when he had to make his way through the woods and water, ten, twelve or fifteen miles to see his patients.

The Maumee Valley Historical Association was organized in 1885 for the purpose of perpetuating the memory and preserving the historical places in the Maumee Valley. Hon. Morrison R. Waite was its first president.

WHAT MIGHT HAVE BEEN

If the Fulton Line Between Ohio and Michigan Had Been Fixed

COLONEL JOHN A. SHANNON indulged in the following probability of Perrysburg's future:
In 1835 was fought the great "Toledo War." Gen. Bell, Gen. Brown, Col. Van Fleet and many others in and out of command of the forces of the state of Ohio, and the territory of Michigan, marched and counter marched their respective commands, and performed feats of valor and strategy which entitle them to a more extended notice than in the limits of this history can be accorded them. The net purport and upshot of the matter was, that the Harris, or present line, between the state of Ohio and the territory of Michigan, was adopted. This left Toledo in the state of Ohio, and lost to Perrysburg the only opportunity she ever had of becoming ultimately a great commercial center.

With Toledo in Michigan, Ohio would have been interested in building up Perrysburg, and it is probable at least, that some effort would have been made to remove the obstructions to navigation, known to exist between Toledo and Perrysburg, and that the fostering care of the state of Ohio would have accomplished for Perrysburg what the state of Michigan afterward accomplished for Detroit, under similar difficulties. It is probably vain to theorize over this matter now, but it certainly does not seem improbable that if the Fulton or southern line, between Ohio and Michigan had been finally adopted, that Perrysburg would have been now a compactly built city, from East Toledo to West Boundary street, with miles of wharves and docks, acres of elevators and depots, and tens of millions instead of tens of thousands of dollars of personal property.

BLOODY WOLF FIGHT

In Which the Dogs Were Badly Used Up by the Vicious Animal

AN issue of the Wood County Sentinel in August, 1877, relates an incident of a black wolf killed a few days prior to that by three dogs near Mr. Willison's house in Jackson Prairie. A steer had died not far from Willison's place a day or so previous, and late in the evening mentioned, Mr. W. heard dogs fighting as he supposed, until finally he became satisfied from the continued barking and fierce growls that the dogs, his own among the number, had some animal at bay. He did not go out however, that night. Next morning Jake Wall's dog was found to be so badly chewed up that he died that day. The other dogs were found to be pretty badly used up also. Not far from the carcass of the steer, the dead body of a wolf was found, a murderous looking brute, and near him were plenty of evidences of a terrible fight between the black monster and the dogs. It is supposed that Wall's dog, which was a gamy, powerful creature, after getting terribly punished by the wolf, had finally got hold of its throat and never let go till he had choked it to death. This is the first wolf killed in this county for several years, and the second instance of the destruction of a black wolf, and the only instance we ever heard of dogs in open battle attacking and killing a full grown wolf. It is supposed there were two wolves, but that the other got away. They usually travel in pairs.

"THE DEVIL'S HOLE"

An Almost Impenetrable Bog—What Was the Origin of the Name? Is It a Den?

A WEBSTER township correspondent wrote the Perrysburg Journal as follows:

"During the year 1813 or '14 a period when the Black Swamp was yet a 'howling wilderness,' well covered by water and occupied by Indians, wolves, bears, raccoons and wildcats, there was a low, wet swampy bog, extending from a portion of Wood county where the Fenton P. O., now is, to a point in Middleton, lately known as the Devil's Hole Prairie —it being a portion of country exceedingly difficult to penetrate owing to the depth of water and massive growth of timber, through which were numerous windfalls that served to render the progress of the pedestrian very difficult and quite uncertain.

"At the time mentioned Gen. Harrison came plunging through the wilds of Sandusky and Wood counties on his march to Fort Meigs, and while passing through the portion of Wood county near where this swamp was located, a scout, whose name the writer is not in possession of, while on the alert for the terror of the forest—the noble red man—became entangled in this man-trap, and only after a day's persistent effort did he succeed in finding the trail of his brave commander, after which he soon caught up with the command. Upon being interrogated as to where he had been, he replied that he had got lost in the "Devil's Hole," asserting that he had truly discovered the home of Satan, and in this trifling manner (although undoubtedly appreciated at the time) originated the name so long attached to what is now one of the most prosperous and prolific portions of this county; a locality that has outgrown its bad name; that has been changed from a dreary wilderness to an enterprising farming community."

The late Mr. C. W. Evers, however, claimed that the name was first given to that locality by the late Mahlon Meeker.

Is It a Den?

The Sentinel, in an issue in September, 1872, indicates that the place may have been used by a band of marauders. It says:

Buried in the heart of the dense woods some miles to the northeast of this place, known as the "Devil's Hole," two men recently discovered a small, low built shanty, covered with bark and entirely obscure from the vision of man or beast by the dense undergrowth, at no greater distance than ten paces. It is off from any road and there is a single path leading to and from it. Just behind it a hole has been dug for water, and near it are troughs cut in a log as if for the purpose of feeding horses. Some hay inside indicates that men have slept there, and there has also been a fire kept in it. Everything about it denotes that the utmost precautions of secrecy have been taken. From its location and other circumstances, persons living nearest the locality are suspicious that it is a rendezvous or stopping place for horse-thieves. Certainly there seems some coloring for such a supposition.

It has been well said that Thomas Jefferson was more than the author of our Declaration of Independence in 1776; he, more than any American, laid down the basis of popular liberty.

There is not a city in Kentucky, there is not a place in all Ohio that did not hasten to the aid of Ft. Meigs nearly a century ago. And all these cities and towns have an abiding interest in these historic grounds.

TOM LONG

A Noted Horsethief of This Region Who Died in the Ohio Penitentiary

FROM the Blade of July 18, 1873, regarding this noted criminal, we quote the following:
Among the names of those mentioned by telegraph in Thursday evening's Blade, as having died of cholera in the penitentiary at Columbus, was that of Thomas Long, sent from Wood county. Long was a noted horsethief, and was serving out his fourth term in the penitentiary, although but just in the prime of life. Perhaps no man in the country was more familiar with the "runways" of horsethieves than he. His range was very extensive, reaching from Central Ohio through Indiana, Illinois and Iowa. It is said that he would start from his home in Wyandot county, and make a through trip to Council Bluffs, stealing horses and selling them as fast as possible. The last horse which he stole was taken from a man by the name of Wilson, living near Portage, Wood county, when he also stole a buggy from a Mr. Roller, living in Portage. This occurred in 1865. He was accompanied on this trip by his brother. The latter was first captured and taken to jail. Tom, who had escaped arrest, although hotly pursued by Sheriff Evers, learning that his brother was in jail, wrote him a letter from some point out west, stating that he would visit the imprisoned brother. This letter fell into the hands of the sheriff, and he was on the alert.

Finally, after the sheriff had about abandoned all hope of securing Tom, two men, one of them a well known citizen of Wood county, called at the jail and expressed a desire to see a prisoner. The present sheriff, Mr. C. C. Baird, was then jailor, and he at once sent for the sheriff. On the arrival of Sheriff Evers, he readily identified the stranger as Tom Long, arrested him and locked him up with his brother. Both were convicted and Tom was sentenced to the penitentiary for twelve years, while his brother got off with ten years. He had, therefore, served out but two-thirds of his time when he died.

Tom Long was a cool, sharp and cunning horsethief. He was quiet, inoffensive to all appearances, and was highly esteemed by those acquaintances who knew nothing of his secret history. With criminal law he was quite familiar and studied it even after his conviction, evidently not for a moment thinking of changing his habits on emerging from the penitentiary. With his arrest and conviction, a large gang of horsethieves was broken up, some of them escaping to Canada, and now believed to be engaged in running stolen horses across the upper end of the lake.

PORTER-RICHARDSON MURDER

Capture, Trial and Conviction of George Porter—Hung at Fort Meigs

THE death of so notorious a man as Richardson, and the sudden and violent manner of his taking off while sitting in the midst of his family, startled and shocked the dwellers by the Maumee. The news of the tragedy spread from the rapids to the lake in a few hours.

Porter, who made no concealment of what he had done, from the first announcement of the murder, seems to have been connected with the deed in the minds of the settlers in the immediate neighborhood who knew of the previous unfortunate state of business with Richardson. But as the effect of the whisky died out and reflection and reason returned, he began to realize what he had done; the instinct of fear took possession of him and he fled, he hardly knew whither nor from whom nor what. He wandered about in the forests like a restless wild beast.

Great search was made for him but without success until the third day when he came out and delivered himself up to Sheriff Webb not far from the river ford below Miltonville. He told Mr. Webb that it seemed the happiest moment of his life when he had delivered himself up and no longer felt that he was pursued. He made no denial of the murder. He said it was the only thing left for him to do to redress his grievances, and admitted that he ought to pay the penalty with his life.

He was confined in the old log jail at Perrysburg for trial. The supreme court was in session with Peter Hitchcock and Judge Brash on the bench.

The prisoner had a right to trial in the common pleas court if he preferred, which would have deferred his trial some months, but he seemed indifferent whether any defense was made at all. He became penitent and zealously religious.

The following are the names of the grand jurors impanelled, there being 16 in all instead of 15 as now, and not one of whom to our knowledge is living today, the late Eber Wilson, who was foreman, being the last survivor:

Nathaniel Jenison, Samuel Spafford, William Bigger, Eber Wilson, James Wilkinson, William Houser, Amasa Andrews, George W. Bennetts, Silas Barnes, David Mills, Hartman Loomis, Willard Gunn, John G. Forbes, Joshua Chappel, J. C. Adams, David Purdue.

Thomas W. Powell, now of Delaware. Ohio, was the prosecuting attorney, and Orish Parish and David Higgins (afterward Judge Higgins) were assigned to the defense of the prisoner. The counsel for the state had of course no difficulty in proving the murder and that George Porter was the murderer, but the counsel for the prisoner set up the plea of insanity and urged it with much vigor, adducing as the strongest evidence the conduct of the prisoner to and after the murder and his behavior in jail and indifference as to his fate. In rebuttal of this position of the defense, the state adopted the theory—(We give Powell's own language):

"That every person is responsible for his acts, whenever he acts upon actual facts and real circumstances. That all that Porter claimed as motives for his acts—the injuries and insults received from Richardson—were all founded upon actual facts and real circumstances. There was no delusion or unreal facts about this case. Whatever motives actuated him, they were like all the rational acts of mankind, founded upon real facts and actual circumstances."

The court took this view of the case and charged the jury accordingly and Porter was convicted.

The names of the jurors selected from a panel of 30 men, none of whom are now living, were as follows:

Robert Shaw, Palmer Kellogg, John M. Jaquis, Aurora Shafford, Reuben Freshwater, Elijah Huntington, Sewell Gunn, Thomas Leaming, Nathaniel Decker, Knowlton Young, Nathaniel Blinn and Andrew Hoover.

The sentence of the court was that he be hung on Friday, the 5th day of the following November. There was a great deal of public sympathy shown for Porter. He had to be sure, taken the life of a fellow man, but that man was a notoriously bad man and the deed had been done under the most provoking circumstances. Porter was crushed and broken in spirit and had no influential friends to intercede for him, a thing he was too dispirited to do for himself, even if he had his liberty. The means of communicating with the executive were long and tedious, beside there were no good grounds, assuming the court's charge to the jury to be correct, upon which to base a petition asking the clemency of the governor. Mr. Webb, a man of kind and humane disposition, formed quite a strong attachment and kindly feeling toward the prisoner on account of his reconciled and submissive conduct, and it taxed his utmost resolution of mind to reconcile sympathy and duty.

Porter was hanged on the west slope of the ravine on the east side of Old Fort Meigs in the presence of a great number of people who had assembled to witness the sad spectacle. His body was buried in the little burying ground just west of the Perrysburg jail.

Whatever may have been the sympathy for Porter, or however much his claim to executive clemency, the execution no doubt had a salutary effect. Nothing is so much calculated to restrain crime as the certainty that punishment and the inexorable execution of the law will follow.
—*C. W. E.*

SIMON GIRTY

Something of the History of That Daring, Treacherous Outlaw

FROM the columns of a copy of the old Toledo Commercial, we clip the following:

There are few localities in the State of Ohio more fertile in historic reminiscences than Henry county. About five miles up the river from Napoleon is what is known as Girty's island, so called from the fact of its having been the abiding place of that notorious white renegade, Simon Girty, whose treatment of white captives was more inhuman and fiendish than even that of the red savages by whom he had been reared from early childhood. The history of Simon Girty is familiar, no doubt, to thousands, but there are features in the family record of the Girty family that always afford fresh food for conjecture. The family in general was shiftless and ne'er do well. There were four brothers, Thomas, Simon, George and James. Each was adopted by an Indian tribe, Simon by the Senecas, the most warlike of all the great Iroquois confederacy.

Simon Girty and Simon Kenton were at one time scouts together, and perhaps the only humane or kindly act in Girty's life was his intercession for Kenton's life in one instance where he had been captured, tortured and sentenced to death by the Indians. Girty, however, after having in every conceivable manner antagonized both Indians and whites by his multiplicity of inhuman and treacherous acts, was compelled to seek refuge and concealment in the territory now embraced in what is known as Henry county. He had wantonly and indiscriminately murdered and pillaged right and left until he became a hunted fugitive, a veritable wanderer on the face of the earth. He eventually sought safety in the famous "Black Swamp" of the northwest, and here opposite the island, on the bank of the Maumee, he erected his cabin, and whenever danger would menace him, would retire into the densely wooded swamp, where it was absolutely impossible to dislodge him. How long he remained here, is not definitely known, or whether his death was the result of the infirmities incident to old age, or more tragic in its character. He was unquestionably one of the boldest and at the same time most treacherous and inhuman outlaws of which American history has any record.

SCRAP-BOOK.

WAYNE'S TWO GRAVES

Mad Anthony Wayne's Burial Places—Story of His Bones

THE Buffalo Express gives the following remarkable incident touching the disposition of Mad Anthony's body: Gen. Wayne is one of the few famous men who have two graves, each equally entitled to commemoration. He died of gout at Erie, Pa., then Fort Presque Isle, in 1796, when he was on his return from his successful Indian campaigns in the northwest. He was buried at the foot of the flagstaff in the fort, and there lay undisturbed for nearly twenty years. Then there came through the woods from the other end of the State, in a sulky, his son in search of his father's bones. He engaged Dr. John C. Wallace, who had been through the Indian wars with Gen. Wayne, to exhume his bones, and pack them in a box, that they might be strapped to the sulky and taken through the woods and over the mountains to the family residence in Chester county. When Dr. Wallace opened the grave he found, to his great surprise, the body in an almost perfect state of preservation. The flesh had not decayed. But it was impossible for young Wayne to carry the coffin and contents in his sulky. So Dr. Wallace, who seems to have been devoid of feeling as one of the Indians whom he fought, decided, on his own motion, and without consulting Mr. Wayne, to separate the General's bones from their enveloping flesh and thus enable them to be removed.

To accomplish this, boiling had to be resorted to, and the bones were then denuded of flesh by the use of knives, and were packed and carried away by young Wayne, and buried near the homestead in which Gen. Wayne was born and in which his descendants still live. This account of the ghoul-like proceedings of Dr. Wallace has an incredible sound, but it is literally and strictly true, and will be corroborated by any old citizen of Erie. Young Mr. Wayne knew nothing of Dr. Wallace's operations until many years after. He was then greatly shocked and declared that he would never have permitted such treatment of his father's remains, but would have returned them to the grave and postponed their removal to a more convenient season. Yet there is no reason to doubt that Dr. Wallace, who was a useful and prominent man in his day, thought he was doing everything for the best, and meant no disrespect to the mortal part of his old friend and patient and army comrade, General Wayne.

Over the General's bones, in Chester county, a monument was raised. But his flesh was returned to its grave at the foot of the flag-staff, in Fort Presque Isle, by Dr. Wallace, and forgotten. The fort—a mere stockade—crumbled away, the flag-staff decayed, and the precise location of the grave was lost.

Some four years ago, however, a digger for relics on the site of the old fort, unearthed a coffin-cover, into which brass-headed nails had been so driven as to form the initials "A. W." with the figures of Wayne's age, date of his death, etc. This determined the location of the grave, and there has since been in Erie a feeling that it should be marked by a monument of some sort. It has, in fact been surrounded by chains, supported by four pieces of superannuated artillery, and also marked by a flag-staff, but something more permanent is desired, and will doubtless be built—if not by legislative aid, then by local subscription.

The last tribe of Indians to remove from Ohio was the Wyandot of Upper-Sandusky, who ceded their lands in 1842, and the following year left for the west.

BURNING OFF A PRAIRIE

How the Flames Swept the Grass for Many Miles

HERE is an incident in Middleton township history published in the Sentinel in 1883:

James Robertson came from Scotland and located in the eastern part of Middleton township in 1836. One morning after he had selected the land for his future home, Mr. Robertson and two of his sons started from Perrysburg for their land for the purpose of selecting a building site, with a horse and wagon, hauling a tent and some other material. They came by a blazed wagon track and pitched their tent in the edge of Hull's Prairie, arriving just at sundown. About 15 minutes after they had arrived at their destination they were startled by the sudden appearance of five Indians on horseback, who had followed up their trail, and the Indians seemed as much surprised as they. After surveying the situation a moment the Indians gave the Robertsons to understand their mission was to "scotto," that is to burn off the prairie. They then proceeded about three miles to the southwest, touched fire to the grass which had not been burned for two years. The flames spread like the wind and Mr. Amelius Robertson states that it did not seem over ten minutes before it had traveled the intervening distance between where it was set and the edge of the woods where they were encamped, and that the smoke almost suffocated them in their tent. He also says that the flames went nearly as high as the trees, and that the streets of Perrysburg 5 1-2 miles distant were so lighted by the fire that they could see to pick up a pin, and that all the grass on Hull Prairie covering hundreds of acres, was licked up by the flames in twenty minutes. Mr. Robertson built a cabin on his land the next spring, 1837, and moved in with his family.

A HUNTER'S PARADISE

Forests of the Black Swamp Abounded in Game—How a Savage Old Boar Was Captured

IN a communication to the Tribune, Mr. J. F. Dubbs says:

Wild hogs were very plentiful in the forests, but while they afforded the settlers a temporary resource at times, to replenish the pork barrel, they were at other times not only troublesome, but dangerous neighbors. They would mingle with tame hogs in the woods and toll them away often, where the tame ones would soon be as wild as their forest kin. Then too, if man or beast should suddenly come upon a band and disturb them in their bed or disturb the young, every hog would instantly become a savage, bristling, furious assailant and the intruder was lucky if he happened to be near a tree which he could climb quickly. Among the bands that roamed the woods was one enormous

Savage Old Boar

With murderous tusks, which was alike a terror to hunters and dogs. This dangerous brute—a veritable king of the forests—was as wily and cunning as a bear, but like all kings and rulers, all his ways were not the paths of wisdom. He got a notion of slipping in nights and lodging with the Dubbs herd till the chickens crowed in the morning, when he would rise, shake himself and join his wild brethren in the forest.

The Dubbs discovered what was going

on, and at the time there was quite a strife in the settlement as to who should be the lucky captor of the big boar. One morning the Dubbs, father and sons, with their two dogs, stole a march on the old woods patriarch, and as he passed out the dogs were turned loose, and after a sharp race his hogship came to bay and faced the dogs. When the men came up the brute again fled, but the dogs at once fastened on him; one dog laid hold at the elbow of the fore shoulder; the other at the ear; the latter was instantly hurled into the air with a ghastly slash across its throat from which the blood poured in a stream. The other dog, a powerful fellow, was able to stop the boar, and the brute could not reach him with its deadly tusks.

Neatly Captured

By this time, Henry Dubbs, James' father, a stout resolute man, came up, furious at the fate of his faithful dog, and seized the boar by its long tail and at once took a turn around a small sapling where he could easily hold the hog. The plan was to capture, confine and feed the boar until he was fat; at that time Mr. Dubbs' son, John, came up, the hog was tied and thrown, his nose lashed, his tusks cut off, after which he was hauled in on a stone boat, and imprisoned in a high, strong log pen.

When he found he could not escape, his gnashing of teeth and hideous aspect was startling to witness, but in all the scrap from first to last not a cry or squeal did he make, except enraged grunts. For days the old fellow would not eat; then he would eat in the night. At last he began to gain, and though when butchered and sold at Perrysburg he was not fat, yet he was a monstrous big porker.

These wild hogs are supposed to have sprung from strays from some of the army quartermasters' droves brought here in the war of 1812. They were quite numerous here from 1830 to 1842.

REMOVING THE INDIANS

Gathered from Many Points—Mission Station on the Maumee River

AN old pioneer, writing to the Sentinel, says:

Between the years 1835-40, the Government began to move the Indians to their reservations in the West and the tribes becoming broken up, were scattered over a large portion of Northwestern Ohio and Northeastern Indiana, and part of Michigan, reaching from Ft. Wayne, Indiana, to Sandusky, Ohio, and including Crawford county, which was named after Colonel Crawford who was so brutally butchered and murdered at the stake by Simon Girty (a white man), after having been deserted and left by General Knight, who made his escape and left Colonel Crawford to suffer because of his, Knight's, treachery.

The tribes and parts of tribes that used to inhabit this part of the country, were the Ottawas, Pottawatomies, Kickapoos, Shawnees, Wyandots and Miamis. After General Harrison's victory at Fort Meigs, and the treaty was effected and peace was declared again, many of them remained and they were considered friendly, and indeed were so as the old settlers well know. A mission station was made on the Maumee river; Rev. Isaac Van Tassel was sent as a missionary to preach to them, and I believe he taught school among them for a while. The largest settlement as I remember, was in Sandusky county, and the largest in Wood county was at the station and at Tontogany, which is an Indian name and I think named after one of their chiefs. They had one small settlement on Beaver creek in Henry county, and a few stragglers were camped for a while in Milton township, this county. In the fall they would go from their camps in Sandusky, Seneca and Wyandot counties, to Wood and Henry counties to camp out for the winter and hunt, and when the spring would open they would return again with their pelts and furs taken during the winter season. In the summer they would resort to the rivers and lakes where they could fish, that being their favorite and principal diet during the summer months.

H. L. Hosmer's Account

The remnant of the Maumee Ottawas were at this time assembled at Buttonwood island, a mile above Perrysburg, preparatory to removal to the country assigned them west of the Mississippi. Robert A. Forsyth was entrusted by the Government with the undertaking. The Indians made a pleasant camp on the island for a month or more, and were visited daily by the citizens of the towns below. They had been sadly demoralized by intercourse with the whites; but a few of their chiefs and leaders retained enough of the old ancestral spirit to inspire them with considerable energy and enterprise after they were settled in their new home. Ottoca, the head chief, was a fat, good-natured fellow, a favorite with his tribe and very social with the whites. His half-brother, Noteno, was greatly his superior in executive ability, and at this time probably the most intelligent man among them. Petonguet, a tall, slender graceful man, with features of a Roman cast had been the hero of a tragedy some years before in the neighborhood of Roche de Boeuf. He was much esteemed for bravery and very popular with his tribe. But a hundred in all remained of this once powerful people, and they were "like strangers in a desert home." A day or two after the tornado, Ottoca, while passing the ruins of the hotel, remarked, with significant gesticulation:

"White man's shanty—no good—too big—he all whish when the big wind come."

After their removal these Indians abandoned their habits of savage life, engaged in agriculture, adopted civilized customs, and became a substantial, orderly community. They accumulated property, erected schools and churches, and to-day I believe they are regarded by the people of Kansas as among their most quiet, law-abiding citizens. Rev. Peter Jones was their leading clergyman, and he was a lineal descendant of Pontiac, who little more than a century before was King of all the country from the Maumee to Mackinaw, and disputed inch by inch its settlement by the whites.

NAVIGATION

Ship Building at an Early Date on the River at Maumee and Perrysburg

AT a Pioneers' meeting held at Fort Meigs, in 1880, Charles E. Bliven gave an address, from which we glean the following facts regarding ship building on the Maumee river. He says: A small steamer, called the Phenomenon, remodeled from a canal boat, was built at Rochester, N. Y., in 1834, and brought to the Maumee river, being towed through Lake Erie in 1836. She was then called the Sun and was commanded by Capt. C. K. Bennett.

Old records reveal the fact that many vessels were built on the Maumee river. Among them the Detroit, 240 tons, was

BURIAL GROUND OF COL. DUDLEY AND HIS MEN

On May 11, 1813, the Bodies of Col. Dudley and About 130 Kentuckians Were Brought to Ft. Meigs and There Buried. They Were Massacred Six Days Before

SCRAP-BOOK.

built at Toledo in 1834; Don Quixote, 80 tons, in 1836; Indiana, 434 tons, in 1839. At Delaware creek, the Chesapeake, 410 tons, in 1838.

At Maumee vessels were built as follows: Miami, in 1838; Gen. Harrison, 293 tons, in 1839; James Wolcott, 80 tons, in 1840; St. Troy, 547 tons, in 1845; G. P. Griffith, 587 tons, in 1846; Albion, 132 tons, in 1848; Minnesota, 749 tons, in 1851-2; Globe, 380 tons, in 1843.

At Perrysburg the following were built: Commodore Perry, 382 tons, in 1834; Anthony Wayne, 390 tons, in 1837; Wabash, 44 tons, and Marshall, 51 tons, in 1838; Gen. Vance, 75 tons, in 1839; St. Louis, 618 tons, in 1844; Superior, 507 tons, in 1845; John Hollister, 300 tons, in 1848; Samson, the first propeller built on Lake Erie, 250 tons, in 1842; Princeton, in 1854, and the Maumee Valley, in 1862-3, which was the last vessel built there.

The Griffith, built at Perrysburg, it will be remembered by our older citizens, was destroyed by fire on the lake, and a number of her passengers perished in the disaster.

FREEDOM TOWNSHIP

Names of Early Settlers—Township Organized and Named by Hiram Pember

IN the year 1833, Isaac Cable and his three sons, Silas, Benjamin and Jonathan, also Michael Miller and Michael Myers, from near Canton, Stark county, Ohio, settled at New Rochester. Almost at the same time a party of settlers, among whom were Henry Nailer, Michael N. Myers, Christian Shelley, Ashael Powers, Henry Hahn, and several others came in from Lorain county and settled at Pemberville and above on the north fork of the river.

Most of the lands below the forks had been bought up by speculators, but most of the settlers at that time, could get good lands near the river at government price, $1.25 per acre. Wood county was at that time in the Delaware land district. The Pembers came the next year. James Pember had previously married the daughter of Ashael Powers, which circumstance, no doubt, was the cause of his locating in Wood county, as his father-in-law was the chief landed proprietor of what is now Pemberville.

They encountered untold hardships at first, and indeed for a long time, chills, shaking ague and intermittent fevers visited them each year, and at times there were not enough persons in the settlement to take care of the sick. But still they hoped for a better day, and kept courage and faith.

Late in the fall of 1834, there were barely enough able abodied men to raise a log school house at the Forks. At this raising, a petition was drawn up and signed, asking the commissioners for a separate township organization. Mr. Hiram Pember, who now lives in Pemberville, and whom we hope may be spared many years yet, gave the township its name.

At the following December session, the commissioners, Guy Nearing, James Wilkinson and John Pray, and John C. Spink, Auditor, heard the petition, and ordered the township set off in a separate organization, and that an election be held at the house of Michael N. Myers, the first Monday of the following April. Freedom at that time was a part of Perrysburg township. It is in date of organization, the sixth township in the county.

Troy and Montgomery townships were organized at the same time, and held their first election on the same day.— *C. W. Evers in Log Cabin Sketches.*

AN ATHLETE

Battered Badly by a Mob of Stalwart and Ruffian Irishmen

UNCLE GUY NEARING took a subcontract from Contractor Beebe, on the Miami and Erie Canal. Contractor Beebe drew the money and appropriated it to his own use. He failed to pay Nearing, who was thereby ruined, having mortgaged his property. While his canal work was going on he became involved in a difficulty with some of the canal men, and while passing up the river with a team he was attacked by seven Irishmen with clubs. He whipped five of them, but had seven of his ribs broken and dislocated from the backbone, from the effects of which he died about a year after, in 1840. Before being taken down with the fever at Providence, he had made great preparation to take part in the big Harrison gathering at Fort Meigs. He had a buckeye log cut on Girty's Island above Napoleon. The log was of large size and 50 feet long, which he sent to Fort Meigs.

BITTEN BY A SNAKE

After a Physician's Failure the Victim Cured by an Indiam

IN the year 1820, Anthony Ewing, a young lad, was bitten by a snake, and was badly poisoned. Doctor Conant of Maumee, was sent for, who came up to Waterville, and called for a guide to take him across the river over the Rapids. Noah Reed, then a boy, mounted a pony and brought the Doctor over. The boy was most terribly swollen and spotted, and Dr. Conant failed to give any relief. About this time an old Indian came over from the Indian village opposite. The Indian proposed to cure the lad for a gallon of whisky, and his proposition was readily agreed to. The Indian soon began to gather some herbs, and administered his restorative to the boy. The cure was a success. But the Indian concealed his operations in effecting the cure from the white medicine man. Dr. Conant afterwards gave the Indian three gallons of whisky for his recipe.

THE MAUMEE RIVER

The Grand and Picturesque Stream Not What It Once Was

THE glory of the Maumee with its pirogues, boatmen and fur traders; its Indian hunters and trappers with their canoes, peltries, pappooses and squaws, is a thing of the past. Even the sturgeon, muscalonge and ponderous catfish of other days are gone, and the waters of the old river, whose name is rich in Indian romance and historic lore—on whose banks the honor of our nation's flag and the fate of the great northwest hung in the balance, amid the clash of arms and roar of cannon, is now polluted and muddy from vast black alluvial deposits sent in by the interminable cordon and net work of artificial water courses and ditches tributary to its channel. It is no longer its natural self. It is a destructive, raging, mad torrent to-day; to-morrow its naked rocks and unsightly, slimy bed scarce deserve the name of river.

Its primitive glory has gone and the recollections of the river, as our fathers saw it, survive only as a memory.—*C. W. E.*

SIMON KENTON

Probably No Frontiersman Had Ever Passed Through so Many Dangers

IN the editorial correspondence of the Sentinel in June, 1876, we find the following from Rush Sylvania:

Not far from this town is Rush Lake, and not far from that is the head waters of the Scioto and Mad rivers. Near by, too, the Auglaize, the head source of the Maumee, starts on its tortuous course to Lake Erie. It was on a high peak on this divide where Wayne's faithful scouts lay secreted and discovered the massing of the Indian forces under Little Turtle, to crush Mad Anthony, then marching his army to the Maumee country, as he had previously done to St. Clair. The wily chieftain, however, never got an opportunity to ambush Wayne, nor ever caught him napping.

Near by, too, is the site of the old Indian town of Wappatomica, now Zanesfield, where is to be seen

The Grave of Simon Kenton

in a rude picket inclosure.
"Tread lightly! This is hallowed ground, tread reverently here!
Beneath this sod in silence sleeps the brave old pioneer
Who never quailed in darkest hour, whose heart ne'er felt a fear."

The iron nerve of this remarkable man during the soul trying adventures of 40 years' experience among hostile Indians in the wilds of Virginia, Kentucky and Ohio, would suffice for a regiment of ordinary heroes. During his captivity among the Indians, he was made to run the gauntlet eight times, and three times he was tied to the stake for torture by fire. At this very little town, Wappatomica, he was once condemned to die. His face was painted black, and he had resigned himself to his fate. He sat tied hand and foot on the ground in the council house, surrounded by his savage persecutors, a dejected, friendless being. He understood not a word of what his fiendish captors said, but knew the dreadful import of their proceedings. At that time a white man came in from a distant expedition with some scalps and learned of the preparation for the torture of a white prisoner. He addressed the prisoner in English and asked him his name. When he heard Kenton's name he fell upon his neck and cried aloud. It was the

Renegade, Simon Girty

He and Kenton had been fast friends and scouts together in the Dunmore war. The Indian warriors looked on the scene with amazement. What a theme for an artist's brush the portrayal of that scene would afford, or what a startling stage scene. Girty, who was a bloodthirsty enemy of the whites, rose to his feet, and in the most earnest appeal to the savages in behalf of the prisoner, an old friend and brother whom he had not seen for many snows, succeeded in getting up a division of sentiment and saved the life of the prisoner, though a portion of the savages were crazy mad for the torture to go on. This is the only instance recorded of Girty in which he showed mercy to a prisoner. In a few days thereafter Kenton was again condemned and sent to Sandusky for execution, but this time a British agent saved his life. It seems a little strange that the old hero should leave Kentucky in after life and settle down in the very village where his narrow escape from a horrid death occurred 40 years before. Perhaps this very fortunate escape made him regard the spot with a kindly feeling.

November 8, 1900, a monument was unveiled at Mansfield, Ohio, in honor of "Johnny Appleseed," whose unselfish character made him so true to his mission of planting nurseries and sowing the seeds of medicinal herbs in Ohio.

SHOCKING SUICIDE

How Benjamin Waite Was Mentally Unbalanced by the Possession of Too Much Money

IN one of his Log Cabin Sketches Mr. Evers relates the following:

Soon after James Pember's arrival in 1836 in Freedom township, he purchased a tract of land from a man named Benjamin Waite, paying him for it $600, which sum proved to be the only perceivable cause for the man's suicide.

No sooner had Waite become possessed of the money, than he was seized with the insane belief that he was pursued by robbers. He counted and recounted his money. He grew to distrust his wife. She was no longer a safe guardian of his pelf. Avaricious spirits and wood demons haunted his footsteps in the forests, and red-handed pirates haunted his fitful slumbers in apparitions more dreadful than the "spectre bridegroom."

Gloominess and melancholy gradually took the place of a once cheerful mind. On other matters he seemed right enough. But that he should be robbed he was certain, and nothing could dissipate the delusion from his mind, and finally he lost confidence in all earthly things except his dog.

It was in this state of mind that he and his wife started back to Lorain county where they had come from. The first night out they stopped at Sherwood's tavern at Green Creek, Sandusky county, still pursued by robbers, as he thought. In the night, his wife missed him, and began to feel uneasy on account of his absence, but he returned and told her that he had been out to hide his money. As soon as it was light in the morning, she went with him to get it. He went nearly a mile as she thought, into the thick woods, as direct as if he had been following a path, where they found the dog tied to a bush with his master's necktie. Near by under a root he dug up the money. What seemed still stranger than all, was the fact of the night's being exceedingly dark and his being wholly unfamiliar with the woods. The next night they reached Vermillion river, where they stopped at a tavern again. His wife lay awake and watched him for a time. He seemed to be resting well and finally overcome with weariness, she fell into a light sleep, only to be startled in a short time with a heavy fall on the floor, in the room where they slept. She instantly perceived that his place in bed was vacant, and hastened to get a light. She found him lying on the floor, red with his own blood and with what little strength and life yet remained, he was still dealing himself deathly stabs with a butcher knife. One almost imagines the poor victim in the same state of mind as Poe, in Lenore:

"Up from the damned earth,
 To friends above, from fiends below,
The indignant ghost is driven—
 From Hell unto a high estate
Far up within the Heaven—
 From grief and groan to a golden
  throne
Beside the King of Heaven."

In 1776 England was the most advanced of all the ages in constitutional liberty, but when we went to war "For No Taxation Without Representation" and created a new nation, we reached a higher plane in the advance of civilization.

In the latter part of the Eighties a bill was introduced into congress and pushed to a vote. This bill provided means for erecting monuments to perpetuate the memory of Perry's victory, Ft. Meigs, Ft. Miami, Ft. Industry and the battle of Fallen Timber. This bill was finally stricken from the appropriations bill.

SCRAP-BOOK.

WOOD COUNTY IN WAR

Her Sturdy Boys Ever Ready to Respond to Their Country's Call to Arms

WE have no data at hand to give any account of volunteers, if any, from Wood county during the Mexican war, as the county was then sparsely settled, there being a population of not over 13,000 probably in the entire county. But in the war of the rebellion, and that of the war with Spain she gave abundant evidence of her patriotism and loyalty.

In the War of the Rebellion, thousands of her sons enlisted in the various regiments, and hundreds gave their lives in the defence of their country. Her brave boys were distributed in the 14th, 21st, 49th, 55th, 57th, 67th, 72d, 100th, 101st, 111th, 123d, 144th, 185th, 186th, and 189th regiments of Ohio Volunteer Infantry. Aside from these Wood county had its representatives in cavalry, artillery, battery and naval service, while many of her sons were enlisted in regiments from other states. Then when the county had been well stripped of its able-bodied men, hundreds more, known as the "squirrel hunters" of 1862, hastened to the relief of Cincinnati when threatened by the invasion of Kirby Smith and his rebel legions.

Then in the war with Spain in 1898, Wood county furnished 222 men in Companies H and K of the 2d Ohio Regiment. The boys entered the service in April, 1898, and were mustered out in February, 1899, returning home without a man missing.

NEWSPAPER HISTORY

The First Newspaper in the County—These Publications Increase and Keep Pace with Its Progress

THE first newspaper published in Wood county was the Miami of the Lake, Jessup W. Scott, editor. The first number of this paper was issued December 11, 1833, and the paper continued to be published under this name until the 18th of August, 1838, when the name was changed to The Ohio Whig and continued under this name until the first of June, 1844, when the name was changed to the Fort Meigs Reveille and under this name it was published till the 10th of March, 1853, and was then changed to the Perrysburg Journal. It was started as a Whig paper and so continued until the fall of 1854, when the Republican party drove the old Whig party from the field. The Journal became an advocate of the principles of the Republican party, which it continues to maintain.

The next paper issued in Wood county was the Wood County Packet. This paper was Democratic in politics, and it was said to have been ably conducted during the brief period while it existed. It was started in the year 1838 or 1839, and closed in the year 1841, or immediately after the memorable hard-cider and coon-skin campaign.

Soon after another Democratic paper started at Perrysburg about the year 1845, but there remains nothing from which its history can be learned.

In the year A.D., 1853, Albert D. Wright commenced the publication of the North Western Democrat, a Democratic paper, as its name indicates. The first issue of this paper was on the 22d of May, 1852, and Mr. Wright continued the publication until his death by cholera in the summer of 1854.

At the resumption of business after the cholera, the publication of the North Western Democrat was resumed and its publication continued till the 22d of January, 1855, when the name was changed to the Maumee Valley Democrat, and continued to be published under that name until September 3, 1857, when the name was again changed and from that time to the 7th of October, 1858, it was published under the name of The Democrat, when for want of support its publication ceased.

In the year 1862 the Independent was started at Perrysburg, and continued to be published when it was removed to Toledo and the name changed to the Democratic Record.

The Buckeye Granger, a paper as its name sufficiently indicates, was started at Perrysburg on the 10th of November, 1874, for the purpose of advocating the principles and advancing the interests of the "Grangers." It was neutral in politics, but finally became the Democratic organ of the county, continuing as such until its collapse.

The contest between Perrysburg and Bowling Green in the year 1866, over the removal of the county seat, called into existence the Advocate at Bowling Green, the publication of which was discontinued a short time after the election in the above named year. In January, 1867 the first number of the Sentinel was issued and subsequently the name was changed to the Wood County Sentinel. This paper from the beginning advocated the principles of the Republican party.

In the fall of 1874, J. D. Baker commenced the publication of the Wood County Democrat, but discontinued after about four months, and sold the press to Bowling Green parties, who began the publication of the Wood County News, in May, 1875, and which paper had a lively existence until in November, after the election, and at the age of six months the News office was merged with the Wood County Sentinel, and was numbered among the things that were.

The Weston Avalanche. The first issue of this paper was on the 3d of June, 1874, and the publication continued till 1875, when it ceased, and shortly after the Weston Free Press was started to take its place.

The New Baltimore Enterprise was commenced in March, 1875, and its successor, the Wood County Democrat was issued in December, 1878, by D. E. & B. L. Peters. In 1880 it passed into the hands of Wm. B. and Russell T. Dobson; in July, 1889, Henry Holterman took the paper and in September, 1890, Henry S. Chapin became the proprietor, and continues its publication up to the present time. D. C. Van Voorhis became connected with the paper in 1892, and is still with the paper. The Democrat was published as a daily in the campaigns of 1894 and 1896. It has a wide circulation throughout the county.

Other papers that have had a brief existence in Bowling Green, were the Bowling Green Journal, The Wood County Republican, The Bowling Green News, Wood County Agitator, The Reporter, The Wood County Gazette, The Daily Gazette, The Wood County News, The Wood County Free Press.

Besides these other papers in the county are The North Baltimore Times, successor to the Bairdstown Times, The Bloomdale Derrick, Wood County Tribune, Evening Tribune, Weston News, Weston Avalanche, The Free Press, The Weston Reporter, The Weston Herald, Pemberville Independent, Pemberville Brick Block, Pemberville Reporter, Wood County Index, Pemberville Leader, Pemberville Presbyterian, Farm and Fireside, Grand Rapids Triumph, The Cygnet Globe, The Cygnet Gusher, The Christian Review, Tontogany Weekly Herald, The Weekly Graphic, The Bradner News, Prairie Depot Observer, and The Bradner Advocate.

SCRAP-BOOK.

A HORRIBLE TRAGEDY

A Crazed Wife Kills Her Husband in Milton Township in 1836

MR. HUTCHINSON'S first work as Constable in Milton township was summoning a jury to hold an inquest over the body of a man by the name of Simmons, who was killed by his wife in the spring of 1836, and who lived on a place in the northeast corner of Jackson township, at that time a part of Milton. Mr. Simmons had moved there with his family against the wishes of his wife. She disliked the dismal situation as it then was, and in brooding over her condition her mind probably became deranged. Several times she made the attempt to run away, but each time was brought back by her husband. She at last, as she afterwards expressed it, resolved "to get rid of her husband" and go back to her old home, and therefore watched her opportunity. One Sunday morning Mr. Simmons rose early, built a fire, and then laid down to rest for a while on a bed containing his three children and went to sleep. His wife, evidently perceiving a good time to carry out her purpose, arose, took a broad-ax from under her bed and with one blow literally cut his head off. The jury summoned found a verdict in accordance with the foregoing facts, and Mrs. Simmons was afterwards taken to an asylum, where, after lingering some time, death put to rest the crazed brain.

WILLARD V. WAY

A Pioneer Lawyer and One of the Wealthy Men of Wood County

MR. EVERS, in 1875, gave an extended sketch of Willard V. Way, who died at his home in Perrysburg in the latter part of August of that year, at the age of 68. Mr. Evers says: Mr. Way was born in Otsego county, New York, in 1807, and was a graduate of Union College, after which he read law for a time, when he removed to Painesville, Ohio, finished his law studies and located in Perrysburg in the year 1834.

Mr. Way was an attorney by profession and though not an eloquent jury lawyer he attained the reputation of being an excellent and safe counselor. He held several county offices, among others that of Auditor and in every position he occupied he showed both care and ability. He was at an earlier day a politician of considerable foresight and sagacity and did more probably than any other man to build up the Democratic party in Wood county.

On the authority of Mr. Michael Hays, an early Democratic associate of Mr. Way, the latter was a leader in the party and a convention had been called at which Mr. Way was a candidate for the State Senate. The convention folks from the river were coming out in a two horse wagon and had stopped at the Strickland place to "take something."

About this time John C. Spink, the leading Whig spirit of the county, drove up and asked Mr. Hays to get in his buggy and ride out with him. Mr. Hays said to Spink, "What are you going out to a Democratic Convention for?" "To raise the devil," said Spink, and sure enough, remarks Mr. Hays, he did raise the devil. Way got mad at the way things went and was further irritated at his defeat, by what he considered unfair means in the Senatorial Convention. Mr. Hays says that he was never more surprised than when a few days after Way rode along by his place in company with Asher Cook who was then reading law with him and called Hays to him and said with much warmth of feeling, "Hays, I have built up the Democratic party in Wood county and now so help me G—d I will tear it down." In later years he acted with the Republican party.

It is estimated that his real estate alone is worth $80,000 and his estate is estimated at $150,000 to $175,000. He was of a literary turn of mind and took a great interest in educational matters and the pioneer history of the Valley. He wrote and published in pamphlet form a history of the "Michigan War," an amusing and rather interesting account of the State boundary line contest.

Shortly after his location on the Maumee Mr. Way returned to Buffalo and married Mrs. Sophia Hodge.

In his will the Union School of Perrysburg in perpetuity is given $5,000, the interest of which is to go toward defraying the College expense of some well recommended graduate of said schools.

His homestead and six village lots are left in custody of his wife, so long as she lives, then it goes to the town for a public park. $15,000 is set apart as a perpetual fund, the interest only of which can be used in the support of the library. All the rest of the proceeds of the estate may be used in the purchase of a lot and the construction of a suitable building and the purchase of books as and in such manner as the town Council may think best, but for no other purpose.

THE WOODBURY HOUSE

The True Story of This Building, Once Famous in Wood County History

IN a letter to the Wood County Republican, C. W. Evers, at the request of the editor, gave the following facts regarding the Woodbury House, correcting the many prevalent errors regarding it. Mr. Evers says:

The village of Woodbury was surveyed and platted by Hiram Davis, a pioneer surveyor of Wood county, May 4, 1837, for John Thompson, Henry B. Gibson and Jabez B. Larwell. The location was at a point where the east and west line dividing Liberty and Henry townships, Wood county, intersects the Findlay pike. Two years prior to the survey or in 1835, a postoffice had been established, kept in a log store room by Joseph Thompson. After the survey General Thompson built the frame house which has been the theme of so many stories uncanny and otherwise. After General Thompson's dream of a city growing up there had been dissipated by a few wet, sickly seasons, the house stood vacant at times for want of a tenant, and seems to have only been occupied by some chance comer who had no other place to go. Now you know how soon a house of this sort will, deservedly perhaps, get a bad name—get "haunted," etc. Some time in the 60's, it burned to the ground, no doubt by design of some one to abate a nuisance. The postoffice was moved about in the settlement still retaining the name "Woodbury" until 1876, when it was dropped from the rolls and is now only a reminiscence.

So far as can be verified by historical records or by Indian tradition, the Miami tribe of Indians were the original "pioneers" of the Maumee Valley. They were always true to the confidence reposed in them, and in their chiefs, from time immemorial, were second in ability to none of their time.

A NIGHT WITH INDIANS

Intense Hatred and Jealousy of a Savage Inspired by Whisky

J. F. DUBBS of Milton township, in 1883, furnished a startling incident for Mr. Evers' sketches. He said that in February of the year 1838, his uncle, John Dubbs, lived in a cabin in Jackson township, and he lived with him, being a small boy at that time. A lad named Simmons about my age also lived there.

There was an Indian shanty on his uncle's land occupied by four Indians, two men and two squaws; the men were brothers; John and Bob were their names; the old squaw was the mother of the two men, the young squaw was Bob's wife. She was young and handsome, and Bob was very proud of his wife. John was always mad at Bob because he had a wife and he, John, had none. The day preceding the night in question, it had snowed about eight inches deep and turned very cold.

Mr. Dubbs says: About 9 o'clock at night the Indian family came to our cabin and asked for admittance, for they were very cold. Uncle John opened the door. I can look back through the mists of time and see those Indians walk in with their blankets around them and with their knives in their belts. The men were over six feet tall and built in proportion. They took their seats around the fire place while we occupied the back part of the cabin. All was quiet for a little while. A man by the name of Rowan had a notion store and kept whisky about one mile from our cabin. The Indians had been there and procured a jug of whisky, of which they had partaken quite freely. When they began to thaw out the whisky began to take effect, and caused the spirit of Cain to rise in John, so he wanted to slay his brother, for he hated him because he had a wife. All at once the stillness was broken by Indian John pouncing upon Bob with all the fierceness of a tiger, grappling him by the throat and felling him to the floor, smashing the chair on which he was sitting; then the squaws took sides with Bob; they were all in a pile before the fire. The fight was fierce, but Bob soon cried murder! He said John has a knife and will kill me.

Uncle John Dubbs no sooner heard this than he ordered us to open the door, which we did; then he sprang and caught Big John by the legs and tumbled him heels over head out of the cabin. Uncle John lit on top of him, and told him if he didn't lay still he would kill him in a minute. Uncle John held him by the hands and told Simmons and me to run to the stable and bring his plow lines, which we did quick as we could in the dark. Soon Big John was thoroughly bound from head to foot.

Then Uncle John began to feel that he was monarch once more and that the red man had no business his rights to dispute; he told Simmons and me to go and bring some straw which we did, and he rolled Big John in the straw, and said, now lay there and freeze until you can behave yourself. The cold soon made John beg hard to be let loose; he said "me be good Injin, fite no more." When he was punished enough Uncle John let him loose and sent them home to their shanty.

It being now about twelve o'clock, and the excitement of the evening being over, we retired to rest. We had not been in bed more than one hour when the dogs began to bark and soon the piteous cries of some one was heard at the door pleading to be let in. Uncle John's patience being pretty well exhausted he yelled at the top of his voice for them to go home and not bother him any more. But the cries continued more pitiful, saying John has most killed me and I will die if you do not let me in.

By this time the whole house was aroused again, and Uncle John got up and struck a light and opened the door, and there stood the young and once beautiful squaw with her face literally cut to pieces. She was covered with blood from head to foot, and nearly frozen, the cold causing her wounds to bleed very profusely. Uncle John and the girls warmed some water and washed and dressed the wounds the best they could. I think there were about four or five bad cuts on her face and head. She soon felt better, and said she guess John kill Bob. The girls got her something to eat, and it was so near morning it was not worth while to go to bed again.

Soon as it was daylight Uncle John took the squaw and started to the shanty to see the slaughter there which he expected to find, but to his surprise he found the old squaw, John and Bob all laying with their feet toward the fire sound asleep. He woke them up and told John what he had done, and how he had broken his promise, and now they must leave his place, and never come back, which orders they promptly obeyed, and we never saw this Indian family any more.

THE BLACK SWAMP

A Region Once So Dreaded Now the Garden Spot of Ohio

YEARS ago, when the tide of emigration was strongly settling to the then Western States of Michigan, Illinois and Iowa, no locality, says the Toledo Blade, was better known or more dreaded than the "Black Swamp." The limits of this "Swamp" were never very well defined, but the largest part of it is embraced in Wood county. At the time when this "Black Swamp" was enjoying its reign of terror, prior to the construction of Western Reserve & Maumee Stone Road, movers passing from the East to the West found the greatest difficulty in going from the Portage river, at Woodville, to the Maumee river, at Perrysburg. While all of this distance was not properly "Swamp," two or three stone ridges rising out of the mud and water to cheer the weary traveler, the greater portion of the fifteen miles was emphatically a "Swamp," covered with water nine months in the year, and affording almost bottomless mud and mire from January first to December thirty-first.

Old settlers relate many amusing incidents connected with travel through the "Swamp" in those days, and the hardships endured by "movers" can probably never be too strongly colored. "Taverns" were located along the line of the traveled road in great numbers, not more than one-half a mile or a mile apart. It is related as a fact that "movers" would frequently travel hard each day for three days in succession and put up at the same "tavern" each night. It was called "Black Swamp" because the soil was black, and it was exceedingly difficult to pass through it, because this black soil, or loam, was of great depth and thoroughly impregnated with lime, forming a tough, waxy mud which would adhere to the wheels of wagons with great tenacity.

But things have changed, and that which years ago was regarded as a great curse, is to-day esteemed the greatest blessing. Clearing up the land and ditching it, has redeemed the "Black Swamp," and the soil to-day is unsurpassed for productiveness. It is easily

SCRAP-BOOK.

tilled and yields the largest crops of grain and the best samples of fruits. The "Black Swamp" farmers see no evidences of the once dreaded "Swamp," except in the deep, rich, black loam into which their plows sink and which yields such abundant returns for the husbandman's labors. Artificial drainage has accomplished what natural drainage has failed to effect, and the "Black Swamp" to-day, where properly under-drained and provided with ditches, will stand a drought or a flood better than any other section of Ohio. The land is much stronger than it possibly could have been but for the level surface of the earth, which gave it the appearance of a vast "Black Swamp."

HULL'S SURRENDER

Graphic Description of the Event—Hull an Imbecile from Drink

GEN. SANDERSON, who was present at the surrender thus describes the situation:

It was late in May, 1812, when General Hull arrived at our camp at Dayton, and Governor Meigs relinquished command. A few days after we were on the march for Detroit. The road was a difficult one to travel, but by the aid of efficient guides, and the protection of Divine Providence we arrived safely at our destination, after much suffering and many stoppages on the way. For nearly two months after our arrival, we engaged in the performance of no extraordinary military duty the general routine of camp life being the order from day to day. In August the British and Indians arrived, and soon after the scene occurred which produced such indignation at the time, and about which histories do not agree. My company, belonging to Cass' regiment, was surrendered with all the Ohio volunteers, Miller's regulars, and a large force of militia. I shall never forget the scenes which then transpired. My opinion of General Hull's conduct, formed at the time (and events since have not changed it) was, that General Hull was an imbecile—not a traitor or a coward but an imbecile, caused by the excessive use of ardent spirits. He was a constant and heavy drinker. On the day before the surrender, his son, Captain Abraham F. Hull, came among my men in a beastly state of intoxication. On the day of the surrender I saw General Hull frequently. His face about the chin and mouth was covered with tobacco juice, and I thought, in common with other officers, that the General was under the influence of liquor. His personal appearance indicated that he had been drinking. The general was surrounded, in camp by a military family, the members of which were fond of high living, wines, liquors, etc. I know us poor volunteers wondered how they could keep up such luxuries, but our surgeon relieved my mind by informing me one day that Hull's officers drew all the liquors from the hospital stores, on continued complaint of illness, Hull's surgeon (one of the party) certifying to the requisitions.

When the news of the surrender was known to the troops, they were scarcely able to restrain their indignation. Hundreds of horrible oaths and threats ascended, which I hope has not been set down by the "Recording Angel." McArthur broke his sword, as did other officers. General Hull was repeatedly insulted to his face, and soon hid himself away. The members of his military family, especially the General's son Abraham, received some pretty tall abuse from us Ohioans. After the surrender and before the enemy had entered, many officers, myself among the number, implored Colonel Findlay to take command of the

American forces, and resist the enemy, but he declined. Colonel Jas. Miller was importuned the same as Findlay, but he was unwilling to assume the responsibility, saying as near as I can recollect, "Matters have gone too far, but had General Hull signified to me his intention of surrendering, I would have assumed command, and defended the fort to the last." Miller would have done so and so would McArthur had he been in the fort.

Some little time after Hull had ordered the white flag, August 16, 1812, Colonel Isaac Brock, the British commander, entered the fort attended by his staff and several Indian chiefs. The American troops were ordered to the parade ground and there piled up their muskets, swords, pistols, knives, cartridge boxes, etc. A heavy guard was placed over us, and we were then sent to the "citadel" where we were kept until released on parole. Hull and the regular officers were sent to Quebec.

A MADMAN'S FRENZY

Orson Cross, a Veritable Demon, and His Remarkable Recovery After 20 Years' Confinement

IN the old Perrysburg jail when the insane patients of Wood county were confined in it, a stalwart middle-aged man with dark hair and beard was confined in the first cell near the entry to the crazy department, and few who ever saw him in his crazy frenzy with that demoniac expression of the eye which at times seemed to emit fire while his mouth was choaked with foam, will have forgotten it. He was one of the most dangerous men ever put under lock and key. When in a frenzy his rage knew no bounds and his strength seemed almost superhuman and he exerted both to the direst extent on any object within his grasp.

On one occasion he dragged a young dog through the bars of the cell door, crushed its head on the brick floor and licked up the blood. C. C. Baird, who was then Deputy Sheriff and jailer, assisted by the best man he could select, undertook the dangerous job of entering his cell. Mr. Baird got his head seriously hurt with an iron vessel with which Cross assailed them, roaring the meanwhile like a lion.

At another time he got a new hat belonging to another patient, in his cell and refused to let it be taken out. It took the strength of two men to force the door open which he held with all his strength, until of a sudden he let loose when both came in nearly falling on their knees. Cross instantly grappled one of the men, pushing him over the iron bedstead against the wall while the other seized hold of the mad man's throat with an iron grip. His eyes protruded from their sockets and his tongue from his mouth, and his face grew black before he released his grasp on the man, which he finally did completely exhausted, after which he was docile as was invariably the case when overpowered.

Cross seemed to pass through three stages or paroxysms of insanity. During the first he was ferocious, noisy and dangerous, sleepless and moving nearly all the time like a caged beast, muttering constantly to himself, more especially repeating in a disconnected way a portion of the multiplication table, but no matter what the numbers multiplied he always got around to the same product, 27. He dwelt especially on numbers 9 and 27. During this time he ate nothing,

THE HARRISON WELL
Which Supplied the Garrison with Water, Fort Meigs

SCRAP-BOOK.

and these spells lasted sometimes for a number of days. At such times he would break all the glass from the window if he could get a stick to reach through the bars, and push his bedding out no matter how cold the weather.

The next stage was a long, almost deathlike sleep, from which it was nearly impossible to arouse him. Then followed a wakeful stupor in which he was sullen and cross, and in which he remained for some time, and during which time he had a ravenous appetite. From this he would come to his natural self, in which he was agreeable, talkative, and a pitiful being to behold. His pale, emaciated, imploring look would excite sympathy in the coldest heart. At such times he was frequently allowed to spend an hour or so in the open air in a back yard inclosed by a high fence. This of course was somewhat risky, as his spells of frenzy did not recur regularly. One afternoon Mr. Baird requested him to come in, which ordinarily he did with the submissiveness of a child, but this time he told Baird to go to h—l. Mr. Baird was powerless to compel him to do so, nor dare he leave a moment for the safety of his family. Cross was already frothing at the mouth. In the dungeon part of the jail among the prisoners was a powerfully built Irishman

Named Pat Shady

Charged with robbery. Baird closed the front doors and called Shady out. Cross closed in with him the moment he came into the yard. It was the struggle between two giants. Cross was, before his troubles and disease, the best wrestler in Wood county, and was struggling with all the fury and wild energy of a mad man. Shady, who was not a whit his inferior in size or strength, was nerved by the hideous appearance of his antagonist. After a terrific struggle of some minutes, Cross threw Shady, but the Irishman proved stronger when down than on his feet even, and turned Cross by main strength, at which time Baird came to his assistance and they got the infuriated man to his cell.

The cause of his insanity is something of a mystery as is usually the case. About 20 years before he was a hale, hearty young man and we believe in the employ of R. W. Kelly, on his farm near Millgrove and not far from where the Cross people lived. It was thought that he injured himself while wrestling one night at a spelling school. He was

Sent to Newburg Asylum

Where he was the terror of the institution, and from which place he was sent back to Wood county as incurable, and was confined in a cell in jail from the time of Sheriff Guyer's term until the establishment of the Wood county infirmary, to which he was removed in 1867. Here he was kept in the same manner until the Northwestern Asylum near Toledo was established, when he was removed there and put under care of Dr. Wright, who sent him out a well man. And he has been back to visit some of his relatives, and is now at work in Michigan, or perhaps at the Asylum, for wages.

Wright, we hear, discovered the cause of his insanity to be in the derangement of his stomach, and by watching closely the approach of his paroxysms and administering powerful cathartics followed by other treatment, succeeded in breaking the force of his attacks until he finally showed no further bad symptoms. This would seem to be strong proof of the astonishing and sympathetic relation of the brain and stomach, and is one of the most remarkable recoveries we have ever heard of.

In his 20 years of prison life, confinement, exposure and abuse of health and the reversal of all laws of health, he had endured that which would have killed 99 men in every hundred. He is to-day to all appearances, a well man of sound mind.—*From Evers' Log Cabin Sketches.*

NOTED BEAR HUNT

Fifty-Five Years Ago in the Black Swamp—Over 200 Miles Chase in Four Days and Nights

IN the Sentinel in 1881, Wm. E. Carothers gives an interesting account of a strenuous bear hunt in December, 1854, with Jim Rowland. In three days they had captured and killed two bears weighing over 400 pounds each. After letting their dogs rest a day, they started on the last day's hunt which is thus described by Carothers:

We started early in the morning, and for a time the dogs left us far in the rear, but we could discover traces of frequent fierce conflicts, and a little after noon the dogs were crowding the game hard. The bear's feet were so torn and lacerated on the bottoms, that he left blood in every track. We were now approaching the Jackson prairie or swamp, the skirts of which were covered with wind-fall and dense brush and thickets, all bent over every which way by the lodged snow. Into this old bruin plunged. It was next to impossible for a man to get through this place. When we at last reached the open space beyond we came in full view of the dogs and game in a savage contest. Bruin was on a log that lay up from the ground, mopping and striking at the dogs, which were closed up in a circle all around him. It was one of the most wild, exciting, sporting scenes a hunter could wish to see. The dogs would either pull the bear off the log or cause him to jump from it, when they would all attack him and the snow would fly in clouds. The fierce growls and groans of rage of the bear could be heard above the din raised by the dogs, which was deafening.

Pretty soon old bruin made a savage rally and broke from his blood-thirsty tormentors, but within a few rods had again taken to a log. Rowland and I had rushed up with all possible haste. Jim, who was watching with great anxiety, expecting every moment to see a dog killed, suddenly stopped and leveled his rifle, and we saw the bear tumble off to the far side of the log. Every dog bounced him instantly. Jim began reloading; but what was our consternation when we heard one of the dogs giving a terrible cry of distress and saw the shaggy, black beast standing on his hind legs, with one of the best dogs in his deadly embrace, while with one paw he was beating and crippling the dogs with frightful ferocity. I rushed up within 20 feet unnoticed by the bear, and shot him in the head, killing him instantly. The dogs all laid hold of the beast with terrible vengeance and fully satiated their wrath for all the trouble and cuffs and bites they had suffered. I took off my hat and yelled loud and long, and never felt better in my life; and though the weather was pretty cold I seemed to be fairly melting and the steam rose from my head in wreaths high as the tree tops.

We were, dogs and all, pretty well used up; the poor brutes lay down and licked their bloody feet, and had hard work to get home; they would lay down and whine and wag their tails as if in the greatest distress. This bear was a fine three-year-old, and weighed about 400 pounds.

Although I have done some hunting since, that was my last bear hunt and it was about the last of Rowland's hunting. He told me years after that he never got over the effects of that chase —that it was more than flesh and bone could endure. Jim was almost a man of iron. Closely knit, compact, large-boned, broad-chested, active as a deer, strong and with an endurance in his younger days almost incredible, he had few equals as a woodsman and hunter; I can now think of one other, his brother, Bob Rowland.

Providence seemed to have allotted each man his proper sphere in the great universe, and this class of men—the pioneers of the Black Swamp, bravely and faithfully fulfilled their mission. The law of necessity gauged all their comforts to the very fewest and plainest. The cares incident to a luxurious state of living, the turmoil of business, the frivolities of fashion, the struggle for social supremacy, were unknown to those early pioneers. They lived more for each other than people do now, but they were only the fore-runners of a higher civilization.

A GHASTLY CRIME

Carl Bach Hanged for the Murder of His Wife—One of the Most Brutal in History of Wood County Crime

ON the night of the 10th of October, 1881, Carl Bach, a farmer of Milton township, most savagely murdered his wife, which was the culmination of a long period of domestic discord. On the morning of the 11th, the murderer voluntarily walked to Bowling Green and surrendered himself to the sheriff.

The Sentinel of October 12, 1883, says when the coroner reached the scene of the murder, in the middle of the room in a pool of blood, lay the body of a woman, covered with a sheet. The floor, walls and ceiling were smeared and bespattered with blood; giblets of flesh, tufts of hair, brains and fingers were scattered over the floor.

On lifting the bloody sheet from the body the sight was still more shocking. The back part of the woman's head was all hacked to a jelly. The left shoulder had been nearly severed by one terrific blow. The side of the head was cut open from the mouth back. An arm was nearly cut off and several fingers were severed on one of the hands. Such a horrible butchery it would be hard to paint in the imagination. The woman when first attacked lay in bed with her six-year-old child, and to her struggles to avoid the murderous blows and get free, is partly attributable her strangely mangled condition, and the blood marks of her hands on the wall. She was doubtless dead before the infuriated murderer ceased hacking her body.

With his three children, aged 13, 11 and 6 years, he slept until morning in an adjoining room and very early in the morning he took the children to the house of a neighbor, Mr. Heinzie, about a mile distant. He told what he had done—that he had killed his wife and that he must go to Bowling Green and give himself up, and requested Mr. Heinzie to take care of the children and left with him also a sum of money for the burial of his wife. Mr. Heinzie was startled at his strange conduct and disbelieved his shocking story, but told some of the neighbors and together they went to the house and found their worst fears more than confirmed.

On the 5th of February, 1882, Bach was indicted for wilful murder. The trial took place in June, 1882, and on the 16th of that month he was found guilty as charged, and sentenced to be hanged October 13, 1882.

Bach's counsel prepared a bill of exceptions and a short time prior to the time set for the execution, filed a motion in the Supreme court for leave to file a petition in error. The motion being argued was sustained by the court and a stay of proceedings granted until the hearing of the petition at the January term 1883, at which time the judgment of the court of Common Pleas was reversed for the reason that said court erred in empanelling the jury. The cause was thereupon remanded for a new trial and at the February term, 1833, of Wood Common Pleas, it was ordered to be again placed on the trial docket of said court, and assigned for trial at the May term thereof, viz: on the 11th day of June, 1883, when the second trial began, and on the 27th of that month the jury brought in a verdict of guilty. He was then sentenced, and on the 12th day of October, 1883, Carl Bach paid the extreme penalty of his crime, being the second and last murderer hanged in Wood county.

A STRANGE STORY

Woman Finds Her Father After a Separation of Over 30 Years

A NUMBER of years ago the Sentinel related an incident regarding an intelligent, plainly dressed woman, above the middle age, who arrived from an eastern state and stopped at one of the Bowling Green hotels. She looked up a livery man and after making some inquiries about prices, she made cautious inquiry for a family whose name need not be given. The livery man knew several persons of that name in the south part of the county, and together they started, and after some inquiry found the man for whom she searched. The balance of the story as reluctantly told by the lady herself is this: Thirty-six years before that time, when she was a child six or seven years old, she lived with her father and mother on a beautiful stream beyond the Alleghanies. She had several brothers and sisters, but she was the favorite of her father. A dark cloud and domestic unhappiness came over the household and her father fled and became lost to his family entirely. The mother obtained a divorce and married again. The children grew up and married one after another, and finally the subject of this sketch became a widow. Some months before her arrival she accidentally heard of a man of the same name as her long lost father, and from some circumstance related she was more than half convinced that it must be he and that he lived in Wood county, Ohio. With a woman's curiosity and tenacity of purpose she resolved to go and search for him.

As she drove along the road in the vicinity of where he lived on a farm less than ten miles from this place, she met a couple of men of whom she made inquiry. One of them answered to the name of the man she sought. The man gazed at her intently for some time. Perhaps he saw in her face something familiar. Perhaps she resembled her mother, once his wife. She nervously disclosed to him a part of her errand, when he walked around the carriage to the side where she sat and extending his hand said, "Sarah Jane, I am your lost father." We will not attempt to describe the meeting of this long separated father and daughter, but conclude after stating the fact that the old man had lived in Wood county a number of years, and had eleven sons and daughters, most of them married and settled. He was then living with his third wife, the mother of his second set of children having died some years before. Wife number one was still living in comfortable circumstances and perhaps ignorant of the whereabouts or fate of her long ago forgotten husband.

SCRAP-BOOK.

INDIAN DANCES

Indian Rivals Have a Tragic Ending—A Young Lady Has No More Use for an Indian Ball

WILLIAM EWING was especially recognized among the Indians as one of their white friends or advisers and has settled many of their disputes. He says he has probably attended as many as a hundred Indian dances in his time. Their dances were of two characters, one called "Manatoo" a religious dance, and the other their war dance. Their "Manatoos" would be held at their camp, at which six or eight hundred Indians would sometimes assemble, dressed in their finest costumes and wearing their brightest jewelry. They would build what might be called a bower, about 30 by 60 feet in size, for the occasion, with center posts, around which the Indians would travel in procession repeating a chant and going through all sorts of antics; one Indian would sit in the center and beat a "one-headed drum," made by stretching a skin over a cut from a hollow log. The medicine man was always a prominent guest, always dressed in the finest furs and carried a wampum belt in his hand. He traveled in an opposite direction to the rest and would occasionally single out a favorite dancer at whom he would point his wampum, and who would drop to the ground and again rise and join the dance after receiving a blessing from the medicine man.

Ewing once attended a war dance at a camp at the mouth of Tontogany creek, the occasion being a little local difficulty. Two young Indians named Nauquezike and Pamquauk, rivals, got into difficulty at the dance over a young squaw, and Nauquezike killed Pamquauk by stabbing him with a knife.

Ewing relates that himself and another young man once attended a dance with two bright young belles of their neighborhood and were invited to join in the services, which invitation they accepted. Ewing's lady became so badly frightened at the maneuvers of the Indians when about half way round the bower, that she "broke" and ran as though for her life. The Indians were so amused at her discomforture that all joined in a hearty demonstration of mirth, which frightened her still more and she nearly went into spasms, and left, resolving that she would never attend another Indian ball.

A SAD CHAPTER

Poor Fanny Deering—Harrowing Tale of Cruelty, of Crushed Hopes and Black Despair

THE Sentinel of March 23, 1882, contains one of the saddest chapters probably in the annals of Wood county, written by Mr. C. W. Evers, who made a thorough investigation of all the circumstances connected with the tragedy. The account follows:

On the morning of March 14, 1882, near the Plain church, four miles west of Bowling Green, Fanny Deering, a young lady of 27, cultured and intelligent, shot herself with a revolver. This is the legal verdict.

But is there another, darker, more awful verdict in this case? Was the trembling hand that held the pistol to the beating heart of Fanny Deering and pulled the fatal trigger the only hand raised against her life? Are there others who, at the final judgment, must be held responsible for her blood?

We will give the facts as near as we have been able to get them from different neighbors of the Deerings and other sources which seem to be credible.

The Deerings

J. K. Deering, the father of Fanny, was of a good, respectable family in Maine, and was given a college education and put into the ministry. At a synod meeting he met an educated young lady and an accomplished musician and after a short acquaintance, married her. Their life was not happy; he was a poor excuse of a husband, scarcely able to provide for himself, let alone a family, while she was proud-spirited and ambitious. They continued man and wife until five children had been born to them, when a decree of divorce on the grounds of incompatibility was given them by the court, and Deering kept the oldest child, Fanny, then thirteen or fourteen years old.

Fanny had, in the meantime, the advantages of schools and was a very bright, apt child. Soon after, Deering took Fanny and went to Michigan where one of his sisters lived, and where Fanny soon after taught school, her father, as she said, appropriating most of her wages, which was almost a necessity to him, as he seemed incapable of maintaining himself in any degree of respectability. He seems to have been too proud and impractical or lazy to work and was not a success as a preacher.

Fanny had a great adaptability and love for music, and after a time entered Oberlin College, and after two years of self denial and deprivation, during which time she taught, she graduated in the Conservatory of Music. Through her proficiency and adaptability as a teacher, good address and good recommends, she had no trouble in securing employment, and through the advice of a classmate she went to Toledo and found profitable patrons in some of the best families in the city, and was organist in one of the city missions, also a beloved teacher in one of the Mission Industrial school classes.

Mrs. Hurlburt, matron of the school, writing of Fannie since the trouble between her and her father and step-mother began, says:

"I visited them (Fanny and her father, who kept house in a rented room.— Ed.) often, and never detected any signs of neglect or indifference to the needs or comforts of her father on the part of Miss Deering, whom I have always given credit for being a most dutiful daughter, continually laboring far beyond her strength, under great disadvantage of delicate health and other unfavorable conditions. I am convinced that if she had been less unselfish and devoted to his interests, she would to-day be far better off in health and pocket than she now is.

"From a close and friendly intercourse with Miss Deering, extending over nearly eight years, I can truly say that I believe her to be truthful and worthy of the respect and confidence of all whom she may meet."

Equally strong commendations come from Col. Slevin, Mrs. A. T. Babbitt, Mrs. Whitney, and others, who were well acquainted with Fanny.

Mrs. Babbitt says:

"I know that previous to the marriage of her father to his present wife, she (Fanny) cared for and supported her father by her own labor, when physically, he was much better able to do it than she was to do it for him.

"Miss Deering has been a member of my family for several months and I know her to be truthful and honest to the last farthing. I also know her character to be spotless and her conduct without reproach."

These are the disinterested testimonials of Christian people and we produce them to silence the tongue of calumny put in motion by Deering or some of his apologists, that Fanny was undutiful, quarrelsome, bad disposition, etc. All who knew her speak of her as a kind, sympathetic, sweet dispositioned girl. She seems to have mostly supported her father for a time until about 1876, when he married a woman at Perrysburg, who now became her step mother and borrowed Fanny's money as fast as she earned it. Fanny still taught music and practiced the greatest economy and self denial, going on foot, lame as she was, from house to house to visit her pupils rather than pay street car fare, in order that she might accumulate a little sum of money with which she could visit Germany and graduate in music, which was the one great aim and ambition of her life. The energy of her whole being centered in this one object. She took lessons in the German language and studied nights until her eye sight began to fail and she had to wear eye glasses. She progressed rapidly and soon she could read and write and converse in German. Thus it was she toiled on night and day that she might fulfill her musical ambition.

In the meantime her step mother continued to borrow her money giving notes therefor and assuring her that it would be forthcoming when she got ready to go to Germany. She represented, that she had an abundance of property and it was thrice secured. The sum now amounted to over $1,400 and Fanny had set a time to go, notifying her step mother, who wrote her the money would be all ready. Music pupils were dismissed, business matters arranged and she was ready to depart.

The Money Gone

But what was the poor girl's chagrin and disappointment when she called for her money and was told there would be a little delay in getting it. There was no help for it and she had to wait; the date was fixed anew when she could get it and also a new date for the journey.

That time came but still no money—nothing but promises. It was about this time she heard the further unpleasant fact that her step mother was so fixed financially that the money was not collectible by law and that there was but a remote possibility of her ever getting it at all.

This was a crushing blow to Fanny; all her bright anticipations dashed to naught—all her days and nights of toil and privation—broken health—tired body and mind all endured in vain—nothing but black disappointment.

Driven from Her Father's Roof

This discouragement and her naturally frail condition of health, together with the mental strain, affected her health so that she did not feel able to teach. In this condition she went sometime last July to her father's at the Plain parsonage four miles west of this place where Deering had preached for two or three years past.

She thought to rest, regain her health and perhaps plead with her step mother to get her at least a part of her money, which Fanny fully believed she could pay if she would. She soon began to realize that she was none too welcome even in her own father's house. They had her money but did not care to be troubled with her presence. From coolness of treatment came bitter words, until at last Fanny received cruel blows and was driven from her father's roof, her trunks put in the wagon shed and the doors locked and even nailed against her and she was told they would not pay her.

To get her away peaceably her father engaged her board at a near neighbor's, Mr. Lowes, for a short time, but Fanny at last had to become responsible for the payment. This cruel treatment on the part of her father, seemed to crush her proud spirit and she seemed heart broken. Matters went on in this way until January, during which time Fanny had been heard to express intentions on her own life.

On January 12, she went in desperation to her father's again, and went to a chamber room she had been in the habit of occupying, and some time later it was noised among the near neighbors that she was very sick and dying. She had taken laudanum enough to kill two persons, and after three days of careful nursing and care she was restored, although for a time it was supposed she was past help.

She had made all preparations for death, and among the papers left, sealed and addressed to a neighbor woman, was one addressed to her step mother. It shows the extent of her sufferings for the deep wrong that she felt had been done her, and is sufficient to draw tears from a cast-iron monument. It may be proper to say here that the lady never sent the letter to the step mother.

We extract as follows:

* * "You knew that I had denied myself of all that a girl and woman craves, and worked myself all but to death to gain just one chance, and yet you deliberately robbed me of the fruit of seven years' toil for that one object. You snatched my last, only hope from me, and now you tell me you have done nothing you regret or would have done differently! Oh, what can you be made of? Though you knew that my strength was broken and worn out in labor to support you and your husband, that you had torn away my last hope and motive for life, and left me broken-hearted and despairing, yet, not content with refusing me the barest necessities of life, you pursued me with a relentless brutality. You knowingly goaded me on to desperation and death by every means your two natures could jointly devise. Night after night have I heard you two conjure upon ways and means to torment and injure me." * * *

Deering was admonished then that something should be done to prevent her taking her own life but he made a cold, unfeeling reply and he even refused to build a fire to warm the room where she lay, and the ladies who were trying to save her life were so uncomfortable that they could not remain long in the room at one time. He seemed to feel indifferent.

After this, Fanny was treated harsher than before. When she got well enough and went back to Lowe's near by, the doors at the parsonage were kept constantly locked and nailed up. Her trunks were out in the shed and when any one knocked at the door Deering or his wife first looked out of the window to see who was there.

The Thursday previous to her death Mrs. Deering had invited a few members of the church society to spend the evening. Each one noticed as they came in that the door was locked behind them. Later in the evening as they sat talking, the back door opened quietly and who should enter but Fanny looking like a hunted deer. She was greeted cordially by the guests, but hardly a look of recognition did she receive from her step mother, who, the moment of the girl's entry, stared at her with a look of spasmodic agitation. Deering could conceal his feelings better and nodded a good evening. No one asked Fanny to a seat or to take off her hat. All the time Fanny was there Mrs. Deering seemed to tremble from head to foot with excitement and agitation.

Did that woman, Mrs. Deering, know at that time what Fanny came there for? She acted as if she did. She knew that Fanny carried, and had carried for weeks, a pistol with her in a little box. The neighbors had noticed that box.

Was She Urged to Suicide?

Mrs. Deering certainly knew what was in that box and must have guessed pretty certainly what it was for; she did not fear violence on herself or Deering as will be seen by an incident farther on. No; in our belief she feared the girl wanted to take her life, and, of course, did not wish to have it happen in her house.

If she thought poor, friendless, robbed Fanny was on the verge of suicide—we say if she thought so—Deering must have shared her suspicion. And if they thought so, did they care? Did they realize what it was that was driving the broken-hearted being on to desperation? —that she knew they were fixing to go to Minnesota soon, and that her father, whose slave she had been and who was her only natural friend and protector on earth, had inhumanly steeled his heart and hand against her, that his wife had got all her hard, hard earnings, and that lame, broken in heart and penniless, this proud-spirited, ambitious girl was to be turned adrift on the world alone, to struggle on as best she could or go to the poor house.

Beaten Like a Dog

If they did think of these things then their sins will be greater, for instead of offering balm to her bleeding heart she was subjected to further degrading, cruel, inhuman treatment—to blows, like a brute. We relate an incident as giving a probable clue to the life the girl had been subjected to while under her father's roof and from the woman who had taken her money from her. It was not enough that the food was hidden from her, that she was denied fire to make her comfortable—she was beaten, beaten like a brute, for the most trivial offense.

Knocked Her Down

The Saturday before Fanny's death Mrs. Carr called at the parsonage to spend an hour, and while there Fanny asked her if she was fond of hickory nuts. She went and brought some, and, finding nothing to crack them on, she thoughtlessly cracked one or two on the heavy stove hearth. Without a word of warning the step mother sprang like a tigress from her chair at the sewing machine, a few yards away, and beat Fanny about the head brutally, and finally knocked her over so she fell in her visitor's lap, and the shameful scene ended, Mrs. Deering saying: "I'll teach you to crack nuts on my stove hearth."

The following Monday morning the step mother left for Elmore because, as is believed by many that she was, as we hinted previously, apprehensive of what would happen and left. The next day, Tuesday,

Fanny was a Corpse

Shot through the heart by her own hand. About the middle of the forenoon Mr. Carr, who was engaged on his place adjoining the parsonage, happened to look up from his work and saw Fanny's face at the window, where she seemed to be kneeling, whether in the attitude of prayer or not he did not know. A short time after, he heard a pistol shot, but not very distinctly, to which he paid but little attention, thinking it some boys in the road beyond the house. That was the last time Fanny was seen alive and was the last time she gazed on the light of day or on an unkind world which she bade a last farewell.

Mr. Carr says her pale, sad face as he saw it through the window glass is, in the light of what followed, engraven on his memory like an image, never to be effaced by time.

She had risen in the morning, combed her hair, and attired herself neatly, having the previous evening written to several intimate friends and given minute directions as to the disposition of her personal effects, also of her body.

A Letter of Farewell

One of these letters, to Mrs. Harvey Condit, which begins with allusions to another friend, Mrs. Prentice, and which was published in the Toledo Bee, is as follows:

"Don't let her know of my death till

it is necessary. She and many others will mourn my said error—as they will call it—but they must remember that one cannot judge correctly of a person's error unless they are familiar with his understanding. They would feel differently if they knew the greatest and best part of me. All joy and hope was dead long ago.

"It is better that the fragment left, go with the rest. I cannot live without the love and tenderness that may never be mine. If I could have attained my ambition and fitted myself for some position of usefulness that I could fill, it might—probably would—have been very different; but now I only know enough to be a drudge all my days, and I have no heart or strength to drudge, even if there were any use in it.

"I could never go into the world again to endure and contend with all a lonely woman must. I have for years—ages it seems—felt that some day it must come to this, but could not give up till I came here. This summer has showed me more plainly what I already knew—that there was nothing else for me. God only knows how desperate and bitter the struggle has been, and I am tired to death. My furniture is willed to a friend who will not care for my stove I think. * * *

"I should be so glad to help dear Mrs. Carr. If I had it to do again I would distribute my few things differently than I have, but I can not change without more bother than it is really worth, for I have but little for any one. When you see Minnie Minton, give her my love, and tell her I look eagerly for a letter from her until the day I die. I am so disappointed not to hear from her again. Her friendship and sympathy have been much to me. The gold pin I spoke of giving her I have given to another friend for whom I seemed to have nothing else. Minnie will have enough to remind her of me.

"I thought of giving some books to Ben (Minton) but as I haven't very many it seems best that they should go together. Please give the German papers to Mrs. Prentice. * * * *

"Your company has lightened and cheered many sad hours for me. I owe you much. I can make no return, but I am grateful for all the kindness and sympathy I have received here. Farewell.
"F. L. Deering."

The above was written in pencil, but the following postscript was written in ink.

"I beg you to do what you can to keep the manner of my death a secret, as far as may be. I believe you will do this for my sake. I never intended that any one should know about it when I used to think about it, but it cannot be helped now. I realize and feel the disgrace as keenly as anybody possibly could."

To Her Father

The letter addressed to her father, which shows the deep sense of wrong she felt, concludes as follows:

* * * "You are, undoubtedly, the one person living who hid his daughter's food in the house, even to hickorynuts and walnuts picked by her, and told her you begrudged her every mouthful she ate, after her whole life had been sacrificed to your selfishness. Live to remember that you did all this, and infinitely more, to me the day before I died; that you forced me to spend my last days on earth in hunger and wretchedness. The time will come when this will be impressed on you, but not in this world. Remember that one sign of honor or uprightness, one fatherly look even, would have saved me from this. When I was sick here I heard you say I ought to be pounded half to death, and you wished you could pound me to death. You have killed me by inches. Are you satisfied?"

These letters were all addressed and sealed up in a large package and sent by a neighbor's child to Mrs. Lowe, so that they reached her house about the time of Fanny's death or soon after.

So Ends the Sad Chapter

Who is to blame, and how far the responsibility for the dead, rests on the living the reader must judge. We have no comments further than to say that Fanny was shamefully wronged by her father and step mother, and they can render to the public and to God to whom they must answer, no adequate justification.

We know it may be said that Fanny was of age and had no legal claim for a home and support from her father; grant this to be all true. Yet she was his child, sick and homeless, made so by efforts to support him and help him and if the embers of human sympathy had not been dried and burned up in his heart he would have shared the last crust of bread with her instead of turning her away.

And his wife, what shall be said of her? Had she dealt even as one despised Jew deals with another, given Fanny the money she had taken from her, Fanny Deering would today be alive, a happy, useful woman.

The broken-hearted girl died in the belief that her step mother had deliberately planned to incumber her property with trumped up mortgages to her sons in order to prevent the collection of this money which she grudged to see the girl get. As to the truth of this we do not pretend to know or say. We are simply relating this to show the influences that worked on the unfortunate girl's mind. That she was insane or ever showed the least symptom of shattered reason the neighbors do not believe. They say it is a trumped up story to break the force of damning sentiment, which lies against Deering, justly or unjustly.

Doubtless the girl had brooded over her disappointment, her ill treatment and desertion till it affected her already shattered health and became a constant sorrow and burden which she could not shake off. She was kind and gentle to all, but especially to children and aged people, and there appears to be not a person who has ever associated with her but what loves and respects her, except her father and step mother, who deliberately drove her to despair.

The sentiment in the community there since the tragedy has been very strong against Deering and his wife and on Saturday night a Ku Klux crowd visited his house but found no occupants. He had prudently absented himself, but there were plenty of signs left that the party was well supplied with tar and feathers.

THE LOOMIS MURDER

Long Search for Arthur J. Grover, the Murderer—Pays the Penalty at Columbus —Story of the Crime

ON May 14, 1886, at the Columbus penitentiary, Arthur J. Grover paid the extreme penalty of the law, by hanging for the murder of Granville G. Loomis. From the Wood County Sentinel of May 16, 1886, the following account of the murder is condensed:

Saturday afternoon, about 2 o'clock May 9, 1885, a man was found lying dead in a pasture lot about half a mile northeast of the Empire House, Stony Ridge, Wood county. Every indication showed that the man had been most foully and deliberately murdered. His body lay on the sod at full length, his right leg crossed over his left, his hands folded over his breast, and his head resting on a rock cropping out of the surface of the ground. The face and head were mangled beyond recognition, evidently for the purpose of preventing identification. A large boulder weighing over twenty pounds was on the ground near by, on which there were traces of blood and hair. With this rock the mutilation had evidently been accomplished.

The body was conveyed to the Empire House and the clothing all removed in search of some clue that would lead to identification. The stockings were peculiar in their construction, and on each one was discovered a strip of white cloth about two inches in length, on which was printed with a stencil the name of "G. G. Loomis." This was the single clue that led eventually to the discovery of the murderer.

The body had evidently laid where it was discovered a number of days, for the grass under it was yellow. The cool weather for a number of days previous had evidently delayed decomposition.

Many theories were advanced regarding the tragedy, after the inquest, and the fact was pretty clearly established that the unfortunate victim had been murdered for his money. On the 13th, Sheriff Brown received a letter from Edwin Goddard, of Ashtabula, saying a man answering the description of the dead man and bearing the name of Granville G. Loomis had been staying at Orwell, that county. The next day a letter came from Will F. Babcock, Orwell, giving the minute description of Loomis, and stating that he had left Orwell on the 27th of April in company with a man named Arthur J. Grover, a chap who bore a pretty hard name, and also that the two had fled in the night, to escape some debts about the town, and that they had driven a cream colored Texas pony, hitched to a buck-board.

About this time, a party of four gentlemen from Ashtabula county came here to look into the matter. They were R. E. Stone and Z. C. Parker, of Orwell and Frank Luce, a brother-in-law of Loomis, and deputy-sheriff S. A. Squires, of Ashtabula. They immediately identified the clothing of the murdered man as Loomis' and expressed the opinion that he had been murdered by Arthur J. Grover. This point settled in the minds of the officers, the next question was how to catch the murderer. The Ashtabula county parties stated that prior to their departure from Orwell Grover and Loomis had talked a good deal about going to Dunn county, Wisconsin, where Grover claimed to have some land. Sheriff Brown and Prosecutor R. S. Parker became convinced that if Grover was the murderer he would drive the horse and buck-board through to Menominee, Wis., where his parents and brothers and sisters lived. It was thereupon agreed among the officers and friends of the murdered man, that Sheriff Brown and deputy Sheriff Squires of Ashtabula, should proceed to Wisconsin and wait for the man to come. Accordingly on May 19th, the two officers left this place quietly and for the next month Sheriff Brown was somewhere in search of Loomis' murderer.

It is too long a story for us to repeat here, the many trials, vexations, and disappointments they passed through during their long search among the swamps, huckleberry brush, mosquitoes and sand flies of northern central Wisconsin. How they had to travel about from one place to another, constantly on the lookout for their man, and yet daring to make but few confidants; how, in order to elicit certain facts they were all the time in a feverish state of internal excitement and hope, which they seldom dared express, lest Grover's friends might learn their mission and warn their man in time for him to escape. Had Grover committed the crime one day sooner or one day later in the course of their travels, we will venture the assertion that he would now be at large, and his victim occupying

SCRAP-BOOK.

an unknown grave. But it so happened, that he murdered his man within the jurisdiction of the officers of Wood county, and when he was captured in the far off woods of Wisconsin, he awoke to a knowledge of the fact that he had been hunted down by a man who did not know what it was to give up a chase.

On the 17th of June, Mr. Squires gave up all hope of catching their man, and started for home. Soon after Squires had started for home, Grover was caught by a man named Sam. McCahn, a gentleman to whom they had confided their story, at Fall Creek, a small town about 40 miles from Menominee. McCahn knew Squires had started home and so telegraphed him and Sheriff Brown at Prairie Farm, where he had gone that day. Both men arrived at Fall Creek that night, where they found Grover, with Loomis' pony, buck-board and a host of small trinkets and belongings, which were subsequently identified as the property of Granville G. Loomis.

Sheriff Brown arrived home with his man on Wednesday, June 24th, having come from Madison, Wis., without sleeping and almost without eating. Then came the most difficult task of all. The collecting of sufficient circumstantial evidence to convict their man.

Prosecutor Parker obtained the services of F. A. Baldwin to assist him in the case, and they with Sheriff Brown and deputy Dunn spent many days and nights in consultation and in weaving the web of testimony that eventually brought the murderer to the gallows. When the grand jury met in September Grover was indicted for murder in the first degree.

The Trial

Was like the unraveling of a strange and dreadful romance. All who heard it said it was the most fascinating case they had ever heard. The testimony of the witnesses for the state was like the leaves of a book. All were necessary to the complete work, and all were placed in just where they belonged; and when every page had been carefully read to the jury, and the book was closed, it was plain to everyone who had heard it throughout that the doom of Grover was sealed. So perfect was the chain of evidence as adduced by the state, and yet so justly and fairly handled during the trial, that Messrs. Parker and Baldwin were highly complimented by Judge Dodge, and the Judges of the Circuit Court before whom it came, as was also Sheriff Brown for the gallant work he had done in bringing the criminal to justice.

After very able pleas by all the attorneys in the case, and a charge from Judge Dodge, which was marked by its fairness and showed a great depth of thought over the trial, the jury retired and were out 20 hours, when they returned a verdict of guilty of murder in the first degree. Judge Dodge then sentenced Grover to be hanged on April 9, at the penitentiary.

Grover's attorneys argued a motion for a new trial before the Circuit Court at Tiffin, in March, but the court found no error in the case, and, as they had granted a suspension of sentence, ordered the sentence to be executed on May 14th. Messrs. Tyler and Canary went before the Supreme Court and there argued a motion for a new trial, but that court also refused to interfere, and so the sentence was executed as above stated.

Gen. Anthony Wayne was not the reckless, daring commander, which might be supposed from the names given him by the Indians "Mad," "The Thunderer," "The Whirlwind." On the contrary, he was prudent, far seeing, methodical in his preparations, but when in action, no obstacle was allowed to thwart his purpose.

ROCHE DE BOEUF

Its Historic Glamour Destroyed by the Largest Solid Concrete Bridge in the World.

THE Lima & Toledo Traction Company has erected at Roche De Boeuf a bridge of one unbroken mass of steel and cement from shore to shore. In giving an account of its construction, the Toledo News-Bee says:

"That historical and famous up-river landmark, Roche De Boeuf, has been practically obliterated by the construction of this bridge. All the glamour and beauty of this famous rock has been taken away by commercialism, in the shape of a traction bridge. This famous beauty spot of Northwestern Ohio is now hemmed in on one side by a string of twenty-two ice-breakers, 12 feet square, and on the other side by one of the bridge piers, which actually cuts out about 15 or 20 feet from the side of the rock. Its beauty as a landmark is gone, and now, instead of towering out majestically at the head of the Rapids of the Miami, as it was wont to do during centuries past, it seems to be creeping and hiding its head in shame back of a pile of concrete and steel, well calculated to dispel forever the glamour of legendary romance that has hung about the famous rock from time immemorial."

UP THE MAUMEE

Unsuccessful Attempt in Running a Steamer on the Upper Maumee

THE story that a steamboat once went up the Maumee past Waterville, Otsego and Gilead, seems to us of to-day like a legend, based mostly on fiction. The Maumee of to-day with its naked projecting rocks, dams, rapids and riffles and muddy water, is not the Maumee of 50 years ago. Once the river and its banks on either side were the highways of a vast commerce between the Lake and the Wabash country.

Scows, pirogues and canoes, ladened with valuable stores, brased its current from Fort Wayne to Perrysburg, and in winter or low stages of water, the carrying of stores, passengers and merchandise gave employment to a vast army of teamsters, horses and wagons. The distance from Fort Wayne to Perrysburg was 100 miles. The round trip with team and loaded wagon usually occupied 8 or 9 days, and various expedients were resorted to by shippers to avoid this slow and expensive way of shipping goods, previous to the building of the canal.

The Steamer Sun

It was in the summer of 1837 that an enterprising man, a captain, brought to the river a little canal-boat-built steam craft, constructed at Rochester, N. Y., and astonished the natives along the river by the bold declaration that he was going up the Maumee. After passing Fort Meigs, Buttonwood Island, and the Presque isle riffles, the little boat's shrill whistle loudly proclaimed her presence at the lock in Nearing's dam just below Miltonville.

After much trouble and by the assistance of ropes and tackle block, and much pulling and puffing, the Sun got into the mill pond above the dam, where, on the 4th of July, 1837, she was employed in giving the assembled people free rides back and forth across the river. When, finally she resumed her up-river course she met trouble again at Rush-te-boo rapids. A part of her freight was taken off and hauled around to Otsego by

ROCHE-DE-BOEUF
As It Appeared Before Building the Cement Bridge Over It—Here Was Held Wayne's Council of War

wagons. A rope and fall block was carried off to the boat from a tree at the shore and then horses were hitched to the rope, and in this way and with the assistance of men on shore the little craft ascended successively, Rush-te-boo Rapids, Wolf Rapids and Bear Rapids at Otsego, and finally landed safely in deep water above Gilead, where for a time she plied between that point and Flat Rock, below Defiance.

Funeral Incident

At Gilead later in the season, the Captain was taken sick with the Maumee fever and died. There was so much sickness that there were hardly well ones enough to take care of the sick and bury the dead. Daniel Barton, now of Milton, and Capt. Alva Gillett, who had a line of hacks on the mail route, sent a team to take the dead Captain to the grave near John Kimberlin's. When the burial party arrived, the two men who had been sent forward to dig the grave were found lying near a tree shaking with the ague and the grave was not dug. Some of the men took the spades and went to work in the hard clay. It was a very hot day and the mosquitoes and flies were so bad that they nearly drove horses and men crazy. Before the grave was completed some more of the men took the shakes, and Mrs. James Donaldson, whose husband was one of the party, carried water for the sick and for those at work at the grave, and it was with much difficulty that the burial was finally made.

The little steamboat stood the Maumee racket better than her master, and after a time ran down the river again and plied between Perrysburg and Vistula, now Toledo.

Another small boat called the Crockett attempted the ascent of the river, but never got above the Miltonville dam, and thus ended all attempts at steam navigation on the Maumee above Perrysburg.
—*C. W. E.*

INDIAN CHARACTER

No Mercy for a Murderer—They Will Not Be Burdened With the Old and Helpless

AMONG his many interesting reminiscences, J. F. Dubbs relates the following, taken from the Sentinel:

If any member of the Indian tribes committed a murder and escaped, they would follow him from year to year if necessary, until they would capture him, and then he would be condemned to die. The rule was that the nearest relative to the murdered man would have to take the life of the murderer. I believe that an occurrence of this kind took place at Tontogany. The wife of the murdered man was selected to slay her husband's murderer, and when the time came, she stepped forward and seized the long knife made for the purpose with its long shining blade, and standing in front of him she raised the knife and plunged it into his heart. They were following out the old law which said, "An eye for an eye and a tooth for a tooth; and he who sheds man's blood by man shall his blood be shed." And as Paul says, "Those having not the written law, make a law among themselves."

When one of them gets old and sick so that he cannot hunt or fish, they would kill him so that they might not be burdened with him in their oft removals and excursions. I recollect one day an old Indian came to my father's. He could talk a little so we could understand him. He said, "Indian sick." Mother asked him, if sick why not stay with his people and have them take care of him. He said, "If Indian stay me die." And he was asked why and he said, "They will kill Indian;" that "when Indian get sick and old and no hunt and no fish any more, they kill Indian."

We gave him something to eat and he went off and we saw him no more; but only a short time afterward a new made Indian grave was found near their camp and we always supposed that they found him and killed him as he said they would. Some one may ask how we could know that it was an Indian grave. It was known by the peculiar marks on the trees and by the trinkets found on the stakes around the grave. Any of the old pioneers can give a minute description of an Indian grave; when they bury one of their number they put all the paraphernalia for hunting and war in the grave; the bow and arrow, the tomahawk, and the scalping knife and belt, for they say they will need them to use in the "Happy hunting grounds beyond the River."

PRESBYTERIAN JUBILEE

Celebration in 1905 of the Fiftieth Anniversary of the Presbyterian Church in Bowling Green—Poem by Mrs. C. W. Evers—Mrs. Baldwin's Letter

THE jubilee services at the Presbyterian church celebrating the fiftieth anniversary of the organization of the church, were held in the latter part of November, 1905. In his address Rev. E. E. Rogers gave an interesting history of the church, from its organization of thirteen members, no one of whom were then living in Bowling Green. Many letters of regret were read from members in distant localities.

Among the proceedings Robert Dunn, Sr., read the following poem by Mrs. C. W. Evers:

The fiftieth anniversary, and the Jubilee tonight
Bring to mind a little village, that has long been out of sight.
No bells disturbed the quiet, no shrill whistles filled the air,
No steam cars and electric, no machinery, rumbled there.
The pathless woods surrounded, the habitations few,
And flowers wild abounded, 'til the city limits grew.
We can scarce believe the fact it was once our Bowling Green,
Where this church was organized, with the number of thirteen.

We are here to tell the story, as each has seen or heard,
Of the progress and the glory, of God's own Holy Word,
Will bring from memory's pages, those whose hands the work begun,
With hearts all full of love, for the betterment of man.
That little band of Christians worked with zeal and iron will;
They are resting from their labor, but their good works follow still.
Boys and girls in countless numbers have been guided to the right,
And will testify in honor, of the sleeping ones tonight.

Could those dear old charter members scan the hamlet from above,
It would be to see great churches in harmony and love.
Six thousand souls are wanted, and the workers at the wheel
Are praying without ceasing, in one earnest long appeal.
They would see the brave Endeavors, that sturdy branch who thrive,

SCRAP-BOOK.

With wondrous untold power, within
their active hive—
The outgrowth of example that will never
cease to be
And they're marching grandly forward
to the next great Jubilee.

The Sabbath school's broad mantle protects the young today,
The seed so early sown, shows no sign of
a decay.
Knowledge gained along the pathway,
has never yet been feared,
And the hosts of its instructors, are
doubly more endeared.
Faithful ministers and choirs, that have
toiled night and day,
While many, O! so many, have been
gently laid away,
From the work that never falters, but
like the surging sea,
With its billows rolling onward, to all
eternity.

Mrs. Baldwin's Letter

A letter was read, written by Mrs. Jane Baldwin, wife of the first minister of the church. At that time she was over eighty years of age. From that letter we quote:

With pleasure I comply with your request that I write some account of the early history of the church my husband organized and was for ten years the first pastor of—a history full of delightful reminiscence and events which are as fresh and distinct in memory as are the scenes of yesterday.

Fifty years ago Bowling Green had but one building that could by courtesy, be called a church. This was small and unattractive and was used during the week for entertainments of various kinds and often on Sabbath morning the odor of the atmosphere indicated the character of the gathering of the previous evening.

Families could "walk to the House of God in company," but at the church door there was a separation for the men seated on one side and the women on the other. Hymn books were few in number and the hymn, if not a familiar one, was generally "lined" by the minister.

The building was owned by the Methodist church and we were kindly permitted to occupy it, on alternate Sabbaths, and our congregations were practically the same, as there was no other service in the town.

We had a large union Sunday school and Mr. Solon Boughton was the faithful and beloved superintendent from its formation.

Family reunions and social gatherings were frequent and informal. The quilting bee and the husking party varied the monotony of country life. In time of sickness or when the Angel of Death brought distress and affliction neighborly kindness and sympathy were unfailing and abundant.

From its beginning Bowling Green constantly, and more or less rapidly, increased its population and was fast becoming the business center of the surrounding country and even at that early day, some, with prophetic vision, were inclined to look forward when it would become the county seat of Wood county. Our church shared in its prosperity and increased in members and in influence.

With growing impatience we eagerly looked forward to the completion of our house of worship, which with great self denial and sacrifice, was being erected on the lot where the present beautiful church now stands.

It was an occasion of great joy when we felt that we had a home of our very own. It was dedicated February 8, 1860, with no indebtedness except for the $200 loaned by the Church Erection Board, and this was paid in annual installments. At the evening service of the dedication, I well remember our delightful surprise in finding our church lighted with kerosene oil. It seemed like a blaze of glory in comparison with the dim light of the tallow candles to which we were accustomed.

Notes

Mr. and Mrs. S. L. Boughton were among the most prominent and active members in the building up and the welfare of the Presbyterian church. Mr. Boughton assisted in the organization of the Sunday school, on the 8th of April, 1860, was its first superintendent, and as such continued for a period of 25 years or more.

The first instrument used in the church was a little melodeon. Later, Miss Mary Day, who had a relative who was an organ dealer, was instrumental in securing a reed organ, which for some years she played.

The first communion set used by the church was the gift of Mr. Baldwin. This was in use for eighteen years, until 1873, when the church received the present of a communion set from the Sunday school of the First Presbyterian church of Utica, N. Y.

The bell which is still in use, was the present of Mr. P. J. Latchaw in the name of his wife, and was presented in April, 1874.

LIFE OF A RECLUSE

Abram D. Edgerton Among the Earliest Pioneers—Peculiar and Eccentric—Sad Romance of His Life

AMONG the few who settled on the sand ridges which skirt the old Keeler Prairie in Plain township, was Abram D. Edgerton, a young man, about 22 years of age, who came out from Ashtabula county with his father and stepmother in the year 1834. The Edgertons, like the Hollingtons, found shelter with the Mitchells, who had just come in until they built a cabin, which stood on the north side of the Weston ridge road at the place known as Carr's corners. The father of young Edgerton soon sickened and died, and some years after he and his step-mother sold out their possession to Joshua Carr, and the step-mother went to Michigan friends, where she died.

A Great Favorite

Abram, who was quite a general favorite among the early settlers, remained here, for he had no other home; in fact no relatives except a brother who had located at Baton Rouge, Louisiana. Edgerton was of a very social turn at times and was a mechanical genius; just such a man as was invaluable in a pioneer settlement. He could "tinker" a clock, solder a tin pan, fix a gun, set and splint a bone, lance an arm or carbuncle, tell a good story, sit up with the sick, teach writing school—in fact, do almost anything that was necessary to be done, and "Brom," as he was called, was welcome to dinner or a night's lodging wherever night chanced to overtake him in the settlement. When Bowling Green started up he engaged in the capacity of clerk in the store of L. C. Locke for some time, after which he taught a term or so of school. He was a fair English scholar and an elegant penman. He then engaged in house-painting as a trade, and accumulated considerable property. At one time he made an expensive tour south in search of his brother, who had died in the meantime of yellow fever. After learning this fact he returned and was more unsettled than ever. This left him without father, mother, brother or sister—in fact, without any kinsmen except some New York cousins whom he had never seen.

Avoided Society

He had no bad habits; neither was he

ever known to express any religious views and he seldom, in later life, attended worship. He was singularly shy and reticent in the presence of women. He was social and pleasant to those females of his early acquaintance, but preferred if possible to avoid the general society of women. It could hardly be called an aversion, but it amounted to almost that for it grew upon him and for the last 15 years of his life he lived by himself wholly alone, without the company of man, woman, dog or cat. He did his own cooking, washing and mending; occupying his spare time at odd jobs of clock "tinkering" and other light mechanical work. He seemed perfectly contented and happy and but seldom would accept the hospitality of friends, and then only as he made one of his periodical visiting rounds among the old settlers.

At Station Island

At one time he became infatuated with the gilt-edged stories told of Florida and her orange groves, sold his little property and like the adventurer Ponce De Leon, made a fruitless trip in the "Land of Flowers," only to return moneyless and disgusted with the home of the mosquitoes, alligators and countless swarms of gnats and midges in that semi-tropical country. He then "bached" it in a little shanty near town and some years after took charge of the Findlay club house at Station Island on the Maumee, at the request of the owners, and seemed to pass an easy, hermit-like life in fishing and shooting; making a few dollars for "pin money" by letting out club boats to little pleasure parties through the warm season.

His Last Days

He became impressed with the idea that a large portion of the Station Island was yet in the United States government, and was so strong in the belief that he borrowed money and made a journey to Washington to investigate the title, but he was disappointed and his projected possession came to naught and left him in quite straitened circumstances. To make matters worse a dropsical affection seized upon him from which time he was crippled in his limbs and gradually failed until he was unable to leave the club house. In this extremity the proud-spirited old man was a pitiable object.

He dreaded the thought of the poor house or of being an object of charity. He declined to be removed to the home of any of his old friends lest he should make them trouble, for which he could not compensate them. A kind neighbor, Mr. Vollmer, for some weeks went each night and remained with him till morning, lest he should die alone, and each day sent him such necessaries as he thought would be acceptable. He grew worse but still refused to be removed until at last, his old friend, John Whitehead, of Tontogany, went to the club house with a wagon and bed, determined to bring him away.

The old man bowed his head and broke into tears, crying like a child, the first time he had ever been known to give up. After a few moments he quietly gave some brief directions about some of his affairs, and consented to go with his friends, where he was kindly cared for and nursed until his death in 1880. He was bright and cheerful, and remained conscious until the last.

A Cherished Relic

He was a man of many singular peculiarities. He possessed a high order of intelligence, in many respects was devoted and faithful to his friends, and especially devoted to the memory of his deceased mother, who died when he was less than 20 years old. He had in one of his trunks, what was once a beautiful silk dress, the property of his mother, and the dress in which she was married. This he treasured as carefully as if it had been gold or precious gems. It is said, by those who knew him best, that there was

A Secret Romance

Connected with his early life—a love affair, which, if known, would explain much of the singular life of this old man whose last days were saddened with the thought that he was without home, kinsmen or natural protectors.

In the old Plain cemetery in an almost forgotten grave, rests the ashes of a lady, who was once the bright, cherished idol and admiration of him whose sad story we have told. He loved her with a devotion that knew no bounds and could brook no disappointment, and the gossips of that day say that she did not regard him with indifference, but he failed to gain her hand more through what a cavalryman would call a lack of soldiery dash, than through any other cause. Edgerton, like many other young men, lacked the courage to make a gallant, bold dash in cavalier-like style, such as would carry the heart and hand of a black-eyed, black-haired maiden of those pioneer days. This prairie belle was not without suitors, one of whom soon supplanted the bashful, hesitating Edgerton and carried her off.

She lived many years and seemed happy, but not so he who once loved her and still in the depths of his heart loved her and when she died the canker of sorrow preyed upon him, but no murmur escaped his lips. A few words which he dropped a short time before his death to an old acquaintance and friend furnishes a key to his untold secret and explains somewhat the story of his fickle, purposeless, though harmless career. His book is closed forever. He will be remembered kindly among all the old pioneers as a kind neighbor, a faithful friend and an inoffensive citizen.—*C. W. E.*

SUCCESSFUL SCHEME

Didn't Propose That Henry County Should Benefit by a Wood County Wolf

A WOLF incident is told in the Wood County Tribune by J. F. Dubbs, illustrative of the schemes the settlers sometimes resorted to, to make an honest dollar in those days when money was so scarce. Across the swamp in Jackson township, lived his uncle, John Dubbs, who raised stock and the wolves gave him much trouble. He finally located their hiding place in the wilderness where Deshler now stands, and built a wolf pen of logs, so that when a wolf jumped down through a hole left in the top, to get the bait, which had been placed inside to appease his hunger, he could not get out.

One day as the great bear hunter, Sam Edwards, and his son, were passing that way on one of their great chases, he came to a halt at the wolf pen where Uncle John had a wolf entrapped which he was trying to take alive.

"Why not kill him and save the bother," said Edwards. "Well, sir," said Uncle John, "I find that my pen is across the Henry county line. Wood county gives a bounty of $10 and Henry county does not, and I am not going to bring Wood county wolves over to Henry county to kill for nothing."

The wolf was taken alive by Uncle John, carried over to Wood county, where it no doubt had been boarding on Uncle John's live stock, and its thieving scalp soon after adorned the wall of Uncle John's cabin.

SCRAP-BOOK.

A LOAD OF COONS

Brought Relief and Made a Handsome Payment on Land

THAT old-time pioneer, J. F. Dubbs, of Milton Center, had a wide experience in the hardships of Wood county's early days, and could tell many reminiscences of the hard winters, the sickly season, the loss of crops, the destitution, the lack of roads, markets, schools, or medical aid when sickness or accident came, all of which bore on the new settler with disheartening weight. Some perished from disease; some fled; others staid and fought it out.

In writing to the Wood County Tribune, Mr. Dubbs says when his father died, he and his brother John, both young fellows then, bought together 160 acres of land in Jackson township, on easy terms of payment.

They worked hard and got out 40 or 50 acres of crop, but a wet season swept away all their labor and seed and a payment of $200 and interest at 6 per cent on $1,000 was to be met the following spring. They didn't know what to do. There were no employment bureaus then —no chance to sell one's labor for cash— nobody had any cash in fact.

So the boys possessed themselves of a couple of hunting dogs, one of which had been trained to locate a coon-tree by scent—that is, the keen-scented animal, in passing through the forests day time or night, would locate the trees where the coon had taken up its winter home. The wet seasons in Liberty prairie, while not favorable to grain crops, were very propitious for the frogs, and that means a good coon, muskrat and mink crop. By spring when their notes were due they had caught over two hundred coon, besides other varmints wearing valuable fur. They started early in the morning and came in late at night. The coon would be frozen so they could not be skinned, by the time they reached the cabin at night. So the boys threw them in the wagon box at the cabin door and covered them, and soon the wagon box was full of unskinned coons.

One day a fur buyer came along and gave them $280 for the lot, and the note and interest was paid, and John and Jim were happy and had a lot of sport as well as hard work.

"JOHNNY APPLESEED"

Quaint Old Pioneer of the Early Northwest Has a Monument

JOHNNY APPLESEED has a monument, says the Chicago Times-Herald. Future generations shall know of the unique mission of John Chapman, the Apostle of Apples. Mansfield, Ohio, has rescued his memory from oblivion and embalmed it in a statue. The story of his gentle, beneficent life is the record of one of the quaintest, sweetest characters produced in the pioneer west. Next to his religion, "Johnny Appleseed" held apples to be the choicest blessing vouchsafed to man. He believed in the salvation of health by apples. He preached the gospel of apples, and he practiced it. He made the young lands in Ohio and Indiana bloom with the fragrant white blossoms of countless apple trees. He added untold wealth and happiness to generations born and unborn. Sage and simple, crank and genius, seer and vagrant, "Johnny Appleseed" was a penniless philanthropist, a humble benefactor of millions.

The cider mills of Pennsylvania were his Mecca, and appleseeds his quest. From every pilgrimage to the east he brought back precious sacks of seeds. With his own hands he cleared forest space for his nurseries, and when the trees were two or three years old, he distributed them broadly, sometimes in exchange for a bit of clothing, but more often as a gift. Gentle and lovable, friend of white and redskin, the apple missionary was as one crying in the wilderness. He went whither he would, welcomed by all, and he dotted the woods and prairies of his kingdom with apple orchards.

"Johnny Appleseed" carried on his work of distributing apple trees and appleseeds through Ohio and the Maumee Valley for twenty years or more, and then he followed the star of empire westward to continue his mission in the newer field of Indiana, where he died in 1845.

"Appleseed Johnny" was a hero, too. During the war of 1812 Mansfield was frightened by rumors of a hostile attack. The nearest soldiers were at Mount Vernon, 30 miles away, where Capt. Douglass had a troop. When a call was made for a volunteer to carry a message to Mount Vernon, "Johnny" stepped forward. The journey had to be made at night over a new road, that was little better than a trail, and through a country swarming with blood-thirsty Indians.

The unarmed Apostle of Apples sped through the woods like a runner, and came back in the morning with a squad of soldiers. It was an incident worthy a poem, but has been almost forgotten.

The death of this strange missionary was in keeping with his life-work. The latter years of his life were spent near Ft. Wayne, where, although 70 years old, he continued to grow and scatter apple trees. He learned that some cattle had broken down the brushwood fence of a nursery he had planted. It was winter, and the nursery was twenty miles away, but the brave old crusader started out on foot to save his beloved trees. He worked for hours in cold and snow, repairing the fence, and started to walk back home. He fainted from fatigue and took refuge in the cabin of a settler. It happened the pioneer had come from Ohio, and knew of "Johnny's" work in that state. He welcomed the weak old man, who asked only a bit of bread and a place on the floor to sleep. The next morning "Johnny" was delirious, and soon afterward he died of pneumonia. He was buried near by and a rude board placed over his grave, but it has long since crumbled into dust, and the site of the burial is unknown.

"Johnny Appleseed"

The following was written by James Newton Matthews, and dedicated to the American Horticultural Society, and read at a meeting in Austin, Texas, by Miss Regan:

There's a hero worth the singing that no
    poet's lips have sung,
A prophet of the wilderness whose deeds
    have found no tongue,—
A homely, humble-hearted man—a gen-
    tle spirit sent
To cheer the world and plant the newer
    gospel as he went,—
A specter of the solitudes, whose bare-
    feet, where they pressed,
Prankt with never-dying beauty the dark
    borders of the West,—
A Druid of the Valley, but as worthless
    as the wave,
Scorning comfort—seeking nothing for
    the good things that he gave,—
A poor old, plodding pilgrim of a brave,
    unselfish breed,
God showed the way, and shod the feet
    of Johnny Appleseed.

SCRAP-BOOK.

I touch the stainless record with a deli-
  cacy due
To the reverence that bows us, when
  the great soul comes to view—
How pales our petty passions and ambi-
  tions, when we scan
The garnered love that glitters from one
  guileless-hearted man;
And such was he to whom we pay the
  tribute of a tear,
The orchard-planter of the West—our
  oldest pioneer,
Whose only weapon of defense against
  a war-like race,
Was the glow of childish innocence that
  gladdened in his face —
And so no knight of any age that ever
  mounted steed,
Went forth to battle better armed than
  Johnny Appleseed.

We frame him in our fancy like a figure
  in a dream,
A specter on a phantom boat, a-floating
  down a stream—
A little fat-faced fellow, with a ruddy
  cheek and chin,
And a funny little "mush-pot" that he
  poked his round head in—
With hair as black and frowsy as a bat's
  wing dipped in tar,
And eyes as sharp and sparkling as the
  twinkling of a star—
With a body plump and pudgy, as the
  picture of a Turk,
And a sprightly Puck-like motion, punc-
  tuated with a jerk—
Such seems the meager outline of the
  man of whom we read,
In the legends handed down to us of
  Johnny Appleseed.

So tender was the heart of him, so gentle, and so just,
He would not harm the vilest thing that
  wriggled in the dust;
He quenched his camp-fire on the hills,
  for fear the beetles might

Get scorched against the flames of it in
  their uncertain flight;
'Tis said he even spared the snake whose
  venomed fangs he felt,
And all the air was soft with love and
  pity where he dwelt;
The pappoose prattled on his knee—the
  panther on the limb
Seemed conscious of his harmlessness,
  and only glared at him—
And thus along the world he went, as
  destiny decreed,
And happy in the life he led, this Johnny
  Appleseed.

Thro' every forest where he passed he
  scattered germs that grew
To blooming benedictions, as he drifted
  on into
The gloomy regions farther west, that
  swallowed him from sight,
As a cloud absorbs a star-beam, in the
  silence of the night;
He sank into the solitudes, like some re-
  membered strain,
That warmed the heart an instant, and
  was never heard again;
But when the pippins glimmer in the
  brown October days,
Ohio's hills and valleys pulse the old
  apostle's praise.
And the people pushing after him, with
  lifted voices plead
For purposes as pure as those of Johnny
  Appleseed.

A song for Johnny Appleseed! who left
  a living trail
Of beauty everywhere he went, in moun-
  tain and in vale;
Thro' many a vanished summer sang the
  birds and hummed the bees
Amid the bending blossoms of his broad
  old appletrees,
Before the tardy vanguard of the foremost pioneers
Came to pluck the welcome fruitage in
  that wilderness of theirs;

A health to Johnny Appleseed! and may
his glory be
Regrafted in the years to come, on Life's
eternal tree,

And as long as poor humanity stands
naked in its need,
God send us souls as white as that of
Johnny Appleseed.

MAYOR ANDREW ROACH

One of the Strong, Energetic Executive Officers of Perrysburg

AFTER a long and painful illness, Mayor Andrew Roach passed from life at his Perrysburg home on Saturday morning, September 14, 1901, diabetes being the cause of death.

Mr. Roach was born in Ireland, in 1833, and had he lived until the 5th of November, would have been 68 years old. His parents moved to Kingston, Canada, in 1837, where he lived for 10 years. In 1848 he moved to this state, and for several years was engaged in railroad building, and in 1859 located in Perrysburg, where he has since resided.

He was twice married. To the first union three daughters and two sons were born, all of whom preceded him to the world beyond except one son, Edward, aged 43, who resides in Dayton. His second wife died a number of years ago leaving one son, Andrew, Jr., now Sheriff of Wood county, who with Edward Roach of Dayton, are the only children who survive the father, and they, with one sister of the deceased, Mrs. Birk of Dayton, were present at his bedside at the time of dissolution.

During his life Mr. Roach had been a very active citizen. In politics he was an ardent Democrat and at various times held the offices of Mayor, Councilman, member of school board, library board, and gas trustee. In every position he held he has been a credit to himself and the people he represented.

He was a member of Phoenix lodge No. 123, Free and Accepted Masons, since February 16, 1863, and for three years was Secretary of the lodge, and during this long term had always been held in high esteem by his brethren.

In his earlier life he was engaged in railroad building, and was in charge of the construction of the Dayton and Michigan railroad from Lima to Toledo and for more than 30 years was roadmaster for the company.

The first engine used on the road, he brought overland from Mad river, and Archie Rider of Tontogany, was the engineer.

The funeral services were conducted at the late home on Sunday in charge of Phoenix lodge of Masons with Rev. Adams as chaplain and Bro. A. R. Williams as acting Master.

The services were attended by a large number of people from Perrysburg and neighboring towns—the members of the council, Clerk and Marshal attending in a body.

An Error Corrected

One writer, in describing the sieges of Ft. Meigs, makes the statement that after the first siege, which ended May 8, 1813, Gen. Proctor embarked his troops and sailed away to Malden, but that he returned ten days later, with a force of 5,000 whites and Indians, and that the second siege was abandoned May 28. This is an error. The fort was invested the second time on July 21. On the 26th Tecumseh resorted to the trick of a sham battle expecting to draw out the garrison, but his scheme failed, and on July 27, 1813, the second siege ended.

FORT MEIGS
The Natural Ravine Where the Soldiers Were Quartered During the Siege of 1813

SCRAP-BOOK.

THE RIVER RAISIN MASSACRE

One of the Bloodiest Tragedies in the Annals of the War of 1812

THE ignominious surrender of Detroit by Gen. Hull in August, 1812, caused the whole Michigan Territory, for the time being to pass under the control of the British. Under these conditions to recover and hold possession of the territory which Hull's unfortunate surrender at Detroit had transferred to British domination, and expel the invaders therefrom, and at the same time protect the helpless pioneers from the torch and scalping knife, was the task imposed upon General Harrison, a task which a less fearless and intrepid leader would have looked upon with apprehension and dismay.

Senator Burrows says the execution of this plan involved the penetration of an almost trackless wilderness, invested on every side by hostile savages intent only upon murder and rapine. General Harrison was not oblivious to the difficulties and dangers of the situation. Replying to an inquiry as to when the army would advance, he said: "I am not able to fix any period for the advance of the troops to Detroit. It is pretty evident that it cannot be done upon proper principles until the frost shall have become so severe as to enable us to use the rivers and the margin of the lakes for the transportation of the baggage upon the ice. To go forward through a swampy wilderness for nearly 200 miles in wagons or on pack horses, which are to carry their own provisions, is absolutely impossible. My present plan is to occupy Upper Sandusky and accumulate at that place as much provision and forage as possible, to be taken from thence upon sleds to the River Raisin."

In the execution of this plan, General Winchester was assigned to the command of the advance with a force of some twelve hundred men, composed of the Seventeenth United States regulars, and the First, Second and Fifth Kentucky Volunteers, and the First Kentucky Riflemen. It will thus be seen that the troops of Kentucky bore a most conspicuous part in the initial movement of the campaign.

At the Rapids

It had been determined by the General in command as a step in his advance upon the enemy, to concentrate his forces on the Maumee, and to that end General Winchester was directed to take position at the Rapids, fortify the place and hold it as a depot for supplies and a base of operations of the army in its advance into the enemy's country.

On the 10th of January, 1813, Winchester, in the execution of his orders, reached the Rapids of the Maumee, established and fortified his camp and awaited the arrival of supplies and the remainder of the command. While thus encamped, disquieting rumors came from the inhabitants of Frenchtown, a little hamlet of less than thirty families, and where the thriving city of Monroe now stands, to the effect that the British forces at Malden, across the border, only eighteen miles distant, were about to move on the defenseless inhabitants of Frenchtown. Upon the confirmation of these rumors an appeal was made to General Winchester to go to the defense of the panic-stricken people. General Harrison was sixty-five miles away, and therefore could not be consulted, and the troops were impatient for the advance, and General Winchester, responding to the humane impulse of his troops, on the 18th of January, 1813, ordered Colonels Lewis and Allen, with 660 men, "to hasten to their defense, attack the enemy, beat them and take possession of Frenchtown and hold it." When the

American forces reached Frenchtown they were confronted by 200 Canadian militia with their 400 Indian allies, prepared to resist the consummation of this purpose.

A Temporary Victory

Though confronting an enemy superior in numbers, Winchester's forces crossed the River Raisin on the ice and in a fierce engagement drove the British and their savage allies from the town and took possession of the abandoned camp of the enemy. The conduct of our troops on this occasion elicited from the historian the declaration that the discipline of the troops "amply supported the double character of Americans and Kentuckians." The twelve Americans killed and the fifty-five wounded testify to the severity of this engagement.

Although a temporary victory had been won, yet the position of our troops was exceedingly perilous, being only twenty miles from Malden, the headquarters of the enemy, from which point reinforcements would be readily and swiftly forwarded. Yet the heroic band, after an informal council of war, deliberately determined to hold the place at all hazards and await reinforcements.

Winchester was immediately advised of conditions, and on the 19th of January, with 300 men, hastened to the support of his decimated forces at Frenchtown, arriving there on the 20th. On the following day, the 21st, news was brought to Winchester that a large force of British and Indians had left Malden and were on the march towards Frenchtown and had already reached Stony Creek, and would be at the village before daylight the following morning. General Winchester refused to credit these rumors and confidence and repose settled down over the doomed American camp. Before the break of the following day the report of a sentinel's musket sounded the alarm and dispelled the illusion of security, and the roar of shell and rattle of musketry, mingled with the yells of the savages, proclaimed the presence of Proctor's forces, and sounded the

Death Knell of the Americans

Let History record the slaughter that followed: "No rule of civilized warfare was observed. Blood and scalps were the chief objects for which the Indians fought. They seemed disposed not to take any prisoners. A party of fifteen or twenty, under Lieutenant Garrett, after retreating about a mile, were compelled to surrender, when all but the young commander were killed and scalped. Another party, of forty men, were more than half murdered under similar circumstances. Colonel Allen, who had been wounded in the thigh in the attempt to rally the troops, after abandoning all hope, and escaping about two miles in the direction of the Maumee, was compelled, by sheer exhaustion, to sit down upon a log. He was observed by an Indian chief, who, perceiving his rank, promised him protection if he would surrender without resistance. He did so. At the same moment two other savages approached with murderous intent, when, with a single blow of his sword, Allen laid one of them dead upon the ground. His companion instantly shot the Colonel dead. 'He had the honor,' it was said, 'of shooting one of the first and greatest citizens of Kentucky.'"

Proctor's Infamy

The last act, however, of this horrible tragedy was yet to be performed. In the struggle Winchester had been taken prisoner, and Proctor, by threats of further slaughter and extermination of his entire command, induced Winchester to sign an order directed to Major Madison, the next in command, and who was still heroically defending his position, to surrender the entire force as prisoners of war. This order borne by one of General Winchester's staff, accompanied by General Proctor himself under a flag of truce, was carried to Major Madison, who refused to obey the order, saying, "It has been customary for the Indians to massacre the wounded and prisoners after a surrender; I shall, therefore, not agree to any capitulation which General Winchester may direct, unless the safety and protection of all the prisoners shall be stipulated." To this refusal Proctor replied, "Sir, do YOU mean to dictate to ME?" Madison answered, "I mean to dictate for myself, and we prefer selling our lives as dearly as possible rather than be massacred in cold blood."

Thereupon Proctor promised protection to all the prisoners, and pledged his honor as a soldier to the performance of the obligation. It is needless to say that the pledge was not redeemed.

Without relating the story of the massacre of the helpless prisoners after the surrender, in shameful disregard of Proctor's plighted faith, and without reciting the deeds of individual heroism, which characterized the actors in this final scene, the awful truth stands recorded that on this field, out of a force of 934 Americans, only 33 escaped, while nearly 400 were massacred and the balance taken prisoners.

Thus ended a conflict which will go down the ages as one of the bloodiest tragedies in the annals of war. The result here, although our forces were defeated, opened the way later for the advance of our army, the recovery of Detroit, the invasion of Canada and the defeat of the British forces on the Thames, with the death of Tecumseh.

Ann Austin, of Cygnet, aged 102 years, died some years ago. She was one of the band of Wyandot Indians who came to Wood county nearly 70 years ago. She was the queen of the little Indian settlement.

THE BATTLE IN CANADA

The Scenes That Closed the Memorable Conflict and the Death of Tecumseh

IN an address by Col. Bennett H. Young, delivered at Monroe, some years since, he thus describes the closing scenes of the battle of the Thames that ended Gen. Harrison's remarkable campaign:

Shelby and his Kentucky army reported to Gen. Harrison at Perrysburg on the 14th of September, 1813, and remained at Put-in-Bay until the 27th, when leaving their homes at Portage river, they embarked on Commodore Perry's fleet, landed at Malden on English soil and began the pursuit of Proctor and Tecumseh, who after Perry's glorious victory began a retreat eastward toward Hamilton.

With the 3,000 Kentuckians Gen. Harrison and Gov. Shelby began on October 1st the hunt of Proctor and Tecumseh in earnest. The dismounted militia vied with Johnson's regiment in making the pursuit vigorous. Many portions of the march were passed at half run, and one day they covered twenty-five miles. Thamesville was a small settlement east of Detroit on the English highway from Hamilton to Detroit, 63 miles east of the latter place and 12 miles from Lake Erie. Here on the afternoon of October, 1813, the English and Indians were brought to bay.

Proctor had with him the 41st British

regiment. They had been at Raisin. These he placed on the main road; Tecumseh had 1,800 Indians; these were assigned to a place in a swamp at right angles to the main road. Johnson's Kentucky mounted riflemen, 1,200 in number, held the front line of the American advance, while the five brigades of dismounted men were a few hundred feet behind. Proctor was with the British forces 1,500 feet away from the front of his line.

Pursuit of Proctor

The hour for action had come. Behind, weary marchings of four hundred miles, full of self-denial and unchanging privations, before them, enemies arousing an immeasurable hate. Every heart was full of memories of savage brutality and cruelty to relatives, friends and fellow citizens for a quarter of a century. The horrible massacre of the Raisin, its indescribable barbarity and its fiendish inhumanity was painted on every soul, and the spirit of its slain victims seemed to ride side by side in martial procession with these living horsemen, fate's avengers, chosen to inflict punishment on its ferocious perpetrators.

The atrocities of Fort Meigs were not forgotten, and the cry of the Kentuckians, tortured and murdered by the savage red men within the sight of British officers, and coolly tomahawked or shot while helpless and defenseless in their very presence, seemed to beseech heaven for a just and complete revenge upon those guilty of such unspeakable horrors.

Among Kentuckians now aligning for conflict were men who had looked upon all that was awful at Raisin and terrible at Fort Meigs. Some had shared in the humiliation of Detroit's surrender, and had witnessed their country's flag and honor sullied by Gen Hull's cowardice and imbecility, while others had endured the trials, insults and torture of British prisons. All were animated by the highest courage and truest patriotism. The generous impulses of brave and chivalrous souls impelled every man to the noblest discharge of duty, and every ear was listening with absorbing interest for the sound which should call them to battle with their detested foes.

"Remember the Raisin!"

In the fierce charge there was but one cry oft repeated, but rising each time in sharper and quicker tones; "Remember the Raisin—Remember the Raisin."

These avenging warriors, catching the enthusiasm and delirium of combat, rose high in their stirrups, and plunged their spurs into the flanks of their chargers as they approached their enemy, still more furiously, waved their guns aloft and with their voices made stronger and stronger by the excitement of their impetuosity, cried the more vehemently, "Remember the Raisin." "Remember the Raisin."

A quarter of a mile away at the rear, in the edge of the forest, along the trail, was the commander of the British regulars. General Henry A. Proctor, who was responsible for the revolting butchery and brutality at Raisin and Meigs, came to Canada as the Colonel of a British regiment, and his atrocities have never been reproved by his government. For his conduct at Raisin he had been promoted to a brigadier-general.

His ear was quick to detect danger. He knew his fate if the Kentuckians (many of whom had sworn that he should not be taken alive) should capture him.

Proctor's Flight

He distinctly heard the tramp of Johnson's mounted men, and his ear caught that portentous and to him fateful cry, "Remember the Raisin." Dismayed, he watched and waited for the result. He saw one line brushed out of the path of the horsemen or rush in confusion upon the second line. He beheld this last line disappear and the black hunting shirts and grey hunting breeches of the Kentuckians as they dismounted and turned upon his stricken and helpless grenadiers, and then with his cowardly conscience impelling him, he turned his horse's head eastward and accompanied by a small guard of horsemen precipitately fled toward Burlington. Hard pressed by Major DeVall Payne, he abandoned his baggage and followers and fled through the forest to escape capture. His ignominious conduct brought upon him the contempt of his associates. He was tried by court martial, disgraced, and deprived of pay for six months, and was publicly reprimanded by his superiors by order of his government.

A Bloody Conflict

A sterner conflict and more sanguinary fate awaited the second battalion of Johnson's regiment.

This was formed in two columns, on horseback, while one company was dismounted and on foot placed in front of the right column, which was led by Col. Johnson. The front of each column was something like 500 feet. At the head of the column led by Johnson was a company on foot. While in front of those mounted was what was known as the "Forlorn Hope," in the courage and gallantry of which on that day was written one of the most heroic and sublimely brave acts which had ever been recorded of Kentucky men.

The "Forlorn Hope" consisted of twenty men. Col. Johnson himself rode by its side. It was led by the grand old pioneer, William Whitley.

These twenty men with Col. R. M. Johnson, and the pioneer William Whitley, at once advanced to the front. The main line halted for a brief space, until this advance could assume position, and when once they were placed, at the command, "Forward, march," they quietly and calmly rode to death.

In the thickets of the swamp, in which lay Tecumseh, and his red soldiers, they peered in vain for a foe. Not a man stirred, but the ominous silence betokened only the more dreadful fire when the moment of contact should come.

Along the narrow space they advanced. Stunted bushes and matted and deadened grass impeded their horses' feet, but these heroes urged their steeds forward with rapid walk, seeking the hidden foe in the morass that skirted the ground upon which they had aligned.

Fate of the "Forlorn Hope"

A loud, clear, savage voice rang out the word "Fire." The sharp crackling of half a hundred rifles was the response, and then the deafening sound of a thousand shots filled the air. The smoke concealed those who fired the guns but the murderous effect was none the less terrible. Of the twenty, one alone escaped unhurt or failed to be unhorsed. A mass of fallen, struggling horses, a company of wounded, dying men lay side by side. The bleeding beasts whinneyed to dead masters, and wounded masters laid their hands on the quivering bodies of their faithful steeds. Of the twenty, fifteen were dead, or to die. Their leader with a dozen wounds, still sat erect, his judge advocate, Theobald, close to his side. The remainder was lost in the battle's confusion.

The "Forlorn Hope" had met its fate. Its mission was to receive the fire of the savages, when their fellows and comrades might safely charge upon the red men with guns unloaded. Its purpose had been fulfilled.

The five hundred and fifty men of Johnson's battalion were reinforced by quite a number of volunteer infantrymen from Trotter's, Donaldson's and Simrall's regiment, who hearing the firing and the shouts both of the Indians and white men, rushed to the assistance of their comrades.

For a quarter of an hour the result of the battle seemed in doubt. Eighteen hundred Indians in the swamp and on their chosen battlefield, behind trees and fallen logs, did not hesitate to throw down the gage of battle to the six thousand Kentuckians who now advanced to the assault.

As the lines were pushed along through the morass, Col. Johnson saw behind a fallen tree, an Indian chief, who with vigorous words of command and loud cheers and most earnest encouragement was urging the red men to stand firm against the assaults of the white men.

Death of Tecumseh

At the head of the column opposing these men, Johnson still sitting upon his white mare, rode around the tree and advanced upon the red man. At the first fire he had lost by a wound the use of his left hand, in which he would carry his bridle. The Indian placing his gun to his shoulder immediately fired and added another to the many wounds already received by the gallant Kentuckian and then having exhausted his trusty rifle, with uplifted tomahawk, he advanced upon the white man, who, although wounded, was now riding upon him fearlessly and rapidly. The savage jerking his tomahawk from his side, and waiting for no assistance except his own strong arm backed by his courageous soul, rushed upon Col. Johnson to strike him from his horse, but when he had advanced within four feet, Johnson letting his horse loose, seized his pistol from his helpless left hand and fired its contents into the breast of the Indian. Being loaded with one bullet and three buckshot, at such close range, and piercing the heart of the Indian, he instantly fell dead. Some said it was Tecumseh.

He was certainly a great leader, and it was at this time that somebody in the battle killed Tecumseh.

The red men with amazement looked upon the sudden and unexpected death of their valiant chief. They heard no more his shouts of encouragement, saw no more the gallant wave of his hand, and with utter alarm and despair, and with a great cry of disappointment they rushed from the battlefield.

A Crushed, Defeated Foe

Tecumseh was dead. The Indian power was crushed. Proctor was in cowardly flight and disgrace as a man and soldier. The red men had by a lesson never to be forgotten, felt the power of the white man's strong arm, and learned that no British agency could save him when the white man undertook his punishment. The red men were humbled and their hopes destroyed. The great northwest was free. Michigan was the white man's possession by right of conquest, and by the power of the sword had been made forever a part of the American Republic.

The British soldiers who had command at the shameful massacre of these knightly Kentuckians, were now prisoners and were to march as captives over this battlefield, where their barbaric cruelty and brutality had done so much to blacken the name and honor of their nation, and in the end to be prisoners of war in the penitentiary of the state whose soldiers they had ruthlessly allowed to be murdered, while their savage allies whom they had incited to kill, burn and scalp, while men, while women and even children, whose only offense was to be an American, were hiding in the pathless woods of Canada and Michigan to avoid the white man's wrath.

Raisin was remembered; Raisin was avenged.

JAMES H. PIERCE

Life and Death of One of Wood County's Sterling Citizens

JAMES PIERCE, of Perrysburg, ex-commissioner of Wood county, to whom more than any other individual are the farmers of Wood county indebted for the present magnificent system of ditching, died very suddenly and unexpectedly at his home on Sunday afternoon, May 6, 1894.

Whether through premonition, or otherwise, is not known, but previous to Sunday Mr. Pierce had requested that all members of his family be invited to dinner on that day, which was accordingly done.

In the forenoon he repaired to a room on the upper floor, which he was wont to occupy during the daytime, either to read or sleep. At dinner time his grandson went to summon him, but finding him asleep, he returned and the meal was eaten in his absence. An hour and a half later his daughter Mattie went to the room, and seeing her father lying in a reclining position she approached him, only to be horrified by the discovery that he was dead.

Drs. Hamilton and Rheinfrank were immediately summoned but found that life was extinct; he had probably been dead about an hour, death coming as a sweet sleep without pain or struggle.

Mr. Pierce was a native of New York State, where he was born December 19, 1831. When three years of age his parents moved to Blissfield, Mich. In 1846, he moved to Shelby county, where he commenced life in a practical way, and from the age of 12 to 26 years he was employed on the Wabash canal, the latter part of which time he was captain of a packet boat, the "Sidney Belle."

On March 6, 1855, he was united in marriage to Miss Sarah Guy of Sidney, Ohio, who with a family of six daughters survive him. In 1857 he came to Perrysburg township, and located on the pike where he engaged in the lumber business, and continued in it until 1872, when he was appointed Commissioner to fill the unexpired term (3 months) occasioned by the death of Commissioner Eber Wilson. At the expiration of this term he was elected Commissioner for two years, and was afterward re-elected for two 3-year terms, and has been regarded as one of the very best Commissioners who ever filled that important office in Wood county.

After that he served as Mayor of Perrysburg, and member of Board of Education of that village, and was again elected to the Union school board at the spring election and at the time of his death was also a member of the Board of Township Trustees.

For several years he was proprietor of the Exchange hotel of Perrysburg, and was known throughout the country as a genial and popular host.

His family consisted of a kind and loving wife, six daughters, Mrs. Emma J. Norton, Mrs. Carrie A. Thompson, Mrs. Jennie E. Priest, and Misses Frances A., Martha A., and Cora M. Pierce, all of whom were present at the time of his death.

Mr. Pierce was a member of Phoenix Lodge, No. 123, F. & A. M. of Perrysburg, and his funeral services were conducted by the members of that order, under the direction of Master John H. Thornton, the sermon being delivered by Rev. G. A. Adams, the chaplain of the lodge. A large number of the members of Phoenix lodge were in attendance and visiting members from neighboring towns were also present.

James Pierce was a man of character in every station in life; honest, courageous and a whole-souled man wherever you found him. He was one of the best known men of Wood county and filled a niche in public affairs which few men have had the honor to fill. For a number of years he had retired from active work, and was living contentedly, surrounded by most of his children.

The funeral was one of the largest ever held in the village. The floral offerings being numerous and of beautiful designs—the last tribute to a beloved and departed citizen, neighbor and friend. Every business house in the village was closed during the funeral.—*Perrysburg Journal.*

JUDGE H. H. DODGE

Sketch of His Life—Tributes of Respect to His Memory

AFTER a lingering illness of several months the life of Hon. H. H. Dodge came to a peaceful close on Monday, May 16, 1904, about 3 o'clock p. m. Of late, says the Perrysburg Journal, Mr. Dodge had seemed to be in better spirits and health than for some months and a few days prior to his death visited relatives in Bowling Green in company with his wife, when he had a most enjoyable time. On Friday, May 13, he was stricken with paralysis from which he did not recover, but sank rapidly until death came as a happy release.

Henry H. Dodge was born February 4, 1830, at Pompey Hill, Onondaga county, New York. He received his early education in his native town and at the age of 16 was sent to the St. John's College, conducted by the Jesuit Fathers, New York City, from which he was graduated in 1849. After a couple of years spent on the farm with his father he began the study of law with Victor Birdseye of Pompey Hill.

He came to Perrysburg in 1852 and finished his law studies with the firm of Spink & Murray, being admitted to the bar in 1855. Upon the death of Mr. Spink, Mr. Dodge became a partner of James Murray, which partnership continued until Mr. Murray's election as Attorney General of Ohio, in 1859. In 1860 he associated himself with the late James R. Tyler until 1869, then with Edson Goit, now deceased, and Jasher Pillars of Bowling Green.

In 1877, Mr. Dodge was elected Judge of the Common Pleas court, holding this position for a term of ten years with marked distinction.

Upon retiring from the bench he formed a partnership with John W. Canary of Bowling Green, which lasted until his removal to Perrysburg in December, 1897. Here he thought he might retrieve his health surrounded by the familiar scenes, in his old homestead, on the banks of the beautiful Maumee.

In 1857 he was united in marriage with Sarah Hodge Wilkinson, and to them were born two children, Mary E. the older, wife of Ernest G. Miller of Creede, Colorado, died in December, 1893, leaving two children Hobart and Mary to the care of her parents. Frederick G., the younger, general agent for the Bloch Bros. Tobacco company of Wheeling, West Virginia.

Judge Dodge was a devoted husband and father and was never happier than when surrounded by his family. He was a member of the Catholic church, strong in his religious beliefs, a consciencious character.

The Wood County Democrat pays the following tribute:

"Politically he was an ardent Demo-

SCRAP-BOOK.

crat of the Jackson school, and his counsel and assistance was always eagerly sought by and freely given to his co-laborers in the cause of the party whose principles he espoused. He was always courteous and manly in his demeanor, warmly cherished friendship, and detested treachery with all the force of his strong mind.

"He enjoyed the highest esteem of all who were favored by his acquaintance, and he will be greatly missed by the bar and in the everyday walks of life. It can truthfully be said that mankind has been ennobled and the world made better by the life of Henry H. Dodge, who has gone to his rest with the universal respect of the people among whom he labored, and who were witnesses of the honor and uprightness of his daily life."

The funeral services were held at the St. Rose de Lima church Friday morning at half past nine o'clock.

The Reverend Father Griss of Fostoria, celebrated requiem high mass assisted by the Reverend Father Schriener of Bowling Green, as deacon, and the Reverend Father Mertes of Maumee as sub-deacon, who spoke feelingly on the life of the deceased.

On account of the prominence of the deceased the funeral was one of the largest ever held in Perrysburg, being attended by a large concourse of friends and admirers from his home county and neighboring counties. The members of the Wood County bar, some accompanied by their wives, attended the services in a body. Those present from Bowling Green were W. S. Haskell, Jas. O. Troup, F. A. Baldwin, A. R. Campbell, E. G. McClelland, Thos. F. Conley, B. F. James, G. C. Nearing, L. C. Cole, E. M. Fries, Robert Dunn, J. E. Shatzel, R. S. Parker, J. W. Canary. Those present from Tiffin were Judge Geo. E. Seney and Judge John McCauley. From Findlay, Judge Geo. F. Pendleton, Col. J. A. Bope, A. Zugschwert, Jason Blackford and Aaron Blackford.

The pall-bearers all ex-judges who associated with Judge Dodge at various times were Judge Geo. E. Seney and Judge John McCauley of Tiffin; Judge Geo. F. Pendleton of Findlay; Judge Frank Taylor, North Baltimore; Judge R. S. Parker, Bowling Green, and Col. Bope.

The remains were laid to rest in Fort Meigs cemetery.

TECUMSEH'S CONTEMPT

It was at Ft. Miami that a quarrel occurred between Gen. Proctor and the Indian Chief Tecumseh. In the presence of Gen. Proctor and other British officers, the Indians robbed and tomahawked the American prisoners. It is said that the number killed without Proctor's interference at the close of the battle, fully equalled those slain on the field of battle. When the prisoners were inside the fort the Indians commenced loading their guns for a general slaughter. At this juncture Tecumseh rode up and inquired for Proctor.

"There he is," said an Indian ally, pointing to the British general.

"Why don't you stop this?" inquired the Indian chief.

"Your Indians cannot be restrained," said the Englishman.

"Go put on petticoats," retorted Tecumseh. "You are not fit to command men."

Just above Waterville, at the lower end of Station Island, is a solid block of granite in a private burial ground. It is the resting place of the remains of "Robert Dunlap, Soldier of the Revolutionary War," born July 28, 1752, died July 25, 1836.

MAJOR GEORGE CROGHAN

A Gallant)Youngster, Not 22, After Service at Fort Meigs, Became the Hero of Ft. Stephenson

ON August 2, 1906, Fremont, in a splendid manner, commemorated the defense of Fort Stephenson so gallantly and successfully accomplished by the valiant Major George Croghan. The event was attended by thousands, and among them some of the most prominent men in public life. On that occasion the Croghan Bank directors issued the following sketch of the life of the hero of Ft. Stephenson:

COLONEL GEORGE CROGHAN
HERO OF FORT STEPHENSON
AUGUST SECOND, 1813

George Croghan was born of distinguished ancestry, near Louisville, Kentucky, November 15th, 1791. He was a boy of manly appearance and intelligence, and at a very early age developed a strong desire for military life.

He graduated at the college of William and Mary, Virginia, July 4th, 1810, and entered upon the study of law. In 1811, however, he enlisted as a private with the Kentucky volunteers under Gen. Harrison; but before the decisive battle of Tippecanoe he was made an aide-de camp to Gen. Boyd, the second in command. Croghan displayed such remarkable courage in battle that, on the recommendation of Gen. Harrison, he was appointed a captain in the 17th U. S. Infantry.

In August, 1812, his command was ordered to accompany the troops under Gen. Winchester, which started from Kentucky to the relief of Gen. Hull at Detroit. Owing to Hull's disgraceful surrender, the plan of campaign was changed, and Winchester's command marched through the wilderness to assist Harrison in the relief of Fort Wayne, and then down the Maumee to Fort Defiance, in September, 1812. In December, Winchester started on the disastrous expedition which ended in the massacre at the River Raisin, January 23, 1813, leaving Croghan, in spite of his extreme youth, in command of the important post of Defiance.

Captain Croghan, with his command, joined Gen. Harrison at the newly constructed Fort Meigs, on the Maumee, and participated most gallantly in defending that fort against the combined assaults of Gen. Proctor and Tecumseh. During the siege, Croghan distinguished himself greatly by a sortie made against a British battery, in an effort to afford Col. Dudley's unfortunate Kentucky volunteers an entrance into the fort. As a result of Harrison's report of this battle, Croghan was promoted to the position of major in the 17th U. S. Infantry.

Early in July, 1813, Major Croghan, with his battalion, was sent to take command of Fort Stephenson, erected in 1812, at Lower Sandusky (Fremont), which guarded the approach to Fort Seneca, where Harrison had his headquarters and stores. After an inspection of the fort by Gen. Harrison, Croghan proposed to shift its location to higher ground on the east side of the Sandusky

SCRAP-BOOK.

river. Harrison refused consent to this, for the reason that the British were momentarily expected; he thereupon ordered Croghan to retreat to Huron or Fort Seneca, should the British appear in sufficient force to indicate the presence of heavy artillery.

Just previous to the battle of Fort Stephenson Croghan wrote to a friend as follows: "The enemy are not far distant. I expect an attack. I will defend this post till the last extremity. I have just sent away the women, the children and the sick of the garrison, that I may be able to act without encumbrance. Be satisfied. I shall, I hope, do my duty. The example set me by my Revolutionary kindred is before me. Let me die rather than prove unworthy of their name."

On July 30 Gen. Harrison, after a council of war, ordered Croghan to destroy the fort and repair to headquarters. To this order Croghan replied, confidently expecting his letter would be intercepted by the British: "We have decided to maintain this place, and by Heaven we can." Gen. Harrison immediately sent Col. Wells to relieve Croghan of his command and order him to report at headquarters. There Croghan satisfactorily explained his insubordinate letter and was promptly restored to his command.

About 700 British Regulars, many of them veterans of Wellington's peninsular campaign, arrived on gunboats of Commodore Barclay's fleet; while Tecumseh's Indians, 2,000 strong, swarmed through the woods from the vicinity of Fort Meigs. Gen. Proctor at once sent a messenger to the fort demanding immediate surrender, thereby avoiding, as he thought, the massacre that must surely follow. To this was returned the defiant answer: "When this fort is taken there will be none to massacre."

Firing began August 1st from the British gunboats and howitzers on shore.

Croghan had but one piece of artillery, which was shifted from place to place to induce the belief that he had several. During the night of the 1st the British landed three six-pounders, and on the morning of the 2d opened fire from a point about 250 yards distant, directing their fire against the northwest angle of the fort. A redout and tablet on State street, opposite Park avenue, in Fremont, now marks this memorable spot. Late in the afternoon under cover of the smoke, the British assaulted with about 300 men of the 51st Regiment, while the Grenadier battalion made a feint against another portion of the fort. The assault was most gallantly made under command of Lieut. Col. Short, who, as they leaped into the ditch, commanded to "give the Yankees no quarter." Croghan, with only 160 men, reserved fire until the red coats had entered the ditch, when he fired with such fatal precision that the British faltered. He then turned his battery of a single gun upon them, and the ravine through which they were approaching was shortly filled with the dead and dying enemy. The British loss in killed and wounded was about 150, while that of Croghan was one killed and seven wounded.

Thus, on the second day of August, 1813, at the age of 21 years, the heroic Croghan against a vastly superior force, won the victory that proved the turning point in the war of 1812. For this exploit he was breveted lieutenant-colonel by the President of the United States; Congress awarded him a gold medal; and the ladies of Chillicothe, then the capital of Ohio, presented him with a beautiful sword.

In 1825 Croghan was made inspector general, with rank of colonel, and served as such with General Taylor in Mexico, 1846-47.

Colonel George Croghan died in New Orleans, January 8, 1849. To keep alive his memory, Fremont, through these succeeding years has continued to celebrate the second day of August.

Fort Stephenson Park comprises the original fort as reconstructed by Croghan, and contains within its stone walls its one cannon, "Old Betsy;" it also contains the monument in honor of Croghan, his men and those of the war of the Rebellion. At the base of this monument was placed, August 2, 1906, the remains of Colonel Croghan, brought from the family burying ground in Kentucky through the instrumentality of Col. Webb C. Hayes.

Fort Stephenson is unique in being the only fort in this country preserved in its original dimension, with its original armament and with the body of its defender.

Prof. Hulbert, in his history, claims that the first settlement of whites, in the limits of Ohio, was made near the present site of Maumee City, in 1679.

The west wall of the Ottawa county court house is decorated with the scene of Commodore Perry's great victory.

After the battle of Fallen Timber, Gen. Wayne returned to what is now the city of Ft. Wayne, and on October 22, 1794, established a garrison. After firing a volley from the cannons, it was named Ft. Wayne, in honor of the gallant commander.

In the vicinity of Mackinaw Island three forts have been erected at various periods in sight of one another. One is preserved for the education and pleasure of future generations, while the ruins of the other two can be traced in the crumbling walls at St. Ignace and Mackinaw City.

AN OLD CEMETERY

Burying Ground of Indians Long Prior to the Time of the White Settlers

IN conversation with Mr. John E. Gunckel, some days after he had attended the flag-raising ceremonies at Ft. Meigs, he said he stopped at Maumee and while in conversation with several citizens, a lad hailed him with, "Say, Mr. Gunckel, you ought to go on the other side, just above Ft. Meigs, down on the flat. The boys are gathering hundreds of bullets, washed out by the flood; and, say," one boy found a copper cent dated 1813." The locality was visited by Mr. Gunckel, who found it to be just as the boy had said. It appears that down near the water edge, the soil had been washed off probably 18 inches or more, leaving a gravely bed. The bullets were strewn in a very small area.

Mr. Gunckel's theory is that this deposit of bullets was the result of a severe skirmish occurring in that locality between 400 Kentuckians under Gen. Clay, who cut their way through British and Indians to reach the fort. It will be remembered by those who are familiar with Ft. Meigs history that the Kentuckians were divided—one portion led by the heroic Dudley to his doom, and the other fighting their way to Ft. Meigs. These bullets were undoubtedly mute reminders of that desperate struggle.

An Indian Burial Ground

In this connection may be said a word in regard to the unearthing of human skeletons at Orchard Grove, just opposite Perrysburg, and just below the site of Ft. Miami, brought to view by the action of the flood. The indications are that at one time there was a burying ground at that place. It may have been used by the garrison occupying the fort. The daily press of Toledo at that time in giving an account of the discovery, stated that no one of all those who had lived in that locality all their lives can re-

FORT MEIGS—(HARRISON POINT)
Where Gen. Harrison Stood Watching Colonel Dudley's Attack on the Opposite Side of the River

member of hearing a rumor that there had been a burying ground there.

In the latter part of the Sixties or early in the Seventies, the Perrysburg Journal recorded the fact that many human bones had been unearthed at that point, and the theory was then advanced that they were the bones of Indians, and that a burying ground had existed there probably many years before there was a settlement of whites in this region. No attempt was ever made at excavation, and in course of time the matter was forgotten.

Opposite Waterville, in Wood county, there is evidently another burying ground which may ante-date the time of the Indians by many years. Its history may reach back to the mound builders, evidences of whose works are scattered throughout Ohio. To these builders may also be attributed the mound that was some years since unearthed on the banks of Ottawa Creek on the Michigan boundary line, and from which seven human skeletons were taken. These skeletons were of a giant type, above the ordinary height of Indians. The history of that mound may reach back several centuries —a history involved in the vague mysticism of the past.

Col. Dudley's Dead

As far as can be ascertained, the names of those who were killed in Col. Dudley's command were as follows:

Col. Wm. Dudley,
Thomas Burrough,
Nicholas Moran,
Edward Dyhouse,
Benj. Helberson,
Robert Helberson,
Corp. Anthony Sammal,
Capt. John C. Montson,
Sergt. Joseph George,
Capt. Thomas Lewis,
John Stevenson,
Silas Fitzgerald,
Joshua Weathers,
John Daugherty,
Lieut. McClintock,
Wm. Martin,
Jesse Polly,
George Clark,
Daniel Sloan,
Ewel Wallace,
Joseph Statin,
Henry White,
James Pebles,
Joseph Clark,
James Elliott,
John Johnson,
Walter Gregory,
Theodore Mass,
James Simpson,
Sergeant Scott,
Winfield Bamm.

A MEMORABLE ADDRESS

Delivered by Gen. Harrison at the Great Fort Meigs Celebration in June, 1840

ELSEWHERE in this volume has been given a succinct account by Mr. Evers of the celebration at Ft. Meigs in 1840. But one of the notable features of that day was the address of Gen. Harrison, which can not fail to produce something more than a passing interest in every lover of the historical incidents of the Maumee Valley. The address was stenographically reported by a representative of the New York Tribune, and was given in full as follows:

Fellow Citizens—I am not, upon this occasion, before you in accordance with my own individual views or wishes. It has ever appeared to me, that the office of President of the United States should not be sought after by any individual; but that the people should spontaneously, and with their own free will, accord the distinguished honor to the man whom they believed would best perform its important duties. Entertaining these views, I should, fellow citizens, have remained at home, but for the pressing and friendly invitation which I have received from the citizens of Perrysburg, and the earnestness with which its acceptation was urged upon me by friends in whom I trusted, and whom I am now proud to see around me. If, however, fellow citizens, I had not complied with that invitation—if I had remained at home—believe me, my friends, that my spirit would have been with you; for where, in this beautiful land, is there a place calculated, as this is, to recall long past reminiscences, and revive long slumbering, but not wholly extinguished, emotions in my bosom?

In casting my eyes around, fellow citizens, they rest upon the spot where the gallant Wayne triumphed so gloriously over his enemies, and carried out these principles which it seemed his pleasure to impress upon the mind, and in which it has ever been my happiness humbly to attempt to imitate him. It was here, fellow citizens, I saw the banner of the United States float in triumph over the flag of the enemy. There it was where was first laid the foundation of the prosperity of the now widespread and beautiful West. It was there I beheld the indignant eagle frown upon the British lion. It was there I saw the youth of our land carry out the lesson they imbibed from the gallant Wayne—the noblest and the best an American can acquire—to die for his country when called to do so in its defense.

(At this moment the speaker's eye fell upon Gen. Hedges, when he said: "Gen. Hedges, will you come here? You have stood by my side in the hour of battle and I cannot bear to see you at so great a distance now." Immense cheering followed this considerate recognition, and the cries of "raise him up," "place him by the side of the old general," had scarcely been uttered when Gen. Hedges was carried forward to the stand.)

The general continued: It was there I saw interred my beloved companions, the companions of my youth. It was not in accordance with the stern etiquette of military life then, to mourn their departure; but I may now drop a tear over their graves at the recollection of their virtues and worth.

In 1793, fellow citizens, I received my commission to serve under Gen. Wayne. In 1794 I was his aide at the battle of Miami. Nineteen years afterward I had the honor of again being associated with many of those who were my companions in arms then. Nineteen years afterwards I found myself commander-in-chief of the northwestern army; but I found no diminution in the bravery of the American soldier. I found the same spirit of valor in all—not in the regular soldier only, but in the enrolled militia and volunteers also.

What glorious reminiscences does the view of these scenes around me recall to my mind! When I consented to visit this memorable spot, I expected that a thousand pleasant associations (would to God there were no painful associations mingled with them) would be recalled—that I should meet thousands of my fellow citizens here—and among them many of my old companions—met here to rear a new altar to liberty in the place of the one which bad men have prostrated.

And, fellow citizens (continued the general), I will not attempt to conceal from you that in coming here I expected that I should receive from you those evidences of regard which a generous people are ever willing to bestow upon those whom they believe to be honest in their endeavors to serve their country. I receive these evidences of regard and esteem as the only reward at all adequate to compensate for the anxieties and anguish which, in the past, I experienced upon this spot. Is there any man of sensibility, or possessing a feeling of self-respect, who asks what those feelings were? Do you suppose that the commander-in-chief finds his reward in the glitter and splendor of the camp? or in the forced obedience of the masses around him?

These are not pleasures under all circumstances—these are not the rewards which a soldier seeks. I ask any man

SCRAP-BOOK.

to place himself in my situation, and then say whether the extreme pain and anguish which I endured, and which every person similarly situated must have endured, can meet with any adequate compensation, except by such expressions of the confidence and gratitude of the people, as that with which, you fellow citizens, have this day honored me? These feelings are common to all commanders of sense and sensibility. The commanders of Europe possess them, although placed at the head of armies reared to war. How much more naturally would those feelings attach to a commander situated as I was? For of what materials was the army composed which was placed under my command? The soldiers who fought and bled and triumphed here were lawyers who had thrown up their briefs—physicians, who had laid aside their instruments—mechanics, who had put by their tools—and, in far the largest proportion, agriculturists, who had left their ploughs in the furrow, although their families depended for their bread upon their exertions, and who hastened to the battle field to give their life to their country if it were necessary, to maintain her rights. I could point from where I now stand, to places where I felt this anxiety pressing heavily upon me, as I thought of the fearful consequences of a mistake on my part, or the want of judgment on the part of others. I knew there were wives who had given their husbands to the field—mothers who had clothed their sons for battle; and I knew that these expecting wives and mothers were looking for the safe return of their husbands and sons. When to this was added the recollection that the peace of the entire west would be broken and the glory of my country tarnished if I failed, you may possibly conceive the anguish which my situation was calculated to produce. Feeling my responsibility, I personally supervised and directed the arrangement of the army under my command. I trusted to no colonel or other officer. No person had any hand in the disposition of the army. Every step of warfare, whether for good or ill, was taken under my own direction and of none other, as many who now hear me know. Whether every movement would or would not pass the criticism of Bonaparte or Wellington, I know not; but, whether they would induce applause or censure, upon myself it must fall.

But, fellow citizens, still another motive induced me to accept the invitation which had been so kindly extended to me. I knew that here I should meet many who had fought and bled under my command—that I should have the pleasure of taking them by the hand and recurring with them to the scenes of the past. I expected, too, to meet with a few of the great and good men yet surviving, by whose efforts our freedom was achieved. This pleasure alone would have been sufficient to induce my visit to this interesting spot upon this equally interesting occasion. I see my old companions here, and I see not a few of the Revolutionary veterans around me. Would to God that it had even been in my power to have made them comfortable and happy—that their sun might go down in peace! But, fellow citizens, they remain unprovided for—monuments of the ingratitude of my country. It was with the greatest difficulty that the existing pension act was passed through congress. But why was it restricted? Why were the brave soldiers who fought under Wayne excluded?—soldiers who suffered far more than they who fought in the Revolution proper. The Revolution, in fact, did not terminate until 1794—until the battle was fought upon the battle ground upon which my eye now rests (Miami). War continued with them from the commencement of the Revolution until the victory of Wayne, to which I have just alluded. The great highway to the west was the scene of unceasing slaughter. Then why this unjust discrimination? Why are the soldiers who terminated the war of the Revolution, in fact, excluded, while those by whom it was begun or a portion of them, are rewarded? I will tell you why. The poor remnant of Wayne's army had but few advocates, while those who had served in the Revolution proper had many friends. Scattered as they were over all parts of the Union, and in large numbers they could exert an influence at the ballot-box. They could whisper thus in the ears of those who sought their influence at the polls: "Take care, for I have waited long enough for what has been promised. The former plea of poverty can no longer be made. The treasury is now full. Take care; your seat is in danger." "Oh! yes, everything that has been promised shall be attended to if you will give me your voice." In this way, fellow citizens, tardy, but partial, justice was done to the soldiers of the Revolution. They made friends by their influence at the ballot-box. But it was different with Gen. Wayne's soldiers. They were few in number, and they had but one or two humble advocates to speak for them in congress. The result has been, justice has been withheld.

I have said that the soldiers under Wayne experienced greater hardships even than the soldiers of the Revolution. This is so. Everyone can appreciate the difference between an Indian and a regular war. When wounded in battle, the soldier must have warmth and shelter before he can recover. This could always be secured to the soldiers of the Revolution. In those days, the latch string of no door was pulled in. When wounded, he was sure to find shelter and very many of those comforts which are so essential to the sick, but which the soldiers in an Indian war cannot procure. Instead of shelter and warmth he is exposed to the thousand ills incident to Indian warfare. Yet no relief was extended to those who had thus suffered.

After the war closed under Wayne, I retired; and when I saw a man poorer than all others, wandering about the land, decrepid and decayed by intemperance it was unnecessary to inquire whether he had ever belonged to Wayne's army. His condition was a guarantee of that—was a sufficient assurance that he had wasted his energies among the unwholesome swamps of the West, in the defense of the rights of his fellow citizens, and for the maintenance of the honor and glory of his country.

Well, fellow citizens, I can only say, that if it should ever be in my power to pay the debt which is due these brave but neglected men, that debt shall first of all be paid. And I am very well satisfied that the government can afford it provided the latch string of the treasury shall ever be more carefully pulled in. Perhaps you will ask me for some proof of my friendship for old soldiers. If so, I can give it you from the records of congress. When the fifteen hundred dollar law was repealed, I opposed it, as I opposed changing the pay of members of congress from six to eight dollars, until we had done justice to and provided for these soldiers. You will find my votes upon this question, among the records of congress, and my speech upon it, in the published debates of the time.

I will now, fellow citizens, give you my reasons for having refused to give pledges and opinions more freely than I have done since my nomination to the presidency. Many of the statements published upon this subject, are by no means correct; but it is true that it is my opinion that no pledge should be made by an individual when in nomination for any office in the gift of the people. And why? Once adopt it, and the battle will no longer be to the strong —to the virtuous—or the sincere lover of the country; but to him who is prepared to tell the greatest number of lies, and to proffer the largest number of pledges which he never intends to carry out. I suppose that the best guarantee which an American citizen could have of the correctness of the conduct of an individual in the future, would be his conduct in the past, when he had no temptation before him, to practice deceit.

Now, fellow citizens, I have not altogether grown gray under the helmet of my country, although I have worn it for some time. A large portion of my life has been passed in the civil departments of government. Examine my conduct there, and the most tenacious democrat —I use the word in its proper sense; I mean not to confine it to parties, for there are good in both—may doubtless discover faults, but he will find no single act calculated to derogate from the rights of the people.

However, to prove the reverse of this, I have been called a federalist! (Here was a cry of "The charge is a lie—a base lie. You are no federalist.") Well, what is a federalist? I recollect what the term formerly signified, and there are many others present who recollect its former signification also. They know that the federal party was accused of a design to strengthen the hands of the general government at the expense of the separate states. That accusation would nor cannot apply to me. I was brought up after the strictest manner of Virginia anti-federalism. St. Paul himself was not a greater devotee to the doctrines of the Pharisees than was I, by inclination and a father's precepts and example, to anti-federalism. I was taught to believe that, sooner or later, that fatal catastrophe to human liberty would take place—that the general government would swallow up all the state governments, and that one department of the government would swallow up all the other departments. I do not know whether my friend, Mr. Van Buren (and he is, and I hope ever will be, my personal friend), has a throat that can swallow everything; but I do know that, if his measures are carried out, he will lay a foundation for others to do so if he does not.

What reflecting man, fellow citizens, cannot see this? The representatives of the people were once the source of power. Is it so now? Nay. It is to the executive mansion now that every eye is turned—that every wish is directed. The men of office and party, who are governed by the principles of John Randolph, to wit: the five loaves and two fishes, seem to have their ears constantly directed to the great bell at headquarters to indicate how the little ones shall ring.

But to return, I have but to remark that my anti-federalism has been tempered by my long service in the employ of the country—and my frequent oaths to support the general government; but I am as ready to resist the encroachments on state rights as I am to support the legitimate authority of the executive, or general government.

Now, fellow citizens, I have very little more to say, except to exhort you to go on peacefully if you can—and you can —to effect that reform upon which your hearts are fixed. What calamitous consequences will ensue to the world if you fail! If you should fail how the tyrants of Europe will rejoice. If you fail, how will the friends of freedom, scattered, like the planets of heaven, over the world, mourn, when they see the beacon light of liberty extinguished—the light whose rays they had hoped would yet penetrate the whole benighted world. If you triumph, it will only be done by vigilance and attention. Our personal friends, but political enemies, remind each other that "Eternal vigilance is the price of liberty." While journeying thitherward, I observed this motto waving at the head of a procession composed of the friends of the present administration. From this I inferred that discrimination was necessary in order to know who to watch. Under Jefferson, Madison and Monroe, the eye of the people was turned to the right source—to the administration. The administration, however, now says to the people, "You must not watch us, but you must watch the Whigs! Only do that and all is safe!" But that, my friends, is not the way. The old fashioned Republican rule is to watch the government. See to the government. See that the government does not acquire too much power. Keep a check upon your rulers. Do this, and liberty is safe. And if your efforts should result successfully, and I should be placed in the presidential chair, I shall invite a recurrence to the old Republican rule, to watch the administration and to condemn all its acts which are not in accordance with the strictest mode of Republicanism. Our rulers, fellow citizens, must be watched. Power is insinuating. Few men are satisfied with less power than they are able to procure. If the ladies whom I see around me, were near enough to hear me, and of sufficient age to give an experimental answer, they would tell you that no lover is ever satisfied with the first smile of his mistress.

It is necessary, therefore, to watch, not the political opponents of an administration, but the administration itself, and to see that it keeps within the bounds of the constitution and the laws of the land. The executive of this Union has immense power to do mischief, if he sees fit to exercise that power. He may prostrate the country. Indeed, this country has been already prostrated. It has already fallen from pure Republicanism, to a monarchy in spirit if not in name.

A celebrated author defines monarchy to be that form of government in which the executive has at once the command of the army, the execution of the laws and the control of the purse. Now, how is it with our present executive? The constitution gives to him the control of the army, and the execution of the laws. He now only awaits the possession of the purse to make him a monarch. Not a monarch simply, with the power of England, but a monarch with powers of the autocrat of Russia. For Gibbon says that an individual possessed of these powers "will unless closely watched, make himself a despot."

The passage of the sub-treasury bill will give to the President an accumulation of power that the constitution withholds from him, thus providing the requisites of a monarch. This catastrophe to freedom should be and can be prevented by vigilance, union and perseverance.

("We will do it," resounded from twenty thousand voices, "we will do it.")

In conclusion, then, fellow-citizens, I would impress it upon all—Democrats and Whigs—to give up the idea of watching each other, and direct your eye to the government. Do that and your children's children, to the latest posterity, will be as happy and as free as you and your fathers have been.

At the close of General Harrison's address the vast multitude of hearers gave "three times three" with a vim, an earnestness and an unanimity that eloquently voiced the truth and beauty of the sentiments so forcibly portrayed by the honored speaker.

This monster demonstration at Fort Meigs was well calculated to give even additional force and character in the further progress of that remarkable

SCRAP-BOOK.

campaign. Not a political meeting of any consequence was held throughout the country that did not bring out delegations in wagons and vehicles of every description, reaching sometimes a mile in length. These wagons were trimmed in many fantastic designs, and always accompanied with martial music.

On General Harrison's return from Fort Meigs he visited a number of towns in Ohio, among them Columbus, Springfield, Dayton, Germantown, Cincinnati and other places.

At Germantown there were some unique preparations for his reception. Among the features were thirteen lads, of whom the writer (F. J. Oblinger,) was one, representing the thirteen original states. These lads were dressed in blue hunting shirts with coonskin caps, and sang campaign songs from the Log Cabin Song Book. Among the airs were Dan Tucker, Rosin the Bow, Buckeye Brawn, John Anderson My Joe, Auld Lang Syne, etc.

Another ornamented wagon contained a number of girls dressed in white, and these represented the stars in the Union at that time.

Many similar spectacular features, processions, patriotic displays and illuminations characterized the campaign of 1840 in every town and village of note throughout the country, north and south—a campaign that has never had its counterpart in our political history.

OTTOKEE
An Indian Chief Who Opposed War, Was Always Friendly to the Whites, and the Last to Leave the Valley

RANDOM NOTES

Gleaned From Wood County Records and Reminiscences.

WOOD COUNTY'S present area is 598 square miles, comprising 382,856 acres.

Bowling Green is 635 feet above sea level, and 70 feet above Lake Erie.

In 1823 Samuel Ewing was killed in a fight at Rushteboo, by a man named Lewis, who afterwards escaped from the jail in Maumee. This is probably the first known murder in the county.

Guy Nearing, took the contract in 1832, to carry the mail from Perrysburg to Lima. Most of the time Noah Reed carried the mail.

First Presbyterian church in Perrysburg was organized 1833-34.

In 1821 a mail route was established from Piqua, by way of St. Marys, Fort Wayne, Defiance and Waterville to Perrysburg, 200 miles, with Thomas Diver as mail carrier.

The convention of Territorial Ohio assembled November 1, 1802, and by the 20th of that month completed its work of framing a constitution, and in the following February, 1803, Congress admitted Ohio as a member of the sisterhood of states.

The first regular mail in the Maumee Valley was carried by Horace Gunn in 1808. Benoni Adams carried the mail in 1809 from Cleveland to Maumee, requiring two weeks to make the trip, partly through the Black Swamp on foot.

Rev. Joseph Badger was a missionary among the Indians in the Valley as early as 1808. He was at Ft. Meigs a part of the time during the war of 1812.

Hull's trace struck Wood county on the south line of Henry township, zigzagged into Bloom, again into Henry, continued north through Liberty, into Portage, then north through Center, Plain, and Middleton into Perrysburg, leaving the county at the foot of the Rapids.

Harrison's trail struck Wood county on the east boundary of Freedom, zigzagging along Portage River, then through Webster, through Perrysburg to Ft. Meigs.

Mr. Joel Foote says that when his father, E. Foote, in 1830, went back to York State to marry his second wife, he had not enough money to bring her back. So he took with him a portion of his wheat crop and sold it in the Buffalo market. The wheat was raised on the island opposite Waterville, and was the first wheat grown and marketed from the Maumee river country. This Mr. Foote gave as a fact, within his own recollection.

Under an act of the legislature, February 12, 1820, Wood county was outlined and what is now Lucas county, was a part of its territory.

The first sessions of the grand juries would, in good weather, be held in the shade of some generous tree or in some nook in the then wilderness close at hand, and intruders were kept away from the jury and witnesses by the prosecutor and court constable, as best they could.

Wood county's first court house, was built of hewn logs. Daniel Hubbell and Guy Nearing were the contractors and the job was let to them March 3, 1823, for $895. This building was paid for by the sale of 105 lots granted by the government for that purpose and were to be sold for $20 or more each.

The first court which was held within the limits of the present Wood county was held at the residence of John Hollister at Orleans, March 27, 1823.

The first brick court house was erected in 1843 at a cost of $20,000, the contractors being Brigham & Curtis. After the county seat was moved to Bowling Green this building was burned in 1871 and the present Perrysburg town hall built on its site.

SCRAP-BOOK.

JOHN WEBB

A Veteran Pioneer of Perrysburg—Brief Sketch of His Active Life—Died on the Ninetieth Anniversary of His Birth

THE sketch of Mr. Webb's life that follows was compiled from memoranda found among the papers of the late Francis Hollenbeck, Esq., and is well worthy of record:

John Webb, the father of the subject of this sketch, was born upon the banks of the Susquehanna river, in Pennsylvania, and resided, though a mere boy, near Wyoming, at the time of the terrible Indian massacre at that place. Immediately after that horrible tragedy, John Webb, sr., moved with his father's family to Berks county, Pa., where he learned the trade of a hatter at Reading, the county seat. About February, 1794, he married and moved to New York City, and manufactured and retailed hats in a shop on Maiden Lane, residing in the same building. At that time, nearly all the hats in the city were made and sold upon that street.

In that little building, on August 27, 1795, John Webb, jr., the subject of this sketch was born, and after several changes during the years that followed, moved nine miles west to Miflinburg, where he resided until 1814. It was here that John Webb, jr., learned the trade of hat manufacturing, having commenced his apprenticeship in 1811, at the age of sixteen years. In 1814 the family removed to Canton, O., where father and son worked together at their trade, until 1820.

Mr. Webb took a trip east into Union county, Pa., and there, on March 8, 1821, became united in marriage to Miss Elizabeth Charles. He immediately returned with his wife to Canton, Ohio, and then went into partnership with his father. He remained there until November 1, 1822, when he started with his wife and son Charles, for Perrysburg, arriving at his destination on the 6th of the same month, after passing through many difficulties while enroute.

He first went with his family and household goods, to Portland (now Sandusky City) by wagon, expecting to take a vessel there for the Maumee river, but no vessel was there. Leaving his goods there to be shipped forward at the first opportunity, he, with his wife and child, took a horse boat (or "mud scow") for Lower Sandusky (now Fremont) where, by previous arrangement, he met his brother Thomas Lincoln Webb (then a young lad) with two horses and a sidesaddle. Thomas R. McKnight (a brother-in-law of Mr. Webb, who had come from the Maumee river to meet them) and Mrs. Webb rode the horses and carried the babe, while Mr. Webb and his little brother Lincoln, and a man by the name of Hawley (who had been waiting for company through the swamp) followed on foot.

Starting from Lower Sandusky, they went down the Sandusky river two miles and then took the trail for the West, arriving on the night of the first day, at "the crossing" of the Portage river, now Elmore. The trail was well beaten, and this was the only place where the river had a rocky bottom and could be forded. The next day, they came through to Perrysburg, striking the river at Rock Bar, about one and one-half miles below the town. At that time, no wagon had ever traversed "the swamp." Perrysburg was entirely uninhabited, except by beasts and birds of the forest, and "The Future Great" had not yet been conceived.

After leaving Lower Sandusky the solitary travelers discovered no habitation until they reached "the crossing" (now Elmore), where there was one log cabin, where the wayfarer might be fed and sheltered over night, for at that time it was impracticable to journey overland from Lower Sandusky to the Maumee River in one day. The next habitation they met with was that of Victory Jenison, on the south bank of the Maumee River, in the bend below the present site of Perrysburg. He had made a little clearing about his cabin, but cultivated a small tract of bottom land which had never been grown over with timber or brush. John Noel and Thomas Leaming were living in small cabins in the bushes on the hillside, on what afterward became the farm of Judge David Ladd, and cultivated a portion of the bottom lands at the foot of the hill.

Arrived at Perrysburg

The town of Perrysburg had been surveyed and platted by the United States Government in 1817, five years prior to Mr. Webb's arrival, but at that time no one was yet living upon it, and no portion of it was at that time cleared, excepting in-lot No. 144, now occupied by the residence of the late Francis Hollenbeck, Esq., and the logs from the felled timber were piled upon it, intended to be used by Thomas R. McKnight for the erection of a dwelling. Mr. Webb took up his quarters in a small frame building standing at the bottom of the hill at the head of the bayou and near the extension of West Boundary street (known as Green Lane) over the flats. He with his family, thus became the first inhabitants of the Perrysburg town plat. At this time, Messrs. Thos. R. McKnight, Aurora and Samuel Spafford, Jacob and James Wilkison, Mrs. Omans and one other person, resided at Orleans of the North, a village located on the flats, under Fort Meigs hill. Immediately after his arrival, Mr. Webb aided in erecting Mr. McKnight's log residence on in-lot 144, carrying up one of the corners, and "chinking" and "daubing" the structure, and Mr. McKnight moved into it the following spring (1823).

The county seat was then at Perrysburg, and Thos. R. McKnight was Clerk of the Court, but the first terms of court were held at Maumee, for the reason that there was no building in Perrysburg in which to hold them. Subsequently, three or four terms were held in the second story of a warehouse at Orleans, owned by John Hollister. Hollister, at that time, lived in Maumee, but owned the warehouse, occupying the ground floor as a store room; afterward he removed these goods to the building in which he was doing a retail business at Orleans.

Soon after his arrival Mr. Webb fitted up a shop for the manufacture of hats in the basement of his dwelling, but did not commence working at his trade until 1824, being unable to sooner obtain the necessary tools. He manufactured the first hats ever made in the Maumee Valley, and the only other establishment of the kind in the West was one at Detroit. The next fall he purchased three rods front on the north side of Front street, at the head of Walnut street, extending to the river, where he at once put up a log shop. He commenced business in this building in 1824, and worked industriously there for about three and one-half years, paying, with the proceeds of his labor, for the tract on which his shop stood, and also for the lot on which he afterward erected the dwelling in which he died. Both of these real estate purchases were made from Seth Doane.

In the autumn of 1822, Samuel Spafford commenced preparations for the erection of the Exchange Hotel, which he completed and moved into during the next fall, coming down from Orleans, which village was being abandoned for higher ground, owing to the river floods. About the same time Judge Thomas W.

SCRAP-BOOK.

Powell, late of Delaware, O., erected the dwelling on Front street, afterward purchased and occupied by Mr. Jonathan Perrin. From this time buildings continued to be erected here and there over the town plat, and Orleans was gradually deserted, the inhabitants locating at Perrysburg.

Held Many Offices

Mr. Webb was elected Sheriff of Wood county in 1826, and again in 1828. In May, 1831, he was appointed Clerk of the County, and continued in office about eleven years, when he was succeeded by Joseph Utley, who appointed him his Deputy. He was again elected Sheriff in 1842 and re-elected in 1844.

George W. Porter was executed November 5, 1830. Mr. Webb being at that time Sheriff, and performing the duties of the office (the particulars of this crime are given elsewhere in this volume).

When Mr. Webb first realized that he would be obliged to execute a fellow-being, his whole soul recoiled from it. Mr. Porter was under his care for about six months, and during that time talked freely of the act he had committed, always declaring that he was ready and willing to die, not desiring to live with such a load upon his mind. He was always calm and greatly regretted the commission of the deed. While in prison no fetters of any kind were placed upon him, nor was he confined to a cell, having the free range of two large rooms. Richardson was regarded by the whole community as a bad man, while Porter was esteemed as a kind-hearted, well-disposed citizen, who, under great provocation and excitement, had committed the fatal act. The sympathizing citizens of the community desired to secure a pardon, but he would not allow them to do so. He was executed on the flats at the foot of Fort Meigs, so that the spectators might occupy the hillside and all witness the execution. Among the large crowd present, were many from Michigan, Pennsylvania and New York, who came expressly for the occasion. This execution is celebrated in history as the first in the annals of the Maumee Valley.

In 1848, Mr. Webb, was again elected County Clerk, and held the office until 1860, when he retired to private life. Since the latter date, a large portion of his time was occupied in setting up the numerous accounts which had accumulated during his long terms of office, and looking after his farm, which he had leased. He employed the most of his time in reading, and his mind was a storehouse of information, both regarding the early history of the country and current events. He always took a great interest in politics, and, since the organization of the party, has been an earnest Republican. He has been married three times: March 8, 1821, to Elizabeth Charles; July 18, 1834, to Mary Dean; February 23, 1851, to Mary A. Jones, the latter two of Perrysburg.

There is probably no citizen of the valley who had more warm friends, in whose hearts his memory will be kept green.

For many years, nearly every one in the community has fondly called him "Uncle John," and it is doubtful if he had an enemy in the world. His name will be inscribed among the most worthy of the old Maumee Valley pioneers as one who, by his industry, gained a competence for himself and family and never committed a dishonest or dishonorable act.

The territory northwest of the Ohio river, by virtue of the Ordinance of 1787, was the first, within the present limits of the United States, dedicated to universal liberty.

CHOLERA VICTIMS

As Its Ravages in Perrysburg Were Described by the Journal in the Year 1854— List of Deaths

THE Perrysburg Journal suspended publication for four weeks in July, 1854, and in its first issue after the suspension, dated August 12, 1854, it gave the following particulars:

"It is four weeks to-day since the last number of the Perrysburg Journal was issued. Up to that time we tried to believe that the worst phase of the cholera had been reached, but each succeeding week brought a greater number of victims, and all business having ceased, this paper and the M. V. Democrat suspended publication, both from choice and necessity. Hands could not be employed to work when everybody else who could leave was deserting the town, nor did it seem desirable to work much when death was decimating our numbers. We have been through two or three cholera seasons before but never have we seen such fearful and fatal results.

"We are happy to announce that the dreadful disease has now almost, if not entirely, subsided here. There have been perhaps two or three modified cases within the past week, but the dreaded fatality which characterized it hitherto has passed away, to return here, we hope, no more.

"The following is as nearly a complete list of the deaths by cholera in this place and immediate vicinity as we can at this time procure. It is probably not far from correct:

"Geo. Jones' child, Stephen Williams, Judson Tocker, Frederick Lucas, wife and five children, Peter Laney, Henry Bason, Mrs. Perkins, Jacob Snyder, Geo. Schuler, William Bellville's child, Mrs. James Perrin and child, Miss Lucy Bellinger, Miss Cronewald, Mrs. Rebecca McKnight, Lewis Mundy, Celia Simonds, Mrs. Hernia Irwin, Miss Julia Irwin, Miss W. Gates, J. W. Lang, W. Mead, Geo. Burns, Esther Burns, F. Zanger, Mrs. Abner Brown, Wm. H. Courser, Rosanna Ferdig, Mrs. Huffman, John J. Cook, Elijah Huntington, Mr. Wolfley, Henry Pfleghart, Findley J. Ross, Stanley T. Ross, Dr. James Robertson, Cornelia Spink, John J. Spink, Mr. Huffman's boy, Mrs. J. A. Hall, Geo. Clemens, Christian Eichholz, Lawrence Hircel, Mrs. Brown, Robert Chambers, Mr. Hamilton, Jarvis Spafford, Mrs. Shannon, Frederick Dortion, Margaret Hircel, Mary Crain, Edward Lee, Jacob Rufly, Theresa Oscam, George W. Bloomfield, Jacob Kingfield, A. Coster, Naomi D. Kelley, Samuel Webb, Adaline Frederick, August Rhodae, Thomas Atkinson, Mr. Zimmerman, H. D. Right, John Reiser, Mrs. Asher Cook, Richard Atkinson, Mr. Arne, Mr. Shaw's boy, Zimmerman's boy, Mrs. Goodwin, Mr. Shannon's child, Johanna Reisly, Sophia Blinn, Mrs. Rhodae, Mrs. Catherine Reiser, Christina Rhodae, child of Wolfley, Mr. Kelp, Mrs. Jane Crook, boy Keider, Miss Eichholz, child of Osburg, child of John Reiser, Mrs. Persis Peck, Margaret Schuckmeal, Geo. Schitz, James Shannon, Mrs. Shaw, Mrs. Wolfley, Wory Hoelzly, John Neiderhouse, Margaret Wild, Philip Riley, Nicholas Reiser, Theresa Reiser, and child—104.

"We are indebted to the politeness of Mr. John Yeager, the sexton, for the foregoing list."

Tecumseh's wild dream was inspired by his brother, the Prophet, who with his wonderful visions foretold the capture of Harrison at Ft. Meigs, the destruction of the western forts, and the grand confederacy of all the Indian tribes and their final supremacy in the west.

FORT MIAMI
Facing the Maumee River

SCRAP-BOOK.

AMOS DEWESE

One of the Pioneer Settlers of Weston Township—His Early Life and Privations in the Black Swamp

AMOS DEWESE was one of the pioneer settlers of Weston township, and one of the sturdy, reliable men, whose character was one of moral worth and integrity. He was well known throughout Wood county, and was a man thoroughly alive to its prosperity. Amos Dewese was of Revolutionary stock.

His great grandfather, Samuel Dewese, was a soldier in the war of the Revolution. He was wounded and captured at the siege of Ft. Washington and thrown into one of the filthy British prison ships. Afterwards he re-entered the Colonial army and died of disease in a military camp, Allentown, Pa.

After his death his son, Samuel, while a mere boy, tramped through the snow to Valley Forge where he enlisted and subsequently became a captain of militia in the First Battalion, 36th regiment of Maryland Troops. At the close of the Revolutionary war he was made captain of a volunteer military company.

Capt. Dewese's brother, Thomas, who was the grandfather of the late Amos Dewese, was a school teacher in early life, and later became a farmer.

Samuel Dewese, the father of Amos Dewese, at the age of 20 years enlisted under Capt. James Drennan for the war of 1812, and served under Gen. Harrison. He was discharged at Detroit, May 14, 1814. When enlisted he first went to Cleveland and later to Ft. Stephenson, at the present site of Fremont, arriving there just a day after Major Croghan's gallant defense of the little stockade. While at Detroit he was sent by Gen. Harrison as a scout to the Thames river in Canada. The mission was a dangerous and difficult one but he accomplished his object.

His Early Trials

Amos Dewese came to Wood county from Hancock county, February 17, 1843, and of his early experience here he gave a graphic account in an article contributed to the Weston Herald, on the occasion of the 40th anniversary of his advent into the "Black Swamp." He wrote:

The snow was 18 inches deep when l started from Hancock county without a cent of money, but a few clothes, and a dry chunk of bread constituting my pack; my shoes out at the toes and carrying a few books.

In the evening I crossed the line and saw a hunter riding an old horse, to the tail of which was tied a large deer. I followed a trail and came tô a Mr. Robbins, of Bloom township, where I staid all night. Early next morning I started for Mr. Frankfather's at Bloom Center, found my old friend, Joseph Shelia, and made my home with him, and went to chopping to get a pair of boots. Mr. Shelia, and I rode through the woods to Risden and Rome (now Fostoria) for an ax. We found a few, but as they wouldn't trust either of us, we had to return without it. Then I went back to Hancock county, got my ax and was rich. I took a job of a Mr. Buisey to chop seven acres, for which he gave me a rifle and some second-hand clothing. I finished my job March 24, when the mercury was 20 degrees below zero, that winter being still known as the "hard winter."

Jonathan Stull

I began work for Mr. Solether April 1; snow and ice on the ground, and sleighing. He gave me a watch. While working there Mr. Jonathan Stull came into the clearing. He had a bag on his shoulder with a peck of corn that he had got from a Mr. Daniel Milburn. Mr. Stull was much depressed and discouraged on account of the hard winter. He talked on Adventism, as the Millerites said the end of the world was at hand. Mr. Stull said he prayed for it every day, as he had seen all the trouble he wanted to see. He said he had eight head of horses, and all had died; 28 head of cattle and 260 head of hogs, and all were dead. I had to pass Mr. Stull's cabin often. He told me they had been married 12 years and that they had 10 children, all of whom were almost nude. Not one had a full suit of clothes. They hadn't a bed or a window in the house.

He was the owner of a three-quarter section of good land. "There," said Mr. Stull, "I have one peck of ears of corn in this sack, and when I take it home and grind it in the hand mill and mix it with water, bake it and eat it with my wife and ten children, God knows where the next will come from. They must starve." He wept like a child. (Mr. Stull was the founder of Jerry City).

A Severe Winter

Mr. Dewese said that during that winter nearly all the wild hogs perished from cold. Later Mr. Dewese worked for Mr. Whitacre two weeks, for which he received $3.25. Continuing he says:

I then went to Milton Center and cleared five acres for James Hutchinson for a pair of two-year-old steers. In July I went to James Bloom, and worked for Bloom and Henderson Carothers, helping to cut 45 acres of wheat and cut and haul 100 tons of tame prairie hay, for which I received one pair of boots and 50 cents in money—a sum total in money for the year of $3.75. In the beginning of the year 1843 I went to Ralph Keeler's to work for my board, and to go to school in the old log school house at Weston. Mr. Keeler took sick, and as I had to take care of him and the stock I lost the benefit of the school. I worked for him three months for $25, to take my pay out of the store.

The teacher, Mr. Jesse Osborne, of New York State, received 25 cents a day or five dollars a month. The scholars were Miss Mary Taylor, George Lewis, Thomas and William Taylor, Samuel McAtee, Olmstead, Amelia and Melicent Keeler. The teacher was paid by the parents, there being no school fund at that time.

Mr. Taylor lost about 45 head of cattle, Mr. Keeler 75 head, while the Salsburys, Sargents, Ellsworths and Greens lost about the same proportion during that terrible winter, never to be forgotten by the old settlers. Many had to move out of the "Black Swamp" before spring. So ended my first year as a pioneer.

In March 1851 Mr. Dewese entered the land which now forms a portion of the Dewese estate. On this he built a log house and began to make for himself a home.

On November 3, 1853, Mr. Dewese was married to Miss Sarah Green, who was born August 17, 1829, in Liverpool, England, and came to this country with her parents in 1834.

Mr. Dewese was a whole-souled, public spirited man, whose ambition was honorable citizenship and financial independence. He was an upright citizen, a kind neighbor, a devoted husband and a loving parent.

The hospitality of the Dewese home was known far and wide, and Mr. Dewese found great pleasure in entertaining his many friends at his fireside and sumptuous table.

The corner stone of the first court house in Bowling Green was laid July 4, 1868. The cost of the building was about $23,000 and Norton Reed was the contractor.

SCRAP-BOOK.

JOSEPH B. NEWTON

One of the Prominent Figures in Wood County History That Will Long Be Remembered

ON the morning of April 10, 1905, there passed away from earthly scenes one who had long been a prominent factor in Wood county history—Captain Joseph B. Newton.

Captain Newton was born in Chenango county, N. Y., in 1837, and with his parents came to Ohio in 1840, locating in Center township, and later on moving to Bowling Green. While a young man, he taught school and was corporation clerk of Bowling Green. At the outbreak of the War of the Rebellion Mr. Newton volunteered in Co. A, 14th O. V. I., and won promotion by faithful and efficient service to Corporal, Sergeant Major, Second Lieutenant, Adjutant and Captain. He never was absent from his command but once on account of sickness. He was with the army in Sherman's march to the sea, and in the final review at Washington at the close of the war—literally starting at the beginning of the war and holding out through all the dangers and vicissitudes in camp and field, in skirmish and battle, to the end.

After the war he returned to Bowling Green. He was elected auditor of Wood county for two terms. Owing to a change in the terms of county officers, Mr. Newton served nearly five years as county auditor. Some time afterward while engaged in farming he became interested in the glass industries of Bowling Green and Indiana, holding prominent positions in the management of that industry. He served as Secretary of the Wood County Fair Company, and at the time of his death was a member and president pro tem of the City Council of Bowling Green. He was also a member of Wiley Post G. A. R., of I. O. O. F. Encampment and of the Loyal Legion.

Captain Newton and Miss Maggie Black were married in 1868, and his wife and three sons and one daughter survive him. The funeral services took place at the family residence and were conducted by Rev. Thos. Barkdull, of Toledo, who had been a friend of the Captain from his early boyhood. He spoke feelingly of his associations and recollections of the dead. These services were attended by the city officials, members of council, Grand Army members, county officials and a large number of personal friends. The pall bearers were C. W. Evers, J. D. Bolles, A. E. Royce, I. L. Hankey, J. E. Merry and M. L. Case. Under the Grand Army ritual the remains of Captain Newton were placed in beautiful Oak Grove cemetery.

One who for a number of years was closely and intimately associated with him, claims that a more even tempered, serene, patient character is seldom to be found. Under the most trying ordeals in official life, calm, patient, self-possessed, he was ever unruffled—ordeals that would exasperate and confuse any one less masterful.

In his business relations he was thoroughly methodical and systematic. He inspired confidence among all who came within his influence, and was affable and courteous to all. Whoever sought his counsel in perplexity, whether rich or poor, high or low in station, his advice was freely given, and often too at the expense of both time and money on his part.

He gave a patient, respectful hearing to all, and it was this trait in the man that to a large extent brought about the high esteem in which he was regarded by his fellow men. In the discharge of his duties as auditor there were many trying circumstances. At many meetings of the commissioners, when diverse interests were in clash before the board Newton was ever calm and unruffled and throughout all he was unswerved, self-poised, fearless, confident in his well studied and matured judgment.

He was ever ready to help his fellowman, and it is of such material that good citizenship is made, whether in the domestic and social circle or in the wider arena of civic duty.—*Cor. of Wood Co. Democrat.*

NATHANIEL H. CALLARD

One of the Veteran Journalists of Wood County—One Who Lived Much of His Life for Others

IN the death of Nathaniel H. Callard, there passed away a man who was identified with the growth of Wood county and the prosperity of the Maumee Valley for nearly half a century.

Mr. Callard was born in Devonshire, England, February 3, 1819, where he grew to manhood's estate, leaving England and coming to America in 1848. He resided several years in Detroit and Toledo, finally making his home in Perrysburg in 1853, where he resided until his death, January 5, 1900.

In 1854, when the cholera raged with such violence that it seemed to baffle all medical skill, when scarcely a family escaped from the dread pestilence, when the fortitude of the bravest was tested in this crucible of disease and death, Mr. Callard, with unflinching devotion, gave his energy and skill unreservedly to his fellow citizens stricken with the plague. For the time he abandoned his business, and day and night found him ministering comfort to the sick and dying and providing necessities wherever needed. In that time of gloom his services were in constant demand and no appeal was ever made to him in vain.

The panic of 1857 swept away his business prospects as it did that of thousands of others in that financial distress. In addition to this the loss of his wife by death in the same year greatly increased the burden of his afflictions, leaving him with three motherless children. In 1861 he chose a second wife, Miss Ellen McNaughton, who proved a devoted mother to his children.

During the early years of the war he was an editorial writer on the Perrysburg Journal and directed the policy of that paper. He was an enthusiastic supporter of Hon. James M. Ashley and advocated the vigorous prosecution of the war for the preservation of the Union, and was a strong adherent to the principles of the Republican party as advocated by the leaders of that period.

In 1875 he established the Buckeye Granger in Perrysburg, a weekly paper, advocating the principles of the Patrons of Industry, and for six years that paper was conducted with signal ability, wielding an influence for good throughout Northwestern Ohio. Subsequently he was a frequent contributor to many newspapers in Toledo and Wood county. He was a close political student and as a writer he was concise, forceful and logical.

In his political views of men and measures, he was thoroughly independent. If he favored any measure of public policy, he did so irrespective of any political party. The only question with him, in regard to any political issue, was "Is it right; or wrong; is it just or unjust?" His sympathies were ever with the people. Whatever would benefit his fellow citizens received his active support. He was free in the expression of his opinion. There was no subterfuge in his make-up. In all his relations with his fellow man he was courteous and affable. He was ever generous to a fault. His cheery smile and hearty greeting were genuine, coming from a heart overflowing with sympathy for all.

The funeral services were largely attended by Perrysburg citizens and many from a distance. The services were in charge of Rev. D. Stecker, pastor of the M. E. church, assisted by Rev. G. A. Adams, who had been the friend and associate of the deceased for nearly half a century. The remains were laid away in Ft. Meigs cemetery.

Thus ended the earthly career of one who in spite of most discouraging business reverses always remained cheerful and hopeful, whose long life proved a benison to his fellow men—a man of sterling integrity—a broad-minded, open-hearted, generous, consistent Christian gentleman.—*F. J. O.*

SETH HUNT FAIRCHILD

A Cultured Gentleman of the Old School of the Legal Fraternity

ONE of the oldest members of the Wood county Bar Association at the time of his death, was Seth H. Fairchild, beloved and respected by all who knew him. He had been in feeble health for a number of years, before he passed into the Unseen. The funeral took place from the residence of his daughter, Mrs. Stanley Thurstin, and was largely attended by the citizens of Bowling Green. The remains were interred in Oak Grove cemetery beside those of his wife who had preceded him a decade before.

Mr. Fairchild was one of the old pioneer lawyers of Northwestern Ohio. He possessed a number of quaint ways, and was of a methodical manner in the conduct of his affairs. He could properly be termed a gentleman of the old school, courteous and friendly in manner. He was the dean of the Wood county bar, being the oldest member in point of age.

Mr. Fairchild resided in McComb previous to his moving to Bowling Green. He owned a large grist mill there, and served that place as mayor and justice of the peace for many years.

In 1869 he went to Bowling Green and applied himself strictly to the practice of law, attaining a good practice. He also served Center township as justice of the peace for several terms. On account of poor health, he was obliged to give up his profession, after which he lived a quiet life alone in his home on Prospect street.

During the county seat fight he became quite a conspicuous figure among the most active workers in behalf of Bowling Green.

The Wood county bar in the expression of its esteem records the following:

"In the removal of brother Fairchild our association recognizes the loss of a member largely entitled to our respect and esteem, and a prominent link in the chain uniting the old with the more modern practice of our profession in this state.

"Brother Fairchild, in his courteous demeanor towards the members of the bar, as well as in his high appreciation of the principles of equity, was a model which the younger members of the profession would do well to imitate; and we can all see much to admire in the simplicity and strict integrity of his character."—*C. W. E.*

The famous chief, Little Turtle, in 1812, died at Fort Wayne, where he had come to be treated by the army surgeons.

ALFRED M. RUSSELL

A Prominent and Influential Citizen Who Had Filled Important Official Positions in the County

AFTER many months of paralytic suffering, Alfred M. Russell passed away at his residence in Bowling Green, on Tuesday morning, June 13, 1899, leaving a wife and two children— Charles H. Russell and Mrs. Frank Reed—together with a host of friends in Wood county.

Mr. Russell was born March 7, 1835, and was the youngest of a family of ten children. He was educated at Antioch and Oberlin, after which he spent a number of years as a school teacher. At the breaking out of the Civil war he enlisted as a member of Co. G, 14th O. V. I., and was made first lieutenant. He was discharged at the end of three months on account of injuries received, and re-enlisted as a private in Co. C, 68th O. V. I., in 1863, and was made sergeant-major. He was discharged from the service in 1866, and soon after located in Bowling Green, where he continued to reside, with the exception of a few years spent at Perrysburg.

He has filled various positions of trust and responsibility having been twice elected county treasurer and having served several terms as deputy county treasurer and deputy county auditor.

The deceased enjoyed a wide acquaintance throughout the county and was honored and esteemed by all who knew him as an upright citizen and public official. He was a member of Phoenix Lodge F. & A. M., of Perrysburg, and of Crystal Chapter R. A. M., of Bowling Green, and was also a member of the Grand Army of the Republic.

The funeral was held Thursday afternoon at 2 o'clock, at the Presbyterian church. The services were under the direction of the Masonic fraternity, of which Mr. Russell was a prominent member. Rev. Adams, of Perrysburg, assisted by Rev. Dillon, had charge of the church services. The remains were interred in Oak Grove cemetery.

HON. E. W. POE

In the Prime of Life, One of Wood County's Worthy Sons, Passed to His Reward

AT the age of 52 years, stricken with apoplexy, Hon Ebenezer W. Poe, one of Wood county's worthy sons, passed away at his home 691 Bryden road, Columbus. The summons of the dread Messenger came Sunday morning, June 19, 1898, at 11 o'clock.

He was stricken early Saturday evening, while down town with some friends, and never regained consciousness. He was conveyed to his home in an ambulance, where he was given the most skilful medical attendance, but all to no avail and he passed away peacefully as stated above, without being able to recognize any of his family, all of whom surrounded his bedside.

Mr. Poe was a self-made man in all that the term implies. He was born and reared on a farm near Van Buren, in Hancock county, and in his boyhood days was fitted for the sturdy responsibilities of life by hard work on the farm. He made the best of every opportunity that presented itself for advancement, and his efforts were crowned with success.

He was twice elected auditor of Wood county and made a most competent and obliging official. Later he served two

SCRAP-BOOK.

terms as auditor of state, in which position he acquitted himself commendably. At the time of his death he was a member of the board of trustees of the Boys' Industrial Home at Lancaster.

Mr. Poe was a member of the Masonic fraternity and of several other secret societies, and he numbered his friends by the score in all parts of the state. He was of a genial disposition, simple and unostentatious in his manners and a true and trusted friend. His taking off in the prime of life was universally lamented by his legion of friends in Wood county and throughout the state.

The funeral was held from the residence the following Tuesday afternoon. Rev. Macafee, of the Broad street M. E. church, of which Mr. Poe was a member, conducted the services at the house. The Masonic fraternity had charge of the services at the grave. The interment was made at Green Lawn, the beautiful Columbus cemetery.

HON. GEORGE LASKEY

At One Time State Senator and for Many Years Identified with Wood County Interests

HON. GEORGE LASKEY, one of the prominent pioneer citizens of the Maumee Valley, after many months of paralytic suffering, passed away at his home in Toledo, August 11, 1899, and in this final ending there passed from earth the soul of a grand man, a devoted father and a whole-souled public-spirited citizen. He was honest, energetic, upright in every phase of life—a man of sterling integrity who enjoyed the unshaken confidence of all who knew him.

The Toledo Bee in announcing his death gave the following brief sketch of his busy life:

Hon. George Laskey was born in Devonshire, England, near the town of Bristol, August 23, 1824. His parents, George and Ann (Southard) Laskey, came to this country in 1833, landing in New York. Coming to Ohio, they settled in Lucas county, then a wild, uncultivated state, and proceeded to make a home among the early pioneers of Ohio.

In 1837, at the age of 13 years, the subject of this sketch started in the world for himself. Going to Grand Rapids, Ohio, he accepted a position as clerk in the store of Francis Hinsdale. Industrious, energetic, reliable and thoroughly honorable in his relations to his employer, he showed while still a boy the sterling qualities that were so marked in his later life, and at the end of nine years' time was admitted to a partnership in the firm, which made a marked success. In 1851, five years after young Laskey had become identified with the firm, Mr. Hinsdale died and Mr. Laskey continued to carry on the extensive business, looking after Mrs. Hinsdale's interests in connection with his own. Later he and his brother bought out Mrs. Hinsdale and the firm name was changed to Laskey Bros. Being energetic, wideawake young men, possessed of more than ordinary business ability, they became the most popular merchants of Grand Rapids and won many friends. In 1866 they sold out and retired from the mercantile business, becoming interested in real estate.

After retiring from his mercantile career, Mr. Laskey became interested in agricultural pursuits, having previously purchased large tracts of land in Wood, Henry, Putnam and Lucas counties. At the time of his death, he owned several thousand acres in these counties, most of which is laid out in fine farms and under a high state of cultivation. This venture proved markedly successful and he continued in the occupation until September, 1877, when he removed to Toledo.

In 1859 Mr. Laskey was elected to the Ohio state senate, to represent the six counties of Lucas, Wood, Hancock, Henry, Fulton and Putnam, serving a term of two years. While in the senate he was one of the committee on railroads, and chairman of the committee on ditches and roads, doing more than any other man in Ohio toward inaugurating the drainage system that has reclaimed so many acres of wet land. He had always taken an active part in the drainage system and in all public affairs, being an important factor in the growth and improvement of the community in which he made his home. He served as commissioner of Wood county for six years.

Mr. Laskey and Antoinette Howard were united in marriage January 1, 1848. The union was a happy one and was blessed by six children, four sons and two daughters. For many years they attended the Congregational church of Toledo, and were among its most active members.

THE HOOD FAMILY

Reminiscences of These Worthy Scotchmen So Well Known to Our Older Wood County Citizens

SOME years ago Mr. N. H. Callard furnished the Wood County Democrat with the following reminiscences of the Hood brothers:

The Hood family comprised five sons and one daughter. They were natives of Midlothian county, Scotland, and after landing in the city of Montreal, came to Ohio in 1851, settling in the village of Perrysburg. They had all been well educated, and in all their personal and public services have shown the highest characteristics of integrity and public spirit.

The writer located in Perrysburg in 1853 and is familiar with their life record, and its services from that time to the period when five members of this worthy family has passed away, and two others who had been allied with them by marriage.

In 1853 when I came to Perrysburg James and William Hood were owners of the brick building on Front street, Perrysburg, which subsequently was purchased by the corporation of Perrysburg, and has been used since then as a council room and engine house. The partners had a large miscellaneous stock of goods and were then doing a profitable business.

In 1854 the scourge of cholera prevailed in the village but the Hoods bravely stood their ground in the midst of it.

Thomas Atkins, an Englishman, and his son, at that time kept a saloon and grocery. The older man was taken down by an attack of cholera in its worst form. He died in a short time and his son immediately followed.

The Hoods performed the kind duties of humanity for them and as an administrator of the Atkins estate, managed it through the action of Asher Cook, who then was probate judge, so that the Atkins children in England participated in their father's estate, instead of its being held by those who had asserted a claim to it in this country.

Another instance in which the Hoods were useful in the cholera time was that of a poor inebriate Scotchman named John Anderson. He was a working blacksmith for Mr. Lawrence and made his home on the river bank in a dilapi-

SCRAP-BOOK.

dated house on Front street, opposite what then belonged to Mr. Lindsay.

Information was brought me as a member of the committee of the M. E. church which together with a similar committee of the Presbyterian church, was charged with the duty of visiting the sick and the dying, and to aid them all to the best of our ability.

I at once went to the house where he was lying alone without food, and in an exceedingly dirty condition, as he had merged into the second stage of that terrible disease. I obtained a change of under-clothing for him from Mr. William Hood, also some medicine from Dr. Smith and with incessant labor the poor inebriate was restored to health.

In this and other cases the Hoods performed good service for the public. Shortly after this event William Hood removed to Bowling Green and as the second merchant in that place became a leading factor in its mercantile affairs, and subsequently when the change of county seat from Perrysburg to Bowling Green was rife, he became one of the most active, resolute and liberal factors in the accomplishment of the removal.

He was a leading factor in the construction of the Tontogany and Bowling Green railway, and the citizens of Bowling Green placed the name "William Hood" on their first locomotive. He died many years ago.

James Hood's services in aid of the old plank road brought to light the ways and methods by which selfish partisans then as well as now, saddled the taxpayers with unjust and unscrupulous burdens. He left Perrysburg and removed to the Hull Prairie farm in 1856, where he subsequently died.

Henry Hood, another of these five brothers, was a practical agriculturist. His personal record of integrity, of public usefulness, and of liberal views in both politics and in religion commanded the respect and confidence of his fellow citizens at large in Middleton township. He was elected trustee and treasurer of Middleton township during several terms, and at all times he was favorable to public improvements when they were honestly conducted.

Henry Hood, together with David Whitney, John Ulrich, James Robertson and some others were instrumental in the establishment of the Wood County Fair, which became a source of much good to the agriculturist and the citizens generally of Wood county. It has been merged with the Bowling Green Fair, the results and influence of which are now felt by the citizens of adjoining counties.

At the time of his death it was found that Henry Hood had bequeathed a fund for the purchase of a lot on the Prairie, and the erection of a church, that under the control of trustees should be held in perpetuity regardless of sectarianism, for public worship.

John Hood resided in Perrysburg until his death, which occurred a few years since.

THE IRONSIDE MURDER

WILLIAM IRONSIDE was killed at the head of Station island. Two men named Griffin, Orrin and Ben, had a kind of fish hut for catching cat fish, both drinking men and hard cases. William Ironside was a half breed from Canada where he had been educated in a mission school. He was engaged in trapping around the island. The Griffins saw him lifting his trap and supposed that he was taking fish from their lines. They were somewhat intoxicated at the time and began to threaten him and finally chased and struck him with a boat oar. After a hard fight Ironside was killed. The Griffins were sent to penitentiary for the murder. This took place in 1835. Ironside was harmless, intelligent and peaceable.

HON. ASHER COOK

In Spite of Almost Insurmountable Obstacles He Became a Leading Member of the Wood County Bar

IN Richland county, Ohio, on May 3, 1823, the subject of this sketch first saw the light of day. In his early childhood his parents came to Perrysburg. The father was a stone mason and plasterer. The son, Asher, with a meagre education obtained from the common school of that day, learned his father's trade and for a short time followed it. Later he worked with the force of laborers employed in the construction of the Maumee and Western Reserve turnpike, which at that time was the main line of overland transportation from the east to the Maumee Valley. Still later he worked as a common laborer in the construction of the Mad River railroad. Not content with the lot of a common laborer he changed his occupation to that of a sailor under Capt. W. H. Wetmore then engaged in lake traffic. When that popular captain took command of a steamer, Asher Cook went with him as wheelsman.

But nature and his studious habits endowed him for a wider field of usefulness. In spite of poverty and the absolute necessity for constant and severe toil, he finally secured a most thorough knowledge of the common and some of the higher branches of learning. He had a special liking for the study of different languages, and became quite proficient in Latin, French, Spanish and German. He engaged in the study of law under Hon. Willard V. Way, one of the strong pioneer lawyers of that day, and in 1849 he was admitted to practice. It was not long until he took a leading position at the bar of Northwestern Ohio. He met on equal terms with his former preceptor, and held his own with such men as John S. Spink, James Murray, Samuel M. Young, Morrison R. Waite and other noted lawyers of that time. When Mr. Waite became Chief Justice of the United States, he said, "In knowledge and understanding of the fundamental principles of law, Asher Cook has no equal in the Maumee Valley."

Soon after his admission to the bar, he was elected prosecuting attorney of Wood county, and in 1851 was elected probate judge. He was married in 1853 to Amanda Hall, sister of Augustus and Manning Hall, pioneer merchants of Perrysburg. His wife died during the cholera epidemic in 1854. Soon afterward Judge Cook spent a year in Europe, studying in Paris and in Heidelberg. On returning to Perrysburg he took up the practice of his profession, and in 1858 married Sophia A. Hitchcock, daughter of W. J. Hitchcock, a prominent merchant of Perrysburg.

Originally Judge Cook was a Democrat, and took an active part in politics. On account of his pronounced anti-slavery sentiments, he could not consistently continue with that party. He was the leading spirit in a meeting held at Portage, Wood county, and at which resolutions were adopted embodying the identical principles afterward announced in the Pittsburg platform. He was a member of that famous Pittsburg convention, out of which the Republican party had its birth as a national organization, and which has cut so large a figure in the political history of the United States.

In the early part of the Rebellion Judge Cook raised and commanded a company of the 21st Regiment O. V. I., and later commanded Company F in the 144th Regiment O. V. I. He was a member of the convention that first nominated Gen. Grant for the Presidency. He was elected, in 1873, a member of the convention to revise the constitution of Ohio, and was made chair-

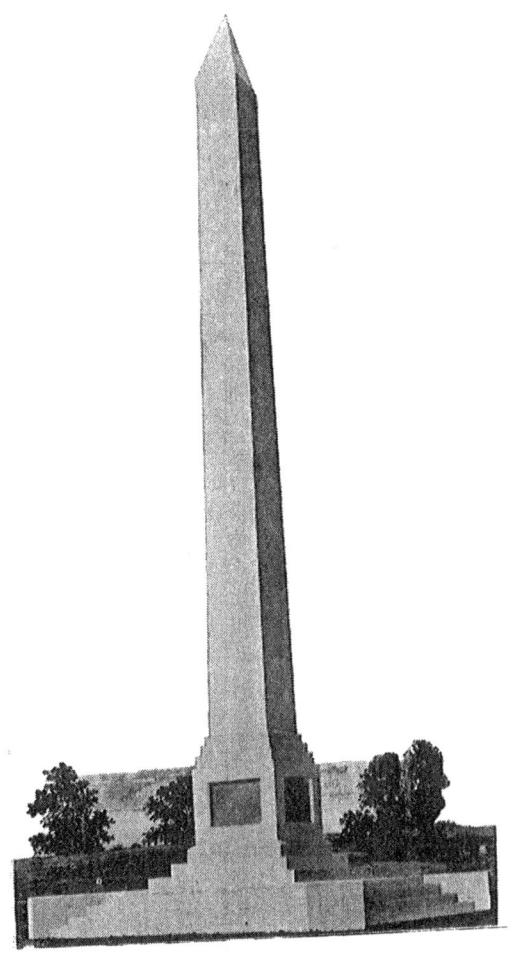

FORT MEIGS MONUMENT
Dedicated by Gov. A. L. Harris, Sept. 1, 1908

SCRAP-BOOK.

man of the committee on education in that convention. With his wife, he spent a year in 1879 in traveling in Great Britain and continental Europe. In 1883, he repeated the trip, extending his travels, however, so as to include Egypt and Palestine. Whether in private conversation or in public address, it was a pleasure to hear him recount the many interesting reminiscences with which his memory was stored.

His strength of mind, his scholarly attainments, his varied experience, his genial courtesy, his unquestioned integrity secured to him an unusual influence with courts and juries, and won the profound respect and esteem of his brethren at the bar as well as that of all who knew him. In his daily life he exemplified all that is best in the teachings of Free-Masonry of which fraternity he was a loyal member. In his intercourse with his fellowmen he was public spirited, and was ever ready to aid any movement adapted to the mental and moral advancement of the community. His domestic and social life was one of sympathetic tenderness. He was unassuming. His character was a strong fibre—fearless, progressive, typical of that army of pioneers, whose purposes carried out transformed this valley from a wilderness into a garden.

As the bells proclaimed the birth of the year 1892, at midnight, Judge Cook laid down life's burden, and his soul passed into the Unseen.

AMELIA WILKISON PERRIN

WHEN a child she came with her father, Jacob Wilkison, to Orleans before the war of 1812. Later the old settlement of Orleans was abandoned as unsuitable for a town, when a removal was made to Perrysburg, then an unbroken forest, and she afterwards saw the town in all its stages of growth up to 1898. Identified with this Valley during her long, useful life she could not be persuaded to leave it and make her home elsewhere.

She was married to Jonathan Perrin, and together they did their share in helping to build the town of Perrysburg. Mrs. Perrin kept fully abreast with the times. She was ever alive and interested in the topics of the day, and was well informed in all that pertained to the history of the country. She was descended from Revolutionary stock, and was a member of the Daughters of the American Revolution.

She was loyal to her country. Her time, her strength and means, and above all, her son, Wilkison D. Perrin, were given to the saving of the government in the Civil War. Her son gave his life in battle just before the close of the war, and although bowed with grief at his fall, she rejoiced in the final triumph of our arms.

Her memory will long be cherished by those who knew her.

The sword of John Paul Jones, the naval commander, now rests in the library of the naval department at Washington. It was presented to Jones by Theodosia Burr, the daughter of Aaron Burr.

Mrs. Mary A. Skinner, formerly Miss Spafford, who died, aged 88, at West Unity, was born in the old block house at Fort Meigs, September 7, 1819. Her girlhood home was the old Exchange Hotel in Perrysburg, and there she was married.

The old Mission House on the Maumee river, above Waterville, was built in 1822. It was a massive log frame about 60 feet in length and 16 feet wide, and two stories high. By many repairs that have been made since its erection, it is in a fair state of preservation, as a memorable relic of the past.

CHARLES W. EVERS

His Own Sketch of His Birth and Parentage---The Life, Labors and Character of the Man as Gleaned from Those Who Knew Him

AMONG the papers of Mr. Evers we find the following written by himself:

Johnson White, the pioneer ferryman on the Maumee river between Waterville and Miltonville had two daughters, Margaret and Celinda. The Whites, who crossed the Cumberland Mountains from Virginia into Tennessee, shortly after the war of 1812 were of English and Welsh stock. Mrs. White was a Fuller. It is not known in what year they came to the Maumee, but the records show that Mr. White served as one of the judges at the first election in Middleton township, November 17, 1832.

About the year 1835, John Evers, a carpenter and cabinet maker, who had recently located on the Maumee, and Celinda White were married. The Evers side was of German extraction. The family moved from Maryland to Western Pennsylvania where John's mother died, leaving three daughters and four sons. His mother, in her childhood, had been taken captive by the Indians, with whom she lived for seven years. From Pennsylvania the family moved to Wayne County, Ohio, and John was later apprenticed to learn a trade, after which he came to the Maumee to grow up with the country.

His son, Charles W., the subject of this sketch, was born at Miltonville, July 22, 1837. A couple of years later the family moved to Plain township where Mr. Evers had bought a 40-acre tract of land of Neptune Nearing in section 34, for which he hewed out and framed the timber and inclosed a 30x40 foot barn. The shingles were made from a white oak tree standing almost on the identical spot where a big oil well is now located. Mr. Nearing, who came from Otsego, was an excellent citizen, and by this trade got a new barn and a new neighbor.

Neighbors were scattered wide apart in Plain township. Lee Moore lived in a cabin on what is now South Main street. Where Weston is now, Thomas Taylor lived on the sinuous woods trail over ridges and across swales. Between Moore and Taylor, 9 miles, lived five families, Daniel Eldridge, about two miles east of Taylor's; on the Hollister land two miles from Eldridge lived an Irish family named Gatehouse, and two and one-half miles from there was Nearing and joining farms with him was Evers; next east a mile was the Missionary, Rev. Isaac Van Tassel, on what is since known as the Leonard place. From there to Moore's there was no cabin. The St. Johns and Edgertons came on the ridge later.

From Other Sources

In a biographical sketch of the life and character of Mr. Evers, by one who knew him well, we compile the following extracts from the Toledo Post and the Wood County Democrat:

Charles remained at home until 17 years old, and from his father learned

SCRAP-BOOK.

the carpenter's trade, which, with attending school and school teaching, occupied his time until the war broke out. He was a good carpenter, a successful teacher and a brave soldier. He early manifested a studious disposition, and making the most of such advantages acquired a good common school education and for a time engaged with marked success as a public school teacher.

At the age of 19 he made a trip to the West, intending to locate there, but later returned to Ohio and entered Oberlin College. At the breaking out of the Civil War he laid aside his books, donned the uniform of a Union soldier, having enlisted in the Second Kentucky Infantry in which he served three years, taking part in the battles of Perryville, Shiloh, Murfreesborough and Chickamauga. In the battle at the latter place he received a severe bullet wound in the leg, was taken prisoner and starved three months in the rebel pens, and was paroled just in time to obtain proper surgical treatment that saved his wounded leg from being amputated.

Returning home badly disabled, he was elected sheriff in 1864, and discharging his official duties to the entire acceptance of the public was honored by re-election two years later.

Mrs. C. W. Evers

The court house at that time was in Perrysburg at which place he and Sarah C. Bronson were married October 29, 1866.

His wife was the daughter of James M. Bronson, of Eagleville, where she was born, December 20, 1842. Her entire life was spent in Wood county, where her death occurred May 15, 1907. Of this union there are three living children, Mrs. J. A. Murray, of Manchester, O.; Mrs. May Evers Ross, of San Antonio, Texas, and John Evers, now a practicing physician of Flint, Michigan.

Mrs. Evers was a woman of rare culture and fine literary attainments, and many glowing and well deserved tributes were bestowed upon her worth of character by the literary societies with which she was an active participant.

Incidents in a Sheriff's Life

Mr. Evers' experience as sheriff was rather rough and he had several narrow escapes for his life. Once while enroute for Perrysburg on a train, with a desperate character he had arrested, the fellow, though handcuffed, suddenly made a spring and jumped through the car window as the train was pulling out of Tontogany. Mr. Evers sprang after him and was thrown so violently upon a pile of ties lying by the track, he received severe injuries upon the head and breast. Notwithstanding this, on his recovery from the shock he gave chase and after running his man for some distance across the country overhauled him. While bringing him back to town on the railroad track, the fellow, yet handcuffed, suddenly with both hands struck Mr. Evers a violent blow over the head and knocked him senseless. As soon as he had sufficiently recovered Mr. Evers with revolver in hand again gave chase and after firing several shots again halted his man. Greatly fatigued, the sheriff and prisoner, both bleeding from bruises, sank down for a rest within a few feet of each other. In the meantime a posse of men from Tontogany had started after them, and when they came upon the two men and saw Mr. Evers in his bruised and bleeding condition, it was only by threats from Mr. Evers that they were prevented from lynching the prisoner. The fellow was lodged in jail that night, and afterwards convicted and sent to the penitentiary.

Another time Marcellus Fugate and Wm. Wagstaff, two prisoners in jail made a desperate attempt to escape. As Sheriff Evers entered the corridor adjoining the prison cells to lock up the two men for the night, Fugate struck him a terrible blow with a stick of stove wood, at the same time throwing a handful of ashes in his face. Luckily, as was her custom, Mrs. Evers stood by the door and immediately locked the jail door and firmly informed the prisoners she would not unlock the door under any circumstances. On taking in the situation the prisoners made no further attack and were locked in their cells. Mr. Evers was badly though not dangerously hurt.

At another time by his watchfulness, he frustrated a jail full of prisoners from making their escape, whose plans were similar to the one just related. Mr. Evers was a keen discerner of character and had remarkable faculties in detecting criminals.

As a Journalist

Pursuing a natural bent for journalism Mr. Evers acquired a half interest with Robert M. Travis in the Wood County Sentinel and moved to Bowling Green in 1870, assuming editorial management of the paper with marked ability. Upon the death of Mr. Travis Mr. Evers became sole owner of the paper. Desiring to engage in the real estate business which offered a fine opening, he sold the Sentinel to M. P. Brewer, but when the county seat contest was inaugurated he with Dr. A. J. Manville, E. W. Merry and M. P. Brewer founded the News for the purpose of championing the claims of Bowling Green as the logical seat of county government. The News having served its purpose was merged with the Sentinel, and Mr. Evers continued in active journalistic work till 1884, when he sold out to A. W. Rudolph, he having conducted the paper for the four previous years alone.

It is conceded that to Mr. Evers was largely due the moulding of public sentiment which culminated in the building of the county infirmary, the inauguration of an adequate system of public drainage and the advancement of the educational interests of the county.

Mr. Evers was particularly well informed on all matters touching the early history of Wood county and the Maumee Valley.

His latest historical work was the souvenir history of Ft. Meigs which was written for the occasion of the dedication of the Fort Meigs monument.

Passes Into the Beyond

On July 29, 1909, at the age of 72 years, this busy, active and useful life came to an end at Robinwood Hospital in Toledo. For nearly two years he had been in declining health, and three weeks before his death he submitted to a surgical operation for a chronic ailment.

Although the operation was pronounced a success, yet in his weakened condition he was unable to withstand the shock, and his vitality gradually waned till death ensued.

On the following Sunday the remains of this brave soldier and esteemed citizen were taken to the G. A. R. rooms in the City Hall, of Bowling Green, where for several hours they were viewed by hundreds of his old friends and neighbors. The body reposed in a solid oak casket, surrounded and covered with a profusion of beautiful floral tokens, a regulation U. S. flag, an expressive esteem from the trustees of the Maumee Valley Pioneer and Historical Association, being entwined among the flowers.

The funeral services were held in the G. A. R. rooms at 2 o'clock, under the direction of Wiley Post G. A. R., the full ritualistic service of that patriotic order being observed.

Dr. E. E. Rogers, pastor of the Presbyterian church, conducted the burial service of the church, and Rev. T. N. Barkdull of Toledo, a lifelong friend of Mr. Evers, paid a touching tribute to his memory. Appropriate vocal selec-

SCRAP-BOOK.

tions were rendered by a quartet composed of Messrs. E. M. Rose, S. R. Case and B. C. and R. J. Eberly.

Tributes to His Memory

Judge Baldwin says: "He was a man of rare capability, keen perception, indomitable courage, and irresistible will.

"I know of no person whose life labor has left a deeper impress upon every phase of public concern to the entire people of Wood county than that of Mr. Evers. During what may be called the constructive period of the county's history, he was especially active, and much of the prosperity and general welfare of our people may be directly traced to the adoption of policies originating with him.

"At times he was misunderstood, and at times criticised, for his advanced position upon public and civic questions, but almost invariably the correctness of his foresight and the wisdom of his mature judgment were completely demonstrated. It is no disparagement that he encountered much opposition and was subjected to occasional censure, for no man with whom all the people always agree, ever says or does anything that endures. He was in the broadest sense a philanthropist—whose disinterested efforts for the public weal will be more appreciated as the years go by."

The Bowling Green Sentinel says:

"When the ritualistic service of Wiley Post was concluded, when the three perfectly timed volleys rang out from the rifles of Company H and the clarion toned notes of Musician Harry Noyes sounded 'Taps' at the grave of C. W. Evers, Sunday afternoon, the last sad rites were brought to a close for a man whose strength of character and patriotic devotion to the best interests of Bowling Green and Wood county wrought so much good to the community during the past forty years."

The Wood County Democrat says:

"He was always a true friend, and any difference of opinion on political or other questions had not the slightest effect on the harmony of our personal relations. And this fact brings his death home to us as a personal loss."

From the tribute of F. J. Oblinger, a life long friend, we extract the following:

"His influence for all that pertains to the benefit of his fellowmen in honesty, in courage, in loyalty, in industry, in all the activities of social, commercial, municipal and political life, can not fail to prove an incentive to those who are conversant with the story of his career from boyhood to manhood.

"He was ever active, courageous, progressive. Honest in purpose, industrious in endeavor, no labor however arduous, no obstacle however seemingly insurmountable appalled him.

"One characteristic cannot be passed over in silence. He never made a statement, either verbal or written, unless its truth could be substantiated by incontrovertible proof. In this regard he was scrupulously careful and exact, and when once he made an assertion it was undeniable and could be relied upon."

A Fitting Tribute

(From the Democrat of Aug. 6, 1909.)

As an expression of appreciation of the great interest in and effective work accomplished for the Maumee Valley Pioneer and Historical Association, the trustees of that organization at a special meeting held at Fort Meigs last Friday afternoon, unanimously adopted the following Memorial and Resolutions:

"This board learns with sincere sorrow of the death of its fellow worker, Mr. Charles W. Evers, of Bowling Green, which occurred at Toledo, July 29, 1909.

"It is certain that there has not been a more zealous nor a more faithful member of the Maumee Valley Pioneer and Historical Association than he, and not one whose evenness of temper and gentlemanly bearing has so endeared himself to our entire membership than has he. He possessed positive views regarding matters which he had investigated, yet he so maintained them as not to forfeit the respect and regard of those from whom he differed.

"Possessing a cultured mind and being well informed regarding historical matters, particularly those connected with the Maumee Valley, his services in behalf of this association in making a record of the military events, and of pioneer trials and achievements in this section have been of great value. Owing to his enfeebled bodily condition much of this work was accomplished at the cost of great physical suffering, yet with an enthusiasm which told of his love for and interest in the work of the association.

"We recognize in Mr. Charles W. Evers a good man, loyal citizen, kind husband and father and faithful friend, therefore,

"Resolved, That on behalf of the Maumee Valley Pioneer and Historical Association this Board extends to his family its sincere sympathies. Be it further

"Resolved, That this Memorial be spread upon the records of this board, and that a copy of the same be offered for publication, and also that a copy be sent to his family.

"D. K. HOLLENBECK, President.
"J. L. PRAY, Secretary."

SCRAP-BOOK.

263

ERRATA

On page 10 under sub-head "The First Legislature," twelfth line, you find mention of Indiana Territory. It should read INDIAN territory.

On page 13, first column, twelfth line from the bottom, you find 1878 given as the date of the settlement of Marietta. It should be 1788.

CONTENTS

	Page
Amusing Incident, An	125
Appleseed, Johnny	211
Attacked by Savages	82
Attacked by Wolves	78
Athlete, An	176
Badger, Rev. Joseph	137
Battle of Grand Rapids	101
Battle in Canada, The	219
Bell School House, The	87
Benton, The Town of	101
Bitten by a Snake	176
Black Swamp, The	184
Bloody Wolf Fight	164
Bowling Green	83
Burning Off a Prairie	170
But the Shot Missed	116
Catholic Missions	16
Callard, Nathaniel H.	248
Campaign of 1840, The	69
Cemetery, An Old	228
Center Township	35
Chubb, Rev. Rolla H.	153
Cholera, The Dread	110
Cholera Victims	242
Cook, Hon. Asher	254
Croghan, Major George	226
Cygnet's Calamity	140
Day, Colonel Seldon	119
Devil's Hole, The	165
Dedication of Ft. Meigs Monument	32
Dewese, Amos	245
Disastrous Campaigns	18
Dodge, Judge H. H.	224
Dubbs, Henry	107
Early History	24
Early School Days	106
Early Formation	10
Error Corrected, An	214
Evers, Charles W.	258
Exchange Bell, The Old	161
False Alarm, A	141
Fairchild, Seth Hunt	249

	Page
Fierce Battle, A	109
Fish and Ague	67
Freedom Township	175
Ghastly Crime, A	191
Girty, Simon	168
Golt, Edson	150
Going to Mill	77
Grand Rapids	65
Grand Organization	30
Historical Crisis, An	114
Hood Family, The	252
Hollister's Prairie	75
Hollingtons, The	94
Horrible Tragedy, A	181
Hopper, George	162
Hull's Surrender	185
Hunter's Paradise, A	170
Hull's Trace, As to	128
Illustration, An	66
Impregnable Fort	143
Indians Foiled	54
Indian Justice	156
Indian Character	205
Indian Dances	193
Indian Skeleton	107
Indian Associates	96
Ironside Murder, The	253
Jail in the Woods, A	45
Kenton, Simon	177
Last of Big Game	88
Lake Commerce	124
Laskey, Hon. George	251
Land Sharks	62
Little Turtle	57
Liberty Township	126
Life of a Recluse	208
Long, Tom	166
Logical Reasons	51
Lost Child, The	129
Load of Coons	211
Loomis Murder, The	199

CONTENTS—Concluded

	Page
Madman's Frenzy, A	186
Maumee River, The	176
Mail Carrying	136
Manor, Peter	57
Mail Route	107
Maumee Country, The	79
Mercer Settlement	103
Memorable Fourth, A	38
Meeker, Mahlon	62
Memorable Address, A	231
Milton Township	76
Mission Station	150
Miami of the Lake	98
Navigation	172
Navarre, Peter	68
Nearing, "Uncle" Guy	121
Newspaper History	179
Newton, Joseph B	247
Night With Indians, A	183
Not All a Dream	151
Noted Bear Hunt	190
Notable Addresses	156
Odd Genius, An	152
Oil in Wood County	104
Old Time Tragedy	46
Organization of Ohio	128
Passed Away	110
Petersburg Volunteers	40
Perrin, Amelia Wilkison	257
Peck, Erasmus D., M. D.	60
Pierce, James H	223
Presbyterian Jubilee	206
Pittsburg Blues, The	39
Pioneer Families	54
Porter-Richardson Murder	166
Powell, Hon. Thomas W	156
Poem, Johnny Applesced	212
Poe, Hon. E. W.	250
Poem, Our Pioneers	6
Poem, Maumee Pioneers, The	115
Random Notes	238
Recovering a Stolen Horse	126
Removing the Indians	171
River Raisin Massacre	217

	Page
Roche de Boeuf	202
Roach, Mayor Andrew	214
Russell, Alfred M	250
Sage Child Tragedy	74
Sad Chapter, A	193
Salsbury, Jonathan	141
Snaking Scourge, A	163
Shocking Suicide	178
Slater's Curse, Jim	130
Spink, Shibnah	43
Strange Story, A	192
Strange Incident	138
Successful Scheme	210
Summer of Gloom, A	111
Tecumseh, Eloquence of	58
Tecumseh, Described	59
Tecumseh, Death of	60
Tecumseh's Contempt	225
Ten Years' Struggle, A	133
Tinge of Romance	97
Treaty of Maumee, The	13
Traffic in 1833	149
Turkey Foot Rock	90
Two Lost Girls	159
Unbroken Forests	93
Up the Maumee	202
Wayne's Daring Scouts	29
Way, Willard V.	181
Wayne's Two Graves	169
Webb, John	239
Weston Township	80
What Might Have Been	164
Wilkinson, Capt. David	135
Winter of 1842-3, The	73
Wild Hogs	78
Wolf Hunting	148
Wood County Masonry	154
Wood County Born	15
Wood County in War	179
Woodbury House, The	182
Wood County's Birth	7
Wood County Fair	112
Worst of All Roads	123
Wood County Organization	31

ILLUSTRATIONS

	Page
Burial Ground of Col. Dudley and Men	173
Croghan, Major George	226
Evers, Chas. W.	3
Ft. Meigs	145
Ft. Meigs (Harrison Point)	229
Ft. Meigs (Ravine)	215
Ft. Meigs (Monument)	255
Ft. Miami	243
Harrison Gen. Wm. H.	157

	Page
Harrison's Well	187
Maumee River and Valley	117
Navarre, Peter	63
Ottokee	237
Petersburg Volunteer Monument	41
Roche de Boeuf	203
Tecumseh	55
Turkey Foot Rock	91
Wayne, Gen Anthony	19

INDEX

----, John 120 Sarah Jane 192 Theobald 221
ABBOTT, S B 129
ADAMS, Benoni 238 G A 135 223 249 J C 167 Rev 214 250 Richard 42
ALBERTY, G 130
ALEXANDER, Maj 147
ALLEN, Col 217-218 Seneca 11
ALLISON, R 39
AMES, 81
ANDERSON, 37 47 49-50 John 28 46 48 252
ANDREWS, Amasa 167 Andrew 42
ANTHONY, Mad 115
APPLESEED, Johnny 177 211-214
ARBUCKLE, Hugh 127
ARNE, Mr 242
ARNOLD, Emanuel 81 154
ASH, C 105 Mr 105
ASHLEY, James M 248 Mr 61
ATKINS, Thomas 252
ATKINSON, Richard 242 Thomas 242
AUSTIN, Ann 219
AVERY, Mr 88-89 108 Wash 89-90 Wash G 88 Wm 89
BABBITT, Mrs 194 Mrs A T 194
BABCOCK, Will F 200
BACH, Carl 191-192
BACON, Mr 155 S A 155 Selah A 154
BADGER, Father 97 John 159-160 Joseph 97 137 159 238 Lewis 159-160 Mr 97 Nathaniel 159 Stella 159-161
BAIRD, 133 C C 166 186 John 132 Mr 186 189
BAKER, J D 180
BALDWIN, F A 201 225 Jane 207 Judge 261 Messr 201 Mr 208 Mrs 207 P C 74
BAMBER, John 113
BAMM, Winfield 231
BARCLAY, Commodore 58 227
BARKDULL, T N 260 Thos 247
BARNES, Silas 167
BARR, Robert 84
BARTON, Daniel 107 154 205 Sarah 107
BASON, Henry 242

BASSETT, B 113
BATES, John 45 112-113
BEACH, 100
BEARDSLEY, 35
BEAUGRAND, 82
BEEBE, Contractor 176
BELL, Gen 164 George A 154
BELLINGER, Lucy 242
BELLVILLE, William 242
BENNETT, C K 172 Henry 100
BENNETTS, George W 167
BENNEY, J 39
BENTON, Thomas 101 Tom 101
BEYMER, George 85
BIGGER, Thomas B 42 William 167
BIGNALL, John 42
BINGHAM, 124 J J 100
BIRDSELL, James 127
BIRDSEYE, Victor 224
BIRK, Mrs 214
BISHOP, Messr 128
BLACK, Maggie 247 Robert 42
BLACKFORD, Aaron 225 Jason 225
BLALOCK, George 59
BLINN, Julius 72 N D 113 Nathaniel 167 Sophia 242
BLIVEN, Charles E 172
BLOOM, Harriet 98 James 98 113 139 246 Messr 113 Mr 98
BLOOMFIELD, George W 242
BLYTHE, Samuel 154-155
BOLLES, J D 247
BONAPARTE, 233
BONNECAMP, Father 17
BOOKER, Daniel 42 George 42
BOPE, Col 225 J A 225
BORTELL, Allen 81
BOSS, D C 39
BOSWELL, Col 147
BOUGHTON, Mr 208 Mrs S L 208 Solon 207
BOURNE, S 37
BOYD, Gen 226
BRADDOCK, 18

BRADY, Mr 162 Sam 162
BRANDY, Jack 126 Jake 126
BRASH, Judge 167
BRAUCH, Richard H 42
BRAYMAN, Mason 100
BREWER, M P 260
BRIGHAM, 100 238
BRISTOL, Maria 153
BROCK, Gen 143 Isaac 186
BRONSON, James M 259 Sarah C 259
BROWN, Alexander 65-66 77 81 Edmund 42 Gen 114 164 J D 100 Morris 96 154 Mr 65 67 77 Mrs 242 Mrs Abner 242 Sheriff 200-201
BROWNSBERGER, John 112
BRUCE, Seth 111-112
BUCHER, 72 Samuel 71
BUISEY, Mr 245
BURGE, George 42
BURKE, Edmund 17 Father 17
BURN, Geo 242
BURNS, Esther 242
BURR, Aaron 257 Theodosia 257
BURRITT, Dr 138 H 163
BURROUGH, Thomas 231
BURROWS, Senator 217
BURTLEY, John W 42 Joseph R 42
BURTON, William 42
BUTLER, James 39 Robert 42
BYERS, Martin 112
CABANISS, James 42
CABLE, Benjamin 175 Isaac 175 Jonathan 175 Silas 175
CADY, 98 Harriet 98 Horace 97 127
CALLARD, Ellen 248 Mr 248 N H 111 125 252 Nathaniel H 248
CAMPBELL, A R 225
CANARY, J W 225 John W 224 Messr 201
CANFIELD, Dwight 90 George S 135
CARLIN, James 59
CAROTHERS, 160 Henderson 246 W R 159 William 105 Wm E 190
CARR, Joshua 208 Mr 197 Mrs 197-198 Omar C 154
CARROTHERS, Henderson 130
CARTER, John 148 Mr 148 Wm 59
CARTRIGHT, Peter 24
CARY, Henry 42
CASE, M L 247 S R 261
CASS, 185 Dr 142 Gen 14 59 Gov 11 Lewis 13

CHALMERS, James 42
CHAMBERS, Robert 242
CHAPIN, Henry S 180
CHAPMAN, John 211
CHAPPEL, J 100 Joshua 65 111 167
CHARLES, Elizabeth 239 241
CHARTER, Samuel 42
CHENSWORTH, Edward 42
CHESS, J 39
CHILCOTE, Samuel 45
CHUBB, Emily 153 Henry 153 Maria 153 Mary C 154 Mr 153 Olive 153 Rolla H 153
CLARK, 39 George 231 Joseph 231 Mr 130 Mrs 83 Oren 100 Robert 112 Samuel 130 Thomas 42
CLAY, 38 Cassius M 143 Gen 124 144 156 228 Green 147 Messr 119
CLEMENS, Geo 242
CLEMMENTS, Moses 42 Reuben 42
CLOUGH, G T 42
CLYMER, Samuel 123
COFFINBERRY, Count 138 Mr 93 T M 93
COFFINBURY, A C 100
COGBILL, Edward H 42
COLE, L C 225
COLLINS, 144
COLWELL, Billy 68 Capt 68-69
COMBS, Leslie 59
COMMAGER, Mrs Gen 101
CONANT, Dr 138 176 Horatio 11
CONDIT, Mrs Harvey 197
CONLEY, Thos F 225
COOK, 100 Amanda 254 Asher 61 112-113 182 252 254 John J 242 Judge 254 257 Messr 113 Mrs Asher 242 Robert B 42 Sophia A 254
COOMBS, Capt 147
CORLETT, Wm 30 40
CORNWALLIS, 22
CORWIN, Tom 38
COSTER, A 242
COURSER, Wm H 242
COX, Ben 36 Benjamin 35 47 Elizabeth 35 Joseph 35 Lydia 35 Thomas 37 Thos 127
CRAIN, Mary 242
CRAVEN, Doctor 120
CRAWFORD, Col 171
CREPS, David 112 Joseph A 112
CROGHAN, Capt 226 Col 228 Gen 40 George 226-227 Maj 226 Major 245

SCRAP-BOOK.

CROM, Jonathan 81
CRONEWALD, Miss 242
CROOK, Henry 112 Jane 242
CROSBY, A B 137
CROSS, 189 Orson 186
CURTIS, 238 James 154
DAUGHERTY, John 231
DAVIS, 94 Hiram 182 J 39 J D 39 Jeff 120 Jefferson 119 Messr 119 Miss Winnie 120 Mr 119-121 161 Mrs 120 Pi 120 S 161
DAY, Col 119 D M 162 Mary 208 Mr 119 Selden A 119 Selden Allen 119
DEAL, J 40
DEAN, Mary 241
DECKER, 54 78 Jesse 62 149 Levi 149 Moses 149 Nathaniel 149 167
DEEMER, A 40
DEERING, F L 198 Fannie 194 Fanny 193-197 199 J K 194 Miss 194 Mrs 196-197
DELARICHARDIE, Father 17
DELEON, Ponce 209
DEWESE, Amos 245 Capt 245 Mr 246 Samuel 245 Sarah 246 Thomas 245
DEWITT, William 37
DICK, Thomas 59
DILLON, Rev 250
DIVER, O 110 Thomas 238
DOAN, 100
DOANE, Seth 240
DOBBINS, T 40
DOBSON, Russell T 180 Wm B 180
DODD, Ezra S 134 J 40 Mr 135
DODGE, 131 Frederick G 224 H H 224 Henry H 224-225 Judge 201 224-225 Mary E 224 Mr 224 Sarah Hodge 224
DONALDSON, 221 Ann 107 Ebenezer 107 James 81 Jas 81 Mr 81 Mrs James 205
DORTION, Frederick 242
DOUGLASS, Capt 212
DOW, Lorenzo 36
DRENNAN, James 245
DUBBS, Ann 107 Henry 107 127-128 171 J F 159 170 183 205 210-211 James 171 Jim 211 John 130 171 183 211 Lewis 107 Mr 107 130 171 183 211 Sarah 107
DUDLEY, 31-32 52 228 Col 144 147 226 231 William 144 Wm 231
DUNLAP, Robert 225
DUNN, 201 Frank W 133 Robert 225 Robert Sr 206
DUSTIN, Dr 138 Mrs 43
DYHOUSE, Edward 231
EARL, 100
EATON, 87
EBERLY, B C 261 Elizabeth 35 Jacob 35 46-47 Mrs W S 153 R J 261
EDGAR, John 154
EDGERTON, 210 258 Abram D 208 Brom 208
EDWARDS, Sam 210
EICHHOLZ, Christian 242 Miss 242
ELDRIDGE, Daniel 258
ELLIOT, Col 59
ELLIOTT, Col 83 E 113 J 40 James 231 Messr 113 S 39
ELLSWORTH, 49-50 246 Geo 127 John 48
EMERSON, 87
ENGLISH, A 40
ESHON, Daniel 42
ESPY, James P 99
EVERS, C W 34-35 43 51 69 73 83 88 90 130 159 165 182 193 247 261 Celinda 258 Charles W 7 258 261-262 John 75 258-259 May 259 Mr 10 16 30 46 51 84 88 96 107 121 130 178 181-183 231 258-261 Mrs 259-260 Mrs C W 6 206 259 Sarah C 259 Sheriff 166 259
EWING, 38 Anthony 101 176 Henry 71 Judge 153 Minerva 122 Olive 153 Samuel 101 238 Samuel H 59 Tom 73 Uncle Hank 101 W H 15 101 William 193 Wm 112 122
FAIRCHILD, Brother 249 Mr 249 Seth H 249 Seth Hunt 249
FAIRFIELD, N 40
FANE, Hiram 137
FAY, Clinton 54 84 139 Jonathan 84
FERDIG, Rosanna 242
FINDLAY, 186 Col 185
FINLEY, James B 26
FITZGERALD, Silas 231
FLANDERS, 123
FLICKINGER, Nancy 36
FOLTZ, Noah 128
FOOTE, E 238 Epaphroditus 149 Joel 238 Mr 238
FORAKER, Joseph B 34
FORBES, John G 167
FORSYTH, 100 Robert A 172

FORSYTHE, Judge 73
FOSTER, Emily 106 Gov 106
FRANKFATHER, Mr 245
FRANKFAUDER, Frederick 129 Margaret 129 Mr 129-130
FRANKLIN, 99
FRAZER, James W 112
FRAZIER, Margery 100
FREDERICK, Adaline 242 Dr 111 Mrs A E 111 The Great 21
FRENCH, 101
FRESHWATER, Reuben 167
FRIES, E M 225
FRONTENAC, 115 Count 51
FUGATE, 260 Marcellus 259
FULLER, 258
GALLATIN, John 129
GARDENER, Helen H 119
GARDNER, A J 154-155
GARFIELD, Gen 16
GARRETT, Lt 218
GASPERS, Ellen Mcmahan 39 Mrs 39-40
GATEHOUSE, 258
GATES, W 242
GEORGE, Joseph 231
GIBBON, 236
GIBSON, Henry B 182 Wm H 38
GIFFORD, Richard 59
GILBERT, Asa 123
GILLETT, Alva 205 Alvin 154-155 Jay L 154
GINGERY, John 66 77 Mr 67
GIRTY, George 168 James 168 Simon 115 168 171 177 Thomas 168
GODDARD, Edwin 200
GOIT, Edson 150 224 Mr 150-151
GOODMAN, Sharon 13
GOODWIN, Mrs 242
GORDON, James 107 Joseph 85 Mr 86
GORRILL, 163
GORTON, E 113 Edwin 113
GOSSETT, 87
GRAHAM, E 70 J N 65 S 40
GRANT, Gen 254
GREEN, Mrs 83 Sarah 246
GREGORY, Walter 231
GREVES, Mrs 40
GRIFFIN, Ben 253 Orrin 253
GRISS, Rev Father 225
GROVER, 201 Arthur J 199-200

GROVES, Henry 113 127 John 112-113 127
GUNCKEL, John E 228 Mr 228
GUNDY, Chris 101
GUNN, Eliza Jane 54 Horace 238 Sewell 167 Warren 54 Willard 167
GUY, Sarah 223
GUYER, Sheriff 189
HAHN, Henry 175
HALL, Amanda 254 Augustus 254 James 112 Manning 254 Mrs J A 242
HAMER, Mary C 154
HAMILTON, Capt 144 Dr 223 Mr 242
HANKEY, I L 247
HANNON, John 86
HARMAR, 54 115 Gen 8 18
HARMER, 90
HARRIS, A L 34 Gov 33-34 James 139 Seth 139
HARRISON, 38 78-79 97 115 242 Brig-gen 143 Gen 15 39 41 52 60 68-73 114 116 139 143-144 147 159 165 171 217 219 226-227 231 236-237 245 Gov 59 143 William Henry 40 42
HASKELL, W S 225
HASKINS, 37 129 Collister 35 66 84-85 103 107 113 126-127 138 Cynthia 127 Henry 127 Mr 127 Sarah 127 Wealthy 127
HATCH, Sylvester 154
HAVEN, G 39
HAWLEY, 239
HAYES, 33 Webb C 228
HAYS, 182 David 131 133 Michael 181 Mr 181
HAZARD, 100
HECOX, Sally 54 William 54
HEDGES, David 65 101 150 Elias 149 Gen 232
HEDINGER, Jake 89
HEINZIE, Mr 191
HELBERSON, Benj 231 Robert 231
HEMMINGER, George 36
HENDERSON, John 42
HERRICK, Elijah 149
HICKMAN, 29
HICKOX, Ambrose 59
HICKSON, David 84
HIGGINS, David 167 Judge 167
HILL, Billy 76
HILLS, A 100

SCRAP-BOOK.

HINSDALE, Francis 251 Mr 251 Mrs 251
HIRCEL, Lawrence 242 Margaret 242
HITCHCOCK, Peter 167 Sophia A 254 W J 254
HIXON, D L 37
HOAG, T H 61
HODGE, Sophia 182
HOELZLY, Wory 242
HOLLENBECK, D K 30 262 Francis 239-240
HOLLINGTON, 208 Ambrose 95 Joseph 84 95 Mary 95 Mr 94-95 Mrs 95 R D 34 95 Richard 94-95 William 95
HOLLISTER, 12 75 122 124 138 258 B F 44 Frank 162 J 100 John 44 65 99-100 149 238 240 Judge 72-73 152
HOLMES, Samuel 37
HOLTERMAN, Henry 180
HOOD, Henry 112-113 253 James 112-113 252-253 John 89 112 253 William 252-253
HOOVER, Andrew 167
HOPKINS, Mr 136
HOPPER, George 162 Mr 162-163 Mrs 163
HOSMER, H L 172 Hezekiah L 82 152 Mr 83 R W Bro Hez L 155
HOUCK, G F 17
HOUSEHOLDER, Adam 37
HOUSER, William 167
HOWARD, 62 78 Antoinette 252 Edward 81 John 149 R A 81 R M 81
HOWE, Henry 10
HOWELL, Maggie 120
HUBBELL, 46 Daniel 15 150 238
HUBBLE, James R 156
HUBERT, Bishop 17
HUFF, Henry 75
HUFFMAN, Mr 242 Mrs 242
HULBERT, Prof 228
HULL, 57 78-79 82-83 114 155 Abraham F 185 David 59 Gen 109 126 143 185-186 217 220 226 H 40 William 28
HUNT, Gen 13 Harry 126 John E 30 126
HUNTER, Mr 136 Robert W 34
HUNTINGTON, E 112 Elijah 54 167 242
HURLBURT, Mrs 194
HUTCHINSON, Andrew 96-97 James 96 246 James Jr 96 James Sr 96 Mr 96-97 181 Mr Sr 96
INDIAN, Black Hoof 108 Blue Jacket 23 53 90 Bob 183-184 Brandt 23 Dog 57

INDIAN (cont.)
John 183-184 Kantuckegau 14 Kantuckegun 53 Little Turtle 18 23 25 53 57 90 177 249 Logan 57 Mashkeman 14 Massasa 52-53 Nauquezike 193 Noteno 172 Onequit 156 Ottoca 172 Ottuso 53 Otusso 14 Pamquauk 193 Petonguet 172 Pontiac 14 17 53 115 172 Roundhead 23 Sacamanc 82 Sawandebans 57 Snakebones 47 Summundewat 46-51 Tarhe 108 Tecumseh 14 52 57-60 115-116 143-144 147 214 219 221-222 225-227 242 The Prophet 242 Tondoganie 28 57 108-110 Turkey Foot 90 Yellow Hair 57
INDLEKOFER, 81
IRONSIDE, William 253
IRVING, Elizabeth Mansfield 115
IRWIN, James 39 Julia 242 Mrs Hernia 242
JACKSON, Andrew 141 Gen 114 James 42
JACQUES, J M 127
JAMES, B F 38 225
JAQUES, 54 John M 37
JAQUIS, John M 167
JEFFERS, James 42
JEFFERSON, 236 S 113 Thomas 165
JENISON, Nathaniel 167 Victory 240
JENKINS, John E 87
JOHN, Uncle 66-67 184 210
JOHNSON, 219-220 Benj 89 Col 60 221-222 Felicia R 39 John 231 Maj 147 Mr 89 Mrs 39-40 Peter 127 R M 221
JOHNSTON, John 148
JOLLIET, 16
JOLLY, Thomas 113
JONES, 100 G A 44 Geo 242 John Paul 257 Mary A 241 Mayor 40 Peter 172 Samuel 40 Wm M 40
JUDSON, J R 88
KEELER, Amelia 246 Melicent 246 Mr 246 Olmstead 246 Ralph 138 246 Ralph O 66 75
KEIDER, 242
KELLEY, Naomi D 242
KELLOGG, Palmer 167
KELLY, R W 189
KELP, Mr 242
KENTON, Simon 168 177
KIMBERLIN, John 205
KING, Nehemiah 11

KINGFIELD, Jacob 242
KINNAMAN, Dr 110 John 110
KIRTLAND, 100
KLEBER, 53
KLOPFENSTEIN, 37
KNAGGS, 14
KNAPP, H S 135
KNIGHT, Gen 171
LACY, William 42
LADD, David 112-113 240
LAFAYETTE, 22
LAFTON, Herbert C 42
LAMB, J M 84 Samuel 84
LANEY, Peter 242
LANG, J W 242
LANIER, William 42
LARWELL, Jabez B 182
LASALLE, 16 115
LASKEY, Ann 251 Antoinette 252 George 251 Mr 251-252
LATCHAW, P J 208
LATHROP, James W 156
LAWRENCE, 70 Mr 252
LAWSON, Benjamin 42
LAYBURN, George P 42
LEAMING, Halsey W 59 Thomas 59 167 240
LEBAUM, Gen 58
LECARON, Joseph 17
LEE, Charles 22 Edward 242
LEIGH, William R 42
LEONARD, 258
LEORLON, P 40
LEWIS, 144 238 Col 143 217 George 246 J 40 Thomas 231
LIDA, Gen 101-102
LINDSAY, Mr 253
LOCK, L C 113
LOCKE, 87 L C 86 208
LONG, Thomas 166 Tom 166
LONSONG, F 40
LOOMIS, G G 200 Granville G 199-201 Hartman 167
LORAINE, Alfred 42
LORD, 153 Caleb 87 Frederick 152 Judge 152
LOUGHRY, Wm 81
LOWE, 196 Mrs 199
LOWES, Mr 195
LUCAS, Frederick 242
LUCE, Frank 200

LUNDY, 37
LYNCH, Judge 50
LYONS, 47 49-50 James 46 Jim 48 Mrs 48
MACAFEE, Rev 251
MACKEY, 87 Robert 86
MADISON, 236 Maj 218-219
MAGINNIS, David 154
MAHAFFY, 29
MALLORY, Rozer 42
MALONEY, Mr 140 Mrs 140
MANCHESTER, D W 16
MANN, David 42
MANOR, 83 Petar 57 Peter 28 57 82
MANSENBURY, Nicholas 42
MANVILLE, A J 98 260 Eli 98
MARCY, J 39
MARGRY, Pierre 16
MARTIN, Wm 231
MARTINDALE, Eli 139 Elisha 46 54 84 123 Eliza Jane 54 Louisa 54 Mr 54 Sally 54
MASON, Joseph 42
MASS, Theodore 231
MATTHEWS, James Newton 212 N 39
MAXWELL, J 39
MAY, 29
MCARTHUR, 14 185-186 Duncan 13
MCATEE, Samuel 246
MCBRIDE, J H 98
MCCAHN, Sam 201
MCCAULEY, John 225
MCCLARNIN, T 40
MCCLELLAN, Robt 29
MCCLELLAND, E G 225
MCCLINTOCK, Lieut 231
MCCOMBS, Gen 156
MCCORMICK, George 94 James 94
MCCUNE, Capt 147 Robert 135
MCCURDY, Attorney 106
MCFALL, George 40
MCGEE, Mathew 39
MCGIFFIN, N M 40
MCGINNESS, James 112
MCISAAC, Patrick 112-113
MCKEE, O 40
MCKNIGHT, 94 Mr 240 Rebecca 242 Thomas R 239-240 Thos R 240
MCMAHAN, John 113 127-129
MCMASTERS, J 39
MCMILLEN, Major 130 Morrison 154 Mr 130 Orlando 130

SCRAP-BOOK.

MCMURRAY, William 131 133
MCNAUGHTON, Ellen 248
MCNEAL, R 39
MCRAE, Capt 42 Richard 40 42
MEAD, W 242
MEAGLEY, Francis E 112
MEARS, Mr 89 Wm 88-89
MEEKER, Mahlon 62 78 149 165 Mr 62 65 78-79 149 Mrs 62 150
MEIGS, Gov 185 R J 144
MERCER, Abram 104 Caleb 103 127 Charles 104 Geo 127 George 103 John 127 Lucretia 104 Mr 103 Wm 104 127
MERRY, E W 260 J E 247
MERTES, Rev Father 225
MICHAELIS, J P 34
MIDDLETON, Benjamin 42
MILBURN, Daniel 246
MILES, Samuel 42
MILLER, 185 Christopher 29 Ernest G 224 Gordon 82 Henry 29 Hobart 224 Jas 186 Mary 224 Mary E 224 Michael 175
MILLS, David 167
MINARD, Pierre 82
MINTON, Ben 198 Minnie 198 Nate 88 Nathan 113 T W 88
MITCHELL, 208 Joseph 95 127
MONROE, 236
MONTSON, John C 231
MOORE, Lee 84 95-96 113 258 Mr 96
MORAN, Nicholas 231
MOREHOUSE, 101
MORGAN, J C 34 M P 81
MUIR, John 37
MULHOLLEN, 135
MULLEN, Anthony 42
MUMFORD, Edward 42
MUNDY, Lewis 242
MUNGEN, William 85
MUNN, William 37
MURAT, 21 53
MURPHY, A B 38 Robert S 34
MURRAY, James 126 224 254 Mr 224 Mrs J A 259
MYERS, Michael 175 Michael N 175
NAILER, Henry 175
NAPOLEON, 152
NAVARRE, Peter 28 68-69 82 Pierre 68
NAWASH, 121 Big 122
NEARING, 150 G C 122 225 Guy 46 65 121-122 136 149 175 238 Henry 101 122

NEARING (cont.)
  Minerva 122 Mr 258 Neptune 122 258 Uncle Guy 121-123 141 176
NEIDERHOUSE, John 242
NEVARRE, Peter 68
NEVILLE, P 39
NEWMAN, J 40
NEWTON, 248 Capt 247 Geo W 72 Joseph B 247 Maggie 247 Mr 247
NIBELUNG, Carl 75
NOBLE, Joseph G 42
NOEL, John 240
NORTH, Jos 65 Joseph 81 Miss 155 Wm 81
NORTON, Emma J 223 Mr 162 Willis 162
NOWASH, 141
NOYES, Harry 261
NYE, John P 155
OBLINGER, F J 237 261
OLIVER, Major 144
OLNEY, Benj 113 Edward 161 Stephen 161
OMANS, Mrs 240
OSBORNE, Jesse 246
OSBURG, 242
OSCAM, Theresa 242
OVIATT, John 52
PAGE, James 42
PAIN, H H 112
PAINE, Edward Jr 11
PARISH, Orish 167
PARK, J 40
PARKER, M 40 Messr 201 Prosecutor 201 R S 200 225 Z C 200
PARKMAN, Francis 16
PARSHALL, Sall 129 Sarah 128
PATTERSON, Jane 151 N 39
PAYNE, Devall 221
PEACOCK, Emily 153
PEBLES, James 231
PECK, Dr 60-61 138 E D 86 111 Erasmus D 60 H E 73 Mrs Persis 242 W R 113
PEGRAM, Benjamin 42
PEMBER, Hiram 175 James 175 178
PENDLETON, Geo F 225
PENTLAND, C 40
PERKINS, Mrs 242
PERNOT, 129
PERRIN, Amelia 111 257 Jonathan 241 257 Leonard 154 Mrs 257 Mrs James 242 Wilkison D 257

PERRY, 31 114 Commodore 219 228 John 42 Thomas W 42
PETERS, B L 180 D E 180 William 59
PETERSON, James 42
PFLEGHART, Henry 242
PHELPS, Judge 134
PHILLIPS, Adam 36-37 127 Catherine 36 Jacob 36
PIERCE, Carrie A 223 Cora M 223 Emma J 223 Frances A 223 James 223 James H 223 Jennie E 223 Martha A 223 Mattie 223 Mr 223 Sarah 223
PILLARS, James 106 Jasher 224
POE, E W 250 Ebenezer W 250 Mr 250-251
POLLARD, J 40
POLLY, Jesse 231
POOL, Richard 42
POORE, Ben Perley 119
PORTER, 101 168 George 46 166-167 George W 241 Mr 241
POTIER, Father 17 Peter 17
POTTER, John 42
POWELL, Thomas W 12 156 167 240-241 Thos W 156
POWERS, Ashael 103 175 Geo 113 George 113
PRATT, E 40 Forest 121 Wm 81
PRAY, J L 30 33 262 John 15 175
PRENTICE, Mrs 197-198
PREVOST, 114
PRIEST, Jennie E 223
PROCTER, Gen 70
PROCTOR, 60 116 147-148 218 222 Gen 58-59 114 124 143-144 214 219 225-227 Henry A 220
PUGH, George E 143 John 66
PURDUE, David 167
RACE, Andrew 29 59 84
RADWAY, 72
RALSTON, J G 88 Joe 88-89 Joseph 37 Mr 139
RANDOLPH, John 235
RANSOM, Leander 100
RAWLINGS, John 42 William P 42
RAWSON, Abel T 150 L Q 150
READ, J 39
REED, Benjamin 84 Henry Jr 100 L W 137 Messr 128 Mr 150 Mrs Frank 250 Noah 136 141 150 176 238 Norton 246
REGAN, Miss 212

REISER, Catherine 242 John 242 Nicholas 242 Theresa 242
REISLY, Johanna 242
RHEINFRANK, Dr 223
RHODAE, August 242 Christina 242 Mrs 242
RICARDS, F 40
RICE, Ambrose 12 Dr 139-140
RICHARDS, George 42 W 40
RICHARDSON, 101 166-167 241 W 40
RIDER, Archie 214
RIGHT, H D 242
RIGLY, Thomas 129
RILEY, Philip 242
ROACH, Andrew 214 Andrew Jr 214 Edward 214 Mr 214
ROBACK, 143 Dr 142
ROBB, Scott 136
ROBBINS, Mr 245
ROBERTSON, Amelius 112 170 James 61 111 170 242 253 L F 112 Margery 100 Mr 170 Mrs Amelius 100
ROBINSON, David 34 G V 40
ROBY, 138
ROGERS, E E 206 260
ROLLER, Mr 166
ROSE, E M 261
ROSS, 114 Findley J 242 May 259 Stanley T 242
ROWAN, 183
ROWLAND, Bob 191 Jim 190
ROYCE, A E 247 Albert E 151
RUDOLPH, A W 260
RUFLY, Jacob 242
RUSH, Leonard 149
RUSSELL, 100 Alfred M 250 Charles H 250 Joseph 35 37 Mr 250
SAGE, 75 George 74 Valentine 74
SAINTCLAIR, 21 23 53-54 90 Arthur 18 Gen 8 18
SAINTJOHN, 258 S W 75 113
SALSBURY, 246 Jonathan 141-142 Old Man 141
SAMMAL, Anthony 231
SANDERSON, Gen 60 185 George 60
SARGENT, 246 John 127-128 Joseph A 36 Mr 127
SARVIS, Henry 112-113
SAUNDERS, John H 42
SCHITZ, Geo 242
SCHRIENER, Rev Father 225

SCRAP-BOOK.

SCHUCKMEAL, Margaret 242
SCHULER, Geo 242
SCOTT, Gen 114 J A 100 Jessup W 43 179 Joseph 42 Sergeant 231 Thomas G 42
SENEY, Geo E 225
SESSIONS, Horace 100
SHADY, Pat 189
SHAFFORD, Aurora 167
SHANNON, James 242 John A 164 Mr 242 Mrs 242
SHARP, Richard 42
SHATZEL, J E 225
SHAW, Mr 242 Mrs 242 Robert 167
SHEA, Gillmany 17 Mr 17
SHEFFIELD, 153 William 152
SHELBY, Gov 219
SHELIA, Joseph 245 Mr 245
SHELLEY, Christian 175
SHELTON, John 42
SHERMAN, 247 Charles R 11 Gen 11 Senator 11
SHERWOOD, Kate B 115
SHIVELY, Henry 37 113
SHOEMAKER, C W 33 Charles W 30
SHORE, John 42
SHORT, Lt Col 227
SHREINER, Samuel 163
SIMMONS, 183 Mr 181 Mrs 181
SIMONDS, Celia 242
SIMPSON, James 231
SIMRALL, 221
SIZER, 129
SKINNER, Jesse 59 Mary A 257
SLATER, 133 James 132 Jim 130-131 Mr 132
SLATTERY, Francis 140
SLAWSON, James 59
SLEVIN, Col 194
SLIGHT, Thomas Jr 37
SLOAN, Daniel 231
SMITH, 124 162 Addison 43 Dr 253 J W 72 John C 100 John H 42 John Z 48 Kirby 179 Mary A 43 Miss 43 Mr 43
SNYDER, Jacob 242 Samuel 37
SOLETHER, Mr 245
SOUTHARD, Ann 251
SPAFFORD, 12 100 138 Amos 29 59 Aurora 240 J 112 James 149 Jarvis 111 161-162 242 Maj 29 82-83 Mary A 257 Mr 161-162 Samuel 31 167 240
SPATSWOOD, M B 42

SPENCER, G B 80 Geo B 79
SPINK, 138 Cornelia 242 J C 100 John C 43 70 72 125 175 181 John J 111 242 John S 254 Mary A 43 Mr 43-45 126 224 Shibnah 43
SPWALT, John 42
SQUIRES, Mr 201 S A 200 Sheriff 200
STACKHOUSE, Mattie 140 Miss 140
STACY, George 37
STATIN, Joseph 231
STEARNS, Newton 88
STECKER, D 249
STEEDMAN, S H 154
STETSON, Isaac 100
STEVENS, James 42 Robert 42 Samuel 42
STEVENSON, John 231
STICKNEY, 123
STITH, Ezra 42
STONE, R E 200
STONER, Charles 100
STORY, Judge 98
STOUFFER, Jacob 84 86
STOWEL, H C 100
STRAIN, George 131 133
STRAIT, Reuben 127
STROW, H C 96
STULL, Jonathan 245 Mr 246
SWANE, 110
SWARROW, 53
SWIFT, S 40
SYLVANIA, Rush 177
SYPHER, Michael 101 149
TABORN, Jas 128 John 129
TAYLOR, Frank 225 Gen 44 227 Grant S 34 John 112 Levi 81 Mary 246 Mr 246 Thomas 246 258 William 246
THOMAS, Dr 139
THOMPSON, Carrie A 223 Gen 182 John 182 John G 134-135 Joseph 182 N 40
THORNTON, John H 223
THORPE, 29
THURSTIN, Alfred 54 84 87 Louisa 54 Mrs Stanley 249
TIFFIN, Edward 42
TISDALE, Shirly 42 William 42
TOCKER, Judson 242
TODD, M B 97
TRACY, J R 73 113 Joseph R 87 Thomas 84
TRAVIS, Mr 260 Robert M 260
TRIMBLE, David 144

TROTTER, 221
TROUP, Jas O 225
TROVILLS, E 39
TUCKER, 100
TUPPER, Gen 109
TYLER, 131 James R 224 Messr 201
ULRICH, John 253
UNDERWOOD, William 35
UTLEY, Joseph 241 Thos 149
VANBUREN, 69 Mr 235
VANFLEET, Col 164
VANTASSEL, 96 Isaac 74 81 88 171 258 Louisa 54
VANVOORHIS, D C 180
VERNON, N 40
VOLLMER, Mr 209
W, Mr 164
WADE, 137 Hiram 136 Joseph 37
WAGSTAFF, Wm 259
WAITE, Benjamin 178 Morrison R 163 254 Mr 254
WALKER, Geo 89 Henry 84 86
WALL, Jake 164
WALLACE, Dr 169 Ewel 231 John C 169
WARD, Stephen 84
WARNER, Geo 113 Martin 154 Martin Jr 113
WASHINGTON, 22 26 53 President 8-9 21 25
WATERS, Mary 95 Octavius 95
WATT, J 40
WAY, Mr 181-182 Sophia 182 W V 138 Willard V 125 181 254
WAYNE, 24 29 54 58 80 93 102 115 159 233 Anthony 9 21-22 25 53 78-79 108 155 201 Gen 22-23 26-27 57 90 169 228 232 234 Mad Anthony 21 27-28 52 67 169 177 Mr 169
WEATHERS, Joshua 231
WEBB, Charles 239 Elizabeth 239 241 John 46 239 John Jr 239 John Sr 239 Lincoln 239 Mary 241 Mary A 241 Mr 46 167-168 239-241 Mrs 239 Samuel 242 Sheriff 167 Thomas Lincoln 239 Uncle John 241
WEDDEL, Geo 149
WELLES, Wm 29
WELLINGTON, 227 233
WELLS, 115 Col 143-144 227
WEST, Benjamin 81

WESTCOTT, John 72 S D 71
WETMORE, W H 254
WHEELER, Pres 152
WHITACRE, Mr 246
WHITAKER, Mahlon 130
WHITE, Celinda 258 Henry 231 Johnson 258 Johnston 62 149 Margaret 258 Mr 258 Mrs 258
WHITEHEAD, John 75 87 101 149 209
WHITLEY, William 221
WHITNEY, D 113 David 112-113 253 Mrs 194
WHITTLESEY, Chas 16 Col 16
WIDNER, C 40
WILD, Margaret 242
WILEY, John F 42
WILKINS, G 40
WILKINSON, Capt 43 72 135-136 David 43 135 Jacob 135-136 James 167 175 Mr 135 Sarah Hodge 224
WILKISON, Amelia 257 D 100 Jacob 240 257 James 240
WILLIAMS, A R 214 David 42 George 142 J 39 James 42 Jesse 89 Samuel 42 Stephen 242
WILLISON, Mr 164
WILLOCK, J 39
WILSON, 54 138 166 Chairman 34 Charles 149 Chas F 71 Eber 71 149 167 223 J B 33-34 John 65 John B 30 Mrs 65
WINCHESTER, Gen 143 156 217-219 226
WINELAND, D 131
WOHRENDORFF, C 40
WOLFLEY, Mr 242 Mrs 242
WONDERLY, Wm 81
WOOD, A J 155 Brother 155 Capt 15 E R 155 Emelius 113 154-155 Everett R 154 William H 155
WOODRUFF, 100
WOOSTER, John C 113
WORSHAM, Daniel 42
WRIGHT, Albert D 111 179 Dr 189 Mr 179
YEAGER, John 242
YOUNG, Bennett H 34 219 Knowlton 167 Samuel M 254
YOUNT, Gabriel 112
ZANGER, F 242
ZIMMERMAN, Mr 242 Wm 37
ZUGSCHWERT, A 225

www.ingramcontent.com/pod-product-compliance
Lightning Source LLC
Chambersburg PA
CBHW051041160426
43193CB00010B/1020